The Japanese Occupation of Malaya and Singapore, 1941–45

The Japanese Occupation of Malaya and Singapore, 1941–45

A Social and Economic History
(*Second Edition*)

Paul H. Kratoska

NUS PRESS
SINGAPORE

Published by:

NUS Press
National University of Singapore
AS3-01-02, 3 Arts Link
Singapore 117569

Fax: (65) 6774-0652
E-mail: nusbooks@nus.edu.sg
Website: http://nuspress.nus.edu.sg

ISBN 978-9971-69-638-2 (paper)

National Library Board, Singapore Cataloguing in Publication Data

Name(s): Kratoska, Paul H.
Title: The Japanese occupation of Malaya and Singapore, 1941–45: a social and economic history / Paul H. Kratoska.
Description: Second edition. | Singapore: NUS Press, [2018] | Includes bibliographical references and index.
Identifier(s): OCN 1015231110 | ISBN 978-9971-69-638-2 (paperback)
Subject(s): LCSH: Malaya--History--Japanese occupation, 1942–1945. | Singapore--History--Japanese occupation, 1942–1945. | Malaya--Economic conditions--20th century. | Singapore--Economic conditions--20th century. | Malaya--Social conditions--20th century. | Singapore--Social conditions--20th century.
Classification: DDC 959.5103--dc23

First published in 1998 by C. Hurst & Co. (Publishers) Ltd (London), The University of Hawaii Press (Honolulu) and Allen & Unwin (St. Leonards, NSW).

Typeset by: Ogma Solutions Pvt Ltd
Printed by: Mainland Press Pte Ltd

To my parents,

Floyd and Phyllis Kratoska,
With gratitude and love

Contents

Maps

Tables

Illustrations

Cover

When British forces entered Malaya in 1945, they removed as many traces as possible of the Japanese presence. The illustration on the front cover is part of a propaganda poster that survived because of a wartime paper shortage. It was torn into pieces and the back was used for correspondence. It is found in Kedah Secretariat (Setia Usaha Kedah) file 21/2486 (Arkib Negara Malaysia, Cawangan Kedah).

The illustration on the back cover is a safe conduct pass dropped by the Japanese when they invaded Malaya. The text states that Japanese forces have come to bring peace, and that anyone approaching Japanese troops should present the paper. Without it, Japanese troops are not permitted to respond.

Abbreviations

ACTS	Army Central Translation Section
ADO	Assistant District Officer
AJU	Anti-Japanese Union
ALFSEA	Allied Land Forces, South East Asia
AR	Annual Report
ATIS	Allied Translator and Interpreter Section
BA	British Adviser
BMA	British Military Administration
BT	Board of Trade
CAO	Civil Affairs Officer
CBI	China Burma India
CCAO	Chief Civil Affairs Officer
CEP	Custodian of Enemy Property
CLR	Collector of Land Revenue
DO	District Officer
ELB	English Language Broadcast
F of M	Federation of Malaya
FEB	Far Eastern Bureau, British Ministry of Information
FIR	Fortnightly Intelligence Report, Far Eastern Bureau, British Ministry of Information
FMS	Federated Malay States
GSDIC	General Services Detailed Intelligence Centre
IIL	Indian Independence League
INA	Indian National Army
JICA	Joint Intelligence Collection Agency
JM	Japanese Monograph
KL	Kuala Lumpur
KMT	Kuomintang
MB	*Menteri Besar* (Chief Minister)
MCS	Malayan Civil Service

MPAJA	Malayan Peoples' Anti-Japanese Army
NARA	(United States) National Archives and Records Administration
NARA RG	NARA Record Group
NS	Negri Sembilan
OCA	Oversea Chinese Association
OHD	Oral History Department, Singapore
OSS	Office of Strategic Services
R&A	Research and Analysis Branch of the OSS
Pk	Perak
PT	Pejabat Tanah (Land Office)
PW	Province Wellesley
PWD	Public Works Department
RG	Resident General (cf NARA RG)
S of S	Secretary of State
SACSEA	Supreme Allied Commander South-East Asia
SB	Sanitary Board
SEAC	South-East Asia Command
SEATIC	South-East Asia Translation and Intelligence Centre
Sel	Selangor
Sel Sec	Selangor Secretariat
Sel Kan	Selangor Kanbo
SOE	Special Operations Executive
SUK	*Setia Usaha Kerajaan* (State Secretary)
TNA	National Archives of Thailand
WO	War Office

Preface to the Second Edition

Anyone who has written a large and complex book knows that unstitching and re-assembling the text is both difficult and unrewarding. Returning to the present book 20 years after writing it, I have been able to acknowledge work done after its publication and introduce some new material, but the bulk of the contents and the conclusion remain unchanged.

New works that appeared after publication of this book include Alan Warren's *Singapore: Britain's Greatest Defeat*, and three regional overviews, *Forgotten Armies: The Fall of British Asia, 1941–1945*, by Christopher Bayly and Tim Harper, *A Sudden Rampage: The Japanese Occupation of Southeast Asia, 1941–1945*, by Nicholas Tarling, and *In the Ruins of Empire: The Japanese Surrender and the Battle for Postwar Asia*, by Ronald H. Spector. *War, Memory and the Making of Modern Malaysia and Singapore*, by Kevin Blackburn and Karl Hack, and *War and Memory in Malaysia and Singapore*, edited by Patricia Lim Pui Huen and Diana Wong, are part of a substantial literature that examines how the war is remembered by studying oral history interviews, monuments, museum exhibits, public ceremonies, and school textbooks.

There is also a major set of newly translated documents. *The Chōsabu Reports*, edited by Gregg Huff and Shinobu Majima, publishes reports prepared by Japanese academics who carried out research on Singapore during the occupation, providing data on the Singapore economy and related matters.

These books are significant additions to the literature on the war and occupation, but most of them they say relatively little about the experiences of the people of Malaya and Singapore. From a local standpoint, the military situation, international diplomacy and Britain's failure to prevent the Japanese conquest were irrelevant compared to more immediate concerns. People needed to come to terms with new rulers who quickly showed themselves to be unpredictable and potentially violent, and over a slightly longer period, to cope with a deteriorating economic situation and Japanese efforts to introduce a new social order.

One new publication that does explore these issues is Abu Talib Ahmad's superb study, *The Malay Muslims, Islam and the Rising Sun, 1941–45*. This book draws heavily on a rich set of unpublished theses, academic exercises, mini-theses and term papers prepared by students at Universiti Sains Malaysia, along with wartime files of state governments, particularly the Johor religious affairs department, which have previously received little attention from researchers. The book adds a major new dimension to understanding the impact of the occupation.

Between 2009 and 2012, the Singapore National Archives published a massive three-volume set of photographs and texts under the general title *Reflections & Memories of War*. This work, which expands on an earlier pictorial history of Singapore during the war, features photographs and commentary drawn from oral history interviews relating to the Occupation.[1]

Paul H. Kratoska
Singapore, January 2018

[1] *Reflections & Memories of War: Exhibition Catalogue & Resource Guide*. Volume 1: Battle for Singapore: Fall of the Impregnable Fortress (National Archives of Singapore, 2011); Volume 2: Syonan Years 1942–1945: Living beneath the Rising Sun (2009); Volume 3: The Liberation: Resisting the Rising Sun and a New Beginning (2012). See also National Archives of Singapore, *The Japanese Occupation: A Pictorial History of Singapore during the War* (Singapore: Times Editions, 1996).

Preface to the First Edition

This book began, as many such projects do, as an attempt to satisfy my own curiosity. The Japanese occupation was a traumatic experience for the people of Malaya (later Malaysia), and from the time of my first visit to the country in 1971 I heard stories about people being slapped by Japanese soldiers and about the malnutrition that resulted from a steady diet of tapioca. Many people I met could still produce a few Japanese phrases, or snatches of Japanese songs. It was, however, difficult to go beyond these fragmentary recollections. While doing my PhD research in 1973–74 on rice cultivation in British Malaya, I tried to locate documents on the occupation period but found very little, and in my dissertation I followed conventional practice by confining my discussion to pre-war events.

I returned to Malaysia in 1977 to become a lecturer at Universiti Sains Malaysia in Penang, and began teaching a course on Malaysian socio-economic history. As a written assignment I required course essays based in part on oral sources, and some of the essays dealt with the Japanese Occupation. Although the students were only completing undergraduate assignments that were worth relatively little in the final calculation of course results, some of them invested an extraordinary amount of effort in writing these essays, and the oral material in particular was of a very high standard. The students collectively commanded the various dialects of Malay and Chinese, and the Indian languages, used in Malaysia, and their linguistic skills contributed to the value of their interviews. More importantly, they often interviewed family members and personal acquaintances, who answered their questions freely and candidly. In the early 1980s, two of my colleagues, Cheah Boon Kheng and Abu Talib Ahmad, were working along similar lines, and we were so impressed with the essays our students produced that we prevailed on Universiti Sains Malaysia to publish some of the better ones. Three volumes of essays eventually appeared in print.[1]

The University also agreed to support an oral history project on the Japanese occupation, and additional publications appeared under the auspices of this programme. My colleague Abu Talib Ahmad continued asking students to prepare course papers based on oral sources, retaining the better ones with an eye toward eventual publication. He kindly gave me access to his material while I was preparing this volume, and it proved to be an invaluable resource.

---

[1] Paul H. Kratoska (ed.), *Penghijrah dan Penghijrahan*; Cheah Boon Kheng (ed.), *Tokoh-Tokoh Tempatan*; Paul H. Kratoska and Abu Talib Ahmad (eds), *Pendudukan Jepun di Tanah Melayu, 1942–1945.*

The student essays, and material in the papers of the British Military Administration, led me to believe that, at least with regard to economic history, the occupation was less of a watershed than I had thought, and that the widespread practice of stopping accounts of Malaya in 1941, or beginning them in 1945, made the occupation appear more disruptive than it actually was. However, without administrative papers for the period many details remained obscure, and it seemed unlikely that this obstacle could be overcome. After leaving Malaysia to join the National University of Singapore in 1987, I continued doing research on rice in British Malaya, and in the course of this work I came across district office files from the war years that allowed me to construct a general picture of wartime food shortages and provided glimpses of other issues, but even with this material the record remained fragmentary. What finally swung the balance was a visit to the United States National Archives where John Taylor, an archivist whose praises had deservedly been sung by every historian who used the wartime papers generated by the Office of Strategic Services (OSS), directed me to a set of Japanese Monographs held by the US Army Center of Military History. This collection, which consists of studies written by Japanese officers and translated into English by the US Army's Military Intelligence Service Group, supplied much information that was unavailable in Malaysia. Used in conjunction with the OSS papers and a series of articles by Professor Yoji Akashi, which were based on Japanese sources and supplied a great many details that were lacking in British or American papers, these materials helped me make sense of the data in Malaysia, and this book began to take shape.

This volume owes much to exchanges with my former colleagues and students at Universiti Sains Malaysia in Penang. Among the latter I should particularly like to mention Cheah Boon Kheng, R. Suntharalingam, Abu Talib Ahmad, Khoo Khay Jin, Tan Liok Ee, Leong Yee Fong, Francis Loh Kok Wah, Abdul Rahman Ismail, Wong Soak Koon, Yuen Choy Leng and Badriyah Haji Salleh. The work of Cheah Boon Kheng on the occupation is a model of careful scholarship, and his books *Masked Comrades* and *Red Star over Malaya* provide thorough and sensitive discussions of political issues during the period. These studies, and the many conversations I have had with Boon Kheng over the years, have contributed to my own work far more extensively than footnotes could possibly indicate. To the students at Universiti Sains Malaysia, who endured and improved my faulty Malay, and taught me a great deal about the workings of Malaysian society, I owe a considerable debt of gratitude. I would also like to thank Edward Lim Huck Tee, formerly Chief Librarian at Universiti Sains Malaysia, his successor Rashidah Begum, and Wong Sook Jean and Chang Siw Lai of the library staff for various forms of assistance during the decade I spent in Penang, and to place on record my admiration for the library collection they helped to assemble. Staff members of the Malaysian National Archives in Kuala Lumpur were also enormously helpful, producing vast piles of material and handling large photocopying orders with despatch, while branches of the archives at Alor Star and Johore Baru provided access to important records in their collections and congenial working environments. I should like to express a particular note of appreciation to Dato' Zakiah Hanum, the former head of the National Archives, for the kind interest she showed in my work. Her observations on life in Kedah during the occupation, although not directly cited here, helped me to understand conditions in that state.

Other friends and colleagues who have contributed in various ways to the shaping of this book include Yoji Akashi, without whose pioneering scholarship it could never have been written, Hara Fujio, who has done extremely fruitful research on the Chinese population during the occupation, E. Bruce Reynolds, who provided helpful comments on an early draft of the manuscript, and Kobkua Suwannathat-Pian, who draws on both Thai and Malay sources in connection with her research on the northern Malay states which were transferred to Thai rule in 1943.

In Singapore Associate Professors Edwin Lee and Ernest C.T. Chew, respectively the Head of the Department of History and the former Dean of the Faculty of Arts and Social Sciences at the National University of Singapore, supported my research. Rohani bte Kamsan helped me work out the nuances of various Malay expressions, the late Ben Batson translated Thai documents and offered insightful comment on the wartime situation in Thailand, Brian Farrell provided useful suggestions based on his research into military aspects of the Japanese invasion, and Kwan Siu-Hing assisted me with Chinese names and Japanese terminology. I profited from discussions with Yeo Kim Wah and Ng Chin-keong, and Hong Lysa's astute comments helped me in more ways than I could ever acknowledge. The Central Library of the National University of Singapore contains an extraordinarily rich body of research materials, and I profited from its vast collection of microforms, which include a substantial part of the holdings concerning Malaysia and Singapore found in archives elsewhere in the world. I am also grateful to Mrs Chong Mui Gek, a cartographer attached to the Department of Geography at the National University of Singapore, for preparing the maps accompanying this book.

In London the services provided by the Public Record Office (now the National Archives) and the India Office Library (now held as the India Office Records in the British Library) were enormously helpful, and in Washington I received a great deal of assistance from the staff of the US National Archives and Records Administration. I would also like to express my appreciation to Phillip and Patricia Afable Thomas for their generous hospitality in Washington, DC, and to Roger Tuffs, Elayne Sharling, Norman Flynn, and John and Christine Gibson for their friendship and hospitality in London.

While writing this book, I had the opportunity to edit for publication a number of papers written by scholars working on the occupation in other parts of Southeast Asia, and to organize a Symposium on the Occupation which was sponsored by the Toyota Foundation. In particular I benefitted from explanations and interpretations in papers written by Shigeru Sato, Michiko Nakahara, Goto Ken'ichi, Aiko Kurasawa-Inomata, Motoe Terami-Wada, Lydia Yu-Jose, Josefma D. Hofileña, Ricardo T. Jose, Pierre van der Eng, Abu Talib Ahmad, Ooi Keat Gin, Patricia Lim Pui Huen, Henry Frei, Elly Touwen-Bouwsma, Lorraine V. Aragon, László Sluimers, Midori Kawashima, Grant K. Goodman, William L. Swan and Tran My-Van.

While I have benefitted greatly from these and many other contacts during the 20 years I have spent in Malaysia and Singapore, I remain acutely conscious that there is much I still do not know, and inevitably there will be places in this volume where this ignorance shows. For that I can only beg the forgiveness of my many teachers.

On the personal side, Arpudamari d/o Paul provided many insights into the Malaysian Indian community. My mother-in-law Tan Siew Tin, who lived on a small estate south of Taiping during the occupation and tells stories of hiding when Japanese soldiers came to visit, and of seeing her pet dogs suffer from malnutrition, contributed to this book in many ways, not least by preparing countless meals from her vast repertoire of Penang and Thai cuisine. Finally, my wife Louise and our son Adam enrich my life in so many ways that I cannot begin to thank them adequately. I can only hope that Adam will never have to live through anything comparable to the events described in this book.

Paul H. Kratoska
Singapore, April 1997

Preliminary Note

Chapters 8 and 13 include material published in my article "Banana Money: Consequences of the Demonetization of Wartime Japanese Currency in British Malaya", *Journal of Southeast Asian Studies* 23, 2 (Sept. 1992): 322–45. Material in Chapters 11 and 13 first appeared in my article "The Post-1945 Food Shortage in British Malaya", *Journal of Southeast Asian Studies* 19, 1 (Mar. 1988): 27–47. I am grateful to NUS Press for permission to reproduce this material. Crown-copyright material in the Public Record Office (now the National Archives) is reproduced by permission of the Controller of Her Majesty's Stationery Office.

Glossary of Key Terms Associated with the Wartime Japanese Administration of Malaya*

Structure of the Japanese Administration of Kedah (see p. 65)

総務部	Sōmu-bu	General Affairs
官房	Kanbō	Secretariat Chamber
管理課	Kanri-ka	General Administration (district offices, sanitary boards)
教育課	Kyōiku-ka	Education
司法課	Shihō-ka	Judicial Department (courts and prisons)
医務課	Imu-ka	Medical Affairs (hospitals, dispensaries, health)
産業部	Sangyō-bu	Department of Industry
農務課	Nomu-ka	Agriculture
商工課	Shōkō-ka	Commerce and Industry
財務部	Zaimu-bu	Financial and Treasury Bureau
理財課	Rizai-ka	Financial
会計課	Kaikei-ka	Treasury
土地課	Tochi-ka	Land District (land offices, mines, surveys, forests)
関税課	Kanzei-ka	Customs (customs-houses, opium, harbour office)
会計監査課	Kaikeikensa-ka	Audit
交通部	Kōtsū-bu	Communication Bureau
郵政課	Yūsei-ka	Posts and Telegraphs
運輸課	Unyu-ka	Traffic
土木課	Doboku-ka	Public Works
警察部	Keisatsu-bu	Police Bureau

* This glossary is a partial list of key terms used in Malaya and Singapore during the Japanese Occupation. I am grateful to Professor Shinobu Majima of the Faculty of Economics at Gakushuin University for providing the kanji and checking the English translations.

警務課	Keimu-ka	Police Affairs Section
保安課	Hoan-ka	Security Section
特高課	Tokkō-ka	Special Attack Task Force
宗務院	Shumuin	Religious Bureau

Sections within Japan's Wartime Administration

防疫課	Bōeki-ka	Epidemic Prevention Section
文教課	Bunkyō-ka	Education Section
治安課	Chian-ka	Public Security Section
電気課	Denki-ka	Electricity Section
土木課	Doboku-ka	Public Works Section
衛生課	Eisei-ka	Hygiene Section
福利課	Fukuri-ka	Welfare Section
秘書課	Hisho-ka	Secretariat Section
医務課	Imu-ka	Medical Affairs Section
会計課	Kaikei-ka	Accounting Section
管財課	Kanzai-ka	Enemy Property Section
鉱業課	Kōgyō-ka	Mines Section
工務課	Kōmu-ka	Engineering Section
交通課	Kōtsū-ka	Traffic Section
農林課	Nōrin-ka	Agriculture and Forestry Section
専売課	Sembai-ka	Monopoly Sales Section (tobacco, alcohol, opium etc.)
総務課	Sōmu-ka	General Affairs Section
水産課	Suisan-ka	Fisheries Section
食品課	Syokuhin-ka	Food Section
食糧統制課	Syokuryō Tōsei-ka	Food Control Section
庶務課	Syomu-ka	Commercial Affairs Section
郵政課	Yūsei-ka	Posts and Telegraphs Section
税務課	Zeimu-ka	Tax Affairs Section

Other Terms that were Important in Occupied Malaya and Singapore

万歳	Banzai	A cheer; short for Banzai can be raised for anyone not just the emperor
部長	Buchō / Butyo	Chief of a Department

馬鹿野郎	Bakayarō	You Idiot
地方法院	Chihō Hōin	District Court
調査部	Chōsabu	Department of Research
中央護謨工業株式会社	Chūō Gomu Kōgyō Kabushiki Kaisha	Central Rubber Industrial Company
大東亜戦争	Dai-tōa Sensō	Great East Asian War
義勇軍	Giyū-gun	Volunteer Army
義勇隊	Giyū-tai	Volunteer Corps
護謨研究所	Gomu Kenkyū-jyo	Rubber Research Institute
郡長	Gun-chō / Gun-tyo	District Officer
軍政部	Gunsei-bu	Military Government
軍政官	Gunsei-kan	Civilian Administrators within the Military Administration
行政庁	Gyōsei-chō	Administrative Office
八紘一宇	Hakkōichiu	All eight corners of the world under one roof
兵補	Heiho	Auxiliary Soldier / Auxiliary Service Personnel
日の丸	Hinomaru	The Rising Sun [National Flag of Japan]
本部	Honbu	Headquarters
印刷局	Insatu Kyoku	Printing Department
自警団	Jikeidan	Peace Preservation Corps (lit. "Vigilance Corps")
株式会社	Kabushiki-gaisha / kaisha	Joint Stock Company
華僑協会	Kakyō-kyōkai	Oversea Chinese Association
憲兵隊	Kempeitai	Military Police
紀元節	Kigen-setsu	Japanese Empire Day (11 February)
君が代	Kimigayo	Japanese National Anthem
勤労奉仕隊	Kinrō Hōshi-tai	Labour Service Corps
国民儀礼	Kokumin-Girei	National Rites
興南奉公会	Kōnan Hōkōkai	Rising South Association for Public Service
興南債券	Kōnan Saiken	Southern Dream Bond / Rising South Lottery (Government-run Lottery)
厚生協会	Kōsei Kyōkai	Welfare Association

訓練所	Kunrenjyo	Training School
協会	Kyōkai	Association or Society
馬来	Malai	Malay, Malaya
馬来護謨組合	Malai Gomu Kanri Kumiai	Malay Rubber Management Association
民政部	Minsei-bu	People's Welfare Department
日本	Nippon	Japan
日本語	Nippon-go	Japanese language
最敬礼	Saikeirei	Homage to the Emperor
産業奉公会	Sangyō Hōkōkai	Labour Service Corps
参事会	Sanji Kai	Advisory Councils
政庁	Seichō	Administrative Office
宣伝班	Senden-han	Propaganda Team
新聞会社	Shimbun-gaisha	Newspaper Company
昭和	Shōwa	Reign of Emperor Hirohito (25 Dec. 1926–7 Jan. 1989)
州	Shū	Province or State
州長官	Shū Chōkan	State Chief Minister
宗務院	Shūmuin	Religious Bureau
州立中央病院	Shūritsu Chūō Byōin	Central State Hospital
昭南護謨組合	Syonan Gomu Kumiai	Singapore Rubber Association
昭南特別市	Syonan Tokubetsu-shi	Syonan Municipality
敵産管理局	Tekisan Kanri-kyoku	Enemy Property Administration Bureau
天長節	Tenchō-setsu	Emperor's Birthday (29 April)
天皇陛下	Tennō-heika	His Majesty the Emperor
天皇陛下万歳	Tennō-heika Banzai	Long Live His Majesty the Emperor
鉄道愛護組合	Tetsudō Aigo Kumiai	Railway Protection Corps/Associations
隣組	Tonari Gumi	Neighbourhood Association

Map I.1 Malaya, showing state and district boundaries

Map I.2 Singapore

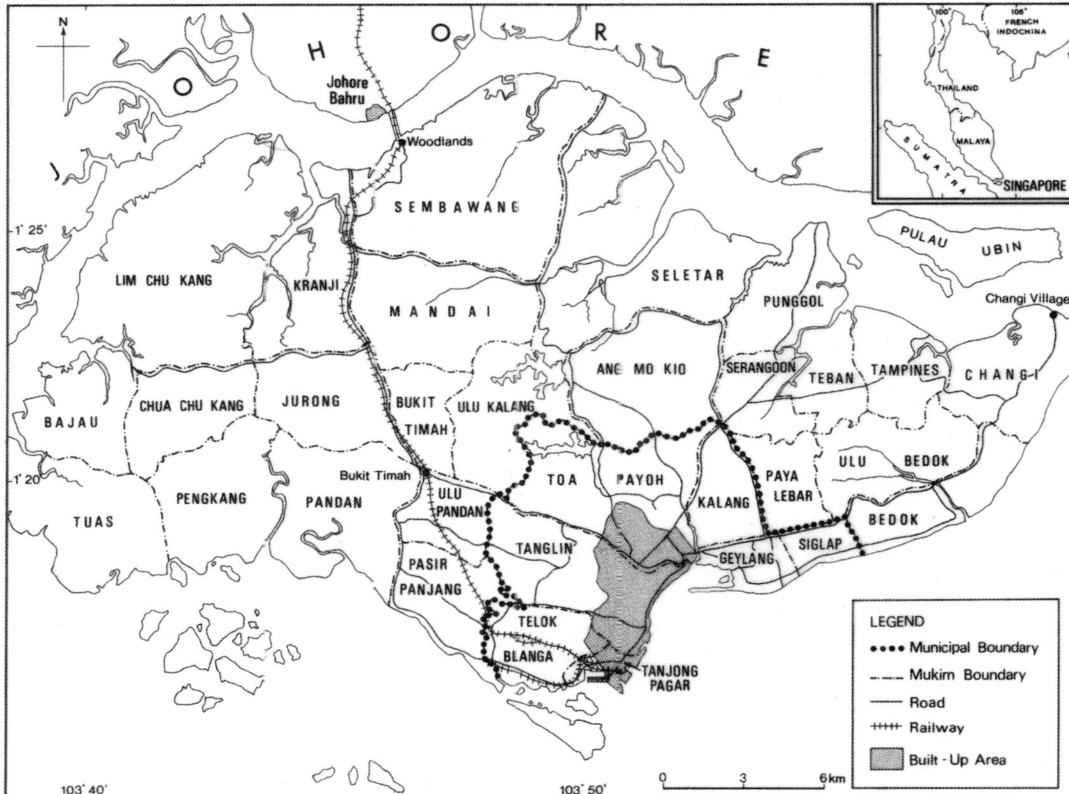

Map I.3 Malaya, showing locations mentioned in the text

Introduction

The Japanese occupation divides the twentieth-century history of Malaysia into two parts, 1900–40 and 1945 onward, and has often been described as a major watershed, an event that put an end to the old order and created a new. However, remarkably little is known about what happened during the years of the occupation, and its significance is often assumed rather than demonstrated. The academic literature on the period deals for the most part with military activity and the ordeal of Europeans held as prisoners of war or as civilian internees, and there are few studies concerning the local population. In Malaysia and Singapore those who experienced the occupation have kept its memory alive, but each succeeding generation finds their war stories less compelling, and young people know little about the events of the war years.

Popular understanding is in any case full of misconceptions: the war caused Britain to abandon its colonial empire; Japan conquered Malaya to obtain the peninsula's rich natural resources; the Japanese ruled autocratically and used terror to control the population; the Chinese were hostile to the Japanese, the Malays collaborated, and the Indians were won over by the promise of support for Indian independence. These interpretations are commonplace, but are partial truths at best and include much that is inaccurate. The Second World War certainly contributed to Britain's decision to give up its empire, but events in Malaya had little to do with that decision, and colonial rule ended in Malaya through a constitutional process twelve years after the Japanese surrender. The natural resources of the peninsula far exceeded Japan's wartime requirements, and the tin and rubber industries were a positive liability because these commodities no longer had a market and the large sector of the economy dependent on their production and export could not be sustained. Japanese rule in Malaya, after an initial period of savage repression that had adverse consequences for the remainder of the occupation, was carried out through communal organizations and pre-war administrative structures. The Japanese themselves, although they are remembered as cold and hostile, emerge from the historical record as somewhat inept, able to impose their will in specific instances but understanding too little of the country and its people, and commanding too little respect to be able to use their power effectively. Most Chinese cooperated with the Japanese, even if reluctantly; Malays tended to be neutral and came to dislike Japanese rule, while many Indians saw Japanese support for the independence movement in India as detrimental to their cause. Nearly everyone collaborated to some degree, but few did so because of a commitment to Japanese objectives as presented by the Japanese.

Japan invaded Malaya on 8 December 1941, and by 15 February 1942 had conquered the entire Malay peninsula and secured the surrender of British forces in Singapore. The occupation lasted until early September 1945, when Malaya was transferred to a British Military Administration under the surrender agreement Japan had accepted on 15 August 1945. The attack on Malaya was timed to coincide with the Japanese invasion of Hong Kong and the Philippines, and the raid on Pearl Harbor, and these actions marked the start of open hostilities. Previously, Japan had placed forces in Indochina under an agreement with the Vichy government in France, and had developed close ties with the government of Thailand. After the fall of Malaya, Japan conquered the Netherlands Indies, Burma and the Andaman and Nicobar islands, and extended their presence in the South Pacific beyond the mandated territories they already controlled, but then the advance stopped, although Japanese forces threatened Australia, and in 1944 launched an assault along the eastern frontier of British India. The captured territories covered a vast area, and Japan found it difficult to maintain supply lines and communications. Moreover, by the end of 1942 the Japanese had suffered the first of a series of defeats which brought the Allies back into Southeast Asia and nearly to the coast of Japan. By August 1945, when the Japanese capitulated, Allied forces had retaken Burma and the Philippines, and an invasion of Malaya was imminent.

The origins of the conflict lie in a set of relationships that had taken shape over the preceding half-century, and in the politics of the 1930s. Japan's industrial economy depended on the import of raw materials and the export of manufactured goods. Despite a general shift toward protectionism in Europe toward the end of the nineteenth century, Asian markets remained open, and Japan prospered in this trade environment. During the Depression, the colonial powers tried to contain as much economic activity as possible within empire trading blocs, and to ensure that there was a balance of imports and exports in trade conducted with places outside of these blocs. Japan sold its exports to Southeast Asia in markets where it bought very little, and steps taken by the British, Dutch and US colonial administrations to limit the import of Japanese goods into territories they controlled posed a threat to this sector of Japanese trade. Far more critical, however, was the question of Japanese imports from Southeast Asia, which included oil and metals vital both to Japanese industry and to the military. Restrictions imposed on these products at the end of the decade pushed matters to the point of crisis.

Although much of Japan's economic success was based on foreign trade, the country also pursued a second strategy during the half century that preceded the Pacific War by laying the foundations for an Asian empire, first taking control of Korea and Taiwan and then moving into Manchuria and northern China. These areas contained important industrial centres, and southern China and Southeast Asia complemented them, offering populous markets along with supplies of food and raw materials. During the 1930s, the right-wing elements in power in Japan responded to the economic pressures the country was facing with an aggressive military build-up and a powerful nationalist appeal, thereby increasing Japan's diplomatic isolation. Japan's move into Southeast Asia was an attempt to ensure that Japanese industry had sufficient natural resources and an adequate market within the ambit of the Japanese political system, and by denying rival powers access to strategic locations in the region. Japan's concept of a Greater East Asian Co-Prosperity Sphere (the term dates only from 1940) presented this policy in a way that suggested benefits for the entire region.[1]

Japan considered Malaya and Sumatra "the nuclear zone of the Empire's plans for the Southern area", and saw the Malay Peninsula as "the economic and communication axis for the entire Southern area".[2] Singapore also had considerable strategic importance because the British naval base located there provided a base for military operations against Japan, while in Japanese hands the naval base would extend the range of the Imperial Navy by some 2,500 miles. Following the conquest, Malaya became a key sector in Japan's defensive perimeter, guarding western approaches to the South China Sea and linking Japanese bases in the Asian mainland with those in the Indonesian Archipelago.[3] Economically, the significance of the occupation of Malaya lay in the denial of its resources to the Allied Forces rather than in the contribution those resources might make to the Japanese war effort, although bauxite, mined on a modest

[1] See J. Lebra (ed.), *Japan's Greater East Asia Co-Prosperity Sphere in World War II: Selected Readings and Documents*, pp. xiii–xvi, 71–2.

[2] Harry J. Benda, James K. Irikura and Koichi Kishi, *Japanese Military Administration in Indonesia*, Document No. 44 (Instructions on the Administration of Malaya and Singapore), p. 169.

[3] An article published in Germany in 1942 stated, "Malaya's chief role is that of a base for military defence, and this must be carried out even if the views of the native populations have to be subordinated." Translation of an article in the *Kölnische Zeitung*, 28 Sept. 1942, CO273/669/50744/7.

scale in Johore and in substantial quantities in the Riau Archipelago, was of considerable importance to Japan.[4]

The concept of an Asian economic sphere, uniting industrialized northeastern Asia with a region that could supply it with raw materials and provide a market for its manufactured goods, could not be realized. The primary task of administrators in the occupied territories was to support the war effort by supplying raw materials as needed, and by ensuring that peace and order prevailed behind the front lines at a time when Japan's combat forces were fully engaged in dealing with the Allied Powers. Far from participating in an integrated economic sphere, territories within the Japanese empire were forced to become self-sufficient. In Malaya the Japanese administration succeeded in maintaining order, but faced an intractable economic situation, characterized by unemployment, inflation, a flourishing black market and ever-worsening shortages of food and basic consumer goods. Japanese activities during the occupation fall into a chronological sequence that begins with consolidation of their power during 1942, followed by economic and administrative reforms in 1943 that moved the country toward centralized economic planning. By 1944, however, food shortages and inflation were out of control, and the administration was unable to deal effectively with either problem. By the end of 1944, Allied planes were appearing in the skies over Malaya, and during 1945 the Japanese were preoccupied with preparing for an invasion which they were unlikely to be able to repel.

For the local population, the sequence might be described differently. In 1941 the country was prosperous and goods were abundant. Conditions deteriorated steadily under Japanese rule, first because hoarding and black market activity pushed prices up and made it difficult to obtain food, clothing and medicines, and later because the supplies which remained were insufficient to meet the country's needs. What began as an irritating necessity to make do with less became for some people a grim struggle for survival.

The occupation is an episode in a large number of different stories—the history of Asia, the history of the British Empire, the history of the Second World War, the history of Malaya, the collective histories of the Malay and Chinese and Indian populations and the individual histories of the 5.5 million people who were in the country during the occupation. The histories of Asia, of the British empire and of the Second World War have been written often and well, and this book will do little to alter established understandings of those topics. It concerns instead the impact of these years on Malaya, on its economy and society, and on the people who lived there.

---

[4] Appreciation of Malaya, BMA 506/10.

For the most part, the Japanese in this book are seen through Malayan eyes. They appear as an alien presence, powerful and threatening, despite conciliatory gestures. They promise a prosperous future free of corruption but oversee an impoverished and corrupt regime. When individuals emerge from this mass, some are brutal and some kind, some clever and some fatuous. There are young men who are homesick and innocent and occasionally fall in love, middle-aged civil servants who struggle with shortages and a faltering economy, scholars who appreciate the art and literature of the Chinese, and racists who despise anyone who does not conform to Japanese standards. There are men who fervently believe in Japan's self-described mission, and men who cynically exploit Japan's momentary supremacy. Lurking in the background is the Japanese military, shadowy but pervasive, taking precedence over all else.

Accounts of the occupation tend to present the people of Malaya as meek victims. Victims they may have been, but they can hardly be described as meek. A substantial proportion of the Chinese population consisted of young working-class men, famous for their coarse speech and truculent disregard for authority. The Malays, living as families in rural villages, presented a quieter facade but were equally ready to ignore Japanese directives that ran counter to their interests, and if the Japanese regime gave the Malays little to oppose, it also offered little they wished to support. Some of the Indian soldiers brought to Malaya by the British to fight against Japan took part in an Indian National Army created to liberate India, but many others suffered and died in detention camps; the tragic fate of Tamil labourers during the occupation was to die in large numbers while working on Japanese construction projects, or from malnutrition and disease while trying to eke out a living growing food on the rubber estates.

Studying the Occupation

The academic literature on the occupation is sparse, reflecting a lack of source materials on the period. The British destroyed files as part of their scorched earth policy, and looters swept through government offices at the time of the invasion, destroying many more papers. The records of the pre-war Federal Secretariat were "completely looted".[5] Records of the Forest Department in Telok Anson perished in a fire, and the Perak State Forest Office lost many files in the process of moving from Ipoh to Taiping and then back again.[6] In Kuala Selangor the District Office building was set alight by the British at the time of their retreat, and while the strongroom survived the fire, "with the exception of the Mukim

[5] S. Ramasamy, Note, 18 Aug. 2602, Sel Kan 106/2602.

[6] State Forest Officer, Pk, to Director of Forests, BMA(M), 15 Feb. 1946, Forests 30/1945.

Registers [a set of massive bound volumes recording land transactions] all other files of documents, books, minute papers etc. which were in the strong room were removed by unknown Chinese by forced breaking open of the strong room. The removed documents etc. were later seen being used as wrappers."[7] When Selangor officials attempted in 1942 to trace service and financial records that the British had taken to Singapore during their retreat, they visited a succession of offices before learning that the building where the British stored these records had been cleared about a month earlier to provide space for the military police. "In conversation with the motor-car driver to the Chief of the Military Police, the party gathered that the records, account books, stationery, typewriter etc., were sold to a Chinese for $300/- who removed them in 30 or 40 lorries to various places for storage or disposal." This man could not be traced.[8]

There was another wave of looting when the war ended, and the Japanese systematically destroyed the greater part of their administrative papers immediately following the surrender (15 August 1945).[9] Many of the materials that survived were subsequently handed over to the War Damage Commission which, when its investigations were finished, arranged for their destruction. For example, in 1953 materials pertaining to banks and estates were taken to the municipal dumping grounds in Kuala Lumpur, sprayed with a chemical to hasten

[7] Investigation of Problems arising out of the Japanese Occupation, Response to Question No. 3 by CLR Kuala Selangor, 5 Jan. 1946, BMA Sel CA436/1945.

[8] S. Ramasamy, Note, 18 Aug. 2602; S. Ramasamy, Question of the recovery of all important Federated Malay States and Selangor Government Records removed from Kuala Lumpur to Syonan by the old regime, 18 July 2602; S. Ramasamy, Report on a Visit to Syonan to recover Government records which were removed from Kuala Lumpur to Syonan by the previous regime, 13 Oct. 2602, Sel Kan 106/2602.

[9] Memo, Dir of Intelligence to Sec/SAC, 10 Dec. 1945, WO203/4942. They also destroyed British records as well. J.M. Gullick, who was in the Malayan Civil Service shortly after the war, describes what happened in Negri Sembilan: "In Seremban … the Kempei Tai took over part of the State Secretariat building. When the Japanese surrender was imminent a Kempei Tai sergeant, with a fatigue party, was sent to destroy the Kempei Tai records. In doing so he also burnt much of the old Negeri Sembilan government records." The British administration left the records of the Selangor Secretariat in a strongroom belonging to the Rubber Department. At the end of the occupation, they were found in a small attic in the Secretariat building opposite the Selangor Club Padang. This is the only set of State Secretariat records to have survived more or less intact, and it has been of enormous importance to scholars working on late nineteenth and early twentieth century Malaya. Introduction to Paul Kratoska (comp.), *A Select List of Files in the Selangor Secretariat, 1875–1955*. Pulau Pinang: Universiti Sains Malaysia, 1984.

decomposition, and buried.[10] However, while vast quantities of records, easily the greater part of the materials produced by the Japanese administration, have been lost, the destruction was not total, and the Malaysian National Archives holds most of the records that remain. The most complete sets of files come from Kedah and Kelantan, which Japan transferred to Thai rule in 1943. Thailand handed the administration of these states over to local Malay authorities, and they rather than the Japanese controlled state records when the war ended. Other materials are from offices that were situated away from the main government buildings, and escaped Japanese destruction parties and the attentions of looters.

As was true under British rule, a majority of the files generated during the occupation concern routine matters—applications for small parcels of land, distribution of estates of deceased persons, applications for licences, the payment of fees. In themselves most of these wartime files are unimportant, although collectively they signal an attempt to adhere to normal procedures in an abnormal time. Some offer vignettes of Malayan life. A Tamil man complained that when cows kept by Indians strayed into Malay kampongs, the villagers tied them up and held them for ransom. The villagers denied doing any such thing. The complaint was written in beautiful English by a professional petition writer on behalf of a man whose haltingly printed signature suggests that he was probably illiterate. In another case an Indian woman ("a poor old woman with the adopted daughter" who affixed her thumbprint at the bottom of a letter drafted by S.D. Rajan, holder of Klang Petition Writer's Licence No. 91/2602, for a charge of 50 cents) complained that a man named Raju was constructing a house on her vegetable patch. Investigations revealed that the vegetables had been planted on a road reserve, and neither party was entitled to use the land.[11]

Surviving administrative papers from the period contain almost nothing written in Japanese. For the first six months of the occupation the titles of nearly all files were in Malay, and correspondence was either in Malay or in English. After that, correspondence in the former Federated Malay States increasingly reverted to English, while in the Unfederated Malay States, where Malay had been the medium used by the pre-war administration, documents continued to be prepared in Malay, generally in Romanized form but sometimes in Jawi, Malay written using a modified version of the Arabic alphabet. Administrative papers for the northern states after the transfer to Thailand were written in Malay

[10] Memo, Director of Intelligence Sec/SAC, 10 Dec. 1945, WO203/4942; Custodian of Enemy Property 133/1952 contains an inventory of records, as well as a list of 256 "Non-Important Books".

[11] Examples are from Klang 543/2602.

and English; a small number of documents are in Thai, but in nearly all cases the files include Malay translations.

Occupation-period records are even more dubious than the usual run of questionable materials used by historians of Southeast Asia. As with any set of official records, these materials tend to concentrate on government activities. Although conditions were deteriorating and there was much inefficiency and corruption, matters had to be presented in a favourable light, and criticism was at the very least circumspect. The problem of documentation for the war years is all the more acute because information available from other sources is of doubtful value. Owing to censorship and the use of the media to spread propaganda, newspapers published immediately before and during the occupation contain much that is inaccurate. Interviews provide a valuable supplement, but are impressionistic and usually vague about details. Intelligence materials and post-war reconstructions of events offer further information, but often include a certain amount of guesswork. No one can use the records without being very conscious of their limitations, of what is not there and of what is suspect about the information that is. Nevertheless, these are the materials that survive, and they provide the foundation for the study that follows.

Note on Malay and Japanese Orthography

The Malay used in this study does not conform to the standards of modern Bahasa Malaysia, the national language of Malaysia, and citations of Malay-language materials have not been adapted to modern spelling conventions, although they will be perfectly intelligible to anyone who knows Bahasa Malaysia. Little would be gained by changing them and much would be lost, since both the language and the spelling help convey the flavour of the period. Bahasa Malaysia is a feature of the post-war world, and played no part in the events of the 1940s.

A similar argument applies to variant spellings of Japanese terms. The Japanese attempted to familiarize the population with the *katakana* syllabary, but as a practical matter had to present Japanese terms in Romanized form. There was no standard way of doing this, and even the premier newspaper appeared with different spellings on the masthead: *Shonan Times*, *Syonan Times*, *Syonan Sinbun* and finally *Syonan Shimbun*.[12] Romanized Japanese terms are presented as they appeared in documents of the period, but will be clear to anyone who knows Japanese.

---

[12] The *Shonan Times* appeared on 20 Feb. 2602, and the name was changed to the *Syonan Times* the following day. The newspaper became the *Syonan Sinbun* on 8 Dec. 2602 (the anniversary of the Japanese invasion) and the *Syonan Shimbun* on 8 Dec. 2603.

Note on Dates

According to the Gregorian calendar the Japanese invasion took place in 1941 and the occupation lasted until 1945. Three other calendars were used in Malaya during this period: the Japanese, Thai and Muslim (see Table I.1). Japanese and Thai (Buddhist Era) dates followed the solar year, and changed to the new year on the first of January of the Gregorian year. The Muslim calendar is based on a lunar year, which is shorter than the solar year by eleven days. Fortuitously, during the occupation the lunar New Year happened to fall close to the solar New Year, and Muslim years nearly coincided with solar years. To make it easier to follow the sequence of events, dates in the main text are given according to the Gregorian calendar, but footnote citations show years from the various calendars as they appear on the original documents. Syowa was the reign name of Emperor Hirohito, whose reign began on 25 December 1926 and ended with his death on 7 January 1989.

Table I.1 Calendar years according to the Gregorian, Japanese, Buddhist and Muslim calendars

Gregorian	*Japanese*	*Buddhist era*	*Muslim (ca.)*
1941	2601 (Syowa 16)	2484	1360
1942	2602 (Syowa 17)	2485	1361
1943	2603 (Syowa 18)	2486	1362
1944	2604 (Syowa 19)	2487	1363
1945	2605 (Syowa 20)	2488	1364

CHAPTER 1

Malaya Before the War[1]

In 1940 the southern portion of the Malay Peninsula was under British rule, and known to the Western world as British Malaya. Although the government was organized along conventional British empire lines, it was made clumsy and complex by the existence of multiple administrative units: the Straits Settlements (Singapore, Penang, Province Wellesley, Malacca[2]), the Federated Malay States or "FMS" (Perak, Selangor, Negri Sembilan and Pahang), and five other states known collectively as the Unfederated Malay States (Johore, Kedah, Perlis, Kelantan and Trengganu). The Straits Settlements were a Crown Colony, while the Federated and Unfederated Malay States were British protectorates. The Governor of the Straits Settlements also served as High Commissioner for the Malay States. This post was filled during the immediate pre-war years by Sir Miles Shenton Thomas. A Colonial Secretary coordinated administrative affairs in the Straits Settlements, and handled the administration of Singapore, while Penang and Malacca were under Resident Commissioners. The FMS had British "Residents" who were nominally advisers to their respective Sultans but in practice controlled the administration; a Federal Secretary served as their link with the High Commissioner. The unfederated states had British Advisers, but there the rulers retained greater control over local affairs. A Secretary to the High Commissioner oversaw administrative activities relating to the Unfederated Malay States.

States were divided into districts under District Officers (see Map I.1), and districts were sub-divided into *mukims*. The most common title for sub-district heads, who occupied the lowest level in the administrative service, was Penghulu,

[1] Information in this section is taken from Malaya – Part I, BMA CAS(M) 506/10; Appreciation of the Economic Position of Malaya under the Japanese, BMA COM/21; *Malaya and Its Civil Administration Prior to Japanese Occupation*; and from standard works on Malayan history, among them Rupert Emerson, *Malaysia*; C.M. Turnbull, *A History of Singapore*; and Barbara Watson Andaya and Leonard Y. Andaya, *A History of Malaysia*.

[2] As a matter of administrative convenience, Brunei, Labuan, Christmas Island and the Cocos-Keeling Islands were also part of the Straits Settlements.

although other terms were used in certain localities. Villages had headmen (for which the most common term was Ketua Kampong) who were not civil servants and worked without fixed salaries, but collected fees for various services, were exempted from the payment of land rent, and received bonuses (the Malay word used was *hadiah*, a gift) for satisfactory work. Specialized government services such as the Department of Drainage and Irrigation, the Department of Agriculture and the Health Department operated at the state and district levels, coordinating their activities with the general administrative service. In cities and towns, bodies known in the Federated Malay States as Sanitary Boards, and in the Unfederated Malay States as Town Boards, were responsible for services such as supplying water and collecting rubbish.

Most legislation for the Straits Settlements consisted of ordinances passed by a 24-member Legislative Council, although the colony was also subject to Acts of the Imperial Parliament and Orders of the King in Council. State councils passed legislation in the Malay states, and laws were promulgated in the name of the ruler in council. In 1909 a Federal Council was formed with power to legislate for the four states which made up the FMS.

The population is conventionally described as consisting primarily of Malays, Indians and Chinese, although these groupings coalesced during the political struggles that followed the occupation and are somewhat misleading as a guide to pre-war Malaya.[3] Prior to 1931, censuses employed an ethnographic classification under which the Malays of the Malay Peninsula and Malays who had emigrated from Sumatra were returned as "Malays Proper", while emigrants from elsewhere in the Netherlands Indies were "Other Malays". The 1931 census sought to differentiate the "politically alien immigrant", and adopted the term "Malaysian" to refer to "all indigenous peoples of the Malay Peninsula and Archipelago". This category was subdivided into "Malays" and "Other Malaysians", the former described as "those Malaysians (excluding aboriginals) who belong to British Malaya", and the latter as immigrants who came to the peninsula from the Netherlands Indies, but enumerators depended on self-identification, and people born in Sumatra often simply described themselves as Malay.[4]

Leadership among the Malays remained to a large extent in the hands of the traditional elite, and in the five unfederated states, where nearly 60 per cent of the Malay population lived, the Malay rulers and aristocracy exercised considerable authority over political affairs. In the FMS, where Malays made up

[3] The "racial" categories used in the 1931 census are described in CA. Vlieland, *British Malaya: A Report on the 1931 Census*, pp. 73–86.

[4] See J.E. Nathan, *The Census of British Malaya*, 1921, pp. 71–6, and C.A. Vlieland, *British Malaya: A Report on the 1931 Census*, p. 75.

just 26 per cent of the total population,[5] the political powers of the traditional elite had become attenuated; the Sultans rarely took part in the day-to-day administration of their states, and their diminished stature is indicated by the fact that in 1927 they ceased attending sessions of the Federal Council. The chiefs retained few administrative responsibilities, while the sub-district heads, the Penghulus, had been transformed from figures of power and influence to salaried civil servants, and were viewed by the British and the local population alike as glorified clerks. Through the Malay College at Kuala Kangsar, children of aristocrats received an education modelled on that offered by British public schools, which qualified them for administrative posts. Most Malays who joined the government did so as members of the Malayan Administrative Service rather than the more prestigious Malayan Civil Service (MCS), which staffed senior positions, but by 1940 a small number of Malays had gained admittance to the MCS and were working in district administration when the Japanese arrived. A second Malay-oriented institution of higher education, the Sultan Idris Training College, emerged in the 1930s as a centre of nationalist political thought, and by the end of the decade some of its graduates were beginning to create a radical, anti-colonial political movement.[6]

The "Chinese" category included people who had migrated to Malaya during the nineteenth century or earlier and were permanently domiciled there and more or less acculturated, along with a substantial body of labourers, mostly men, who were more recent arrivals and continued to identify with China. Groping for appropriate terms and concepts to characterize this population, British census takers referred to subdivisions in the Chinese community, which were based largely on spoken language[7] but incorporated geographic and political features, as "tribes". The principal groupings identified in this way were the Hokkien, predominant in the Straits Settlements where Hokkien was the lingua franca; Cantonese, who formed a majority in the mining centres of Kuala Lumpur and Ipoh; Hakka, Teochew and Hailam. In addition, Kwongsai, Hok Chiu and Hok Chia people were found in sufficient numbers to merit separate mention,

[5] Percentages are based on the "Malay" category in the 1931 Census of British Malaya.

[6] The Sultan Idris Training College opened in 1922 to provide education beyond the primary level for non-elite students, who were expected to become school teachers. William R. Roff, *The Origins of Malay Nationalism*, pp. 142–53, 221ff.

[7] The term "dialect" was not used because distinctions between the speech of the different Chinese groups were too great to be described in this way. "Between what may be called the major dialects or, preferably, the principal languages of China, e.g. the Mandarin, the Cantonese, the Hokkien, etc., lies as great a difference as between European languages." A.M. Pountney, Introduction to the 1911 Census, cited by C.A. Vlieland in the Introduction to the 1931 Census, p. 78.

along with a "Baba Chinese" population whose presence in the peninsula went back several centuries. Mostly of Hokkien derivation, the Babas retained various elements of Chinese culture but spoke little or no Chinese and communicated in Malay with an admixture of Hokkien words. In the nineteenth century the Babas, seizing upon the opportunities offered by the British settlements at Penang and Singapore, had used their capital and local experience to become a powerful force in the new ports. They generally supported British rule.

The Chinese were excluded from positions of authority within the British administration. Chinese community leaders did sit as "unofficial" members on the State and Federal Councils (in contrast with "official" members, who were civil servants), but these councils had little power and the government in any case maintained an official majority throughout much of the pre-war period. The central figures within the Chinese community were usually successful businessmen, and could be found among the office-bearers of secret societies, clan and dialect organizations, clubs, and trade or professional bodies.

Malayan Chinese retained an interest in Chinese affairs, and political organizations in China viewed Malaya as part of their sphere of operations. From early in the twentieth century the Kuomintang (KMT, the Chinese Nationalist Party) had been active in the peninsula, and during the 1920s and 1930s it invited Malayan Chinese to propose candidates for party congresses, and to vote in KMT elections. The British administration suppressed the Malayan KMT in 1925, but under the terms of an agreement worked out in 1931 between the British Minister in China, Sir Miles Lampson, and China's Minister for Foreign Affairs, Wang Cheng-ting, the Malayan government legalized the KMT of China and allowed Chinese in Malaya to take part in its activities, while continuing to proscribe the local KMT. Henceforth, Chinese consulates and Chinese Chambers of Commerce became the focus of KMT activity in the peninsula. The party emphasized education, and as a means of unifying the Malayan Chinese population promoted the use of Mandarin, making it the standard medium of instruction in Chinese schools, and encouraged all Chinese to identify with China. In this way the KMT made some progress in drawing together the disparate Chinese groups, and the Japanese invasion of China in 1937 contributed to this process by giving them a common enemy and a common political cause.

The Chinese Communist Party was also active in Malaya. Communists initially operated surreptitiously within the KMT, but they established a separate organization in Singapore in 1928, and created the Malayan Communist Party in 1930. The British administration decimated the communist organization with a series of arrests in 1931, but around 1934 the party began to rebuild under the leadership of a Comintern agent who used the name Lai Tek, and in December 1936 it formed a united front with the KMT to work against Japan.

The communists, who adopted a particularly strident anti-Japanese line, also began to conduct training for guerrilla warfare.

Malayan Chinese became involved in China's modernization movement during the 1890s and early 1900s, and played an important role in the planning of the 1911 revolution.[8] In 1915, when Japan's "Twenty-One Demands" led to an arrangement giving the Japanese special rights in parts of Manchuria, Mongolia and Shantung Province, Malayan Chinese sent aid to China, and in 1919 they announced a boycott of Japanese goods. Following Japan's attack on Manchuria in 1931, the Chinese community attempted to mount another boycott, but it was short-lived and Japan's share of the Malayan market for manufactured goods actually increased during the first half of the 1930s. By 1935 Japan provided well over half of Malaya's imports of many everyday items, including canned sardines (94 per cent), crockery and glassware (67 per cent), cotton goods (70 per cent), rubber shoes (92 per cent) and bicycle tyres (83 per cent). Following the Marco Polo Bridge incident on 7 July 1937 and aggressive moves by the Japanese against Shanghai, Malayan Chinese again took action against Japanese goods. To avoid diplomatic complications, the colonial authorities did not permit an overt boycott, but they were generally sympathetic and allowed Chinese organizations to create a movement promoting local products, which served the same purpose and resulted in a fall in the value of Japanese exports to Malaya from 71.3 million yen to 22.9 million yen.[9] The Chinese also formed a China Relief Fund Association, which raised large sums of money for China and sent young men to fight against Japanese forces. A Southeast Asia Federation of China Relief Funds, based in Singapore, carried the movement to other parts of the region.[10] At the end of December 1941, as the Japanese were advancing toward Singapore, the Chinese community set up a Mobilization General Council for Overseas Chinese Resistance Against the Japanese Enemy, and created a volunteer Self-Protection Corps, a Propaganda Corps, and a Labour Service Corps to assist in the war effort. Such activity involved thousands of people, and gave the Japanese a clear indication of the hostile sentiments found among the Malayan Chinese population. It also helped identify Chinese who were politically active, and following their conquest of Malaya the Japanese would act quickly to nullify this potential source of opposition.

---

[8] See Michael Godley, *The Mandarin-Capitalists*, and Yen Ching Hwang, *The Overseas Chinese*.

[9] Stephen Leong, "The Malayan Overseas Chinese and the Sino-Japanese War", p. 317.

[10] Denis Koh Soo Jin, "Japanese Competition in the Trade of Malaya in the 1930s", pp. 21–4, 50, 52–61. Tan Kah Kee was chairman of the federation, called the Nan-Chiao Federation of Relief Funds.

More than 80 per cent of the Indians in Malaya were Tamils from southern India, most of whom worked as estate labourers. Other Indian groups present in significant numbers were Telegus, Malayalis and Punjabis (the latter known in Malaya as "Bengalis", presumably because they came from the Bengal Presidency). The Indian population was divided by religion (Hindu, Muslim and Sikh), language, culture, caste and class. Political activity was not widespread, and what there was tended to be concerned with developments in the Indian subcontinent, although a body known as the Central Indian Association of Malaya agitated for increased Indian participation in Malayan affairs. Japanese firms in Malaya often employed Indians and cultivated their support.

Three smaller groups played a significant role in Malaya. There were several thousand Ceylon Tamils (counted as "Others" rather than as Indians in the 1931 Census), most of them educated and working as clerks. There were some 16,000 Eurasians, generally professing the Roman Catholic faith and often claiming Portuguese origins, who lived for the most part in urban areas and particularly in the Straits Settlements. And finally there was a small Japanese community, numbering about 6,400 in 1931, whose members engaged in commerce, mining and plantation agriculture. Upon returning home, many of the Japanese who had spent time in Malaya joined a Malayan Association, and Japan drew upon this organization for manpower and information during the occupation.

War preparations made it impossible to carry out the census scheduled for 1941, and census figures for Malaya are only available for 1931 and 1947, although the Japanese carried out a limited census in 1943. Estimates based on 1931 figures adjusted for births, deaths and migration suggest that the population was around 5.5 million in 1941, and this figure is consistent with Japanese calculations in connection with food rationing during the occupation. At the end of the war the Japanese placed the population at 5,709,204,[11] and the first post-war census, taken in 1947, showed 5,848,910 people in the Malayan Union and Singapore (see Table 1.1). The racial distribution of the population was uneven (see Table 1.2). The Malays were predominantly rural and especially numerous in the northern part of the country. The Chinese lived in cities and towns, and in the mine and estate zone along the west coast. Some 35 per cent were in Singapore and Penang, and these two locations together with Perak, Selangor and Johore accounted for more than 80 per cent of the Chinese population. More than half of the Indians lived in Perak and Selangor, while the rest were scattered throughout the peninsula, often in urban areas.

[11] Hone to G. Hall, S of S (Colonies), 16 Feb. 1946, BMA DEPT/9/4; correspondence in MU Confidential 678/1947.

Table 1.1 Size of the Malayan population

State or Settlement	*Area (sq. miles)*	*1931*	*1941 (est.)*	*ca. 1943*	*1947*
Singapore	220	559,946	769,216	855,679	940,824
Penang	400	340,259	419,047	n.a.	446,321
Malacca	640	186,711	236,087	n.a.	239,536
Perak	7,980	785,581	992,691	n.a.	953,938
Selangor	3,160	533,197	701,552	687,690	710,788
Negri Sembilan	2,580	233,799	296,009	n.a.	267,668
Pahang	13,820	180,111	221,800	n.a.	250,158
Johore	7,330	505,311	675,297	n.a.	738,251
Kedah	3,640	429,691	525,458	567,600	554,441
Kelantan	5,750	362,517	407,981	409,500	448,572
Trengganu	5,050	179,789	205,743	193,100	225,996
Perlis	310	49,296	57,850	57,100	70,490
Total	50,800	4,347,704	5,508,731	n.a.	5,848,910

Source: Figures for 1931 and 1947 are taken from the 1947 Census. Estimates for 1941 are found in Table 4 of *Malaya and Its Civil Administration Prior to Japanese Occupation*. The 1943 figures for Kedah, Perlis, Kelantan and Trengganu were collected by the Japanese administration and are reported in Summary of Economic Intelligence (Far East) No. 132, 29 Oct. 1945, WO208/1532, p. 9. The 1943 figure for Singapore is from a document prepared in Dec. 1943 by the Research Division, Southern General Military Office, and was supplied by Professor Hara Fujio.[12] The Selangor figure is in Food Controller, Sel to Financial Officer, Sel, 27 Mar. 2603, DO Klang 133/2603. Areas of the states are taken from a letter from the Surveyor General of the FMS to the Resident of Selangor, 7 Mar. 1936, in Sel Sec 151/1936. The figures are "approximate" but were adopted as a standard to avoid inconsistency in official references.

The economy of the Malay Peninsula underwent great changes during the century that preceded the Japanese occupation.[13] Britain had created trading stations at Penang (in 1786) and Singapore (1819) to capitalize on the entrepôt trade passing through the Straits of Malacca. The concentration of capital, along with the availability of warehouses, shipping facilities and commercial houses at

[12] For details of the 1943 census of Singapore, see Gregg Huff and Shinobu Majima, *World War II Singapore: The Chōsabu Reports on Syonan*, Chapter 3.

[13] Sources for this section include: Appreciation of Malaya, I – Pre-Japanese Occupation, II – Post-Japanese Occupation, BMA 506/10; Malaya – Part I and Malaya – Part II, BMA 506/10; FEB, "Malaya under the Japanese", Mar. 1945, NARA RG226 128585; John Drabble, *Malayan Rubber: The Interwar Years*; Yip Yat Hoong, *The Malayan Tin Industry*.

Table 1.2 Distribution of population by race, 1941

	Malays	*Chinese*	*Indians*	*Others*	*Europeans*	*Eurasians*	*Total*
STRAITS SETTLEMENTS							
Singapore	77,231	599,659	59,838	9,582	14,585	8,321	769,216
Penang	41,353	166,974	31,916	1,879	2,464	2,374	247,460
Province Wellesley	78,060	63,705	28,587	558	369	308	171,587
Malacca	111,907	92,125	28,282	693	599	2,481	236,087
Total	309,051	922,463	148,623	12,712	18,017	13,484	1,424,350
FEDERATED MALAY STATES							
Perak	335,385	450,197	196,056	5,350	4,113	1,590	992,691
Selangor	152,697	339,707	193,504	8,012	4,978	2,654	701,552
Neeri Sembilan	106,005	125,806	59,270	2,633	1,430	865	296,009
Pahang	128,539	73,925	17,226	1,305	628	177	221,800
Total	722,626	989,635	466,056	17,300	11,149	5,286	2,212,052
UNFEDERATED MALAY STATES							
Johore	302,104	308,901	58,498	4,178	1,264	352	675,297
Kedah	341,294	108,445	60,898	14,009	671	141	525,458
Kelantan	369,256	23,363	7,591	7,522	209	40	407,981
Trengganu	186,580	16,956	1,409	728	53	17	205,743
Perlis	46,441	8,227	1,127	2,042	3	10	57,850
Total	1,245,675	465,892	129,523	28,479	2,200	560	1,872,329
Total Malaya	2,277,352	2,377,990	744,202	58,491	31,366	19,330	5,508,731

Source: *Malaya and Its Civil Administration Prior to Japanese Occupation*, Table 4.

these two locations, which operated as free ports, helped define future patterns of economic growth. By the 1840s, Penang and Singapore had become prosperous financial centres, and the European and Chinese merchants based there were beginning to look to the peninsula as a suitable place to invest their trading profits. Malaya proved to have substantial reserves of tin ore (see Map 6.3), and Chinese investment in the tin industry yielded good returns. Mine owners brought large numbers of Chinese labourers to Malaya, and these men worked in the mines or in associated service industries, creating new centres of economic activity and a non-Malay capitalist class along the thinly populated west coast. In the twentieth century Malaya became the largest tin producer in the world, and attracted European investment. Dredging, a capital-intensive method of production largely confined to European-owned mines, accounted for about two-thirds of Malaya's output, while the balance came from Chinese mines using more labour-intensive hydraulic and gravel pump methods. Although Malays had mined tin for centuries, their activities were carried out on a smaller scale, and they played little part in the new mining industry.

Malaya also produced coal and minerals. Coal was mined by Malayan Collieries at Batu Arang in Selangor (see Map 6.3). The output amounted to almost 630,000 tons in 1937 and was sold, in roughly equal proportions, to the railway, to tin mines, and to other local consumers. The coal was lignite, and Malaya imported some 700,000 tons of hard coal each year from South Africa, Japan and India to supply ships calling at Malayan ports. Iron ore was produced by Japanese mines located in Johore, Kelantan and Trengganu, and the output, amounting to some 2 million tons per annum, was sent to Japan. The Japanese also mined manganese and bauxite in Malaya. Southeast Asia accounted for more than half of Japan's imports of tin, rubber, bauxite and chrome ore, and a substantial proportion of the manganese, tungsten, nickel, copper and petroleum used in Japan.

Petroleum had not been found in the peninsula, but Singapore was a major storage, processing and distribution centre for the oil fields of Sumatra and Burma, and petroleum products accounted for between 10 and 15 per cent of the trade of pre-war Malaya.

Trade and mining were the dominant commercial activities in Malaya until the early twentieth century, when rubber cultivation had a period of explosive growth, first as an estate crop, and after 1910 on smallholdings as well (see Map 8.1). During the 1930s, rubber was the country's principal agricultural product and most important export. Two-thirds of the five million acres of land under cultivation in the peninsula was planted with rubber, and Malaya accounted for more than 40 per cent of the rubber entering world markets. Other commercial crops were insignificant by comparison. They included pineapples (about 50,000 acres), oil palm (75,000 acres) and coconuts (600,000 acres). During the rubber boom, the acquisition of Malay lands by plantation interests reached a level that British officials felt was threatening the traditional way of life, and the administration devised a Malay Reservations Enactment to preserve certain lands for exclusive use by Malays. Conceived as a mechanism to protect established areas of Malay settlement, the Enactment was later used to reserve land for future generations of Malays.

The transport network developed along the west coast to carry tin from the mines in Perak and Selangor to processing and shipping centres in Penang and Singapore suited the needs of the rubber companies as well, and they opened land in areas that gave them access to these facilities (see Map 6.1). The estate industry added a new dimension to the entrepôt trade at Penang and Singapore, and conclusively positioned Malaya's economic centre along the west coast.

Rice was the staple food of the population, but the local crop supplied less than half of Malaya's total requirements, and less than 20 per cent of the rice consumed by labourers involved in export production and the urban population (see Map 8.1). During the 1930s the government attempted to stimulate rice cultivation by constructing irrigation works, distributing selected seeds, and improving milling and marketing arrangements. These efforts more than doubled the size of the crop but the increase did not even keep pace with population growth, and imports rose during the same period. Overall, around two-thirds of Malaya's rice was consumed by those who grew it, while many people who planted rice produced less than they needed for personal use and purchased additional supplies. On the eve of the Japanese occupation, Malaya remained heavily dependant on imported rice.

Fish figured prominently in the Malayan diet, both salt-water and fresh-water varieties, the latter caught in rivers and in rice fields and irrigation canals. Japanese fishermen operating large motor-driven vessels supplied nearly half of Singapore's fish supply. Malay and Chinese fishermen accounted for the rest and for fish sold in the Malay states, often using smaller boats without motors. However, local fish catches only satisfied half of local demand.[14]

Malaya's industries were concentrated in Singapore and in urban areas on the western side of the peninsula, and tended to be in the hands of British and Chinese firms (see Maps 6.3 and 6.4). One major activity was the processing of rubber and tin for export. Drawing supplies from the Malay Peninsula, the Netherlands Indies, Siam, southern Burma, Sarawak and British North Borneo, factories in Singapore and Penang smoked and milled low grade rubber, selling most of the output to manufacturers outside of Malaya. Malayan smelters processed local

[14] Ministry of Economic Warfare. Malaya – Part I. 20 July 1943, p. 15, in FO371/41732.

tin ore, and obtained additional supplies from Burma, the Netherlands Indies, French Indochina, Siam, China, Japan, Africa and Alaska. Local firms also built and repaired ships, and carried out civil, mechanical and electrical engineering projects, particularly in tin-producing areas where foundries made equipment for the mines. Other locally manufactured products included

> ... bricks, soap, candles, pottery, concrete goods, wire nails, steel and rattan furniture, flooring tiles, beer, aerated waters, bedsteads, biscuits, cement products, cigarettes, batteries for electric torches, essential oils, oxygen and acetylene and other gases, earthenware, fertilizers and disinfectants, galvanised buckets and tanks, groundnut oil, ice, inks, iron pans, patent medicines, piping (earthenware and steel), planks, sago-flour, sauces and pickles, steel trunks, sugar candy, tinned pineapples and varnishes.[15]

There were also tanneries, dye works, automobile assembly plants and printing works. Although the list is long, Malayan industries only produced goods for the domestic market and for export to neighbouring countries, and operated on a very small scale compared with those in industrialized countries elsewhere.

Industrial output made little contribution to Malaya's export trade, and the main exports before the war were primary products that had undergone rudimentary processing, including copra, sago flour, pepper, palm oil and coconut oil, tapioca, gambier, pineapples, rattans, tuba root (Derris), rubber and tin. Imports included substantial quantities of tin and rubber destined for re-export, rice, petroleum products and a wide range of manufactured goods (see Tables 1.3 and 1.4).

As the tables indicate, Malaya enjoyed a favourable balance of trade. The range of exports was limited, with tin (categorized in the tables under non-ferrous metals) and rubber accounting for around three-quarters of the total, but the returns on these products were sufficient to offset the cost of substantial quantities of imported goods. In view of what lay ahead, the crucial feature of the trade figures was the country's heavy dependence on imports for basic consumer requirements, such as kerosene and other petroleum products, rice, sugar and cotton piece goods. With the Japanese invasion, imports came to a halt and it proved impossible to supply the deficit in these products from local sources.

The British Colonial Office administered Malaya as a more or less autonomous entity, responsible for its own finances and governed by laws that conformed to general colonial practice but were passed as specifically Malayan legislation. Economically the peninsula was a fragment of larger economic systems, drawing labour from China and India and peasant farmers from the Netherlands Indies, while importing rice from mainland Southeast Asia, and capital from Europe and

15 Malaya – Part I, BMA 506/10. See also OSS Planning Group, Implementation Study for Strategic Services Activity in the SEAC: Malaya, 3 July 1944, NABA RG226 E136 folder 650.

Table 1.3 Malaya's principal exports (× $1,000)

	1931	*1938*	*1939*	*1940*	*1941*[a]
Grain and flour	18,415	19,139	18,619	21,710	18,208
Other food and drink (non-dutiable)	41,220	36,971	41,714	39,850	32,987
Seeds and nuts for oil, oils, fats, resins and gums	41,351	27,453	27,389	24,929	16,108
Rubber and gutta percha	488,680	277,954	377,905	638,240	540,368
Non-ferrous metals and manufactures thereof	190,374	96,644	158,615	284,899	n.a.
Oils, fats and resins (manufactures thereof)	57,919	57,224	55,030	46,347	31,697
Other	59,162	80,930	57,208	69,082	n.a.
Total	897,121	596,315	736,480	1,125,057	n.a.

Note: [a]Figures for 1941 are for January through September.
Source: Malayan Trade Statistics, 1938, 1939, 1940, 1941.

Table 1.4 Malaya's principal imports (× $1,000)

	1931	*1938*	*1939*	*1940*	*1941*[a]
Grain and flour	67,880	71,140	73,340	86,338	86,323
Other food and drink (non-dutiable)	67,752	64,270	68,611	85,625	92,522
Drink and tobacco (dutiable)	25,070	23,370	21,852	29,040	26,842
Rubber and gutta percha	145,612	76,867	114,759	188,018	161,506
Non-ferrous metalliferous ores and scrap	43,081	30,211	56,623	96,961	71,253
Iron and steel (manufactures thereof)	29,208	22,673	21,376	31,466	22,079
Oils, fats and resins (manufactured)	91,832	86,026	92,425	86,862	53,008
Cotton yarn and manufactured goods	30,313	25,940	23,491	35,545	28,956
Machinery and vehicles	37,856	36,415	33,358	32,280	27,048
Misc. manufactured articles	21,986	19,102	18,498	25,014	16,559
Other	119,323	90,596	96,287	126,958	103,749
Total	679,913	546,610	620,620	697,149	679,845

Note: [a]Figures for 1941 are for January through September.
Source: Malayan Trade Statistics, 1938, 1939, 1940, 1941.

various parts of Asia. The country's mines and plantations, and the export trade associated with them, provided employment for much of the population, while the trading ports of Singapore and Penang imported manufactured goods and food, supplying the needs of the people of Malaya and generating income and employment. In most years the value of Malaya's exports was substantially greater than the value of its imports and the territory prospered, but maintaining this prosperity required continued access to overseas markets and overseas suppliers of manufactured goods, and when war reached Malaya this critical feature of the economy disappeared. During the occupation, the country had a surfeit of tin and rubber but insufficient food and clothing.

* * *

Large numbers of people came to Malaya as contract workers, and many of them retained close social and in some cases political links with their homelands. Both Chinese and Indian political activity intruded on the peninsula, but Malaya itself had very little in the way of domestic politics, although during the 1930s a Malay political awareness directed toward preserving and enhancing the position of the Malay population began to take shape. The different elements of the population were to some degree segregated because the states with large Malay populations had relatively small numbers of Chinese and Indians, while the Chinese and Indians occupied separate niches in the areas where they lived in substantial numbers. Even within the "Chinese", "Indian" and "Malay/Malaysian" categories there were major divisions of language, religion and class, and people had little in common apart from the fact that they lived and worked in British Malaya.

CHAPTER 2

The Beginning of the Occupation

The Build-up to the War

Britain and Japan were allies before and during the First World War, but relations deteriorated during the political realignment that took place after the conflict ended. Britain emerged from the war as the world's greatest naval power, but construction programmes in the United States, France and Japan threatened to overshadow the British navy, and the British government, facing pressure to economize on military expenditure, was unable to compete in a naval race. There was considerable harmony between the strategic interests of Britain and America, but Japan and Britain appeared to be on a collision course as Japan attempted to secure a greater share of the resources and markets of Southeast Asia. The British accordingly abandoned the Anglo-Japanese Alliance which had regulated naval affairs in the Far East before the war, in favour of strengthening ties with the United States. The Washington Conference in 1921 stabilized the situation and for the time being put an end to the naval race. The United States, Britain, and Japan agreed to maintain their capital fleets according to a ratio of 5:5:3, and Britain then developed a naval strategy that called for stationing its Main Fleet in European waters, and sending it to other parts of the world should the need arise. This arrangement required secure naval bases from which warships could operate, and a series of defended ports on the principal routes of imperial communication to enable the fleet to reach any possible theatre of operations.

The British government proposed in 1919 to build a major naval base in Singapore, and four years later approved funds for a floating dock that was constructed in Britain and reached Singapore at the end of 1928. Preparation of the site for the naval base began in the same year, but pressures to economize, and moves toward disarmament following the economic collapse in 1929, slowed development of the facility. The pace of work picked up again following the Shanghai incident in 1932, when Japanese troops invested the city for nearly four months. Talks concerning renewal of the Washington Treaty, which was due to expire in 1936, did not produce an agreement because Britain and the United States rejected Japan's demand for parity of naval forces. Construction proceeded in an atmosphere of heightened tension. In February 1938 the British government staged an opening ceremony for the King George VI dry dock, although the naval base was not yet entirely finished and in fact remained unfinished when Singapore fell.[1]

An intense propaganda battle broke out between Japan and Britain in the late 1930s. The Japanese concentrated their efforts on the press, and in 1939 were publishing five newspapers in Singapore, three in Japanese, one in Chinese and one in English.[2] They also distributed news bulletins in Japanese, English and Chinese through the Eastern News Agency (Toho Tsushin Sha), an organization established in 1938 that reportedly received support from the Japanese Foreign Office. Britain's Special Operations Executive (SOE), through its Oriental Mission, disseminated propaganda worldwide through newspaper stories and radio broadcasts originating in Singapore, and regionally by means of Asian-language broadcasts and publications. Some of this activity was carried out on a covert basis.

> Through an agreement reached with a world-wide news organisation it was possible for us to release news presented from "our point of view" and to release rumours on an international basis. Some seventy-two newspapers in British and Allied countries were secretly influenced. Indirectly other major news chains were influenced through this organisation; it was one of our most efficient anti-Japanese weapons.[3]

The Oriental Mission also arranged for the preparation of feature films and documentaries that were released through normal commercial channels. "These pictures—mainly fakes, presented British and anti-Japanese propaganda in a most acceptable form." Plans called for most of the operational units involved in propaganda activities to be transferred to the Ministry of Information's Far Eastern Bureau in the event of war, but the Far Eastern Bureau ceased to function

---

[1] The literature on the Singapore Naval Base and the fall of Singapore is large. See Brian Farrell, *The Defence and Fall of Singapore, 1940–1942*; W. David McIntyre, *The Rise and Fall of the Singapore Naval Base, 1919–1942*; Malcolm Murfett et al., *Between Two Oceans: A Military History of Singapore*; James Neidpath, *The Singapore Naval Base and the Defence of Britain's Eastern Empire, 1919–1941*; Karl Hack and Kevin Blackburn, *Did Singapore Have to Fall?*

[2] These were the *Nanyo Nichi Nichi Shimbun*, the *Singapore Nippo*, a weekly Chinese edition of the *Singapore Nippo*, the *Nanyo Oyobi Nihonjin* (weekly), and the *Singapore Herald.*

[3] Report on Propaganda Activities by the Oriental Mission, 27 Apr. 1942, HSI/226.

when fighting broke out, and was itself taken over by the Oriental Mission to ensure continuity of British propaganda.[4]

Japan was also gathering intelligence in Malaya. Japanese-owned lands in Johore and on Singapore island provided useful vantage points for observing construction of the Singapore Naval Base and coastal defences, while the Japanese fishing fleet, which accounted for nearly half of the fish landed in Singapore, conducted surveys of Malayan coastal areas and took soundings off the beaches, ostensibly because this information was needed to catch fish. Japanese photographers operated studios in many Malayan towns, and some of them took pictures of roads and railways and military installations. Certain Japanese military officers operated incognito; for example, an army colonel named Tsugunori Kadomatsu worked for six years as a waiter in the British Officers' Club. In September 1940 a visit to Singapore by Colonel T. Tanikawa, planning chief of the Japanese Imperial Army Headquarters in Tokyo, led to the arrest and imprisonment of Mamoru Shinozaki, a press attaché at the Japanese Consulate, who had taken Tanikawa's party on a tour of various strategic locations.[5] A Japanese known locally as "Ayah Kawa" was involved in laying pipe to supply water to rice fields in the Pengkalan Chepa area of Kelantan, where the initial Japanese landing took place.[6] Although it is probably true, as Shinozaki contends in his book on this period, that most of the Japanese living in Malaya and Singapore were ordinary businessmen and not spies, Japan collected a great deal of useful information before the invasion, and people throughout the peninsula relate stories about Japanese photographers or barbers who reappeared

---

[4] Ibid. OM/P officers held the following positions: Adviser on Re-organization of the Far Eastern Bureau, Acting Director of the Far Eastern Bureau, Press Attaché and Director of Publicity at Chungking, Ministry of Information Representative in Burma, and Controller of the Research Bureau. In Malaya all propaganda for morale operations originated with and was controlled by OM/P.

[5] Mamoru Shinozaki, *Syonan – My Story*, pp. 1–3. An account of Shinozaki's arrest and conviction in Eric Robertson's The Japanese File makes no mention of Tanikawa's visit, and Shinozaki was arrested in connection with two other episodes. Shinozaki says he was simply a press attaché and not a spy (*Syonan*, p. 4), but Robertson claims that evidence showed him to have been involved in "suborning members of the Services stationed in Singapore", and he was convicted of collecting information "which might be useful to a foreign power". *The Japanese File*, p. 115.

[6] Mohd. Rafdi Mohd. Taha, "Serangan dan Pendudukan Tentera Jepun terhadap Kampung Pak Amat dan Pengkalan Chepa", p. 94. This information was obtained from Dato' Hj. Mohammad Hj. Ab. Kadir, the headman of Kampung Pak Amat at the time, who was well acquainted with the man people called "Ayah Kawa", punning on his Japanese name. "Ayah" is a Malay word meaning father.

during the occupation wearing a military uniform.[7] The British attempted to limit the gathering of intelligence by declaring certain areas to be "prohibited places", and by imposing limits on the movement and activities of "aliens"; the police Special Branch set up a Nippon Section that monitored the movements of Japanese nationals and issued a monthly account of Japanese activities. However, Britain was concerned not to cause diplomatic incidents, and the police only took action when there was a clear violation of the law.[8]

In the late 1930s the Malayan administration began preparing for the possibility of an imminent conflict with Japan. Hospitals were equipped to treat military casualties, and in Kuala Lumpur the General Hospital underwent a major re-organization in 1941, adding an air-conditioned operating theatre, a casualty clearing centre, resuscitation wards and surgical units. From August admissions were limited to those in great need of hospital care, and decrepit wards were evacuated, with temples and the Hong Fatt Mines Company taking charge of most of those removed. In December 1941, with fighting taking place in northern Malaya, all chronic and convalescent patients were discharged from hospitals throughout Selangor, and staff was brought from dispensaries into the hospitals to help deal with war casualties. During the fighting, the General Hospital treated 1,700–2,000 military casualties.[9]

Because Malaya was a rice deficit area, food supplies were a major focus of attention. In July 1939 the Customs Department assumed responsibility for food control, and the Comptroller of Customs, H.R. Jarrett, became Food Controller. To facilitate rationing should this become necessary, the government registered and licensed all rice dealers, and required them to submit monthly reports of stocks and records of transactions, using this information to develop statistics on the movement and consumption of rice. The Food Controller also began creating a rice stockpile designed to meet the needs of the population

---

[7] See, for example, Lee Siow Mong, *Words Cannot Equal Experience*, pp. 24–5. Eric Robertson, a British intelligence officer in pre-war Malaya, suggests in his book *The Japanese File* that photographic studios and barber shops played a minor role in the Japanese intelligence effort.

[8] Ophelia Ooi, "An Inquiry into the Political Activities of the Japanese in Singapore", pp. 39–74; see also Shinozaki, *Syonan*, passim.

[9] State of Selangor, Report of the Medical Department for the Years 1941–46, RC Sel 296/1947.

for six months.[10] Normal consumption of imported rice in Malaya was around 53,000 tons per month, but the target for the stockpile was based on 43,000 tons per month on the assumption that people could reduce their intake by 25 per cent. Since milled rice did not keep well, grain had to be purchased and stored as unmilled rice (padi), which could be stored for up to one year. Padi was bulkier than milled rice, and it required almost 70,000 tons of padi to produce 43,000 tons of milled grain. Existing mills did not have sufficient capacity to process rice at this rate, and in 1939 existing and planned storage facilities could only hold 95,000 tons of padi, or slightly more than one month's supply.[11] Early in 1940 the reserve stood at 80,000 tons of padi. Warehouses built in the course of the year in Kedah and Perlis could accommodate about 20,000 tons of padi, and the government spent $230,000 to construct a large mill at Arau, Perlis, with a capacity of 25 bags of rice per hour and storage space for 10,000 tons of padi. This area would be one of the first parts of Malaya to fall into Japanese hands. Another government mill was erected at Telok Anson in order to handle rice from the irrigation areas that were being developed at Sungei Manik in Lower Perak and in Kuala Selangor, and a mill was planned for Singapore.[12]

Although some rice for the stockpile came from local sources, the greater part was purchased from external sources. During 1939 the Malayan government bought about 30,000 tons of unmilled rice from Thailand for the stockpile, and in 1940 it acquired an additional 250,000 tons.[13] For 1941 the Malayan Food Controller signed a contract with the quasi-governmental Thai Rice Company covering purchases of 420,000 tons of grain, but the contract was accompanied by a memorandum that permitted the Thais to alter the terms of the agreement

---

[10] Revised Report on Singapore Food Supplies, 1938, 21 Dec. 1938, CO852/264/13; History of the First Three Months of the War, section 16 (Food Supply), encl. in Gov. of Malaya secret despatch, 15 Feb. 1940, CO852/327/9. In Malaya the Secretary for Defence, CA. Vlieland, served as Chairman of the Food Supply Sub-Committee. In August 1939 a Food Reserve Stocks Committee, made up of the Food Controller and three leading merchants, had also recommended stockpiling sufficient milk, meat, sugar, salt, flour, and edible fats to meet requirements for three months, but limited storage space and the perishable nature of some of these items made it impossible to carry out the arrangements fully.

[11] Thomas to MacDonald, 27 Apr. 1939, CO852/264/13; Thomas to MacDonald, 3 Aug. 1939, CO852/264/14.

[12] BA Kedah to Secy for Defence, Malaya, 14 Jan. 1940, BA Perlis 653/1358; Food Reserve Held or to be Held in 1940 by the Malayan Governments, CO852/264/14; Executive Engineer Perlis to BA Perlis, 16 July 1941, BA Perlis 172/1360; Belgrave to Stockdale, 17 Oct. 1939, CO852/264/14.

[13] The Anglo-Thai Corporation, Ltd. and The Borneo Company, Memorandum on the Possibilities of Obtaining in Bangkok, Siam, and Moving to Malaya, Large Quantities of Rice during a Post-Hostilities Emergency Period, 6 Sept. 1943, CO852/510/19.

under certain conditions, for example, if the rice crop was poor.[14] The British ambassador in Thailand, Sir Josiah Crosby, warned at the end of March 1941 that the country was "palpably pro-Japanese" and would "prefer Japan to Malaya in case of a short crop".[15] The crop appears to have been normal, but the Thais invoked the provision allowing them to reduce the amount of rice sold to Malaya, and announced in April that they could only deliver 270,000 tons.[16] With prices of Thai rice high and supplies difficult to obtain, the Food Controller turned to Burma to build up the Malayan stockpile, and individual consumers in Malaya also began to favour the less expensive Burmese rice. In 1941 Burma's exportable surplus was approximately 3,700,000 tons as compared with a reported availability of just 900,000 tons in Thailand, and through purchases of Burmese rice the Malayan authorities succeeded by the end of 1941 in meeting the objective of creating a reserve stock sufficient to meet the country's needs for six months.[17]

In addition to buying imported rice, the government launched a campaign to increase local production of rice and other foodstuffs. Expenditure was concentrated on the irrigation works at Sungei Manik in Lower Perak and in the Tanjong Karang area of Kuala Selangor, but the government also encouraged estate managers to interplant stands of young trees with foodcrops, and advised the public to plant tapioca and other vegetables wherever land was available.[18] In 1939 Governor Shenton Thomas reversed a policy adopted at the beginning of the 1930s that restricted grants of rice land to ethnic Malays, and opened rice cultivation to non-Malays, saying that Malaya's domestic production was small because there were too few rice farmers. The change in policy produced a strong reaction from Malay nationalists, and the Malay-language newspaper

---

[14] Memorandum accompanying agreement between the Thai Rice Co. and the Secretary to the Food Controller on behalf of the Government of the Straits Settlements, Dec. 1940, TNA, Ministry of the Prime Minister (2) 0201.57.3/2.

[15] Crosby to FO, 31 Mar. 1941, F2448/1281/40, FO371/28140.

[16] Crosby to FO, 2 Apr. and 7 Apr. 1941 and Coultas to FO, 10 Apr. 1941, F2944/1281 /40, F0371 /28140. The Thai Rice Company at first told the Bangkok Agents acting for the Straits Settlements that they could only supply 225,000 tons, but the Prime Minister increased the figure to 270,000 tons as a gesture of goodwill. One indication that Siam was using the rice trade for political purposes can be seen in the visit to Singapore in June 1941 by Major Vilas Osatanandha of Thailand's Ministry of Commerce, who offered 50,000 tons of rice in exchange for oil supplies. A.G. Baker, The Siamese Rice Trade with Malaya, 27 Aug. 1945, CO852/568/12; see also Crosby to FO, 21 Oct. 1940, FO371/24756.

[17] F0371/13446. There was also sufficient wheat flour for 130 days (24,000 tons), milk for 90 days, sugar for 100 days, and salt for 120 days.

[18] Belgrave to Stockdale, 17 Oct. 1939, CO852/264/14.

Majlis described it as "an outrage of the Malay's rightful preserve and heritage", which would result in their being "swamped out of the padi fields ... literally deprived of their only certain means of livelihood".[19] These dire warnings proved baseless, not least because rice cultivation remained relatively unprofitable; the *Straits Times* stated editorially that "as the actual cash return on a three-acre padi holding is only $45 for six months' work, the Chinese will not exactly flock into this new industry".[20]

The outbreak of war in Europe gave rise to panic buying, hoarding and inflation in Malaya. The Food Controller imposed ceilings on the prices charged for major food items and took action against profiteers, cancelling or suspending their licences and initiating prosecutions in court. These actions were given wide publicity by the government's Information Department and succeeded in bringing prices down.[21] For a time the administration also encouraged the public to prepare for possible shortages by building up private stockpiles. Thomas told the Legislative Council in February 1939 that buying supplies in anticipation of an emergency "was not hoarding but merely a wise precautionary measure", and in April he advised householders and employers to store adequate supplies of food, stating that stocks so accumulated would be considered part of the country's defense arrangements and would not be confiscated. He made a similar statement at the Federal Council meeting in June, but on 23 August, the government reversed its position and issued the following notice:

> It has come to the knowledge of the Government that certain members of the public have been purchasing or attempting to purchase abnormal quantities of food during the past twenty-four hours, presumably fearing a shortage in the near future.
>
> The Government wishes it to be clearly understood that the time has passed when the laying-in of household reserve stocks is to be commended; at the present time such action is definitely against the public interest; it is open to all the objections to hoarding and will be treated accordingly by the Food Control authorities.
>
> The Government desires to impress on the public that there is not the slightest ground for fearing a real shortage of food supplies in the near future, but it is quite possible that a temporary artificial shortage may be gratuitously created if individuals try to buy up and hoard more than the amount of food which they usually purchase at one time.

---

19 Reported in the *Straits Times*, 10 Aug. 1939.

20 *Straits Times*, 9 Aug. 1939.

21 History of the First Three Months of the War, section 16 (Food Supply), CO852/327/9.

The Governor also announced that the immunity from requisitioning announced previously would not apply to stocks acquired after the notice was issued.[22]

The Japanese Conquest

The fall of Malaya and Singapore was one of the most devastating military defeats in British history, and has been exhaustively analyzed both by the protagonists and by historians.[23] The fundamental cause of the defeat was that British military forces in Malaya were too weak to resist the Japanese, while plans to send reinforcements from Europe, and the expectation that America's Pacific fleet would have a deterrent effect on the Japanese, were nullified by the German advance in Europe and Japan's raid on Pearl Harbor. However, studies of this event also call attention to personality clashes, interservice rivalries and civilian-military conflicts, and suggest that the leadership was at least complacent and arguably incompetent.

Military plans developed in the 1920s emphasized the need to protect Singapore, and largely disregarded the Malay Peninsula. Singapore's defences were considered adequate to repel a Japanese invasion, and should Japan lay siege to the island, the main fleet could relieve Singapore within two months. A revised Defence Scheme prepared in 1937 adopted much the same approach, but the worsening situation in Europe soon forced the Malayan Defence Committee to increase the period before relief to 180 days and then to an indefinite period.[24] In 1940, Italy's alliance with Germany and the fall of France forced Britain to abandon altogether the idea that the navy could play a major role against a Japanese offensive in Southeast Asia, and to prepare a revised strategy which shifted the burden of protecting Malaya to the air force and the army. This change made it essential to defend the entire Malay Peninsula so that the air force could operate there, and Japan could not establish forward bases to attack Singapore.

---

[22] K.S. Patton, American Consul General, to S of S (Washington), 24 Aug. 1939, NARA RG59 846 D.5018/4.

[23] See, for example, A.E. Percival, *The War in Malaya*; Masanobu Tsuji, *Singapore: The Japanese Version*; S. Woodburn Kirby, *History of the Second World War: The War Against Japan*, vol. 1 and the same author's *The Loss of Singapore*; K.D. Bhargava and K.N.V. Sastri, *Official History of the Indian Armed Forces in the Second World War, 1939–45: Campaigns in South-East Asia, 1941–42*; Compton Mackenzie, *Eastern Epic*, W. David McIntyre, *The Rise and Fall of the Singapore Naval Base, 1919–1942*; James Neidpath, *The Singapore Naval Base and the Defence of Britain's Eastern Empire, 1919–1941*; Peter Elphick, *Singapore: The Pregnable Fortress*. McIntyre provides a chronological list of 75 books and articles on the Malayan campaign published between 1942 and 1977, and the number has increased substantially since that time.

[24] For discussion of this point, see the Malayan Defence Scheme, 1937, CAB 11/201, and Kirby, *The Loss of Singapore*, p. 281.

The Chiefs of Staff estimated that mounting a successful defence of Malaya, Singapore and northern Borneo would require an increase in air strength in the region from the existing 8 squadrons and 88 first-line aircraft to 22 squadrons and 336 first-line aircraft. Local commanders said even this figure was too low and requested 556 aircraft, but when the invasion took place British forces had just 158 first-line aircraft available for operations, compared with at least 500 used by the Japanese.

Illus. 2.1 Labourers opening cases containing "Long-Nose" Blenheim bombers newly arrived in Singapore.

Source: United States Library of Congress, LC-DIG-ds-04804.

The army commander, General A.E. Percival, considered that 48 battalions constituted the minimum force needed to defend Malaya; he had 32, and few of the combat formations were adequately trained and equipped. Including support personnel, there were about 88,600 men serving in Malaya in December 1941, of whom 37,000 were Indian troops, and 16,800 were Asians recruited locally. British and Australian troops made up the balance (19,600 and 15,200 respectively). There was legislation in place that allowed the government to demand compulsory service from male British subjects and British Protected Persons in the Straits Settlements and Malay States, although when general mobilization came many of these men were exempted to keep Malaya's export industries functioning. Last-minute reinforcements brought the size of the force

Illus. 2.2 Assembling United States-made Brewster pursuit ships in a hangar in Malaya for the use of Britain's Royal air force in the Far East, c. 1941.

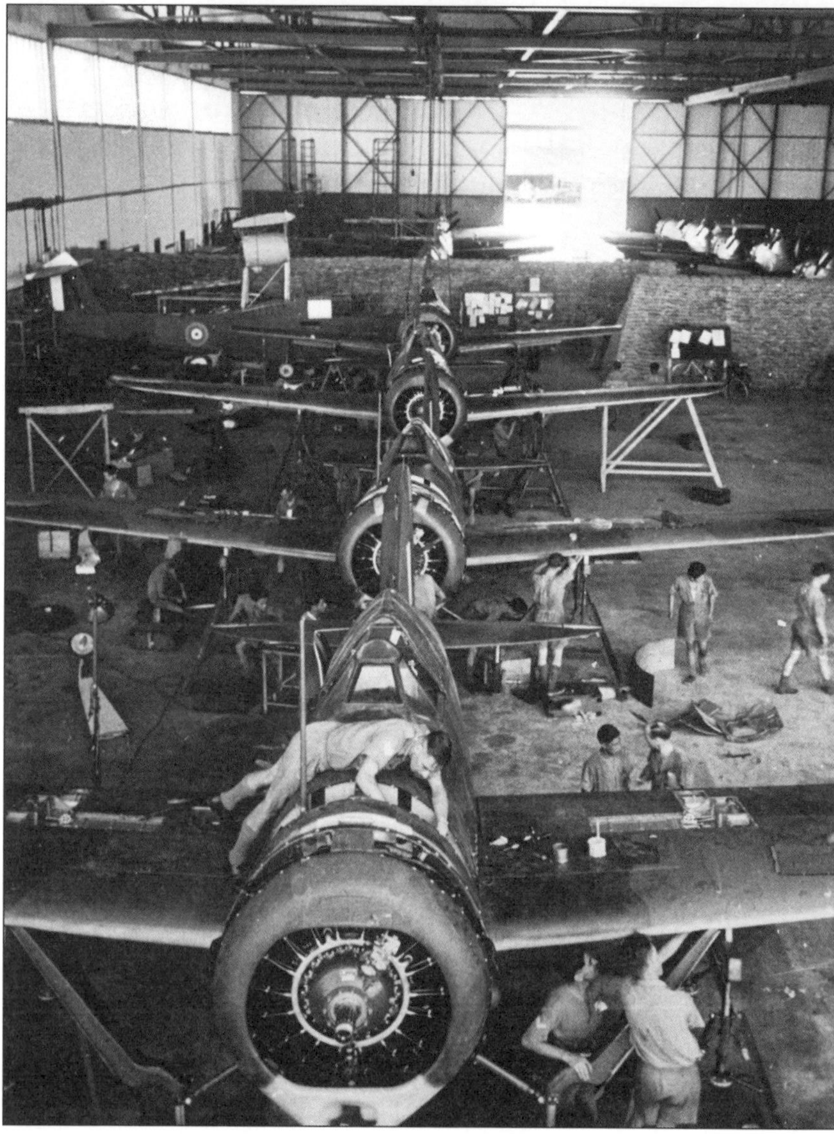

Source: United States Library of Congress, LC-DIG-ds-04819.

to somewhere between 125,000 and 138,000 men, with Australia and India both providing additional troops, but few of the new arrivals were ready for combat.[25] Lee Siow Mong, who was a security warden in Singapore, recalls encountering some newly-arrived British conscripts who asked him what a Japanese looked like. "My answer was that the Japanese looked very much like me except perhaps they were a little shorter. I was puzzled and confused as to how the British could ever hope to fight a war when they could not even recognise their enemy."[26]

Illus. 2.3 American Brewster Buffalo fighter planes over Malaya, c. 1941.

Source: United States Library of Congress, LC-DIG-ds-04801.

The weakness of British military forces in Malaya and elsewhere in the Far East forced Britain to play for time by offering economic concessions to Japan and avoiding open conflict while trying to shore up defences within the region. Japan needed to maintain imports of rice, which it obtained from Indochina, British Burma and Thailand, and imports of oil, acquired from Sumatra, and there was pressure to respond to Japanese aggression in China by imposing a trade embargo, but action along these lines seemed more likely to spark an open conflict than to cause Japan to abandon warlike activities, and the suggestion was not pursued. This assessment of the Japanese response was probably correct, for a Japanese Army-Navy Draft Policy dated 17 April 1941 stated that Japan would attempt to strengthen its defensive position by diplomatic means, but added

---

25 Kirby, *The War against Japan*, vol. 1, and *The Loss of Singapore*, pp. 77, 163–4; Brian Farrell, personal communication.

26 Lee Siow Mong, *Words Cannot Equal Experience*, p. 25.

that if embargoes or other measures threatened the existence of the Japanese empire, military action would be taken. On 25 July 1941, after Japanese forces moved into southern Vietnam, the United States froze Japanese funds, and as other countries including the Netherlands followed America's lead, it became increasingly difficult for Japan to purchase fuel. At the end of August the Netherlands Indies banned exports of oil and bauxite to Japan, greatly restricting Japan's access to these critical commodities.[27] In December Japan seized the initiative, launching coordinated assaults on Pearl Harbor, Hong Kong, Malaya and the Philippines.

Japanese forces landed in southern Thailand and northern Malaya very early on 8 December 1941, opting to approach Singapore overland through Malaya. The British Chiefs of Staff Committee had considered this possibility in 1940 and concluded: "An advance down the Isthmus and across Malaya was fraught with difficulty and should be particularly vulnerable to air attack."[28] Elaborating on this point, the Joint Planning Staff observed that the mountains in Malaya, together with "the rivers which flow in the valleys between them and the almost impenetrable jungle which covers the greater part of the country, form well nigh insuperable barriers to Communications".[29] After the Japanese landing, the Malayan administration issued reassurances, claiming that British forces were well prepared to handle the situation, and that Japan, "drained for years by the exhausting claims of her wanton onslaught on China", was incapable of posing a serious threat.[30] A memorandum prepared by US intelligence on 12 December 1941 continued to show unwarranted optimism about Britain's capacity to resist a Japanese advance. After describing the defences of Singapore (coastal artillery, anti-aircraft batteries, barbed wire entanglements and pill boxes, and 50,000 troops), the document continued:

> The "back door" approach via the Malayan Peninsula is protected by British, Indian, and Malay troops, reinforced by the Volunteers of the Straits Settlements and Malay States and the Johore Military Forces. There are probably more trained troops to the square mile in Malaya than in any neighboring country. The geography of Malaya is also a factor in its defense. The coastal plains average only about fifteen miles in width and their

---

[27] See W.G. Beasley, *Japanese Imperialism*, pp. 225–30; James William Morley (ed.), *The Fateful Choice: Japan's Advance into Southeast Asia, 1939–1941*, p. 303; Jonathan Marshall, *To Have and Have Not*.

[28] War Cabinet. Chiefs of Staff Committee. Minutes of Meeting held 5 Nov. 1940, C.O.S(40) 374th meeting. CAB 122/25.

[29] War Cabinet. Joint Planning Staff. E.P.S.(41)146, 12 Jan. 1941, CAB 122/25.

[30] R. Brooke-Popham, Commander-in-Chief, Far East, and G. Layton, Commander-in-Chief, China, Order of the Day issued on 8 Dec. 1941, in Kirby, *The Loss of Singapore*, p. 525.

> hollows are filled with mango swamps [*sic*, an error for mangrove swamps]. The mountain range which runs north and south … is covered with dense jungle and vast areas are almost unknown, except to forestry workers and surveyors. Roads are few and heavily guarded, so that an invading army would be at the mercy of defenders securely hidden in the jungle.[31]

When this assessment appeared, the Japanese were already enjoying considerable success using the "back door" approach. Units which came ashore in southern Thailand had crossed over to the west coast of the peninsula and on the 12th succeeded in dislodging the British from Jitra, a strong point about 15 miles north of Alor Star. Additional forces had landed in Kelantan and were moving southward along the east coast, a more difficult undertaking because there was no coast road, although they were able to follow the eastern branch of the railway line through the jungle. The Japanese quickly achieved air superiority, and the capture of British airfields in northern Malaya gave them facilities to support their ground forces. A few days earlier, Japanese aircraft had destroyed two warships sent to strengthen Singapore's defences, the *Repulse* and the *Prince of Wales*, which sailed without air cover toward southern Thailand to investigate reports of Japanese transports moving into the area, and were sunk by torpedo planes off the coast of Pahang. Combined with the attack on Pearl Harbor, which caused Washington to withhold American ships of the Asiatic Fleet based at Manila from actions west of Surabaya, the sinking of these two vessels gave Japan control of the seas.

The advance to the south involved a combination of assaults on strong points, and amphibious movements that outflanked British positions. Japanese companies operated behind one- and two-man patrols armed with submachine guns. If these patrols drew fire, they infiltrated the enemy position and then launched assaults on the flanks and the rear as the main body of troops approached. When British units counterattacked, Japanese advance parties allowed them to pass and then struck from behind. Amphibious operations were mounted seven times along the Straits of Malacca, with the Japanese sending troops down the coast in sufficient numbers to cut the British lines of communication. The first of these movements took place when British forces held up the Japanese advance at Kampar, some 90 miles north of Kuala Lumpur. The Japanese used small boats, including craft captured at Penang, to land troops further south in the Telok Anson area where they attacked road and rail links behind Kampar, forcing the British to abandon their positions there.[32]

---

[31] Coordinator of Information, British Empire Section, Special Memorandum No. 16, Singapore, 12 Dec. 1941. OSS R&A No. 34.

[32] Major H.P. Thomas, Report on Malaya and Singapore, 30 May 1942, WO208/1529, p. 4.

American observers with the British forces reported that Japanese soldiers displayed "considerable initiative, vigor, and physical stamina", and an "unusual aptitude for overcoming terrain obstacles". Commanders rarely issued orders once troops went into action, and clear and detailed instructions were obviously given in advance. Japanese soldiers wore khaki or khaki-green uniforms with hobnailed boots or rubber-soled athletic shoes, although some adopted local dress to deceive the British troops. They travelled by bicycle, as a rule in groups of 60 to 70, moving at a rate of 8-10 miles per hour and carrying 70–80 pounds of equipment apiece.[33]

Illus. 2.4 British sappers preparing to destroy a bridge.

Source: United States Library of Congress, LC-DIG-ds-04814.

[33] "Notes on Japanese Warfare on the Malayan Front", Military Intelligence Service, War Department, Washington, DC, Information Bulletin No. 6, NARA RG226 19074; "Notes on Japanese Warfare", Military Intelligence Service, War Department, Washington, DC, Information Bulletin No. 10, NARA RG226 19072. Eyewitnesses to the Japanese assault claimed the bicycles were commandeered in Malaya, but according to Col. Masanobu Tsuji, who planned the operation, each Japanese division was equipped with 6,000 bicycles. Tsuji commented that Japanese-made bicycles were widely used in Southeast Asia, and spare parts were readily available throughout Malaya. Masanobu Tsuji, Singapore: *The Japanese Version*, pp. 183–5.

One reason for the rapidity of the Japanese advance was that the British had not prepared strong defensive positions. Brigadier Ivan Simson, the Chief Engineer for Malaya Command, went to Malaya in August 1941 charged with the task of developing modern defences, but both General Percival and the Commander of the Singapore Fortress, General Keith Simmons, contended that such installations would be bad for morale, and refused to sanction their construction.[34] Air Chief Marshal Sir Robert Brooke-Popham, Commander-in-Chief for the Far East from October 1940 until 23 December 1941, later conceded that it was "a reasonable criticism, that we should have had stronger defences on the North of Singapore Island and down the West side of Malaya, before war broke out". His explanation was that:

> It was a problem of morale and of man hours. I was always on my guard against the fortress complex and against too much reliance on water obstacles, barbed wire and pill boxes & insisted as the principle that troops must make their own field works and obstacles wherever practicable. General Percival rightly pointed out to me that all barbed wire in Malaya had to be replaced almost every six months and that we might reach a stage when most of the Army would be employed on renewing wire. So a division of working hours was agreed upon: training, renewals, new works.[35]

Attempting to explain the catastrophe, various British observers blamed fifth column activity, particularly on the part of Malays, and claimed that local people had been caught placing signals to guide the invading forces. However, the Japanese practice of dressing as Malays makes reports of widespread Malay collusion suspect, and Japanese who had lived in Malaya before the war knew the terrain well enough to act as guides. Noel Barber's account of the fall of Singapore suggests that General Percival contributed to the idea that there was widespread disloyalty when he "made great play of phrases like 'the enemy within our gate', 'loose talk' and 'rumour-mongering'—all calculated to alarm civilians (when in fact there was virtually no 'fifth column')".[36] G.W. Seabridge, editor of the *Straits Times* immediately before the fall of Singapore, also says there was less fifth column activity than many supposed. In his view the Malays did little to assist either side, but very few actively betrayed the British cause. A 1943

---

[34] Simson makes trenchant criticisms along these lines in his book *Singapore: Too Little, Too Late*. See, *inter alia*, pp. 30ff, 69–70, 129.

[35] Air Chief Marshal Sir Robert Brooke-Popham, Despatch on the Far East, CAB 106/40.

[36] Barber, *Sinister Twilight*, pp. 128–9.

enquiry into Malay fifth column activity concluded that allegations of Malay collaboration were largely unfounded.[37]

Illus. 2.5 Japanese bicycle unit engaged in bridging during the invasion of Malaya.

"There were instances when infantry and bicycle units would improvise bridges by felling trees and placing them across deep and fast moving streams and then march on to their objective."

Source: *The Syonan Times Sunday Supplement*, 18 Oct. 2602 (1942).

Abu Talib Ahmad questions this conclusion, writing "scores of Malay youths ... assisted the Japanese during the invasion".[38] He argues that loyalty to their homeland, and patriotism, motivated the Malay community during the Occupation, and that nationalist feeling led individuals on both the Left and the Right toward both collaboration and resistance. Moreover, changing circumstances sometimes altered these calculations, and caused loyalties to shift. In explaining the dilemma of the Malays during the occupation, he cites Mohd

[37] Material on this subject is in CO273/671/50790. For the remarks by Seabridge, see Enclosure to Captain on Staffs Letter No. 1184/081 of 5 Mar. 1942, WO208/1529.

[38] Abu Talib Ahmad, *Malay Muslims, Islam and the Rising Sun*, p. 102. On this point he is quoting Mohd Salleh Daud, *Memoir Bukan Seorang Konformis* [Memoir of a Non-Conformist] (Kuala Lumpur: Dewan Bahasa dan Pustaka, 1998).

Yusoff Ahmad, a junior civil servant before the war, who wrote that "my feelings were somewhat mixed, hatred for the Japanese and anger at the British".[39]

Among the troops positioned in the northwestern sector of Singapore, where the main body of Japanese forces made their landing, was a newly-recruited group of Chinese volunteers known as Dalforce, named after their commander, Colonel John Dalley. Dalforce drew on a number of existing groups, including the communist-led Public Armed Forces, the Singapore Volunteer Forces made up of locally-born and English-educated Chinese, and a volunteer organization established by the Kuomintang Youth Group.[40] Fighting under a Chinese flag, Dalforce inflicted heavy casualties on the Japanese, and it has been suggested that the savage reprisals the Japanese took against the Chinese in Singapore were in part a response to the participation of Dalforce in the battle for the island.

The Japanese had considerable success in subverting the loyalties of Indian soldiers fighting on the British side. Before the outbreak of hostilities, Major Fujiwara Iwaichi had become involved in Japanese efforts to develop links with Indian nationalists active in Bangkok, and in October 1941 he travelled to Thailand to meet with members of the Indian Independence League, including Pritam Singh, the Secretary-General, who handled liaison activities with Indians in southern Thailand and northern Malaya. Immediately after the invasion, Pritam Singh and Fujiwara entered Malaya, where they sent messages to Indian soldiers urging them to abandon the British cause, which was lost, and to support Japan. These activities had little or no effect on the course of the battle, but favourable treatment given to Indian soldiers who surrendered or were captured, and Fujiwara's apparently sincere interest in the cause of Indian independence won him the support of a substantial number of men, including Captain Mohan Singh, who would play a key role in Fujiwara's plans. These trained soldiers provided the nucleus for an Indian National Army (INA) dedicated to the liberation of India, a force born out of discussions held in Taiping on the last day of 1941 involving Fujiwara, Pritam Singh and Captain Mohan Singh, who became the commanding officer. To oversee these arrangements Fujiwara worked through an organization called the Fujiwara Kikan (Fujiwara Organization), or simply the F-Kikan.[41]

---

[39] Abu Talib Ahmad, *Malay Muslims, Islam and the Rising Sun*, pp. 85–149. The quote from Mohd Yusoff appears in his book *Decades of Change: Malaysia (1910–1970s)* (Kuala Lumpur: Pesaka, 1983), p. 205.

[40] Kang Jew Koon, "The Chinese in Singapore during the Japanese Occupation", citing *Dazhan yu Nanqiao – Malaiy zhi bu* [The War and the Nanyang Overseas Chinese – The Section on Malaya] (Singapore, 1947), p. 52.

[41] *Fujiwara Iwaichi*, F. Kikan.

Illus. 2.6 Fujiwara Iwaichi (left) and Captain Mohan Singh (right).

Sources: Fujiwara Iwaichi (藤原 岩市) – Wikipedia.
Mohan Singh – *The Syonan Times*, 21 Aug. Syowa 17 (1942).

By the end of January, Japanese forces moving down the east and west coasts had begun to merge in Johore, and automobiles fleeing southward were, in the words of a Japanese account, "rubbing each other like potatoes being washed".[42] The assault on Singapore began at midnight on 8 February 1942, and the Japanese anticipated an early British capitulation. "Observations of aerial photographs indicate that there are no important fortifications to the rear of the … main zone…. The enemy should surrender tomorrow." Resistance was unexpectedly heavy and the Japanese were running short of ammunition when, on 15 February 1942, "the enemy surprisingly surrendered to our forces".[43]

The understanding in London was that Percival had a fighting force of more than 100,000, and the Prime Minister was unequivocal in saying (on 10 February 1942):

> There must at this stage be no thought of saving the troops or sparing the population. The battle must be fought to the bitter end at all costs.… Commanders and Senior Officers should die with their troops. The honour of the British Empire and of the British Army is at stake. I rely on you to show no mercy to weakness in any form.[44]

---

[42] Ryuichi Yokoyama, *Malaya Campaign 1941–1942* [8 Oct. 1942], ATIS Enemy Publications No. 278, NARA RG165 Entry 79 Box 309.

[43] Commanding Officer of the Battle Command Post, the statement predicting an early surrender was made on 7 Feb. 1942, JM 54, pp. 95–6.

[44] The War Office to C.-in-C., S.W. Pacific, 10 Feb. 1942, in CAB 120/615.

Illus. 2.7 Air raid wardens dousing an incendiary bomb in Raffles Place, Singapore as part of a drill.

Source: United States Library of Congress LC-DIG-ds-04815.

Illus. 2.8 Last days at Singapore. Photograph taken during a Japanese air raid.

Source: United States Library of Congress, LC-DIG-ds-04803.

In his memoir of the war years, John Wyatt described messages of this sort as "Churchill at his maudlin worst", and said such missives were received with "utter disgust".[45]

General A.P. Wavell, the Commander-in-Chief of India Command, replied that Percival only had 60 to 70 thousand troops, and that some of the reinforcements lacked sufficient training. He said that Japanese tactics and their control of the air had given rise to an inferiority complex within the forces defending Singapore.[46] On 14 February, Percival reported extensive damage to the water mains, and said the prospect of millions of civilians having no water had changed the situation. Churchill then told Wavell that he was "the sole judge of the moment when no further result can be gained at Singapore and should instruct Percival accordingly". On the 15th Wavell authorized Percival to cease resistance if he was satisfied that British forces could no longer cause serious damage to the Japanese forces. Percival replied that the soldiers under his command were unable to continue fighting.[47]

Illus. 2.9 A Malayan Chinese couple amidst the ruins of their home which has been bombed by Japanese aircraft.

Source: United States Library of Congress LC-DIG-ds-04806.

[45] Wyatt, *Staff Wallah*, p. 207.

[46] Wavell to Churchill, 11 Feb. 1942, in CAB 120/615.

[47] Printed telegrams relating to the defence of Singapore, CAB 120/615.

General Percival's last message to his troops before the capitulation cited an imminent failure of the water supply along with shortages of food, petrol and ammunition as reasons for laying down arms.[48] The water shortage had become extremely serious. Water piped in from Johore had been cut off in January, but had only supplied covered reservoirs at Pearl's Hill and Fort Canning. The Seletar, Peirce and MacRitchie reservoirs on Singapore Island held sufficient water to provide the entire population with around 15 gallons per person per day. Much of this supply was lost when an attack on a group of Japanese soldiers bathing in the Peirce Reservoir killed and injured several men, rendering water from this source, and from the Seletar Reservoir which flowed into it, unusable. The MacRitchie Reservoir remained available, as did the service reservoirs at Pearl's Hill and Fort Canning, but bombing and shelling caused extensive leaks in the water mains, which in the tropical climate of Singapore had been laid at a shallow level, and on 15 February the pressure fell sharply owing to burst pipes. Although the damage was not great, repairs could not be carried out under prevailing conditions. Some 80 per cent of the water pumped into the system was running to waste, and during the afternoon the supply failed completely.[49]

Many of the first-hand accounts of the fall of Singapore collected by the War Office dispute Percival's statement that Singapore had exhausted its capacity to resist the Japanese. For example, G.W. Seabridge, who based his statement on reports by accredited war correspondents, contended that Singapore had enough food and water to withstand a siege, and huge stocks of oil. He attributed the capitulation to poor leadership, low morale and a failure to take effective action.[50] An account by Major R.G.B. Thompson, part of a group ordered to escape from Singapore shortly before the surrender, confirms that there was a great deal of confusion and disorganization among the soldiers defending the island.

> The Japs landed about the 8th Feb. exactly where everyone expected except apparently higher authority. From then on it was a question of chaos and our Div. Cmdr. and Brigadiers saw their commands taken away bit by bit.
>
> The Foresters put in a counter attack two days later. They covered ten miles through the jungle and got to their objective without opposition when they were heavily shelled by an Australian Bty. who knew nothing at all of what was going on. 'B' Coy. less one Platoon was taken away as div. reserve. Then the C.O., 2i/c part of H.Q. Coy., A. & D. Coys, disappeared for some other job and we never saw any of them again. That left 'C' Coy

---

48 A.E. Percival, GOC Malaya Command, 15 Feb. 1942, WO203/2667.

49 Percival, *The War in Malaya*, p. 66; P. McKerron, "Note on the Immediate Causes of the Surrender of Singapore", BMA ADM/22; Kirby, *Singapore: The Chain of Disaster*, pp. 231–2.

50 "Enclosure to Captain on Staffs Letter No. 1184/081 of 5.3.42", WO208/1529.

> and part of H.Q. and 'B' Ech. We were withdrawn without opposition to the East of McRitchie reservoir at a place called Thompson Village.... There we were joined the same night (11th) by 1st Reinforcement Coy. of ours and the Foresters and about 75 searchlight chaps with rifles. This they pleased to call a Bn. It was a perfectly b-place at the junction of two main roads. Wherever one went one couldn't see more than 50 yards owing to very broken ground and close trees or buildings. We arrived about midnight and I had a wander round to try and see how the land lay.
>
> There didn't seem to be anyone about and I proved that the village had been evacuated, but the next morning the whole place was alive with Chinese and Malays mostly the latter. They proceeded to wander all over the place and it was quite impossible to stop them as there must have been 2–3 thousand of them....
>
> The whole show was a tragedy and the chaos shocking. One example of good organisation. We had one 2½" map in the Bn. of the Island and were crying out for more as the inch maps were out of date and inaccurate. Eventually to the delight of the intelligence section 50 2½" were doled out. On opening them up the Island seemed to have changed shape slightly and it was found that the name was the Isle of Wight. Almost incredible.[51]

In a report submitted to the War Cabinet on 1 June 1942, Wavell listed seven general factors as causes of the British defeat: an inaccurate assessment of the Japanese Army and Air Force, a lack of air support, effective propaganda issued by the Japanese, poor utilization of civilian manpower, a breakdown of civil morale, fifth column activity (although Wavell commented that it was difficult to know how extensive this was), and inadequate cooperation and coordination between civilians and the military. Turning to strictly military considerations, the report called attention to the superior physical conditioning of Japanese soldiers and the fact they had trained in conditions similar to those in Malaya, and low morale among troops fighting against the Japanese, particularly at the end when they were tired and had experienced a numbing succession of defeats: "all had been out-numbered, out-manoeuvred, and never a friendly plane in the sky". Japanese tactics had been simple but extremely effective: infiltration, attacks on the north-south road, use of mortars, low level bombing, noise (including firecrackers, heavy fire from unexpected directions, shouting and howling) and the use of well-trained "stalker-scouts". Japanese forces had also been supported by engineering work of a high standard. British training, on the other hand, had been poor, and ill-suited to Malayan conditions. Troops placed excessive reliance on motor transport, and vehicles had been moved too close to the front lines

---

[51] Extract from letter by Major R.G.B. Thompson, formerly 5 Bedfs and Herts, 17 June 1942, CAB 106/20.

where they were often cut off. Finally, very little intelligence reached commanders in the rear. Just 12 prisoners were captured, including pilots who bailed out of aircraft, and almost no equipment was sent back for analysis.[52]

Illus. 2.10 Japanese victory photograph taken immediately after the surrender ceremony at the surrender chamber, Ford Factory Building, Upper Bukit Timah Road, Singapore on 15 February 1942: General Tomoyuki Yamashita and his officers with Lieutenant-General Arthur Percival.

Source: 20060000785–0010 Lim Kheng Chye Collection, courtesy of National Archives of Singapore.

Conditions at the Start of the Occupation

Following the British surrender, Japanese forces halted their advance outside of the municipality area of Singapore "in consideration of possible outbreaks of disorder and inauspicious events". Military police entered the city proper to restore order, and the Japanese occupied the islands surrounding Singapore without further resistance.[53] On 21 February 1942, the Japanese commander,

[52] War Cabinet. Operations in Malaya and Singapore. W.P.(42)314, 8 Sept.1942. Report by General A.P. Wavell, Commander-in-Chief, India Command, 1 June 1942, CAB 119/208; for another copy see CAB 66/26/44. CAB 120/615 contains several evaluations of the circumstances surrounding the fall of Singapore.

[53] Malay Operations Record, Nov. 1941–Mar. 1942, JM 54, p. 101.

Tomoyuki Yamashita, published the following declaration in the *Syonan Times* newspaper, successor to the pre-war *Straits Times*, announcing and justifying the new regime:

> Singapore is not only the connective point of the British Empire to control British India, Australia and East Asia, but the strong base to invade and squeeze them and Britain has boasted of its impregnable features for many years and it is generally accepted as an unsurmountable fortress.
>
> Since the Nippon armies, however, have taken a military operation over the Malay Peninsula and Singapore, they have overwhelmed the whole peninsula within only two months and smashed the strong fort to pieces within 7 days and thus the British dominating power in British India, Australia and East Asia has collapsed in a moment and changed to, as if, a fan without a rivet or an umbrella without a handle.
>
> Originally, the English has entertained extremely egoistic and dogmatic principles and they not only have despised others, but have been accustomed to carry out the foxy, deceit, cunning and intimidation and they dared to commit the injustice and unrighteousness in order to keep only their own interest, and thus they have really spoiled the whole world.
>
> Now, considering from the military proceeding of the Nippon Army and in view of the British administrations and their results, the traces of the British squeeze on Malayans are very clear and the British Armies, during their operations and also on retreating from the front, have confiscated and looted the treasures, properties, provisions and resources from the populace and sent them backward for destruction and dared to throw the people into severe pains by burning their houses and also they placed the Indian and Australian troops on the front while the English troops, remaining in Singapore, had the former at their beck. Thus the English egoism, injustice and unrighteousness are beyond description and worthy to be called as the common enemy of humanity.
>
> The reason why Nippon has stood up resolutely this time, taking her sword of evil-breaking, is very clear as already explained in several declarations of the Nippon Government and it is needless to declare again. We, however, hope that we sweep away the arrogant and unrighteous British elements and share pain and rejoicing with all concerned peoples in a spirit of "give and take," and also hope to promote the social development by establishing the East Asia Co-prosperity Sphere on which the New Order of justice have to be attained under "the Great Spirit of Cosmocracy" giving all content to the respective race and individual according to their talents and faculties. So, Nippon Army will hereafter endeavour further to sweep out the remaining power of Britain and U.S.A. from the adjoining regions and intend to realize the eternal developments and policies of Malaya after curing the wound caused by British bloody squeeze in the long time past and restoring the war damage inflicted in this war.
>
> Nippon armies hereby wish Malayan people to understand the real intention of Nippon and to co-operate with Nippon army toward the

> prompt establishment of the New Order and the Co-prosperity Sphere. Nippon army will drastically expel and punish those who still pursue bended delusions as heretofore, those who indulge themselves in private interests and wants, those who act against humanity or disturb the public order and peace and those who are against the orders and disturb the military action of Nippon army.
>
> On the fall of Singapore, the above declarations have hereby been given to the populace to indicate the right way for the purpose of eliminating their possible mistakes.[54]

The early restoration of peaceful conditions in occupied territories was a primary objective for the Japanese, who needed to free combat units for operations along the fighting front. The Japanese 25th Army, the force responsible for the invasion, was reconfigured from an attacking force into an army of occupation responsible for the defence and administration of Malaya and Sumatra. To subdue the local population, they employed terror tactics such as beatings and summary executions, particularly in dealing with the Chinese. Lai Ping Khiong, who escaped from Malaya late in 1942, told interrogators that there were few Japanese troops in the country, and that the garrison force included Formosans along with soldiers from Shantung and Korea. Shantung troops, he said, were well behaved, while Koreans were "the worst of all".[55] By June 1942, nearly all military resistance had ceased, and the Southern Army received instructions to concentrate its efforts on popularizing and expanding the military administration in order to promote stability and self-sufficiency.[56] The use of terror subsequently became less prevalent, although the military police, the *Kempeitai*, were extremely brutal in dealing with people suspected of anti-Japanese activity.

The fighting, looting, and Britain's scorched earth policy caused widespread damage in Malaya and Singapore. A newspaper article published one month after the British surrender painted this picture of conditions in Singapore:

> The inhabitants of Syonan woke up on the morning of the 16th of February, from the first undisturbed sleep that they had had for more than a month to a strange and eerie stillness. Those who ventured out into the streets gazed upon a scene of destruction, but a destruction that had taken on a new aspect, an aspect of utter quiet, and the stillness of a grave, after the preceding weeks of nerve-shattering and ceaseless blasts of bombs, the explosions of shells and the rat-tat-tat of machine guns. Everything was still. Peace had come to Syonan.

---

[54] Declaration of the Commander of the Nippon Army, *Syonan Times*, 21 Feb. 2602.

[55] Conditions in Malaya up to October 1942, based on information supplied by Lai Ping Khiong, former Secretary of the Bank of China in Singapore, HS1/114.

[56] JM 103, p. 2.

> The streets were strewn with the debris of shattered buildings, military lorries and cars, private cars and rickshaws, some completely burnt out, others in various stages of destruction and damage, littered the pavements or lay overturned in the gutters and drains.
>
> Others were buried in bricks and broken concrete where they had smashed into the houses. Here and there, grisly and bloated corpses in grotesque attitudes, their sightless eyes staring up at the sky, lay just as they had fallen.
>
> Fires still smouldered in the wreckage of destroyed buildings, and here and there groups of miserable people groped in piles of broken masonry and smashed timbers for the bodies of lost relatives or for some treasured article. The pall of dense smoke which had covered the city for more than two weeks still hung overhead to the north and west.[57]

Illus. 2.11 Destruction of a rubber factory by British forces as part of their "scorched earth" policy in Malaya.

Source: United States Library of Congress, LC-DIG-ds-04808.

One year later the *Syonan Sinbun* published this account of the situation in Singapore shortly after the British surrender:

> It would take a Dante to describe the pandemonium that prevailed in the inferno which Singapore was, in its final comatose condition.

[57] "A Month in Retrospect", by Charles Nell, *Syonan Times*, 16 Mar. 2602.

Whisky and rum flooding the drains; millions of dollar notes going up in smoke; Asiatic women looking for their fleeing British husbands; widows and orphans banging at the closed doors of banks to withdraw funds; factory and office workers risking certain death to get their pay envelopes which never came; prosperous-looking tin and rubber magnates coaxing fishermen to give them a "lift" God knows whither; and preying over all Singapore was the desperate Tommy who fled the last ditch—it was through this hell that the 800,000 people of Singapore lived to greet that sunny Monday morning which saw the birth of Syonan, "Light of the South", a year ago.[58]

Illus. 2.12 "The blowing up of certain sections of the Causeway, linking the Peninsula with the then Singapore by the British defenders a year ago today, signalled the start of the Battle for Singapore. Picture shows repairs being made to breaches in the Causeway, as Nippon military trucks passed by on their way to the frontlines on the island."

Source: *Syonan Sinbun*, 6 Feb. 2603 (1943).

[58] *Syonan Sinbun*, 11 Feb. 2603.

In Kuala Lumpur, according to the 1942 report of the Sanitary Board, conditions were equally bad:

> Nearly three-fourth of the residents in Kuala Lumpur had by [9 January 1942] evacuated to outlying districts. Looting and plundering were rife, bridges were blown off and important business premises and godowns were scorched and as a result of these, the Town was in a devastated condition and chaos prevailed.[59]

Elsewhere in Selangor, looters emptied the godowns (warehouses) and stores belonging to the Public Works Department, and removed furniture and laboratory equipment from the Forest Research Institute at Kepong, where they threw out a large collection of valuable specimens in order to take the cabinets used to store them. At Sentul they carried away "everything that was portable" from the Timber Research Laboratory, and destroyed "what they did not fancy".[60] In Perak looters removed "electrical and sanitary fittings, brass door and window furniture and other tempting articles", and when the occupation began some 137 buildings had been destroyed by various causes. Most buildings were repaired and in use by the end of 1942 but there was little maintenance and efforts to eradicate termites came to an end because chemicals and wood preservatives were no longer available. As a result, some older buildings in Taiping collapsed unexpectedly.[61]

British plans had called for the destruction of key military and industrial installations in the event of an invasion to deny them to the Japanese, but an order issued in mid-December 1941 directed British forces to carry out an unrestricted scorched earth policy throughout Malaya, excluding only facilities required for essential civilian services such as sewerage and running water, along with supply networks for electricity and gas. However, the War Council in Singapore decided against destroying Asian businesses unless they offered particular advantages to the Japanese, and in the event, even this more limited scorched earth policy could not be fully implemented. Field commanders did not have detailed lists

[59] AR KL SB 2602, Sel Kan 108/2603. See also AR PWD Sel 2602, Sel Kan 53/2603.

[60] Report on Forest Administration, Sel, 2602, Sel Kan 89/2603. Situation Report on the Forest Department, Malaya, for Sept. 1945, Forests 30/1914. The British destroyed machinery at the Timber Research Laboratory during the evacuation. A Dr Tanakadate from the Japanese museums organization is credited with saving remnants of the Kepong herbarium, and with arranging for publication of O.F. Symington's *Foresters' Manual of Dipterocarps* (Malayan Forest Record No. 16), which had been typeset and was ready for printing when the invasion took place.

[61] E.A. Gardiner, "Notes on the Work carried out by the Public Works Department in the State of Perak during the Japanese Occupation" (signed T.G. Seshan), 3 Dec. 1945, MSS. Ind. Ocn. S. 172, Weston Library, Oxford University.

of objectives and were expected to arrange demolitions on their own initiative except in the case of very large enterprises, for which reference had to be made to Singapore. The speed of the Japanese advance made it difficult to locate and destroy installations, particularly in the northern part of the country, and in some cases the owners of costly machinery resisted demolition orders. Moreover, even within the military there was a belief that Japanese advances would be reversed within a few months, and that damaged equipment would ultimately impede British activity. The Governor observed after the war that the intention had been "to deny to the Japanese by removing or destroying essential parts while leaving bulk installations in a condition which enabled them quickly to be brought into action when relief arrived".[62]

Both Percival and Shenton Thomas felt that demolitions, like defensive fortifications, fostered a defeatist attitude and had a bad effect on military and civilian morale, a line of reasoning that also lay behind the government's failure to order an early evacuation of European women and children, and its refusal to permit the departure of Chinese who wished to leave.[63]

Percival later complained that he had been instructed to hold Singapore to the end and at the same time to carry out a total scorched earth policy, objectives that were mutually contradictory, and he had decided to give priority to the first of these tasks.[64] Demolition teams did destroy transport facilities, including road bridges and most of the country's railway bridges, about half of the locomotives in service in Malaya and around 500 of the 3,500 goods wagons used by the railway system, and the central railway workshops and stores located at Kuala Lumpur. They also blew up broadcasting equipment and some of Singapore's industrial plant, including the Municipal and Public Works Department workshops, the shops of United Engineers and of Hume Pipe Works, equipment belonging to the Cable and Wireless Company, and stocks of oil. Demolition teams paid particular attention to military facilities, with the goal of rendering Singapore useless as a naval base. However, blowing up the main magazines storing ammunition in Singapore would have produced a massive explosion that would have wrecked many structures in the vicinity, including hospitals. Churchill, who followed developments closely, said if evacuation became inevitable, forces in Singapore should fire as much ammunition as possible at the enemy before destroying the guns, and called for the Naval Base to be "completely wrecked so that the docks and workshops are rendered utterly useless for at least eighteen

[62] Comments by Sir Miles Shenton Thomas on draft War History, quoted in Louis Allen, *Singapore, 1941–1942*, p. 294.

[63] Kirby, *Singapore: The Chain of Disaster*, pp. 228–9.

[64] Allen, *Singapore 1941–1942*, p. 298.

months". Demolitions did cause serious damage to shipbuilding facilities, but the Japanese captured large quantities of serviceable stores and machinery, and they restored much of the equipment that was damaged, including Singapore's huge floating drydock.[65] By early June 1942, Japanese ships were able to enter the naval base, and repairs were well underway, but British intelligence reports suggested that the most important facilities belonging to the naval base, the King George VI Graving Dock and the floating drydock, remained unusable. For the former, demolition teams had used explosive charges to damage all pumps, and to destroy the the independent electricity supply. They scuttled the floating dock by allowing the flotation tanks to fill with water, and using acetylene torches to cut it in various places, but the Japanese refloated it in July 1943, re-christening it the "Hinode" dock.[66]

Most European residents from countries fighting the Japanese were moved into internment camps on 17 February 1942. There were two camps for men (Joo Chiat Camp and Karikal Road Camp) and one for women, and after a week a third camp for men was opened at a French convent beside Karikal Camp. On 6 March the Japanese moved all internees to Changi Prison, which became the Changi Internment Camp. As of 6 March, the Changi Camp held 2,198 men, 349 women, and 55 children, a total of 2,602 individuals. Between 1 and 8 May 1944 the Japanese moved the entire camp population, now numbering 3,453 men, women and children, to Sime Road. Between 17 February 1942 and 27 August 1945, a total of 214 camp inmates would die of various causes.[67]

With the collapse of the British administration, public services came to a halt. In Kuala Lumpur rubbish accumulated in the streets and drains, and "flies and mosquitoes were breeding abundantly every where". A newly created Town Re-organisation Bureau set about restoring the water supply and cleansing the town. Scavenging work was done using bullock carts because serviceable motor vehicles were needed for other purposes.[68]

---

[65] Malaya – Part II, BMA 506/10; O.W. Gilmour, "Appreciation of the probable position in Singapore on re-occupation", BMA ADM/22; Kirby, *Singapore: The Chain of Disaster*, pp. 189–90; Allen, *Singapore 1941–1942*, pp. 294–300; Churchill to Ismay, Personal Minute No. D.16/2, 31 Jan. 1942, and Churchill to Ismay, Personal Minute No. D.20/2, 2 Feb. 1942, CAB 120/615.

[66] Extract from most secret sources information, 6 June 1942, Japanese Official Source, and Copy of a report by Capt. D.H. Wilson, 18 June 1942, and attached Demolition Scheme, and report from the *Hamburger Fremdenblatt*, 19 June 1942, WO 208/1527; *Syonan Sinbun*, 23 July 2603.

[67] D.W.G. Faris, Report on the Working of the Government Health Department – Singapore, Part III, MSS. Ind. Ocn. S. 135.

[68] AR KL SB, 2602, Sel Kan 108/2603.

Illus. 2.13 British prisoners of war marching to an internment centre in Singapore at the start of the Japanese Occupation.

Source: 19980005712 – 0090 David Ng Collection. Courtesy of the National Archives of Singapore.

The Japanese restored the water supply in Singapore within a few days, and the officer in charge claimed that within two weeks sanitary conditions had returned to "almost prewar level".[69] However, in November the population was told to boil drinking water because chemicals to purify supplies drawn from the reservoirs were no longer available. Elsewhere in the peninsula, British forces left water distribution networks intact, but they blew up bridges to slow the Japanese advance and many of the bridges carried water mains. In Selangor alone some 50 bridges were destroyed during the British withdrawal. While the Japanese administration restored water supplies, the quality of piped water soon deteriorated.[70]

The invasion also disrupted electricity supplies. Trained staff systematically put out of action a number of important power stations, including Chenderong in Perak, Bangsar in Kuala Lumpur, and the St James Power Station in Singapore,[71] and repairs were impeded by shortages of staff and materials. Electricity was only

[69] Rural Health University, Boeki-Ka Syonan Tokubetsui, MSS. Ind. Ocn. s. 135.

[70] AR PWD Sel 2602, Sel Kan 53/2603.

[71] Malaya – Part II, BMA 506/10.

restored to Selangor in May 1942, and there was no electric street lighting in Kuala Lumpur until October.[72]

* * *

The Japanese conquest came as a devastating blow to the people of Malaya. The military authorities were aware of weaknesses in their defences, though they appear to have underrated Japanese abilities and once the invasion had taken place to have overrated the strength of the Japanese force arrayed against them. Newspaper reports provided assurances that the Japanese stood no chance of success, and official statements released during the Japanese advance shrouded the true situation. However, people came to realize that these statements were unreliable and that Britain might be losing the war:

> .... at the time of the invasion it was not possible for people living in one part of Malaya to know what was happening in another or to have a comprehensive view of the war situation because of the rapidity of the Japanese advance and the black-out of news which might hinder our war effort. The announcements made by Radio Tokyo and our official communiques were at variance and the confusion was rendered worse confounded by the false rumours afloat.[73]

For a significant element within the Malayan population, which identified with and actively supported the British, the rout was an unmitigated tragedy. For many others, the change of political masters seemed to be of no great importance and offered possible advantages, particularly if the Japanese maintained the flow of cheap manufactured goods they had sent into Malaya during the 1930s. For the country's small group of Malay and Indian political activists, the collapse of British rule heralded the beginning of a new era, a first step on the road to independence. Thus the people of Malaya awaited developments, fearful of Japanese soldiers but curious and even optimistic about what the new regime might offer. They were soon disillusioned, for the Japanese proved to be harsh and overbearing masters, given to acts of gratuitous violence, and unable to supply the basic needs of the population.

[72] AR, KL SB, 2602, and AR Klang SB, 2602, Sel Kan 108/2603.

[73] Chelvasingam-MacIntyre, *Through Memory Lane*, pp. 86–7.

CHAPTER 3

The Japanese Administration of Malaya

Administrative Structures and Procedures

By the time of the British surrender in February 1942, the Japanese had already taken control of local and state administrations in most of the Malay Peninsula. Japanese officials stepped into senior positions, and ordered civil servants to report to work and told them to resume their normal duties while taking appropriate steps to preserve peace, secure food supplies and control prices. In Perak the Japanese set up a military administration for the state in the town of Taiping on 27 December 1941, where it remained until 4 July 1942, when they shifted the capital to Ipoh. A Japanese officer named K. Matsunaga became head of a Government Industries Organisation (Sangyobu), with responsibility for agriculture, forestry, marine, weights and measures, drainage and Irrigation, mines, estates, food control, surveys and electricity. The Japanese re-employed Asian officers and clerical and technical staff and most returned to work as instructed, but not always in jobs they had held previously or for which they were qualified. According to a post-war report on the Public Works Department, "in some case it was more a scramble for power and individual advantage than any attempt to organize the department as a service to the public. Many square pegs established themselves into round holes...." In the Public Works Department, the result was "loose and uncoordinated" operations.[1]

In Trengganu the Japanese followed a similar approach, promising promotions or other rewards to officials who were diligent and industrious while

[1] K.N. Sinnathamby and T.G. Seshan, "Report on work done during the period Jan. 1942–Aug. 15, 1945", 3 Dec. 1945, enclosed in E.A. Gardiner, "Notes on the work carried out by the Public Works Department in the state of Perak during the Japanese Occupation, 1942 to 1945 inclusive", MSS. Ind. Ocn. s. 172 (1), Weston Library, Commonwealth and African MSS, Bodleian Libraries, Oxford University.

warning that complaints would be viewed as a sign of non-cooperation, and that anyone who opposed the administration or did poor work was liable to be expelled from the state or even killed.[2] The Japanese ordered members of the public to hand over all firearms and ammunition to the police, along with items stolen from abandoned houses, and to assist with any work the Japanese military wanted done. They also warned people not to conceal cars, lorries, motor cycles, petrol stocks or bicycles. At the same time, safe conduct passes in local languages offered assurances of Japan's good intentions. One flyer, headed "Passport in Lands Seized by the Japanese Military", promised that the Japanese would provide security to anyone carrying the document, and another told people that "Japanese soldiers are not enemies of people in Asia. The enemies of people in Asia are the English and the Americans."[3] In Batu Gajah, Perak, a "Malay Committee" (Jawatan Kuasa Melayu) announced that the Japanese authorities had instructed soldiers not to enter Malay houses, and advised all Malays to return to their homes. Non-Malay women were advised to seek refuge in the Catholic Church, which was guarded by a Japanese sentry.[4]

Japanese-sponsored Local Government Committees for the Restoration of Peace and Order and Essential Services (also known as Peace Preservation Committees or Peace Maintenance Committees) operated in areas where the British had withdrawn. Among other matters, they dealt with food control, scrap iron collection, rubbish disposal, sanitation, public utilities and the recovery of looted articles. The Japanese gave these committees "some semblance of authority",[5] but their powers and responsibilities were vaguely defined, and in some places there was tension between the Peace Committees and officials of the civil administration. For example, the District Officer for Klang complained that when he attended meetings of the Peace Committee in his district, "he spoke simply as a member of the general public because he did not chair the meeting".

---

[2] Memberitahu kepada Kerajaan Trengganu, 20 Zulhijjah 1360 (7 Jan. 1942), SUK Trengganu 384/1945. The document was signed by the Sultan, Menteri Besar and State Secretary, acknowledging their adherence to its provisions.

[3] Notice headed Tentara Jepon Sudah Datang Menolong Kaom Kaom Semua yang di Tanah Malaya dan Serata di Benua Asia [The Japanese Military has Come to Help All Races in Malaya and in Asia]. See also Collector of Land Revenue Batu Pahat file 4/2602.

[4] Stia [Setia] Usaha, Jawatan Kuasa Melayu, Batu Gajah, Kenyataan, 19 Jan. 1942, and Penolong Pegawai Jajahan Batu Gajah, Kenyataan, 24 Jan. 2602, Batu Gajah 1/2602.

[5] *Penang Shimbun*, 17 Dec. 2603.

These committees were scheduled to be eliminated at the end of March 1942, but some continued to operate until the end of June.[6]

Japan's 25th Army was responsible for the administration of Malaya and Sumatra following the conquest, and the two territories, which were merged in March 1942, became a "Special Defence Area". They were treated as an "integral territory" of Japan, and as such did not fall under the authority of the Greater East Asia Ministry, and were not represented on the Council of Greater East Asia which met in Tokyo in November 1943.[7] In January 1942 the Japanese armed forces despatched a Department of Military Administration (*Gunseibu*) to Malaya to take charge of administrative affairs in areas that fell under Japanese control. In June a General Inspection Bureau assumed overall responsibility for military administrations throughout occupied Southeast Asia, and a Military Administration Inspection Bureau within the 25th Army took charge of Malaya and Sumatra. The Headquarters of the Southern Army moved from Saigon to Singapore on 20 April 1943, and at that time the 25th Army relinquished responsibility for Malaya,[8] which was placed under the office of the Inspector General of the Southern Army Military Headquarters. It proved cumbersome to have military units in the peninsula attached directly to the Southern Army, and a new 29th Army was established in January 1944 to handle military activity between the Kra Isthmus and the Riau Archipelago, and to run the Malayan military administration. The 29th Army Headquarters was located at Taiping, in northern Perak, a place suitable for conducting operations in Kedah and southern Thailand but inconvenient in other respects because of its northerly location. Certain elements of the military administration remained in Kuala Lumpur (the Railway, Communications and Postal Bureaus, and the Supreme Court) and in Singapore (the Broadcast and Maritime Bureaus), making coordination

[6] Minutes, Klang Local Government Committee for the Restoration of Peace and Order and Essential Services, and Mohd Yassin for O-in-C, Peace Making Committee to All Chairman [*sic*] Peace Making Committees, Selangor, excluding Klang and K. Langat, 3 July 2602, DO Klang 3/1942; Pegawai Jajahan Klang to Pegawai Kerajaan Selangor, 13 Mar. 1942, DO Klang 84/2942; Halinah Bamadhaj, "The Impact of the Japanese Occupation of Malaya", p. 134; S. Chelvasingam-Maclntyre, *Through Memory Lane*, p. 102.

[7] JM 103, p. 44.

[8] The 25th Army had previously given up control of British Borneo when a Borneo Garrison Army was activated in April 1942. According to Yoji Akashi, the 25th Army's departure from Malaya was the outcome of a power struggle with the General Headquarters of the Southern Expeditionary Force (GHQSEF), and made it impossible to pursue the strategy for the defence of Malaya that the GHQSEF had itself previously approved. See Akashi, "Military Administration in Malaya", pp. 69–70.

difficult.[9] Southern Army Headquarters moved to the Philippines in May 1944 to supervise operations against the Americans, but it was hard to monitor the situation in Burma from that location, and in November the Southern Army headquarters returned to Saigon.[10] An Order of Battle issued on 13 April 1944 placed the 29th Army under a newly created 7th Area Army, which on 26 April assumed responsibility for the defence of Singapore, and for Johore, which was defined as the Singapore Perimeter Zone.[11]

The civil administration of the country remained in the hands of the pre-war bureaucracy throughout the occupation, with the Japanese military administration exercising overall control and Japanese filling senior positions. Outside the formal administrative structure, communal organizations, neighbourhood associations and paramilitary groups helped control the population.

Throughout Southeast Asia the Japanese expected military administrations to maintain law and order, arrange for the export of commodities needed by the military, and work toward self-sufficiency. In Selangor these objectives were phrased as follows:

> *Policy of the Military Administration of Selangor*
> (a) The fundamental policy is to preserve peace and order which are of paramount importance and each department should strengthen co-operation with other departments in order to enforce this policy strictly while retaining a firm hold on popular public sentiment.
> (b) The reconstruction of industrial enterprises is the special objective of this State and this should be encouraged by every possible means in order to increase the power and resources of the strategy of war and also to meet the shortage of public requirements: these two points are very important. There should also be close co-operation with the Military Authorities in order to achieve the object of destroying the enemies of the Military Administration.[12]

While working to fulfil these objectives, officials were to observe the following guidelines:

> (a) In executing the military administration, the remaining administrative organs of the natives will be used to the best of advantage. In addition, their present organizations and customs will be respected.

[9] JM 103, p. 47; JM 167, pp. 1–5.

[10] JM 24, p. 114.

[11] JM 167, pp. 21–2, 28. The change in April 1944 gave control of the Malayan railway system to the Field Railway Commander of the Southern Army.

[12] Summary of Instructions given by the Governor of Selangor at the Meeting of Judicial Officers including Judges, Public Prosecutors and Magistrates, n.d., DO Ulu Langat 132/2602.

(b) The occupation army will prepare to acquire and develop the resources important to national defense, provided that there will be no trouble caused by doing so.
(c) For the purpose of acquiring the above resources and securing the self-support of the occupation army, it is imperative to cause no great hardship to the natives. Great care will be taken in bringing about a satisfactory balance between the demands of the natives and the above object.
(d) As for the treatment of American, English and Dutch citizens, it is our principle to instruct them to co-operate with us in executing military administration. However, anyone who disagrees with our policy will not be permitted to remain.
(e) Although the remaining enterprises of the axis citizens will be protected, their expansion will be strictly regulated.
(f) Chinese residents will be instructed to sever with Chiang's government and to co-operate with us in our executive policy.
(g) Natives will be instructed to trust the Japanese army to the fullest extent.
(h) The records of the Japanese nationals who immigrate to these territories for the first time will be carefully checked. Former residents of these territories will have first priority for re-passage.[13]

Willing acceptance of Japanese rule was particularly important because Japan needed its combat troops on the fighting front and could not afford to have large numbers of soldiers tied down maintaining order in conquered territories. To secure cooperation, military administrators were told to respect the "customs, habits, and religions" of the inhabitants, allow free enterprise, popularize the Japanese language as a means of achieving mutual understanding, and arrange for local political participation.[14] At the same time, however, the Japanese employed considerable brutality in dealing with people considered hostile, cowing them into submission.

The peninsula was divided into "provinces" with boundaries that coincided for the most part with those of pre-war states. There were ten provinces in all, eight of the nine states that had made up British Malaya (Johore, Negri Sembilan, Selangor, Pahang, Perak, Kedah—incorporating the pre-war state of Perlis—Trengganu and Kelantan) and the former Straits Settlements of Malacca and Penang. Each province had a Japanese governor. Singapore, renamed "Syonan-to", became the Syonan Special Municipality (Syonan Tokubetu-si) under a Japanese mayor, and the pre-war distinction between municipal and

[13] JM 103, pp. 1–2.

[14] Ibid., p. 44.

rural board areas was eliminated.[15] The military administration dissolved the federation which had united Perak, Selangor, Negri Sembilan and Pahang before the war, and reorganized federal departments on a provincial basis.[16] The new rulers changed street names and shops removed English-language signboards. In December 1942 the official name of the country became "Malai", and like the rest of Southeast Asia it was forced to adopt Japanese time, two hours ahead of Malayan time. Office hours were 10 a.m. to "2 noon", 3.30 to 5.30 p.m., and on Saturdays 10 a.m. to "2 noon", making a working day that was shorter than under the British. The reason, according to a government circular, was to give officers a chance "to study Nippon-go [Japanese language] with vigour", but civil servants also needed time to tend their vegetable plots as part of the Grow More Food Campaign.[17]

Illus. 3.1 Removal of English-language signboards in occupied Singapore.

Source: Syonan Times, 23 May 2602.

[15] Military Administration Department Notice No. 45, *Syonan Times*, 30 Apr. 2602, p. 3.

[16] Akashi, "Bureaucracy and the Japanese Military Administration", pp. 56–7; JM 167, p. 2. Regarding Kedah and Perlis, see the *Syonan Times*, 25 Oct. 2602.

[17] *Penang Shimbun*, 10 Dec. 2602; Perak Secretariat Circular 21, 8 Oct. 2602, Pejabat Hutan Perak 56/2602. In May 1943 the afternoon working hours were changed to 3–5 p.m., and in November 1943 offices began to open for two hours on Saturday afternoons.

Illus. 3.2 Tokugawa Yoshichika (left) and Wataru Watanabe (right), Gunseibu-cho (President of the Military Administration, Malaya).

Sources: Tokugawa Yoshichika – Rekishi-Shasin Kai. 歴史写真会「歴史写真（昭和4年4月号）」より。
Wataru Watanabe – *The Syonan Times*, 29 Apr. 1942.

In March 1942, civilians were appointed as governors of the province administrations, which ceased to be referred to as Gunseibu Sibu (Military Administration Branch Offices) and became Shu Seicho (Province Head Offices). The Gunseikanbu or Central Malayan Military Administration remained in overall charge,[18] and the Marquis Tokugawa (Tokugawa Yoshichika), a descendant of the Tokugawa clan that had effectively ruled Japan for over 300 years as Shoguns before the Meiji restoration of 1867, served as Supreme Consulting Advisor to the military administration and as Civil Governor of Malaya. There was considerable friction between military officers and civilian officials, and the Japanese historian Yoji Akashi has described rivalry between these two groups as the "most serious malady" of the administration. According to Akashi, military bureaucrats had been trained to obey orders unquestioningly, and objected when civilian officials did not adopt the same ethos. The lack of respect shown to civilian bureaucrats by military officers contributed to poor relations between the two groups.[19] Some of the civilian officials serving in the upper levels of the Malayan administration came from Japan's powerful Ministry of Home Affairs, and were able to stand up to the military. For example, a conflict between the civilian mayor of Syonan (Singapore), Odachi Shigeo, who was a prominent Ministry figure, and Wataru Watanabe, the President of the Military

[18] Minutes, Meeting of District Officers, 22 and 23 Mar. 2602, P.T. Larut 106/2602.

[19] Akashi, 'Military Administration in Malaya", p. 49.

Administration in Malaya, resulted in Watanabe's departure from Malaya in March 1943. In another context, when the District Officer of Upper Perak raised a question regarding punishments in support of instructions he had issued at the request of the military, the Governor of Perak ("His Excellency" in the following statement) reminded him that:

> ... while it is their duty to co-operate as closely as possible with the Military in their districts for the maintenance of peace and order, District Officers should clearly understand that they are under His Excellency's command and that they should first seek His Excellency's instructions in any matter on which they are unable to use their own discretion or which involves expenditure.[20]

However, circumstances generally favoured the military, and civilian officials often found it difficult to assert their authority. Akashi states that "the supremacy of the military over the civil bureaucracy was undisputed", and even the Marquis Tokugawa found that his influence was limited. Long after the war, he told Akashi in an interview that his advice "was worth no more than that of a field grade staff officer".[21]

Watanabe stated at a press conference in March 1942 that the British administrative system would be retained for the time being, although made subordinate to Japanese military authority,[22] and despite several administrative reorganizations, many elements of the pre-war administration survived the occupation nearly unchanged. The Chairman of the Klang Sanitary Board remarked in his annual report for 1942: "With a few exceptions, where departure from the old method of procedure had been found to be necessary, the general system of administration is practically the same as before", and a survey of various government offices in Kelantan in 1943 produced similar conclusions.[23]

Provinces had considerable autonomy, and laws or regulations varied from place to place according to the views of particular Japanese governors on certain issues, although local civil servants attempted to maintain some degree of uniformity. As the occupation progressed the Japanese tightened their control

---

[20] Minutes, Meeting of District Officers, 5 Nov. 2602, Batu Gajah 69/2602.

[21] Akashi, "Military Administration in Malaya", pp. 72–6. See also Halinah Bamadhaj, "The Impact of the Japanese Occupation of Malaya", p. 134; Japanese Administration in Malaya, OSS R&A No. 2072, p. 8; Brett, "Japanese Rule in Malaya", p. 13; *Syonan Sinbun*, 3 Feb. 2603.

[22] Monitored radio broadcast, 14 Mar. 1942, CO273/669/50744/7.

[23] AR, Klang SB, 2602, Sel Kan 108/2603. The Kelantan survey was carried out after the state was transferred to Thai rule in October 1943. Responses are in Pejabat Menteri Kelantan 79/2486.

over the administration, but their lack of strong central authority and poor coordination impeded the smooth running of the government.[24]

The central military administration began operations with just four bureaus, but by the end of the year the number had grown to eleven (General Affairs, Police, Control, Industry, Judiciary, Finance, Communications, Health, Internal Affairs, Propaganda, Accounting Supervision), overseeing the activities of 25 departments. Reorganization in April 1943 reduced the number of bureaus to just six, but many of the old bureaus simply became departments and continued to function.[25] The most notable Japanese innovation was the General Affairs Bureau, which carried out the coordinating functions of the pre-war state secretariats, and handled local administration and finance.

The police force received immediate attention. Following the British surrender, a Police Affairs Department established branches in each province, and local police officials underwent "re-education" at a training centre in Singapore. The police force was later reorganized under the direction of specialists sent from Japan, and Japanese replaced senior local officers in charge of many police stations.[26] The police had limited powers and could do little to control theft and looting because they were not given firearms, apart from shotguns confiscated from people in rural areas. They had to refer major offenses, such as anti-Japanese or communist activities, to the military police, the *Kempeitai*, who wielded immense authority both within the military and over the civilian population. *Kempei* personnel handled security, discipline and special warfare, and introduced a set of procedures that included registering the local population, monitoring travel passes, and setting up neighbourhood associations responsible for maintaining order. They could only be arrested by their superiors within the *Kempei* organization, and were not subject to control by the local military establishment.[27] Both the regular police force and the *Kempeitai* made extensive use of spies, and newspaper accounts of court cases regularly mentioned rewards paid to informers.

---

[24] JM 103, p. 8; Circulars 1 and 19 of 2602, Sel Kanbo 2/2602; AR Ulu Langat, 2602, Sel Kan 33/2603; Sel Kan 59/2602; Domei ELB, FIR No. 8, 16–30 April 1944, CO273/673/50744/7. See also Appreciation of Malaya: II – Post-Japanese Occupation, BMA 506/10.

[25] Yoji Akashi, "Bureaucracy and the Japanese Military Administration", pp. 54–7.

[26] AR Ulu Langat, 2602, Sel Kan 33/2603; Chief ADO Kinta to Penolong Pegawai Jajahan Batu Gajah, Land Office Batu Gajah 35/2602; Akashi, "The Anti-Japanese Movement in Perak".

[27] The Kempei in Japanese-Occupied Territory, 13 July 1945, OSS R&A 3186S.

In provincial administrations there was initially a trend toward consolidation, but administrative offices proliferated as the war progressed. For example, in Singapore a Food Control Department assumed responsibility for fisheries, livestock, drainage and irrigation, agriculture and forestry in addition to performing the duties of the pre-war food controller, but toward the end of 1942 agriculture and forestry were transferred to a new department, the *Norin-ka*, and in April 1944 fisheries, livestock and manufacturing were handed over to yet another new department, the *Syokuhin-ka*.[28] In Selangor the Labour Department absorbed the former Chinese Protectorate, and was subdivided into three sections dealing with Malays, Chinese Affairs, and Labour. A Rubber Department operated rubber, coconut, oil palm and tea estates owned by enemy nationals, and manufactured petrol from rubber. An Industrial Bureau had overall responsibility for agriculture, commerce and industry.[29] Table 3.1, which shows the administrative structure for Kedah early in the occupation, illustrates the general pattern, although details differed from province to province.[30]

Before the war, British officers held nearly all upper-level administrative positions. The Japanese filled some of these posts with local appointees, generally assigning men to departments where they had previously served, and assigned senior positions to Japanese, having concluded "by experience … that many natives were incapable of administrative duties".[31] However, the number of Japanese available to hold such appointments was far from sufficient and there were many compromises, as can be seen from the following instructions concerning the appointment of financial officers:

> The Sainyu-Tyosyukan (Collector of Revenue), Sisyutukan (Paymaster) or Suitokanri (Sub-Accountant) must be a Nipponese Officer. If there is no Nipponese Officer available, a Malayan Officer may be appointed. In the latter case, it is necessary to emphasize the responsibility upon him and to train and guide him as far as possible.[32]

---

[28] Food Control Department (Syokuryo Ka), no author, n.d., WO203/4499; T. Tojyo, Chief Officer-in-Charge, Industrial & Engineering Department, Agricultural Office, Pahang, Reorganization of the Agricultural Department, Pahang, 31 Aug. 2602, DO Temerloh 207/2602.

[29] AR, Department of Commerce and Industry, 2602, Sel Kan 26/2603.

[30] The Japanese term *bu* has been translated as Department; the word *ka* is probably best translated as "section", but some pre-war administrative departments became *ka* during the occupation, and the old English-language terminology continued to be used.

[31] JM 103, pp. 7–8.

[32] Financial Arrangements with Regard to the States and the Syonan Tokubetusi, DO Temerloh 24/2603.

Officers previously in the government service and all applicants for government positions were required to sign a statutory declaration stating that they would be "most faithful to the Imperial Nipponese Government", and affirming that they were not insolvent, had never been convicted of a criminal charge, and had never resigned or been dismissed from government service.[33]

Table 3.1 Organization of the Kedah head office (*Shusei-cho*)

Bureau (bu)	*Sections / departments (ka)*
1. General Affairs (*Somu-bu*)	Secretariat Chamber (*Kan-bo*) General Administration (*Kanri-ka*) (district offices, sanitary boards) Education (*Kyoiku-ka*) Judicial Department (*Shiho-ka*) (courts and prisons) Medical Affairs (*Imu-ka*) (hospitals, dispensaries, health)
2. Industrial Bureau (*Sangyo-bu*)	Agriculture (*Nomu-ka*) Commerce and Industry (*Shoko Suisanka*)
3. Financial and Treasury Bureau (*Zaimu-bu*)	Financial (*Rizai-ka*) Treasury (*Kaikei-ka*) Land (*Tochi-ka*) (District Land Offices, mines, Surveys, Forests) Customs (*Kanzei-ka*) (Customs-houses, opium, Harbour Office) Audit (*Kaikeikensa-ka*)
4. Communication Bureau (*Kotsu-bu*)	Posts and Telegraphs (*Yusei-ka*) Traffic (*Unyu-ka*) Public Works (*Doboku-ka*)
5. Police Bureau (*Keisatsu-bu*)	Police Affairs Section (*Keimu-ka*) Security Section (*Hoan-ka*) Special Attack Task Force (*Tokko-ka*)
6. Religious Bureau (*Shumuin*)	

Source: Organization of Kedah Shusei-cho, SUK Kedah 298/2602.

[33] Perak Secretariat Circular, 21 Nov. 2602, Hutan Perak, 56/2602.

The Japanese planned to reduce the official establishment to about one-tenth of its size before the war. As a first step they issued instructions that government departments should cut back their staff strength to 60 per cent of pre-war levels, although "Where it cannot be done otherwise this limit may be exceeded."[34] A report on the Johore Public Works Department, which had absorbed the pre-war Electrical Department and the Drainage and Irrigation Department, detailed the vast amount of work that needed to be done, and then added the curious observation that "Owing to the state of the present conditions, the P.W.D. is found necessary to be reorganised, and by that it has been found that the Department has been overstaffed."[35] Some departments substantially reduced staffing levels, but overall the Japanese failed to achieve their objective. Table 3.2 shows the situation in Kelantan before the war and under the Japanese administration, and also during the latter part of the war after the state's transfer to Thailand. The increase in the size of the police force is unsurprising; the increase in the education department reflects Japanese encouragement of Malay education in a predominantly Malay area.[36]

At the district level, the principal change was the appointment of Malays to fill posts as District Officers, which had largely been the preserve of the British. It appears that the Japanese gave preference to members of the aristocracy when making these appointments.[37] In principle District Officers continued to perform the same activities as before the war—controlling district land offices, serving as sub-treasurers, supervising office staff, inspecting and reporting on local conditions—and in addition exercised powers conferred on them by the Military Administration Ordinance. In practice, some pre-war functions fell into abeyance, and in 1943 the District Officer for Ulu Langat summarized his duties as follows:

(i) to encourage the inhabitants of the district to work hard,
(ii) to encourage them to cultivate all the available land with rice and other food stuffs for their sustenance,

[34] Minutes, Meeting of District Officers, 22 and 23 Mar. 2602, P.T. Larut 106/2602; Johore Circular Letter, 18 Apr. 2602, State Secretary 98/2602, cited in Ghazali, *Johor Semasa Pendudukan Jepun*, p. 33; Monitored radio broadcast, 14 Mar. 1942, CO273/669/50744/7.

[35] Report of the Public Works Department, Johore, and "Report", both unsigned and n.d., MB Johor 60/2602.

[36] See Rengkasan Tanggongan Pejabat Setia Usaha Keraja'an Kelantan, Pejabat Mentari Kelantan 79/2486, also Notes on the Procedure of Work in the State Secretary's Office and Office Mentri before the War, and Peringatan bagi Menjalankan Kerja di Pejabat Mentri, Pejabat Menteri Kelantan 87/2486.

[37] See, for example, AR Kuala Langat, 2602, Sel Kan 32/2603, and Minutes, Meeting of District Officers, 6 and 7 July 2602, Batu Gajah 69/2602.

Table 3.2 Staffing levels in government departments in Kelantan

Department	*Staff (pre war)*	*Staff (Japanese period)*	*Staff (Thai period)*
1. Sultan	11	9	11
2. Adviser	25	17	18
3. Menteri*	8	7	8
4. State Secretary	16	Closed	4
5. Education	211	252	247
6. Medical	154	118	118
7. Town Board	29	20	19
8. DO Kota Bharu	79	58	53
9. DO Pasir Mas	54	48	41
10. DO Pasir Puteh	38	29	29
11. DO Bachok	30	25	25
12. DO Ulu Kelantan	59	45	45
13. Customs	171	110	104
14. Treasury	15	14	13
15. Audit	14	11	10
16. Chandu (opium)	3	1	1
17. Police	472	773	724
18. Prisons	49	39	39
19. High Court	15	10	7
20. Central Court	11	8	8
21. Agriculture	16	14	12
22. Drainage and Irrigation	10	9	8
23. Forest	34	25	25
24. Survey	48	30	30
25. Adviser, lands and mines	5	7	7
26. Labour	3	1	1
27. PWD	15	13	14
28. Posts and Telegraphs	59	98	97
29. Mufti Kerajaan	23	20	20
30. Electric	12	Under a Japanese firm	Under a Japanese firm
31. Volunteers	7	Closed down	Closed down
Total	1,696	1,811	1,738

Note: *In the unfederated states, the term "Menteri" referred to the office of the Mentri Besar or Chief Minister, who was the intermediary linking the British Adviser with the state secretariat and the Sultan during the British period. Under Thai rule the office provided a channel for communications between the Sultan and the Thai administrator responsible for the state, the Khaluang.

Source: Number of Government Employees in each Department, Pejabat Menteri Kelantan 79/2486.

(iii) to see that they preserve peace and order,
(iv) to see that they co-operate with the Administration,
(v) to take suitable steps that all official business be dealt with all speed for the convenience of the Administration and the public.[38]

Shortly before the end of the occupation, the Japanese created a new post known as Gun Shidokanho (Officer in Charge of Promoting the District Administration), a sort of super district officer. These officials were to "supervise and control the entire district administration excepting police affairs, by guiding the District Officer in order to adjust and [make] adequate the executions of the latter's duties, and to strengthen the terminal administration". They also served as branch superintendents of the state propaganda offices.[39] According to the District Officer of Kuantan, Dato' Mahmud, Japanese officers frequently interfered with his work before this change, and issued verbal orders that conflicted with the written instructions sent by his head office. Following the appointment of a Gun Shidokan for his district the situation became worse. "This officer insisted on chopping [referring to the affixing of an inked seal to a document] all documents signed by the D.O. and accompanied me wherever and whenever I went on field visits."[40]

The Japanese reduced salaries paid to civil servants according to the following formula:

1. Those who received $50 or less per month before the war continued to receive full salary.
2. Those who received $50–$100 per month were paid $50 plus 80 per cent of the balance.
3. Those who formerly received $100–$200 were paid 80 per cent of the first $100, and 60 per cent of the balance, subject to a $95 minimum.
4. Those who received more than $200 were paid 70 per cent of the first $200, and 40 per cent of the balance.[41]

---

[38] DO Ulu Langat, Report on the Administration of the District on the lines indicated by His Excellency the Governor of Selangor, 7 June 2603, Ulu Langat 216/2602.

[39] Selangor State Rule No. 5 (Rule for the establishment of Gun Shidokan and Gun Shidokanho, 15 June 1605) and Selangor State Rule No. 6 (Rule relating to the duties of Officers attached to the first front line, 15 June 2605), DO Ulu Langat 132/2602.

[40] The quotation is from a statement by the DO Kuantan in BMA 83/1945, and is cited in Halinah Bamadhaj, "The Impact of the Japanese Occupation", pp. 145–6.

[41] Kedah Treasury Circular No. 2/2602 and Amendment to Treasury Circular No. 2/2602, 2 Apr. and 9 Apr. 2602, SUK Kedah 5/2602; see also Ulu Sel SB AR 2602, Sel Kan 108/2603.

Officials who had occupied government quarters free of rent before the war were allowed to continue to do so; others paid a reduced rental calculated on the basis of the new salary scale. The British had supplied furnishings, but many government-owned buildings were looted during the evacuation and the Japanese administration did not refit them.[42] The pay cuts caused discontent, and in November 1942 Singapore adopted a salary scheme similar to that used before the war in order to "allay the fears and uncertainties" of government employees and get them to produce their "best efforts" at work.[43] Some civil servants supplemented their incomes by collecting commissions for performing various official functions, or by reselling consumer goods they purchased at preferential rates (such as medicine, cloth, vegetables and cigarettes) into the black market.

The Japanese repudiated the rules of international law concerning property in occupied territories, stating that: "Existing international law shall not be adhered to, and state and public property of enemy nations shall become the property of the Empire."[44] The office of the Custodian of Enemy Property, a minor department before the war with responsibility for properties belonging to nationals of the Axis Powers, became a large and important operation under the Japanese, holding the titles to a large number of extremely valuable "enemy" concerns, that is, businesses owned by companies registered in countries which were at war with Japan, as well as properties belonging to local residents who had left the country.[45] Managers operated the seized enterprises under the direction of the Custodian, who received the income they generated. Even the Selangor

---

[42] Minutes, Meeting of District Officers, 22 and 23 Apr. 2602, P.T. Larut 161/2602.

[43] *Syonan Times*, 18 Nov. 2602.

[44] Benda et al., *Japanese Military Administration in Indonesia*, Document No. 50 (Instructions of the Superintendent-General of Military Administration, 7 Aug. 1942), pp. 190–1.

[45] Auditor, Selangor, Present Scope of Government Audit in Selangor as compared with that under the Old Regime, 4 Feb. 2603, Sel Kan 117/2603 (originally in Sel Kan 194/2602 and possibly misfiled). Enemy property consisted of the following:

1. Property belonging to people in enemy or enemy-controlled areas (with the exception of Japanese nationals);
2. Property belonging to people imprisoned by the military administration;
3. Property belonging to westerners and enemy nationals;
4. Property belonging to any national who left Malaya after 8 December 1941;
5. Property belonging to anyone who did not hold a "Good Citizen Pass".

The *Syonan Jit Pau*, 2 July 2602, cited by Kang Jew Koon, "The Chinese in Singapore during the Japanese Occupation", p. 25. In Selangor those affected included such well-known figures as Loke Wan Tho, Chan Wing, H.S. Lee, Au-Yong Peng Choon, W.J.P. Grenier, Chan Kang Swi, Loo Yuson, H.M. Lee, Ng Kong Low, Chan Hon Kwong, and Mesdames Lim Ching Kim, Chan Keng Doa, Chan Keng Kwai, Chan Keng Mui, Loke Yuen Peng, Lim Koon Ee and Loo Keng Yee.

Turf Club was confiscated, and the Custodian took charge of 75 "enemy horses". (A local Chinese secured a three-year contract to operate the Turf Club, and racing resumed in July, 1942.) The value of property seized in Selangor was estimated at $278,438,384 (including public buildings—"Administration Offices, hospitals, stores, godowns, factories, workshops, quarters, labourers' lines"—valued at $23,390,286, but not taking into account the railway system, postal and telegraph equipment, and transport and marine facilities). Most of this was immovable property, and by far the greater part (over $145 million) consisted of rubber estates (364,150 acres, assigned a valuation of $400 per acre). The Custodian attempted to collect outstanding debts owed to seized enemy firms, and published announcements in the press stating that people who owed money to enemies were legally obliged to declare those debts. The notices had little effect, but forms sent directly to businesses produced better results, and by the end of 1942 debts worth $250,000 had been reported.[46]

Under the new order, the number of Japanese working for the administration increased rapidly as men were sent to Malaya from government agencies in Japan. Lacking local knowledge and hampered by an inability to communicate in the languages commonly used in Malaya, these officials depended heavily on the Asian staff of the pre-war administration to carry out their duties.[47] For local appointees, the laws and regulations of the British regime, which they understood far better than their new superiors, offered a degree of protection against arbitrary decisions and a modicum of power, and they placed considerable emphasis on strict observance of established procedures.

A draft plan prepared in 1941 for administering the Southern Areas called for retention of the Malay Sultans as nominal rulers under an advisory system, and a policy document approved by General Yamashita in February 1942 stated that the Sultans would in the first instance be allowed to retain their political status.[48] However, following the British surrender, the new regime adopted a hard-line policy that envisaged eliminating the authority of the Sultans entirely. Wataru Watanabe issued instructions in February 1942 that the Sultans should be allowed to retain their positions temporarily, subject to Japanese supervision, but

[46] AR Tekisan Kanri Kyoku, Selangor, Showa 17 Nen (2602), Sel Kan 113/2603.

[47] Gardiner, "Notes on the Work carried out by the Public Works Department in the State of Perak during the Japanese Occupation", 3 Dec. 1945, MSS. Ind. Ocn. S. 172, Weston Library, Oxford University.

[48] See "Outlines on the Conduct of Military Administration" (3 Feb. 1941), "Principles Governing the Administration of Occupied Southern Areas" (20 Dec. 1941), "Principles Governing the Military Administration of the Twenty-Fifth Army", cited in Akashi, "Japanese Military Administration in Malaya", pp. 82, 89. Itagaki, "Some Aspects of the Japanese Policy for Malaya" contains a detailed account of this issue.

Illus. 3.3 Cover for the annual report of the Customs and Excise Department for 2602 (1943).

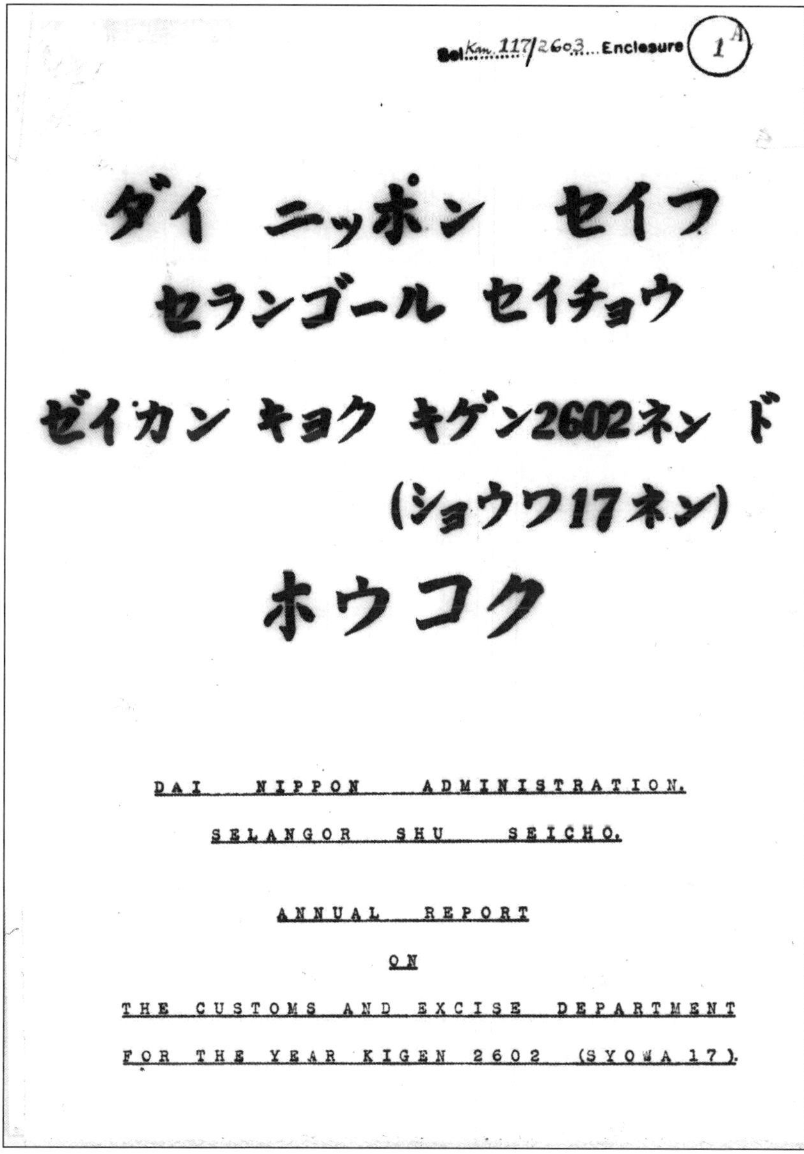

Sel Kan. 117/2603 Enclosure 1A

ダイ ニッポン セイフ

セランゴール セイチョウ

ゼイカン キョク キゲン2602ネン ド

(ショウワ17ネン)

ホウコク

DAI NIPPON ADMINISTRATION.

SELANGOR SHU SEICHO.

ANNUAL REPORT

ON

THE CUSTOMS AND EXCISE DEPARTMENT

FOR THE YEAR KIGEN 2602 (SYOWA 17).

Source: Selangor Kanbo 117/2603.

he strongly opposed the idea of working through them to win the confidence of the population.[49] In May 1942 the Marquis Tokugawa threw his weight behind the policy of ending the political authority of the Sultans on grounds that the Malayan people had become subjects of the Japanese Emperor,[50] and a policy document issued by the Military Administration Department of the 25th Army in July 1942 envisioned the eventual removal of traditional rulers throughout Southeast Asia.

> It is only proper … that the existence of heads of autonomous areas, who claim personal control of lands and peoples, if only nominally, be eliminated. But it is impractical from the viewpoint of civil administration to dispose of them abruptly by force; hence, special plans shall be formulated on the basis of which the heads of autonomous areas shall be induced to surrender voluntarily their political privileges.[51]

Administrators were admonished not to deal with this issue through "direct action" by "flatly presenting the inducement scheme with its basic concepts and concrete program to the heads of autonomous areas and forcing their submission". Instead they were to make the rulers understand that "the future of a Malaya under Japanese sovereignty shall be a unified land and people under benevolent Imperial rule", and to convince them that changes were desirable by using the concept of "*Hakkoichiu*", "the rule of all peoples under one sovereign", or "four corners under one roof'. Once the Sultans understood Japan's determination to eliminate their positions, they were to be persuaded to offer "their titles, lands, and peoples to His Imperial Majesty through the Japanese military commanders", and "voluntarily to set an example for the people by swearing loyalty as Japanese subjects". In return they would receive allowances ("to give them the satisfaction of enjoying a special position" and "enable their utilization for civil administrative purposes"), and would continue to serve as religious leaders. Implementation of these plans was to take place through "top secret covert inducement" in the first instance, while in the second stage "influential heads of autonomous areas (Johore)" were to take the lead in creating support for the new policy.[52] Press comment about the Sultans reflected the hostility of the administration, and a few days after the Sultans visited General Yamashita to express "whole-hearted

[49] Watanabe's views and his role in shaping policy toward the Sultans are discussed in some detail in Akashi, "Japanese Military Administration".

[50] Ibid., p. 85. It is unlikely that this reflected the Marquis Tokugawa's true sentiments. In 1941 he wrote a memorandum that favoured working through "princely states loyal to Japan".

[51] Benda et al., *Japanese Military Administration in Indonesia*, doc. 49 (Items Concerning the Disposition of Heads of Autonomous Areas, July 1942), p. 184.

[52] Ibid., pp. 184–5; see also Akashi, "Japanese Military Administration", pp. 90–1.

congratulations for the brilliant Nipponese successes" and to pledge "whole-hearted co-operation with the Nipponese", the *Syonan Times* published an article, headlined "Sultans who Acquiesced to British Intrigue Now Expecting Nippon to Wave Magic Wand?", that suggested the sultans should devote their wealth and influence to helping the Japanese rehabilitate Malaya.[53]

From July 1942 onward the Japanese paid increasing attention to efforts to cultivate local support. While continuing to affirm that the political authority of the rulers was to be "nullified", the Army High Command abandoned the idea that their positions should be eliminated altogether, and a document issued on 28 November 1942 stated that "Sultans shall be utilized in such a way as to be the central driving force for reconstruction and the leaders for inspiring an Asian consciousness."[54] This policy was reinforced by a telegram sent by the Vice Minister of War complaining that steps taken in Malaya to reduce the importance of the Sultans were "contrary to the policy of the Center".[55] At a meeting of representatives of the Sultans in Malaya and Sumatra held in January 1943, the military administration sought the active support of the rulers, promising in return to restore their pre-war allowances and properties. In April the Sultans became official advisors to their respective governors, and when the Japanese Premier, General Tojo, visited Malaya in July 1943 he said he wished "to give due recognition and profound appreciation" to the Sultans for the services they had rendered "from the very outset of hostilities". He enjoined them, as "accepted leaders of your respective places", to guide the people in creating a new order.[56] In October the Sultans received appointments as Vice Presidents of newly formed state advisory councils, and the Marquis Tokugawa now urged that they be given "membership status in the Japanese Imperial family". He also suggested awarding titles and medals to the rulers as had been done with the feudal lords in Japan at the time of the Meiji Restoration.[57] By this time Watanabe had left Malaya, and his successor, Major General Fujimura Masuzo, pursued a conciliatory approach.

---

[53] *Syonan Times*, Saturday Supplement, 18 Apr. 2602.

[54] This document is cited in Akashi, "Japanese Military Administration", p. 97. The original citation was: [Tomi Shudan Gunseikanbu] Somubu Somuka, *Minzoku taisaku sanko shiryo oyobi setsumei*, 28 Nov. 1942.

[55] Akashi, "Japanese Military Administration", p. 98.

[56] *Syonan Sinbun*, 6 July 2603; *Perak Times*, 7 July 2603.

[57] Akashi, "Japanese Military Administration", pp. 81–4, 89–94, 105–8. In discussing these shifts in policy, Akashi notes (p. 109) that Japanese intelligence had collected information indicating that the Sultans were not uniformly popular with the local population, and that treatment favouring them did not always have the desired effect.

Illus. 3.4 "Members of the Nippon Propaganda Department distributing leaflets and pamphlets to Chinese and Indians who are eagerly waiting to read them."

Source: *Syonan Times*, 2 May 2602 (1942), Saturday supplement.

The advisory councils (*Sanji Kai*) were created in accordance with a suggestion made by Tojo during his visit to Singapore that the local population should play a greater role in administering Malaya. The state governors, and the mayor of Singapore, became council presidents and they appointed the other members, who represented the various racial communities and included a number of individuals who had served on pre-war state councils or in the legislative councils of the Straits Settlements and Federated Malay States.[58] Throughout Malaya the distribution of advisory council members was 58 Malays, 37 Chinese, 19 Indians, 2 Eurasians and 1 Arab.[59]

The Military Administration used the advisory councils to assess public opinion and create a favourable impression on the local population, but did not give them a legislative or policy-making role. In Selangor the regulations for the Advisory Board stated that its purpose was "to discuss over the matters which concerns directly with the daily livelihood of the local inhabitants in order to smoothen their minds [*sic*]", and stipulated that the Council "shall not determine the questions by votes".[60] The administration announced that apart from the chairmen there would be no Japanese council members, although Japanese officials took part in council meetings. For the inaugural session of the Singapore Consultative Board, held on 21 January 1944, the agenda included encouragement of a spirit of service, food rations, economy in the use of cloth, increased production of daily requirements, and cooperation in the defence of Singapore and in the working of public utilities and transport services. The second meeting did not take place until 7 August 1944 and dealt with a similar range of topics.[61] The first meeting of the Johore Council discussed "'universal' labour, wartime livelihood, increase in production of foodstuffs and the maintenance of peace and order", while the initial session in Penang covered food imports and ways of increasing food production, ways of achieving local self sufficiency in daily needs, anti-espionage and defence work, and the supply of labour.[62] The chairmen conducted meetings by making enquiries about various matters; when free discussion was permitted, members generally raised points related to the food shortage.[63]

Apart from the formal administration, the Japanese made use of communal organizations in dealing with the various communities in Malaya. These bodies will be discussed in the next chapter.

---

[58] O.W. Gilmour, Appreciation of the Probable Position in Singapore on Reoccupation, 4 May 1944, BMA ADM/22.

[59] Itagaki, "Some Aspects of the Japanese Policy for Malaya", p. 260.

[60] Selangor Order No. 3: Regulations of the Selangor State Council, 1 Dec. 2603, Ulu Langat 160/2603.

[61] See the account published in *Fajar Asia* for Aug. 1944, and reproduced in Arena Wati (comp.), *Cherpen Zaman Jepun*, pp. 67–8.

[62] Domei broadcast in French, 20 Jan. 1944, cited in FIR 4, 29 Feb. 1944, CO273/673/50744 /7; *Penang Shimbun*, 18 Dec. 2603; FIR 21, 31 Dec. 1943, CO273/673/50744/7.

[63] JM 103, p. 45.

Finances

The Japanese used a military account to meet initial expenditures, but by the end of 1942 finances had been reorganized and Malaya was expected to cover administrative expenses from local sources. Direct taxes were not allowed, leaving monopolies and taxes on trade as the principle sources of government income. In pre-war Malaya, export and import duties had generated revenues of approximately \$55–\$60 million annually, primarily from levies on exports of tin and rubber and on imported liquor and tobacco, but these revenues disappeared entirely after the conquest. Apart from small quantities of goods that passed between the peninsula and Thailand, Sumatra and Burma, there was almost no external trade. The state of Selangor collected \$26,288 on imports in 1942, mostly from levies on matches and dried fish, compared with an average of \$7,884,489 during each of the last two years before the war, and \$3,131 on exports compared with \$5,998,293 before the war.[64]

In an attempt to deal with the deficit, the administration developed new sources of revenue, including:

> re-registration of all Companies, Businesses and Societies; re-sealing of Powers of Attorney, Bills of Sale, Promissory Notes and Court Decrees; registration of Electric Wiring Contractors, Dance Hostesses, Medical Practitioners, Dentists, Pharmacists, Midwives and Physicians (Eastern); licensing of Bicycle Dealers and Repairers, Dealers in Poison, deleterious Drugs and Native Drugs, Milk Vendors, Money Lenders, Motor Vehicles Storage, Wheel Barrows, Liquor Distilleries, Aerated Water Factories and Printing Presses; and collection of excise duty on locally manufactured liquor and aerated water.[65]

Real estate taxes and licence fees for 1942 paid before 15 February were declared invalid, and had to be paid again.[66] Bicycles were registered for the first time, a massive undertaking that forced the offices involved to employ extra clerical staff.[67] The right of civil servants to receive free medical treatment and medicine was withdrawn, and government medical facilities, in the past rarely used by

---

64 AR on the Customs and Excise Department for 2602, Sel Kan 117/2603.

65 Auditor, Selangor, Present Scope of Government Audit in Selangor as Compared with that under the Old Regime, 4 Feb. 2603, Sel Kan 117/2603 (but originally in Sel Kan 194/2602 and possibly misfiled). See also Legal Adviser, Selangor, Re question of Validating Legal and other documents executed on or before 8 Dec. 2601, and Selangor Government Notice of 10 Oct. 1602, amended and published in the Government Gazette on 5 Nov. 2602, Sel Kan 59/2602.

66 Gilmour, Appreciation of the Probable Position in Singapore on Re-occupation, BMA ADM/22.

67 See, e.g., AR KL SB, 2602, Sel Kan 108/2603.

anyone except government employees, were opened to the public on a fee-paying basis. In Perak licensed dart-throwing stalls operated in the early months of the occupation, but following complaints that "it was really a discouraging sight to see young able bodied men spending most of their time at these stalls and neglecting their vocation", the government cancelled all licences except in Ipoh and Taiping.[68] Licensed gambling generated substantial revenues, as did a state lottery and excise taxes collected on liquor. The Selangor government took over management of all shops in the state selling toddy (an alcoholic drink made from the sap of palm trees) on 1 July 1942, and also issued three licences to operate distilleries, meeting a need that was "keenly felt" because foreign liquors were no longer available. Applications for these licences came "pouring in".[69] The Japanese also taxed internal trade and operated customs stations at points of entry into each state by road and rail, but more as a way to limit speculation and control the availability of scarce goods than as a source of revenue. The arrangements were cumbersome:

> While the checking of imports and exports is done by the Customs and Excise Department, the control scheme is actually being done by several departments. In the case of food stuffs, the permits for imports and exports are issued by the Food Controller; engineering stores are controlled by the Public Works Department, certain agricultural products by the Agricultural Department, motor vehicles and parts by the Transport Department, medical supplies by the Medical Department, forest products by the Forest Department and other goods generally by the Department of Commerce and Industry or this Department [Customs and Excise].
>
> Although the control scheme is working smoothly, there is, however, some confusion and traders are put to a great deal of inconvenience by having to apply for permits at several places.[70]

The budget covering the first full year of the occupation was an ad hoc affair, with appropriations made quarterly to meet changing conditions. For the following fiscal year (1 April 1943–31 March 1944), the Military Administration prepared a unified budget that emphasized shipbuilding and salvage of sunken vessels, industrial development, public works (especially roads and harbours) and food

68 Minutes, Meeting of District Officers, 5 Nov. 2602, Batu Gajah 69/2602.

69 AR. Sel Customs and Excise Department for 2602, Sel Kan 117/2603.

70 Ibid. The Superintendent noted in his report that the British had paid rewards for information leading to seizures of contraband, but the Japanese paid rewards only in cases where fines were collected. One informer provided information leading to a major seizure of opium, but the offender could not pay the fine of $18,000, and as a consequence the informer received nothing. Episodes such as this tended to dry up the flow of information.

production. Sources of revenue included tariffs on commodities exported to Japan (described as "the Japanese mainland"), sales of sugar, rice, salt and other daily requirements, sales of public property, a state lottery, and profits from government monopolies over tobacco, railways and postage stamps. Taxes were expected to provide about 40 per cent of total revenue.[71] The budget for the next fiscal year, 1944–45, provided for a "tremendous increase" in expenditure, with funds devoted to industrial development, exploitation of natural resources, shipbuilding, defence and food production. It was designed to achieve "further centralisation of administrative powers into the hands of the Regional Government through fiscal measures" as a remedy for "the existing provincial sectionalism".[72]

The central budget and the various state budgets were separated into a Common Account, Special Accounts (the Headquarters Special Accounts covered Communications, Railways, the office of the Custodian of Enemy Property, Public Utilities, Monopolies and Extraordinary Contributions) and an Emergency Fund—a Japanese innovation "to provide for emergency measures resulting from the country's position as a front-line base". Money could be transferred between accounts as required, and departments could apply for additional funds, but expenditures during any fiscal year had to be covered by revenue received during the same fiscal year. Government offices collected revenue by issuing Orders to Pay, and payments were made directly to authorized banks, which sent confirmations back to the government departments where the funds were recorded. Certain forms of revenue, notably stamp duties, estate duties and some excise taxes, were collected by the states on behalf of the Headquarters of the Military Administration, and held in separate accounts. Government offices paid out funds by cheque, and handled very little cash except in places where there was no authorized bank. The financial year ended on 31 March, but accounts were not closed immediately because payments continued to be received after that date with respect to Orders to pay issued during the old year. During April and May departments had to maintain overlapping accounts.[73]

---

[71] *Syonan Sinbun*, 3 Mar. 2603; *Perak Times*, 4 Mar. 2603; Domei ELB, 2 Mar. 1943, CO273/669/50744/7; Domei ELB, 14 Apr. 1943, BMA PS410 pt l; Malaya under the Japanese, NARA RG226 128585.

[72] Domei ELB, FIR 8, 16–30 Apr. 1944, CO273/673/50744/7.

[73] Outline of accounting procedures, Batu Gajah 109/2603; Financial Arrangements of the Malai Gunseikanbu and Its Differences from the Former Arrangement, DO Larut 270/2603; the quote is in Malaya under the Japanese, NARA RG226 128585, but appears to have come from a Japanese statement.

Government expenditure rose dramatically over the course of the occupation (see Table 3.3), and the figures show a notable increase in the proportion of funds handled under the headquarters account as opposed to the state accounts.

Table 3.3 Japanese government expenditure, 1941–45 ($)

	1941/42	*1942/43*	*1943/44*	*1944/45*
Headquarters	727,798	67,026,973	190,343,597	294,955,108
State accounts	2,611,099	70,025,787	101,205,730	105,141,286
Total	3,338,897	137,052,760	291,549,327	400,096,394

Source: Report on the Actual Expenditure for the Financial Year, 1941–44, 3 MOB SEC SEATIC Translation Report No. 34, Sel CA250/1945. The report bears a note saying the information "is incomplete and actual figures may not check with the totals due to the fact that the information herein had to be extracted from various sources and hastily collated". There are no 1944/45 figures for Kelantan and Trengganu, which had been transferred to Thailand. A 1944/45 figure shown for Kedah, also transferred to Thailand, should probably have been entered against Pahang, for which no figure is given.

Record-keeping was poor in the early stages of the occupation. In Selangor the state auditor observed that before his office resumed operations on the first day of June 1942, not all departments maintained proper records, and irregularities were widespread. Most of the calculating machines, counterfoil books and stock books used by government offices had been stolen or destroyed by looters, forcing officials to improvise various alternatives. Sub-treasuries had stopped functioning—they were only re-opened on the first of July—and the Accountant General received revenue collections in lump sum payments.[74]

The British administration had used small percentage audits to monitor accounts. The Japanese regime abandoned this practice in favour of full audits, and the observations of the Selangor State Auditor concerning the change provide an instructive commentary on the workings of the Japanese administration:

> Formerly computations, correctness of scales of fees, tracing receipts into Registers, etc., were merely "text checked" and no more than 50 per cent (and often less) was audited but certain important considerations have now made it quite necessary to carry out 100 per cent audit, and among such considerations which preclude any degree of reliance being placed upon accuracy to warrant reversion to test checking as in the past, the following may be mentioned:-

[74] Sel, Auditor's AR, 2602, Sel Kan 104/2603.

> (i) *Salaries and Wages* in respect of monthly and daily paid staff and of labourers were in the past paid in accordance with approved schemes or fixed scales, specially approved lists or fixed rates respectively, within the strict limits provided annually for each Department in the approved Annual Estimates of Revenue and Expenditure for the State. It was, therefore, sufficient in the past to audit 50 per cent of the salary vouchers in respect of the monthly and daily paid staff and 1 in 5 of the wages of labourers in each check roll. At present there are no salary schemes, fixed scales or rates in force but salaries and wages are fixed separately for each employee, either on a percentage basis or otherwise and, moreover, there are frequent changes in the establishment lists of most Departments which makes it absolutely necessary to check all paysheets on a 100 per cent basis.
>
> (ii) *Other Expenditure* payments were in the past made in accordance with approved schedule rates or contract rates but payments are now made at arbitrary rates. Building materials and other stores were formerly imported from England and the audit had no responsibility to check the prices at which they were bought but at present large quantities of such materials are bought locally at rates which fluctuate violently from time to time....
>
> (iii) *Accuracy* was formerly assured to a great degree by the use of accounting machines and of the services of employees who had qualified themselves by passing Government examinations designed to test their knowledge of Government accounting procedure, legislation relating to taxes and revenue rates, approved schemes, scales and expenditure rates, etc., but this is definitely not the case now owing to the fact that all the accounting machines formerly employed are now out of commission and there are now a number of employees in various departments who were not previously in Government service and do not possess the required knowledge and experience. These facts make a 100 per cent audit most essential.[75]

The Legal System

After nearly two months when no courts functioned, the Japanese established military or in some cases police courts which heard all cases until the end of May 1942, when civil courts reopened with local appointees serving as judges and magistrates. Military courts retained responsibility for cases involving the

[75] Auditor, Selangor, Memorandum on the Present Scope of Government Audit in Selangor as Compared with that under the Old Regime, 4 Feb. 2603, Sel Kan 117/2603 (but originally in Sel Kan 194/2602 and possibly misfiled).

security of the Japanese army.[76] Lawyers registered before the occupation could resume practice if they re-registered and paid a fee of $500.[77]

Pre-war laws remained in force unless specifically rescinded.[78] However, in June 1943 the Governor of Selangor told a conference of judges and magistrates that while "the old or existing laws may be applied … they need not be strictly adhered to". The spirit of the times had changed, he said, and "*every precaution should be taken not to be misguided into committing a misjudgment* by following the letter of the pre-war laws which are in force for the time being".[79] The Japanese Chief Justice of the Selangor Supreme Court, S. Masuyama, told the same gathering that "except for certain special legislation and subject to non-interference with the functioning of the Military Administration, we are allowed to employ the pre-war judicial machinery and laws". He also emphasized the importance of resisting corruption and pressure in reaching decisions, specifically mentioning the Japanese themselves as a possible source of difficulty. "Great care should be taken not to be influenced by any unreasonable demand or proposals made by any Nippon-jin [Japanese]. Although you may listen to them for the sake of any information of value they may convey yet you must not allow them to interfere with your judgment." Masuyama followed these propositions with some much harsher strictures. Pre-war laws, he said, "were enacted for peace time conditions", and the prescribed penalties were "too lenient and light for war time conditions".

> As a crime is more culpable if committed during war time than in peace time, the punishment of an offender during war time must necessarily be different from the punishment for the same crime during peace time. Offenders in war time should, therefore, be punished more severely as compared with the usual punishment during peace time by the infliction of long sentences or very heavy fines. Short terms of imprisonment are useless as deterrent punishment during war time.

---

76 In Singapore a Military Court was established by a decree dated 7 Apr. 1942; the Criminal, Police and Coroner's Courts resumed operations on 27 May 1942, and the Supreme Court and the Civil District Court two days later. The official ceremony marking the re-opening of the courts, "conducted entirely in Nippon-Go", took place on 2 June 2602 (see the *Syonan Times*, 3 June 2602). In the peninsula courts were reinstated slightly later. For Selangor civil courts began to function on 15 May 1942, and criminal courts on 1 August.

77 Malaya under the Japanese, NARA RG226 128585; *The Good Citizen's Guide*, pp. 51–2, 106; Sel, Auditor's AR, 2602, Sel Kan 104/2603.

78 See, for example, SUK Trengganu 384/1945 for announcements issued in Trengganu on 1 Apr. and 20 Apr. 1942.

79 Summary of Instructions given by His Excellency the Governor of Selangor at the meeting of Judicial Officers including Judges, Public Prosecutors and Magistrates, n.d. but apparently 17 June 1603, DO Ulu Langat 132/2602. Emphasis in original.

He called particular attention to a new Maintenance of Public Peace and Order Law promulgated on 1 February 1943, but strangely—in light of his emphasis on severe punishments—said that while this law "would appear to be very harsh", judges could at their discretion reduce sentences if circumstances appeared to justify clemency. The Chief Justice also suggested that the judiciary could impose punishments even in the absence of appropriate legislation.

> Anyone who commits an offence which is considered to be an impediment to the discharge of the functions of the Military Administration should be severely punished and not allowed to go free merely because there is no special regulation which is applicable to the particular offence. If there is no appropriate regulation, or even if there is any but it is not suitable, the case should be dealt with in accordance with reason....

In interpreting the law, he added, judges should "consider the spirit of the legislation" and not be "tied down to the letter of the law or to any usual formality". Rulings were to be made in accordance with the "Nipponese spirit and the Nipponese laws".

> Many of you are perhaps accustomed, from carrying out your duties during the pre-war regime, to the British judicial system which places emphasis on extreme respect and love for personal property and wealth and on doctrines of liberalism, individualism and egoism. Therefore, unless you change your outlook and gain an insight into the aims and objects of the Military Administration it will be very difficult for you to prosecute and judge in accordance with the wishes of the Military Administration. The paramount object of the judicial machinery of the Military Administration is the preservation of peace and order. All offenses should, therefore, be judged from this point of view. In other words, all those offenses which might lead to the violation of peace and order must be severely punished irrespective of the laws in force. In order to prosecute and judge with the confidence of the public, you must make more use of your common sense and be more sympathetic in addition to acquiring a sufficiently detailed knowledge of the laws and ordinances.[80]

Neighbourhood Associations and Paramilitary Organizations

Under a Family Registration System that the Japanese introduced in April 1942, the police issued "proper citizens" with identification certificates called Ankyosyo. These documents entitled the holder to police protection, and had to be shown

[80] Summary of Speech by S. Masuyama, Chief Justice of the Selangor Supreme Court, 17 June 2603, DO Ulu Langat 132/2602.

when buying rice, sugar and salt. In Singapore permits for the Chinese required a guarantee from a shopkeeper and had to be "chopped" by the Chinese Residents' Association and by the Police, conditions that made it difficult for refugees who had fled to Singapore during the fighting to obtain these documents. Permits for Indians, white for literate persons and red for labourers, had to be counter-signed by the Indian Independence League. Every house had to display a certificate showing the name and occupation of the head of the household, and details of all those who lived there. People wishing to travel had to apply for passes, and obtain Temporary Residence Certificates in order to stay in a place other than their usual home.[81]

Control was further tightened with the creation of an auxiliary police force known as the *Jikeidan*, a scheme launched in September 1942 and extended throughout the country during 1943.[82] Members, who were between the ages of 18 and 45, had to be in good health and display suitable thinking ("*fikiran sempurna*"). There were branches in every town and district, and these were combined into unions ("*Gun Rengodan*"). Substantial numbers of men took part. For example, in the Pasir Puteh District of Kelantan, with 10,830 households and a total population of 47,248, *Jikeidan* enrolment was 4,089.[83] The *Jikeidan* maintained family registers which listed people according to their respective wards, and operated as a sort of neighbourhood watch, handling Air Raid Precaution activities, emergencies such as fires or floods, and apprehension of thieves or others who disturbed the peace. The government instructed *Jikeidan* members to report suspicious persons, anyone without a fixed place of residence, and enemy suicide squads should any appear. They also performed casual labour. With regard to members in rural areas, the Governor of Perak observed that: "it was not necessary to urge them to grow more food crops because it was their duty to do so. In their case, therefore, some such other work as building or repairing roads must be done in addition to food cultivation."[84] To encourage diligence, members were made liable for punishment in the event that activities favourable to the enemy took place in their areas, if it was found that people had hidden offenders from the authorities, if weapons caches were discovered, or if

---

[81] *The Good Citizen's Guide*, p. 61; *Syonan Times*, 19 July 2602; SIPS Proforma 'B'—Tactical: Perak, 12 June 1945, NARA RG226 XL21411.

[82] *Jikeidan* literally means "Vigilance Corps"; in Malay the force was called the Pasukan Pemilihara Keamanan, and in English the Peace Preservation Corps.

[83] Senarai Menunjokan Jemelah Jikeidan dalam Jajahan Pasir Puteh, DO Pasir Puteh 71/2603; Penyata Menunjokan Ra-yat2, Rumah2, Keluasan Tanah Padi … dalam Jajahan Pasir Puteh, n.d., Pasir Puteh 92/2603; *Penang Shimbun*, 19 May 2603.

[84] Minutes, Conference of District Officers, 4 Oct. 2604, PT Larut 161/2602.

anyone damaged railway lines, telephone wires or postboxes. On the other hand, *Jikeidan* members who performed creditably were promised rewards.[85]

In 1944 the District Judge for Klang, Raja Suleiman, praised the *Jikeidan* for helping reduce crime:

> Owing to the good work of the Jikeidan and other welfare organisation, the court is much relieved of the unnecessary and petty cases which are now settled amicably by them. It is clearly observed that the people are gradually imbibing the Nippon Spirit by co-operating whole heartedly for the betterment of the community, leaving aside their selfishness, criminal and quarrelsome nature and thus becoming Law Abiding Citizen.[86]

There are, however, indications that the activities of the *Jikeidan* caused friction, not only because members acted as enforcers and informers within their own communities but also because of conflicts with the regular police. In Kelantan, for example, a notice issued in July 1943 observed that disagreements between the police and the *Jikeidan* were affecting cooperation between the two groups.[87] And in January 1945 the Commissioner of Police for Kelantan informed the state judiciary that *Jikeidan* members were reported to have been involved in cases of theft, receiving stolen property and cheating, and said that anyone found guilty of such offenses should be given a heavy sentence.[88]

In October 1943 the Japanese began enrolling the population in Neighbourhood Associations called *Tonari Gumi*. Modelled on a system used in Japan,[89] the *Tonari Gumi* grouped people together based on their place of residence. In Johore the beginning of the proclamation announcing the new policy read as follows:

---

[85] Peratoran bagi Jikeidan, 23 Feb. 2603, DO Pasir Puteh 71/2603; Director, Public Works, Selangor to Executive Engineer Ulu Langat, 19 Jan. 2605, Ulu Langat 29/2605. In July 1944 (2487) the Kelantan administration introduced Emergency (Vigilance Corps) Regulations under the provisions of The Emergency Regulations Enactment of 1931, apparently reconstituting the *Jikeidan* organization. On 1 Jan. 1945 the Kelantan government activated town residents, requiring them to man police posts from 7.30 p.m. to 6 a.m. Ag DO Ulu Kelantan, Proclamation, n.d., DO Ulu Kelantan 151/2487.

[86] AR, Klang District Court, 2604, DO Klang 7/2605.

[87] Kelantan Keimubutyo (So Jikeidan Tyo) to Pasir Puteh Gun Tyo, "Peratoran kepada Jikeidan2 bagi Menjalankan Pekerja'an-nya", 25 July 2603, DO Pasir Puteh 71/2603.

[88] Commissioner Police Kelantan to Tuan Magistrate, 6 Jan. 2488, DO Ulu Kelantan 151/2487.

[89] The *Tonari Gumi* system was institutionalized by the Japanese Ministry of the Interior on 11 Sept. 1940. See Sato, *War, Nationalism and Peasants*, p. 19.

> It is hereby proclaimed that all citizens must unite, co-operate and work together by way of assisting in the present war for the benefit of the Greater East Asia Co-prosperity Sphere. In order to achieve this important aim, every citizen must help each other in the way of keeping the peace and in the general welfare by adhering to the ... regulations of the working of Tonari Gumi and its good custom and every one should carry this out without delay.[90]

The ideal represented by this arrangement was that "all citizens should work together in the way of helping each other with all sincerity for the prosperity and peacefulness of the Great East Asia, and also to render whatever help is necessary in the present war in order to attain the above aim".[91] *Tonari Gumi* were expected to serve as conduits of information between the administration and the people, to provide assistance during police investigations, and to report anyone who broke the law or contracted a contagious disease. In Singapore 30 families comprised a unit, 10 units a Small Mutual Aid Sector, and 10 small sectors a Large Mutual Aid Sector. The Japanese announced in March 1944 that the 55 headmen on the island were to form a cooperative association through which they would operate two committees, one handling relief measures, including education for children, and one helping overcome food shortages by encouraging increased cultivation of vegetables on barren land and by organizing a patriotic service corps.[92] In Johore, families were organized into ten-house blocks called "*Gumi*". Ten *Gumi* constituted a *Tonari*, and the various *Tonari* of a village, a town, a *mukim* (subdistrict) or an estate or mine formed leagues called *Tonari Gumi Rengokai*. All residents were expected to take part except for those ambiguously described as people "who have particular characteristic".[93] Members of a *Gumi* were held collectively responsible for the actions of other members: "If any one in a Kumi [*Gumi*] committed an offence he will be severely punished by the law, and the heads of his families and of that Kumi will be fined (that is bindary punishment)."[94]

---

[90] Proclamation issued by the Governor of Johore, Tonari Gumi (The Neighbourhood Association), n.d., MB Johor 181/2602.

[91] Ibid.

[92] *Syonan Times*, 5 Aug. 2602; Tokyo English language broadcast 18 Mar. 1944, cited in FIR No. 7, 1–15 Apr. 1944, CO273/673/50744/7.

[93] Introduction of Tonari-Gumi, n.d., MB Johor 209/2602; Tonari Gumi (The Neighbourhood Association); Draft Rules for the Tonari Gumi Rengokai (League of Neighbourhood Associations), MB Johor 181/2602.

[94] Diagram outlining the Re-Organisation of District Organisation and Purpose of Tonari Kumi, MB Johor 209/2602.

Also in 1943, the Japanese established local military or paramilitary organizations to support their regular military forces, first enlisting "subsoldiers" (*Heiho*) in the Japanese Army, and then, in December, creating a Malay Volunteer Army (*Giyu-Gun*; in Malay, Pembela Tanah Air, or PETA) and a Volunteer Corps (*Giyu-Tai*). Collectively the last two organizations were referred to as the *Giyu-Hei*, or Malay Protection Army.[95] The *Heiho*, members of the "*Gunpo*" or Auxiliary Services, wore uniforms and lived alongside Japanese soldiers. Touted as a solution to the problem of unemployment which created "fertile material for subversive elements to exploit their nefarious practices", the *Gunpo* recruited around 8,000 men of all races. *Heiho* were non-combatants who did light work and fatigue duty, and appear in many cases to have been little more than ordinary labourers.[96] According to one account of wartime Chinese affairs, the auxiliary services had little attraction for the Chinese: "Many Chinese lads preferred to proceed to Endau and Bahau [Agricultural] Settlements to work as farm hands rather than turn 'Heihos'. Some of them, sons of millionaires, chose to work as factory hands rather than join the ranks of these 'Heihos'."[97]

The Giyu-Gun, or Volunteer Army, was a true military force consisting of approximately 2,000 men armed with machine guns and rifles confiscated from the British Army. Members, who were recruited from the Malay community, wore uniforms similar to those used by the Japanese army, and officers held comparable ranks. The Giyu-Gun force was based at Johore Baru, and according to a notice in the *Syonan Shimbun*, would not be sent abroad.[98]

The Volunteer Corps, or Giyu-Tai, was "an Army (troops) of semi-soldiers and semi-farmers" formed into "small units ... for the maintenance of peace and order and the performance of defence measures". Members were expected to have a "strong love for the native State", "a brave mind and a strong physic [*sic*]" and "an absolute sense for responsibilities". Burmese and Thais resident in Malaya were not allowed to join, and Indians wishing to become soldiers were expected to join the Indian National Army rather than the Giyu-Tai. Enlistees received "young men's training as in Japan", conducted by Japanese

---

95 An announcement concerning the Giyu Gun and Giyu Tai appeared on 3 Jan. 2604 in *Fajar Asia*. See Arena Wati (comp.), *Cherpen Zaman Jepun*, pp. 62–4. The Giyu Gun and Giyu Tai are discussed in Lebra, *Japanese-Trained Armies in Southeast Asia*, pp. 116–20. The Volunteer Corps was also known as the Local Defence Corps, the Volunteer Defence Corps, and the Self Defence Corps, and in Malay as the Pasokkan2 Volunteer Malai.

96 JM 167, pp. 8–9, 20; *Syonan Sinbun*, 24 May 2603; Cheah Boon Kheng, "The Japanese Occupation of Malaya, 1941–45", pp. 106–10; Ibrahim Ismail, *Sejarah Kedah Sepintas Lalu*, p. 184.

97 Lau and Barry, A Brief Review of Chinese Affairs, BMA ADM/8/1.

98 JM 167, pp. 8–10, 20; *Syonan Shimbun*, 4 Jan. Syowa 19 [1944].

officers. A Malay-language notice calling for recruits stated unequivocally that units would only serve locally, and would not be expected to take part in military activities outside of Malaya, but an English-language version of the same notice qualified this assurance, saying that members were "generally stationed permanently in the district where reconstruction takes place" and "as a rule will not be utilized in other districts nor to march into enemy territories to attack the same". Both documents refer somewhat incongruously to the "conscription" (*kerahan*) of "volunteers", although newspaper reports announcing the formation of these units emphasized that no compulsion was involved.[99] A March 1945 notice concerning recruitment in Kelantan suggested that it was preferable to enlist only genuine volunteers because otherwise the recruits might run away.[100] Units of the Volunteer Corps held training sessions on alternate days, or in some cases alternate weeks, and were armed with confiscated hunting weapons. Their responsibilities included local defence, particularly against parachute landings, coast watching and the general maintenance of peace and order. Members served as air raid wardens, and at night manned police posts, checking all those who passed by between 6 p.m. and 6 a.m. In March 1944 the total strength of the Volunteer Corps stood at around 5,000. Its relatively small size was due to difficulties in recruiting among the Chinese and a shortage of suitable candidates among the Malays, caused in part by the drafting of workers as forced labour.[101]

The Japanese also set up a Railway Protection Corps (*Tetsudo Aigo Kumiai*), made up of Penghulus, village headmen and others living near the railway. The Perak Railway Protection Corps was formed in October 1943, and with effect from December 1943 the administration banned use of the railway line for walking or riding bicycles by anyone except its members.[102] For Pahang

[99] Kerahan Berkenaan dengan Volunteer2, and Regarding Conscription of Volunteers, Ulu Langat 51/2604; *Syonan Shimbun*, 9 Dec. 2603.

[100] Khaluang Tahan Pracham Rat Kelantan to Yang Di Pertua Montri Spa Kelantan, 14 Mar. 2488, Kelantan 211/2488. The notice indicated that volunteers might have to serve outside of Kelantan ("luar negeri").

[101] Appreciation of Malaya, no author, n.d., BMA 506/10; JM 167, pp. 8–9; interrogation of a Captain in the Indian Army, a former INA member, captured on 5 May 1945 in Burma, NARA RG226 XL10747; Lau and Barry, A Brief Review of Chinese Affairs, BMA ADM/8/1; Extract from Weekly Digest of World Broadcasts, 14 Jan. 1944, CO273/673/50744/7; FIR No. 2, 31 Jan. 1994, CO273/673/50744/7; Japanese broadcasts quoted in Manpower in Japan and Occupied Areas, OSS R&A Assemblage no. 45, 26 Aug. 1944, pp. 243–8.

[102] Notes of a meeting in connection with the formulation of Tetudo Aigo Kumiai, 22 Oct. 2603, and DO Kinta to ADO Batu Gajah, Tetudo Aigo Kumiai, 10 Dec. 2603, Batu Gajah 127/2603.

there was a Road Protection Society that included all government employees and local inhabitants in the state. Its functions were to carry out minor repairs to important roads, conduct surveillance of telecommunications lines, and perform other necessary tasks. The state's Public Works Department covered the expenses.[103]

Transfer of the Northern Malay States to Thailand

A joint communiqué issued by Japan and Thailand on 5 July 1943 announced that Kedah, Perlis, Kelantan and Trengganu were to be transferred to Thailand, and a treaty embodying this decision was signed in Bangkok on 20 August 1943. The announced reason for the change was that "Nippon respects the history and tradition of the Thai people"—referring to the fact that Siam controlled this area before 1909, when the four states were transferred to Britain—but it was also a reward for Thai assistance in the period leading up to the invasion of Malaya. To mark the occasion the Singapore administration announced that "today the inhabitants of these four States are reborn as true Asiatics to take their rightful place in the Co-Prosperity Sphere.... We sincerely pray for the inhabitants and the future prosperity of those peoples who have transferred their allegiance to Siam."

The transfer deeply offended Malay nationalist sentiment, for the Malays both in Thailand and in what remained of Malaya became minority groups, the former a small proportion of the population of Buddhist Thailand, the latter outnumbered by the Chinese. In an attempt to blunt this issue the Japanese urged people "to sacrifice parochial affiliations based on religion or culture ... to foster the more important all-embracing loyalty to the sphere of pan-Asianism".[104] The *Syonan Sinbun*, in an opinion piece under the headline "Back to Their Rightful Owners", declared that the move fulfilled Japan's promise to "respect the sovereignty of her allies".[105] In Kelantan, officials were told to emphasize that the four states remained part of East Asia and that their people were citizens of Asia. However, the notice containing this suggestion concluded with a gesture to local nationalism, pointing out that whether under Japanese or Thai rule Kelantan was the homeland of the Kelantanese and the source of their livelihood.[106]

---

[103] Rules of the Pahang Road Protection Society, DO Kuantan 63/2605.

[104] Domei ELB, 20 and 21 Aug. 1943, FIR No. 12, 28 Aug. 1943, CO273/669/50744/7; *Syonan Sinbun*, 21 Aug. 2603.

[105] *Syonan Sinbun*, 8 July 2603.

[106] Pengertian kapada Pejabat2 Jajahan, n.d., Pasir Puteh 180/2603.

The transfer of authority took place on 18 October 1943 (B.E. 2486), and Thailand began administering the territories the following day. On 20 October the Japanese garrison withdrew, although certain key installations (including the *Kempeitai* Headquarters) remained in Japanese hands.[107] On 17 December 1943 Thailand handed over the administration of the four states to their local rulers. Each ruler was assigned a Thai Military Commissioner as an adviser (see Table 3.4), and Japanese Liaison Offices in the towns of Alor Star, Kota Baru and Kuala Trengganu handled Japanese properties and the development of resources within the transferred states. Important decisions were referred to a higher-level liaison office in Bangkok.[108] The Thai government was concerned about Japan's influence in the area, and a memorandum issued by the Dato' Mentri of Kelantan on 14 December 1943 told District Officers that all requests made by Japanese should be referred to the Thai authorities and no action should be taken without approval, an instruction that was later qualified by saying it referred only to non-routine matters.[109] According to a Kedah historian, administrative discipline was lax during this period, and civil servants from the governor down devoted much of their time to personal business activities.[110]

The Thai Military High Commissioner immediately announced that all existing laws would remain in force, that property and individual rights would be protected, and that religious principles and freedom of worship would be

[107] Ibrahim Ismail, *Sejarah Kedah Sepintas Lalu*, p. 186. SUK Kedah 243/2603 has information on the ceremonies held in Kedah on 18 Oct. 1943.

[108] Ch. Chan Chai Chark, Khaluang Taharn Pracham Rath Kelantan, Perkeluaran Perentahan daripada Duli Yang Maja Mulia Al-Sultan dan Pejabat Mentri [translated from Thai], 15 Nov. 2486, and Keraja'an Kelantan Persiaran No. 1 of 2486 (B.E.), 31 Oct. 2486, Pej Menteri Kelantan 6/2486; Military High Commissioner, Kenyataan Military Commissioner Tentera Darat Thai, Perkara Menghadkan Kekuasaan Memerintah dan Tanggongan Ra'ayat Negri, 10 Tulakom 2486 [19 Oct. 1943], SUK Trengganu 384/1945; FIR 15, 9 Oct. 1943, CO273/673/50744/7; Malaya under the Japanese, NARA RG226 128585; Mahmood b. Ismail, Dato' Menteri Kelantan to District Penggawa, 18 Nov. 2486, DO Pasir Puteh 14/2486; Kobkua Suwannathat-Pian, "Thai Japanese Bargaining over the Return of the Four Malay States to Thailand", *Jebat* 17 (1989): 29–38.

[109] Dato Menteri Kelantan to Ketua Jajahan Pasir Puteh, 14 Dec. and 20 Dec. 2486, Pasir Puteh 27/2486.

[110] Ibrahim Ismail, *Sejarah Kedah Sepintas Lalu*, p. 187.

Table 3.4 Thai administrators of the northern Malay states

Name of administrator	*Position*
Major General Kamol Saraphaisariddhikan Chotikasathien[a]	Military High Commissioner
Captain Mom Rajawong Chalermlaph Thaweewon[b]	Chief Adviser to the Military High Commissioner
Police Colonel Jiam Limpichat	Commander of the Armed Police Force, Office of the Military High Commissioner
Tavil Kupterak	Chief Trade Commissioner
Police Major Pramote Chongcharoen[c]	Military Commissioner, Kedah State
Mr Jaroon Na Songkhla[d]	Military Commissioner, Perlis State
1st Lieut. Charn Charnchaichak[e]	Military Commissioner, Kelantan State
Colonel Prayoon Ratanakit	Military Commissioner, Trengganu State

Notes: [a] Formerly Vice-Chief of the Armed Forces General Staff and Vice-Director of the Japan-Siam Liaison Office.

[b] This official was "well respected for his administrative and diplomatic skill. Moreover, he got on well with both the civilians and military". Personal communication from Kobkua Suwannathat Pian.

[c] Pre-war Thai consul in Penang, and suspected by the British of being involved in espionage.

[d] Jaroon Na Songkhla came from a prestigious family which had been involved in the administration of the south from the beginning of the Chakri Dynasty. He was an official in the Ministry of the Interior.

[e] Charn Charnchaichak was a naval officer whose rank was equivalent to that of an Army captain. He was thus of lower rank than the military commissioners in Kedah and Trengganu.

Sources: The appointments were announced in Directive no. 109/86, Supreme Command Headquarters, 7 Sept. 1943 and published in the *Royal Gazette* 60, part 47 (Sept. 1943): 2868–9. I am grateful to Kobkua Suwannathat Pian for translating the relevant portion of the Thai Royal Gazette and for providing information concerning the appointees. See also FIR 14, 25 Sept. 1943, and FIR 15, 9 Oct. 1943, CO273/673/50744/7, Security Intelligence for Planning Section, Proforma 'A' —Strategical, Kedah and Perlis, NARA RG226 XL21421.

fully respected. Officials were told to continue their normal activities.[111] On 8 November 1943 Thai Prime Minister Pibunsongkhram issued an order stating that inhabitants of the annexed territories were to be "accorded treatment equal to that enjoyed by the inhabitants of other parts of Thailand".

> It is not permitted to exercise powers which will engender difficulties, wherefore it is requested that the Government Officers of each department including Military and Civil Officers and also Thai nationals will treat and behave towards the new inhabitants as they ordinarily do towards Thai nationals. Any act which will directly or indirectly cause inconvenience is absolutely prohibited.[112]

For Malays, equal treatment meant the loss of some existing rights, and the Thai national assembly almost immediately passed two bills that offended Malay opinion. One stipulated that, as a means of "eliminating illiteracy in the country", all persons between the ages of 20 and 45 who could not read and write Thai by the end of 1943 would be required to pay a surtax, and the other rescinded the recognition of polygamy for Muslims and banned registration of polygamous marriages.[113]

In January 1944 the Thai government announced the creation of a council known as the "Montri Spa" in each state, with powers "to carry out the executive functions". The Montri Spa was to be "a legislature and concurrently an administrative and executive body which governs the State in accordance with

---

[111] The wording of the provision concerning religion was as follows: "Perkara ugama dan menjalankan dia itu akan di-hormati dan di-benarkan di-dalam segenap perkara-nya" [religion and religious practice will be respected and permitted fully]. Kenyataan Military Commissioner Tentera Darat Thai, Perakara menghadkan kekuasaan memerintah dan tanggongan ra-ayat negri, 19 Tulakom 2486 [19 Oct. 1943], SUK Trengganu 384/1945. For a Domei announcement concerning these matters see CO825/38/55151 (1953). The first circular issued in Kelantan under the Thai regime (dated 31 Oct. 2486) declared that all laws in force before the Greater East Asian War remained in force insofar as they did not conflict with Thai law. There were some changes in terminology. The words "Kerajaan Thailand" (Government of Thailand) or "Khaluang Tahan Phra Chamrat" (properly Khaluang Tahan Pracham Rat, Military Administrator for the State) replaced "Duli Yang Maha Mulia Baginda King" (the Malay equivalent to "His Majesty the King", although use of the word King rather than Sultan is unusual) or "Jajahan Ta'alok British" (Territory under British Rule). Use of the term *rat* (state) rather than *changwat* (province) in references to the Malay states suggests that they were being treated as subordinate but independent territories and not as an integral part of Thailand.

[112] Military Order 147/86, 8 Pruschika Yon 2486, forwarded to the Military Commisioner for Syburi on 5 Tanwa Khom 2486 [5 Dec. 1943], SUK Kedah 63/2486.

[113] *Penang Shimbun*, 21 Aug. 2603; Malaya under the Japanese, NARA RG226 128585; Legal Adviser's Report, 19 Tula Kom 2486–18 Tula Kom 2487 [19 Oct. 1943–18 Oct. 1944], SUK Kedah 790/2487.

the constitution", with powers of appointment and dismissal over members of the administration. In Kedah the proclamation establishing the Montri Spa and laying down constitutional provisions under which it would operate appeared in the official Gazette of 5 February 1944 (5 Kumpapan 2487). It stipulated that the ruler of the state would serve as President of the Montri Spa, and required him to appoint at least four members to the body. Members enjoyed freedom of speech, "and shall not at any time be questioned by Government for anything they have said therein". Resolutions were decided by a majority of votes, unlike the practice in territories under Japanese rule, but any law passed was subject to the approval of the Military High Commissioner.[114] Military Orders promulgated before creation of the Montri Spa remained in force, although the Kedah Food Controller suggested in May 1945 that one such order, controlling exports and imports, had "no force of law" and could not be enforced by the Court because lawmaking powers rested with the Montri Spa.[115]

June 23–25 became public holidays when the population celebrated "National Day", and during this period all houses had to display Thai flags, which they could purchase for $6. On the 24th, National Day itself, activities began with the ringing of bells at Mosques, Muslim prayer houses (Surau) and Buddhist temples. There was then a religious ceremony exclusively for Thai officers, after which processions of school children marched to the tune of the patriotic Thai song "Rak Meung Thai" [Love Thailand]. On all three days there were displays of Thai and Malay dance, theatre and martial arts. In general, the festivities positioned the state within the context of Thai nationalism.[116]

Malayan currency was not withdrawn, and Thai currency did not become the official currency in the northern states, although some circulated there.[117] The Thai government did take over the postal system, and replaced Japanese postage stamps with its own. Post Office Savings Bank Accounts were transferred to Thailand as well, and the Japanese gave the Thais funds covering the amount of deposits plus interest as of the date of the transfer of authority.[118]

---

[114] Proclamation by Military Headquarters of Supreme Command, in the matter of the Administration of the States of Syburi (Kedah), Perlis, Kelantan and Trengganu, signed by Field Marshal P. Phibunsonggram, SUK Kedah 52/2487; Standing Rules and Orders of the Monteri Spa, Syburi (Kedah), SUK Kedah 182/2487; First Part of the Report of the Office of the Legal Adviser for the period from 19th Tula Kom, 2486 to 31st Tanwa Khom, 2486 [19 Oct. 1943–31 Dec. 1943], SUK Kedah 770/2487.

[115] Food Controller, Syburi to Secy to Govt, Syburi, 23 May 1988, SUK Kedah 37/2486.

[116] National Day Celebration, Detail Programme, DO Ulu Kelantan 128/2487.

[117] Summary of Economic Intelligence No. 133, 12 Nov. 1945, BMA DEPT/18/7.

[118] Agreement concerning the Transfer to Thailand of the Postal Services of the Four Northern Malayan States, n.d., SUK Kedah 182/2486. 122 Sel, Auditor's AR, 2602, Sel Kan 104/2603.

For the most part, Japan's Malayan Military Administration continued the practices of pre-war Malaya, and changes in administrative structures were largely superficial. In the beginning, according to a wartime report, "many inexperienced men, in their eagerness to assist the conquerors … elbowed out the men of experience",[119] but the Japanese soon directed pre-war civil servants to return to their posts, and discouraged the hiring of fresh staff except where vacancies made this necessary. The Japanese used the pre-war administration as a matter of expediency, but in doing so forfeited a considerable degree of control over the country. The Selangor State Auditor remarked in February 1943, "It is surprising how soon order has been evolved out of chaos." He gave credit to "the efficiency of His Excellency the Governor and all the other responsible Nippon Officers, and their capability of understanding and accommodating themselves to the difficult conditions", but in the next sentence he mentioned "the language difficulty—to overcome which every effort is being made". Most British officials and local civil servants had shared two languages—English and Malay—and some British officials spoke Tamil or a Chinese dialect. Nevertheless, the British relied heavily on their local subordinates to supply information and to interpret that information for them. Japanese officials knew far less about Malaya, and the language barrier was much greater. Efforts to overcome this difficulty by teaching Japanese proved unproductive, and much of the wartime administration was conducted in English or Malay, which many Japanese administrators did not understand well.

* * *

The occupation brought a shift toward greater government control of the economy, and of the lives of the population. Extra-governmental bodies such as communal and social welfare organizations, the *Jikeidan* and the local defence forces, also played an important role in these activities. However, the government's financial travails, the need to sustain the military, and the difficulties Japanese officials faced in understanding and adjusting to Malayan conditions all weakened the administration, and internal conflicts on the Japanese side compounded these difficulties. By 1944 the Japanese were more concerned with holding on to what they had than with shaping a new social or economic order.

119 Sel, Auditor's AR, 2602, Sel Kan 104/2603.

CHAPTER 4

Ethnic Policies

The Japanese attempted to harness and control the forces of nationalism and ethnicity by promoting an Asian identity, a concept of Asian unity and a pan-Asian nationalism under Japanese leadership.

> Asserting that all the people in East Asia are now fighting not only for their own sake but for Asia as a whole the Tokyo Sinbun states that the cliche "Asia is one" is not a mere slogan but a living reality. The unity of Asia, with Japan as the pivot is bound by a faith which transcends by far any private interests and feelings, and should be the foundation of the forthcoming new world order.[1]

Statements such as these notwithstanding, the Japanese were acutely sensitive to race, and their policies for occupied areas of Southeast Asia had a strong ethnic slant. "The treatment of the residents in these territories varied according to their status: natives, Chinese residents; citizens of enemy nations; citizens of neutral countries; etc. However, it was our policy to guarantee their welfare as a whole and insure their co-operation."[2]

Malay, Chinese and Indian nationalists did not share a common perception of the new regime. Malay activists cultivated ties with the Japanese during the 1930s, and received preferential treatment at the time of the invasion. However, they made little progress toward achieving nationalist objectives under Japanese rule, and the military administration marginalized Malay radicals and developed links with pre-war Malay civil servants and religious leaders. The Indian Independence League became a key institution within the Indian community and attracted anti-British political activists, but its central leadership consisted of men who were involved with nationalist activity in pre-war India and had few connections with Malaya. Chinese radicals, while they opposed British rule, hated the Japanese for invading China, and formed the nucleus of an armed resistance movement.

---

[1] *Syonan Sinbun*, 15 Dec. 2602.

[2] JM 103, p. 2.

Japan and the Chinese Community

The Japanese were extremely wary of the Chinese but recognized their abilities and their significance for Malaya's economic recovery. A document issued in April 1942 laid down the following policy:

> For the present, the overseas Chinese shall be utilized for economic purposes but their social power shall be gradually checked by the application of appropriate political pressures.[3]

A local statement of this principle is found in a speech by the Johore Industrial Administrator a few months later:

> You must always try to guide your peoples to do work according to their peculiar ways but they should not be unequally treated. For instance, the problem of Overseas Chinese; they should not be oppressed but this does not mean that they should be given preferential treatment. You should encourage them to utilize their peculiar economic capabilities so as to assist us in achieving our highest object. On the other hand, if they object to our policy they will be severely dealt with and even oppressed. This treatment does not apply to Chinese alone but to all other races.[4]

The Japanese saw free enterprise as the key to working with the Chinese, whose cooperation was to be secured "by utilizing their greed for profit" and their "speculative spirit".[5] They paid little attention to Chinese religious beliefs, and had a low opinion of Chinese political skills: "The economic potency of the Chinese residents was superior but their political ability was nil."[6] Chinese who refused to cooperate were to be "dealt with by means of extremely severe measures—specifically, confiscation of property and deportation of the entire family with prohibition of reentry—while hostile elements shall be answered with capital punishment". On the other hand, "Those who pledge wholehearted cooperation with Japan not only shall not be deprived of their existing livelihood and interests but shall also be given adequate guarantee for their prosperity." While controls might be required, Chinese businesses were as a matter of policy not to be purchased or confiscated. "There should be no lapsing into the expediency of oppressing and rejecting the Chinese in anticipation of favoring

---

[3] Benda et al., *Japanese Military Administration in Indonesia*, Document no. 44 (Instructions on the Administration of Malaya and Sumatra, April 1942), p. 169.

[4] Speech of the Industrial Administrator, Mr. Mizuno, MS. dated 8 Sept. 2602, MB Johor 209/2602.

[5] Benda et al., *Japanese Military Administration in Indonesia*, Document no. 47 (Principles Governing the Implementation of Measures Relative to the Chinese, April 1942), pp. 179–80.

[6] JM 103, p. 17.

Illus. 4.1 Notice calling on people to surrender looted articles.

通告

各籍人民知悉凡前日有規取別人之家器及雜物等須於七日內携交原處或親自繳交警察所如無送行一經查出依法重辦

昭和十七年
一月廿五日

IMPORTANT NOTICE.

ALL persons having LOOTED ARTICLES either hidden away or in their possession, are hereby asked to return same to their owners (or deliver at the POLICE Head Quarters) within 7 days from date. Failure to comply with this order will result in summary punishment on the offenders by the Local Government Authority.

Klang, 25. 1 42. By order of NIPPON GOVT

KENYATAAN.

Siapa 2 orang yang menyimpan barang 2 kechurian daripada (i) rumah 2 kerajaan — office atau Government Quarters walau pun barang itu ada kepadanya atau tersembunyi hendak lah di hantarkan balek barang 2 itu ka tempat yang di-ambil dahulu. (ii) Barang 2 yang lain hendak lah di hantar kan balek ka tempat yang di-ambil dahulu atau pun di-hantarkan ka-rumah pasong. Di-beri tempoh selama tujoh hari daripada hari ini 25 hari bulan January tahun 1942. Barang siapa yang melanggar hukuman ini akau mendapat seksa yang teramat berat daripada kerajaan baharu ini.

Dengan kebenaran kerajaan
Nippon.

Tertulis pada 25 January 1942.

கொள்ளையடித்த பொருள்களை வைத்திருப்பவர்கள் இன்றுமுதல் ஒருவாரத்திற்குள் அவற்றை அப்பொருள்கள் இருந்த இடத்திலோ அல்லது இப்பகுதியிலுள்ள போலீஸ் வசமோ ஒப்படைத்து விடவேண்டுமென்று கடுமையாக எச்சரிக்கப் படுகின்றனர்.

இக்கட்டளையின்படி செய்யத் தவறினோர் கடும் தண்டனையடைவார்கள்.

ஜப்பான் சர்க்கார் கட்டளைப்படி.

Source: Arkib Negara Malaysia file Klang 24/1942.

inroads by Japanese."[7] Nevertheless, Japanese army units seized some Chinese enterprises, actions the Military Administration deplored because of their bad effect on public opinion, and later in the occupation certain elements which "had their own views and plans and were anxious to obtain results ... arbitrarily impounded or bought the Chinese merchants' plants and materials without obtaining the approval of the 29th Army".[8]

One of the most potent measures used by the Japanese to intimidate the Chinese was summary execution by beheading, and shortly after the occupation began, severed heads were placed at key points in several cities. In Singapore they appeared on the bridges crossing the Singapore River[9] and in Penang on poles in the centre of the market. In Taiping the Japanese cut off the heads of four Hainanese canteen assistants found hiding in the hill station behind the town, possibly because many Communist Party members were Hainanese, and these heads too went on display.[10] Such actions undoubtedly had a salutary effect on the population. Yeo Tiam Siew of the Oversea Chinese Banking Corporation said the display of heads in Penang was "a horrible sight" that left him "petrified with fear", although he never found out who the victims were or what they had done wrong.[11] Aisha Akbar describes the dilemma of the people who had looted her own house and those of her neighbours when they learned of the executions.

> When news of the looting reached the ears of the Japanese, they announced that anyone caught with stolen goods would be beheaded. The culprits across the road who had seen too many heads stuck on poles knew that the Japanese meant what they said. They were understandably panic-stricken; how were they to hide whole sets of furniture, piled high even to the attap [thatched] roofs? How were they to account for the pianos and cars they had so recently acquired? Many of the houses had as yet not been fitted with electricity, and yet, they were full of fridges, radiograms, toasters and electric fans. The thieves could hardly return the things to their rightful owners. If they did not get beaten-up for their pains, the irate owners would certainly report them to the Japanese, who could then be expected to take even harsher action. So the only way out

7 Benda et al., *Japanese Military Administration in Indonesia*, Document no. 47 (Principles Governing the Implementation of Measures Relative to the Chinese, April 1942), pp. 179–80.

8 JM 103, pp. 17, 44; JM 167, p. 17.

9 Ivan Simson, *Singapore: Too Little, Too Late*, p. 118, and Ian Ward, *The Killer They Called a God*, pp. 115–6, both discuss this episode, which is also frequently mentioned in accounts collected by the Singapore Oral History Department (OHD).

10 Cheong Peng Yeap, "Sejauh Manakah Pendudukan Jepun di Taiping Mempengaruhi Kehidupan Seharian Komuniti Cina di Sana?".

11 Yeo Tiam Siew, *Destined to Survive*, p. 118.

> was to dispose of the things as best they could, and the cheapest, fastest and most effective way was to burn the lot.
>
> When we saw what was being done to our belongings, we did not dare do anything. We could have told the Japanese, but then, who wanted to be responsible for the life and death of neighbours, even if they were thieves. So we stayed on our side of the road, gnashing our teeth in frustration, watching in silent rage as our chairs, cupboards, tables, beds, and all manner of electrical goods were stacked in a huge pile and set alight.[12]

There was also a more systematic attempt to deal with possible Chinese resistance. The Japanese detained Chinese leaders who had actively supported the Chungking government and the China Relief Fund, and then carried out a mass "investigation" of the entire Chinese population followed by a process of "purification by elimination", or *sook ching*. In Singapore all Chinese were ordered to gather at various centres, bringing along a week's rations. The Japanese carried out screenings with the help of hooded local informers, and took away a substantial number of young men for summary execution.

> My father was released only toward the end and he had my youngest brother, Yong Chow Wee, with him. He was the youngest son, and very attached to my father—my father's favourite son. As Father walked past the soldiers to leave the camp, this young brother of mine followed, but was stopped by the soldiers....
>
> We didn't know what exactly to do, where to go or whom to ask. If we saw any Japanese soldiers, we asked questions and sometimes we got slapped. We got kicked on other occasions and were made to stand in the sun for hours. But still we persevered. The search went on for a long time, for weeks, with no results.
>
> We heard rumours that the missing males were taken to Changi, where a big hole was dug and all the youngsters were lined-up around the pit and machine-gunned. All buried in one mass burial in one big grave.
>
> But we were not satisfied. We continued to make enquiries. Until today, we still don't know what happened to my brother. He was seventeen. He was still at school. We have no idea why my brother was singled out.[13]

Similar uncertainties beset Siew Fung Fong, whose husband Wan Kwai Pik had disappeared. He had been warned that the Japanese planned to execute all professionals, except doctors. "Pik had laughed at this, saying that the Japanese were an educated people and would not think of such atrocities."

---

[12] Aisha Akbar, *Aisha Bee at War*, pp. 119–20.

[13] Interview with Elizabeth Choy in H. Sidhu, *The Bamboo Fortress*, pp. 127–8.

> Day after day, Pik did not return. Whenever she finished with the children, she would sit by the window facing the main street hoping for his arrival.

Siew Fung Fong sought the assistance of a sympathetic Japanese official, but was advised to give up the search: "It's beyond my control." She moved into a small room in Chinatown and supported her children by selling drinks and cigarettes.

> Throughout the years, Grandmother rarely talked of Grandfather... She told my sister, Bette, that she never thought of him as dead. "I just waited and waited and waited for him to come home, thinking he would be there the next day, but when I realized that he was dead, it was much too late to mourn."
>
> Grandma neither discussed the happiness of her marriage nor the sorrow she went through when Grandfather was taken by the Japanese. She also never spoke of their love letters and his diary. But she kept them protectively in a drawer next to her bed for more than forty years.... Up to the day she died, on June 26 1983, at the age of 78, she wanted all these to be near her.[14]

Those targeted in the operation included people involved with the China Relief Fund, followers of Tan Kah Kee's Nanyang National Salvation Movement, teachers, lawyers, Hainanese China-born Chinese who had come to Malaya after 1937, men with tattoos—assumed to indicate secret society membership, men who had taken part in Dalforce, civil servants who displayed pro-British leanings, and anyone else the Japanese considered a possible threat to public safety.[15] Thio Chan Bee, a teacher at the Anglo-Chinese School who evaded the screening operation, noted that at the Jalan Besar centre men who wore eyeglasses were taken away. Two of his colleagues disappeared. "Both of them wore spectacles. And so did I. Thus I would have disappeared with them had I gone to the camp."[16] According to Mamoru Shinozaki, the pre-war press attaché who served during the occupation as Director of Education and then as Head of the Welfare Department, the Japanese involved in setting up the military administration felt worried about the long-term effects of the operation, which he claims was planned by 25th Army Headquarters and carried out by young, poorly educated soldiers.[17] Ian Ward, who conducted a detailed investigation of the *sook ching* episode, concluded that it was largely the work of Masanobu

---

[14] Wong Moh Keed (ed.), *To My Heart with Smiles*, p. 123.

[15] Akashi, "Japanese Policy towards the Malayan Chinese", p. 69.

[16] Thio Chan Bee, *Extraordinary Adventures of an Ordinary Man*, p. 36.

[17] Mamoru Shinozaki, *Syonan – My Story*, pp. 16–24. Shinozaki himself, then and later, is credited with saving a considerable number of Chinese from ill-treatment.

Tsuji, the Chief of Operations and Planning Staff for the 25th Army, and that neither General Yamashita nor Major General Saburo Kawamura, the Singapore Garrison Commander, was advised of the scheme in advance.[18]

Illus. 4.2 Mass screening centre at the start of the Japanese Occupation of Singapore.

Source: 20050000103-0007 The Nanyang Miscellany Collection, courtesy of National Archives of Singapore.

On 23 February 1942 the *Syonan Times* printed the following statement concerning actions taken against the Chinese:

> It is hereby declared that the recent arrests of hostile and rebellious Chinese have drastically been carried out in order to establish the prompt restoration of the peace of "Syonan-Ko" (port of Syonan) and also to establish the bright Malaya.
>
> Chinese in Syonan-Ko have hitherto been in sympathy with propaganda of Chungking government, and majority of them supported the aforesaid government and taken politically and economically the same action with Britain against Japan and moreover they have positively participated in British Army, in forming volunteer corps and still have secretly disturbed the military activities of the Nippon Army as guerilla corps or spies and thus they have always taken anti-Japanese actions at

[18] See the indictment against Tsuji drawn up by Ian Ward in *The Killer They Called a God*, pp. 98–126. Questions remain about this issue.

> their first front and it goes without saying that they, in spite of being Eastern Race, were indeed so-called traitors of the East Asia who disturbed the establishment of the Great East Asia.
>
> Now, as soon as "Syonan-Ko" has easily fallen into the hands of Nippon Army, a part of Chinese have run away and it becomes very clear that another part of them, disguising themselves as good citizens, appear to try to have a chance of wriggling. Should it remain untouched the bright Malaya would never come forever.
>
> Thus it is the most important thing to sweep away these treacherous Chinese elements and to establish the peace and welfare of the populace.
>
> Now, as already announced in the declaration of the Commander of the Nippon Army, it is hoped, under the divine protection of the universal and imperial glory, to realize the new order and to establish the co-prosperity sphere as well as the eternal development of Malaya.
>
> Anyone who disturbs this great idea is the common enemy of the human race and shall severely be punished without any exception.
>
> Nevertheless, any good citizen who initiatively supports Nippon's great idea and hopes the bright, free and sound development of Malaya, and also co-operates positively with the above idea, or any one who supports the establishment of the New Order after repenting of his past deeds, no matter whether Chinese or not, shall indiscriminately be treated under the divine protection of Imperial glory.
>
> The Nippon army will gladly help to protect lives and properties of the populace and the permanent development of the peace and happiness shall surely be enjoyed by the people as well as their descendants.
>
> The purpose of the enforcement of the arrests is explained as above and anyone, regardless of nationality, who stirs shall severely be punished without single exception.[19]

A newspaper article five days later stated that "All the people of Syonan who indulged in anti-Nipponese movement, shaking hands with Britain and Chungking, and those who carried on espionage activities against Nippon or did actions to profit the enemies of Nippon should rightly be killed", but added that "Nippon's divine mercy has been bestowed upon them" and only those who disturbed the peace of Syonan were punished.[20]

There had been an earlier screening in Kelantan, and the Japanese subsequently extended this campaign throughout the peninsula. On 20 December 1941 Chinese residents of Pasir Puteh, Kelantan, were ordered to gather outside the police station where an examination took place. Five men were executed, including officials of the local branch of the China Relief Fund who refused to

---

[19] Declaration of the Chief of the Syonan Defence Headquarters of Nippon Army, *Syonan Times*, 23 Feb. 2602.

[20] Article "Sword that Kills One & Saves Many!", *Syonan Times*, 28 Feb. 2602.

disclose where the organization's account books were hidden.[21] A mass screening was carried out in the Georgetown area of Penang on 5 April 1942, and elsewhere on the island the next day. Masked informers identified people who fell into four suspect categories: those who had worked against Japan, communists, educated people and criminals. In Penang those selected, possibly as many as 5,000 men, were taken to the prison to await further interrogation. Some detainees were eventually released, some were executed and a substantial number died when cholera swept through the overcrowded cells.[22] In Taiping the Chinese were told to assemble to receive some favourable news. After listening to addresses by members of the local Peace Maintenance Committee exhorting them to be loyal to Japan, the crowd was divided into two groups according to sex, and an examination began which lasted for more than two days, during which time no food or drink was supplied. Those who failed the screening were taken away and never seen again.[23] Following a similar episode in Selama, a town a few miles north of Taiping, a local administrator wrote:

> The examination of the inhabitants on 17th and 18th April relieved the whole population from their anxiety. After the examination the people, especially Chinese, came out to live in the town and began to feel calm, seeing that the bad persons had been removed from their lot.[24]

The harshness of the Japanese assault on the Chinese community stunned people, and no doubt weakened overt opposition to the Japanese, but it left a legacy of hatred and contributed to the support given to anti-Japanese activity. A resistance movement began organizing in Malaya at very onset of the occupation, first with the creation of a Malayan People's Anti-Japanese Union, and then with the formation of a military wing known variously as the Anti-Japanese Union Forces, or the Malayan People's Anti-Japanese Army (MPAJA), which had units throughout the peninsula by the time the occupation ended.

---

[21] Chua Chong Bin, "Japanese Occupation in Kelantan – A Focus on Pasir Puteh", p. 60.

[22] Particulars on Penang are from Lee Kit Yeng, "Sook Ching dan Perkembangannya di Pulau Pinang". The writer interviewed Datuk Oon Chin Seang, Han Kok Foo and Ooi Song Jen, all of Penang. Lee Kit Yeng gives the date of the screening as 6 April, but I have used the date given by Baba Ahmed bin Ahmed, whose journals are published in Ahmed Meah Baba Ahmed, *Suka Duka di Georgetown* (the screening is mentioned on pp. 47–8). The Japanese devoted special attention to ferreting out teachers and pupils of the Chung Ling High School, who had been very active in support of the China Relief Fund. The school building displays a plaque listing the names of those associated with the school who perished at the hands of the Japanese.

[23] Cheong Peng Yeap, "Sejauh Manakah Pendudukan Jepun di Taiping Mempengaruhi Kehidupan Seharian Komuniti Cina di Sana?"

[24] Selama, Monthly Report for April 2602, Larut 145/1942.

The Japanese dissolved many existing Chinese organizations, notably dialect and clan associations,[25] and created an Oversea Chinese Association (OCA) with branches throughout Malaya as their principal agency for dealing with the Chinese community. The elderly and much respected Dr Lim Boon Keng became the OCA Chairman in Singapore, though he remained relatively inactive. Born in 1869, Lim Boon Keng was an extremely influential figure in the Straits Chinese community. After earning his medical degree at Edinburgh University, he had become active in business and politics, and was a founding member (in 1906) of the Straits Chinese Chamber of Commerce, a leader of the Kuomintang in Malaya, a key figure in the Straits Chinese British Association and a member of the Straits Settlements Legislative Council. Between 1921 and 1937 he served as Vice-Chancellor, the substantive head, of Amoy University.[26] One account says that the Japanese spotted him at a concentration centre, and that he only agreed to cooperate after they threatened to harm his wife.[27] Shmozaki claims to have sought out Dr Lim and to have secured his cooperation in creating the Oversea Chinese Association as a way of saving Chinese lives. He says nothing about Dr. Lim's wife, but mentions that his son was being held in a screening centre, and that Shinozaki promised to send the young man home.[28] According to Yap Pheng Geck, Lim Boon Keng "was drunk most of the time during the occupation".

> When I had a chance to converse with him I found out the reason for his unusual behaviour. He confided in me: "Pheng Geck, you must have thought I am a disgrace. If I don't behave like this they will make me do all sorts of things and I can't stand it. The only way I can shake them off is to behave in this way. They can put my name down for anything they like but I am not functioning because I am incapable and drunk most of the time." I felt very sorry for him and respected him all the more after that.[29]

[25] See, for example, Chief ADO Kinta, Notice, n.d., Batu Gajah 1/2602.

[26] C.F. Yong, *Chinese Leadership and Power in Colonial Singapore*, passim.

[27] Y.S. Tan, "History of the Formation of the Oversea Chinese Association and the Extortion by J.M.A. of $50,000,000 Military Contribution from the Chinese in Malaya", p. 1; this story also appears in N.I. Low and H.M. Cheng, *This Singapore*, pp. 33–4.

[28] Shinozaki, *Syonan – My Story*, pp. 25–30.

[29] Yap Pheng Geck, *Scholar, Banker, Gentleman Soldier*, p. 67.

Illus. 4.3 Dr Lim Boon Keng, President of the Oversea Chinese Association (OCA), with Japanese officers and Wee Twee Kim (right), a Taiwanese, at the OCA office.

Source: 20090000504-0185 Courtesy of National Archives of Singapore.

Other leaders of the OCA included S.Q. Wong and Ching Kee Sun in Singapore, Heah Joo Seang in Penang, K.C. Chan in Perak,[30] and Wong Tet San and Choo Kia Peng in Selangor. Their names recur on the lists of leaders of other Japanese-sponsored organizations, including the Peace Maintenance Committees, Grow-More-Food Committees, and the state advisory councils.[31] The OCA leadership consisted for the most part of established business figures whose financial interests and family concerns, and in some cases their past opposition to Japanese aggression, made them vulnerable to Japanese pressure. Some were being held in detention centres when the committee invited them to join the organization.[32]

One of the first tasks for the OCA was to respond to a Japanese demand that the Chinese expiate their past opposition to Japan by undertaking a "Voluntary Contribution Campaign" to collect $50 million, which would be donated to the military administration.[33] The OCA decided that Chinese throughout the peninsula should contribute according to assessments of their property and other forms of wealth as determined by pre-war tax records. Sub-committees were set up according to speech group divisions (Straits Born, Hokkien, Teochew, Cantonese, Hakka, Hailam and North China), and to ensure fairness the examination of properties belonging to one group was undertaken by another (Teochew properties were examined by the Hailam sub-committee, Hailam properties by the Hokkien, and so on). Any Chinese with property worth more than $3,000 was expected to donate 8 per cent of the value of that property.[34] In

[30] A younger sister of K.C. Chan (Ch'en Chi-tsu), Chan Pek Kwan (Ch'en Pi-jun), was married to Wang Ching-wei, President of the pro-Japanese Nanjing government in China, and his brother Ch'en Yaotsu was Governor of Kwangtung Province until his assassination in April 1944. Another brother, Ch'en Ch'ang-tsu was chief director of the Nanjing government's aviation department, while a nephew, Chan Kwok Kheong (Ch'en Kuo-ch'iang), held a senior position in Kwangtung Province. See the *Penang Shimbun*, 29 Dec. 2602, 20 Apr. 2604; personal communication from Professor Hara Fujio.

[31] See Hara, "The Japanese Occupation of Malaya and the Chinese Community", pp. 68–74, for a fuller list of names.

[32] Kang Jew Koon, "The Chinese in Singapore during the Japanese Occupation", pp. 41–2

[33] Instructions for this collection are found in "Principles Governing the Implementation of Measures Relative to the Chinese", issued by the Military Administration Headquarters in April 1942. See Benda et al., *Japanese Military Administration in Indonesia*, Document no. 47, p. 179. The Straits dollar was revalued by the Japanese, and placed on par with the Japanese yen.

[34] Y.S. Tan, "History of the Formation of the Oversea Chinese Association", pp. 7–8; Lau and Barry, A Brief Review of Chinese Affairs, BMA ADM/8/1; Shü Yün-Ts'iao and Chua Ser-Koon (eds), *Malayan Chinese Resistance to Japan, 1937–1945*, pp. 36–42 of the English-language section.

Illus. 4.4 A receipt issued to the Oversea Chinese Association acknowledging a donation to the Japanese authorities.

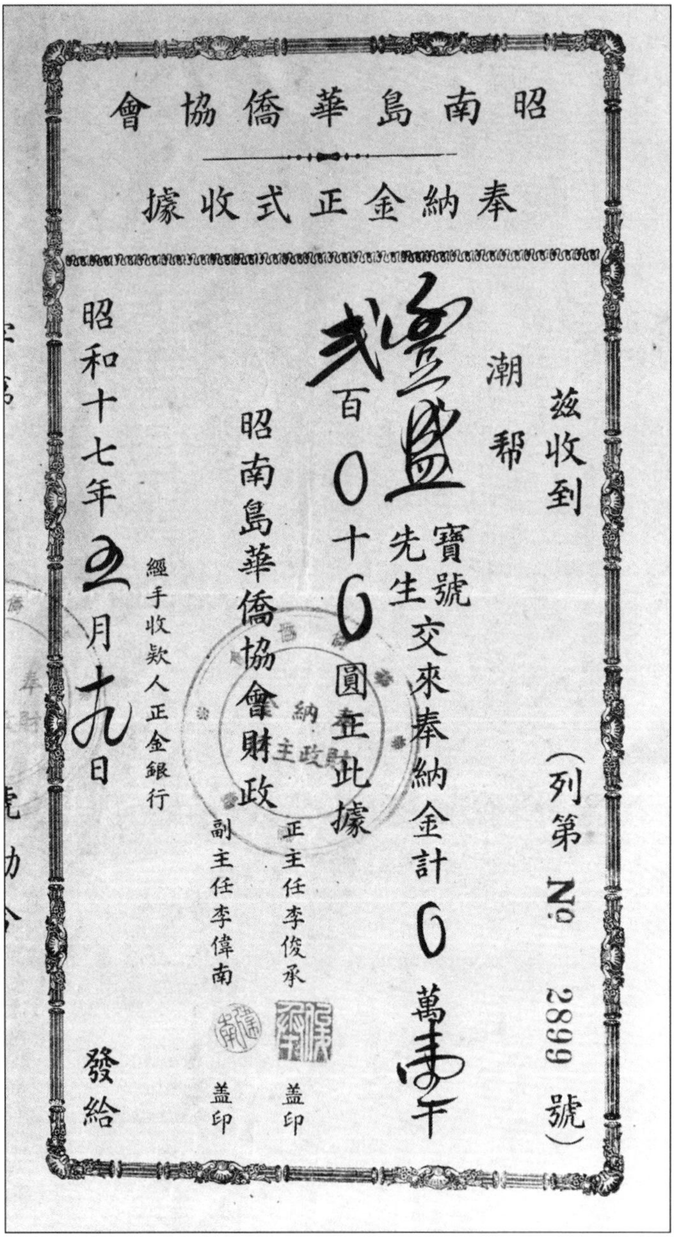

昭南島華僑協會

奉納金正式收據

（列第 №. 2899 號）

茲收到

潮帮 豐盛 寶號 先生 交來奉納金計 6 萬 壹 千 弍 百 0 十 6 圓正此據

昭南島華僑協會財政

正主任李俊承 蓋印

副主任李偉南 蓋印

經手收款人正金銀行

昭和十七年五月十九日 發給

Source: 19980005536-0012 Chew Chang Lang Collection, courtesy of National Archives of Singapore.

Kelantan the OCA imposed a levy on businessmen, and then went from door to door demanding donations from individual households.

> The amount to be contributed by each leading Chinese businessman was assessed against his property and a ... tax of 5 to 12% tax was imposed on it. The shopkeepers were forced to pay a 5 to 12% tax on existing stocks found in their shops; and at family level, each family contributed "head-tax" of about $3.00 per member. This ruling was also extended to employees and coolies employed by firms, guilds and companies. In many instances, there were a lot of duplications in payment, but to whom could the victims complain?[35]

Despite intense Japanese pressure the Chinese community raised just $28 million of the $50 million demanded. The OCA then borrowed the remaining $22 million from the Yokohama Specie Bank, and people who had not yet paid their assessments were considered to be in debt to the Association. In Selangor the government later issued instructions that members of the Chinese community who wished to buy, sell or mortgage landed property had to obtain a certificate stating that they had settled their obligations to the OCA before the transaction could be registered.[36]

The Chinese in Singapore also operated a charitable organization known as the Blue Cross, created by five Chinese "worshippers' groups" after a spirit medium, speaking in the voice of a deity, said that there was great distress on the island and that people should not remain idle and indifferent. The Blue Cross operated mobile kitchens to provide food for the needy, and medical centres where Chinese *sinsehs* (physicians dispensing herbal medicines) offered treatment free of charge. A related organization known as the Black Cross collected and buried corpses found lying in the streets.[37]

Overall, the large Chinese population in Malaya was quiescent during the war, but this post-war assessment makes it clear that the Japanese had no illusions about their feelings.

> Generally speaking the Chinese residents in the southern area were not in favor of the Japanese government. They co-operated outwardly with us since they valued their lives and wanted to gain profits. Accordingly no uprising occurred during our occupation. However some Chinese

[35] Chua Chong Bin, "Japanese Occupation in Kelantan – A Focus on Pasir Puteh", p. 61. Interviewees reported different figures for the assessment, including 5, 7 and 12 per cent.

[36] Tan, "History of the Formation of the Oversea Chinese Association", pp. 10–12 (English-language section); Notification issued by the Selangor OCA, 22 July 2603, Sel CA436/1945.

[37] Yap, *Scholar, Banker, Gentleman Soldier*, pp. 85–90.

> residents with anti-Japanese feelings remained in Malay [Malai] and Northern Borneo and continued their fifth column movement to the last and hindered our administration.[38]

Japan and the Indian Community

The Japanese encouraged Indian nationalist activity directed at winning independence for India from British rule, and supported an Indian Independence League (IIL) as the primary organization for Indian residents. Large numbers of Indians joined the IIL, but not necessarily for the reasons intended by the Japanese.

> … they had to come and they will be issued the passes to go anywhere they liked, you know…. Without these passes they cannot go anywhere. So that made them come there and they all became members of the Indian Independence League. And whenever a Japanese saw an Indian, they immediately asked, "Are you a member of the Indian Independence League?" If they are not, they'll get slapped…. So to avoid the slaps they immediately became members. So that was the League.[39]

The Japanese also supported the Indian National Army (INA), which enrolled large numbers of Indian soldiers following the British surrender. The Indian leadership included local figures such as S.G. Goho and K.P.K. Menon, both lawyers, and A. Yellapa, but the Japanese placed two Bengalis, Rash Behari Bose and after him Subhas Chandra Bose, at the head of the movement. Both men had solid credentials as Indian nationalists but lacked strong Malayan connections.

The relationship between Indian nationalists and the Japanese was uneasy. According to K.R. Menon, a wartime journalist and a member of the IIL, K.P.K. Menon angered Fujiwara Iwaichi during their first meeting by telling him that Indian independence was the affair of Indians, and that they did not want the Japanese to interfere.[40] Fujiwara's own account of his introduction to Menon presents a very different picture: "From the moment of our first meeting, we were able to talk on intimate terms as though we were old friends; we did not need to explain things in detail."[41] To attract support, the IIL staged a series of mass rallies. At the first of these events, which was directed at Indian POWs and took place at Farrer Park in Singapore on 17 February, Fujiwara offered the men a choice between languishing in detention camps or taking part in the

---

38 JM 167, p. 16.

39 OHD, interview with K.R. Menon.

40 Ibid.

41 Fujiwara Iwaichi, *F. Kikan*, p. 187.

movement for Indian independence, and says most of them enthusiastically embraced the second option.[42] The number of soldiers from the British Army who joined the INA is unclear. Mohan Singh claimed 42,000 volunteered and 13,000 did not, while according to Field-Marshal Lord Wavell, 20,000 soldiers joined the INA, and a further 45,000 remained prisoners of war.[43] The soldiers were primarily Sikhs, and the dominant role played by North Indians in the movement lessened its appeal for Malaya's Tamil community. At a Great Indian Independence Rally held at Farrer Park on 12 August, speeches were delivered in Hindi and in English, but a scheduled Tamil translation was not read out because the sound system failed, and the failure to address the crowd in Tamil created an inflammatory situation. A few days later K.P.K. Menon published a statement in the *Syonan Times* which explained what had happened and made the point, whether by way of apology or admonition is not altogether clear, that communalism had no place in the national movement.[44]

Personal and administrative conflicts plagued the Indian independence movement throughout 1942. In March, Fujiwara's operation was taken over by Colonel Hideo Iwakuro, a man less committed to the ideals of the Indian leadership, and the Fujiwara Kikan was replaced by an enlarged Iwakuro Kikan. During the months that followed the IIL grew increasingly unhappy with the Japanese practice of making unilateral decisions on issues relating to Indian affairs. K.P.K. Menon, who worked in the Propaganda Section of the IIL, was concerned that people not think of it as a puppet organization, and chafed under the tight controls the Japanese imposed over the material he wrote. As another former IIL member, K.M. Rengarajoo, explained:

> … whatever you draft, whatever you suggest, whatever suggestions you put to these people they want more clarification on that. And just advising the people "No! You don't do this … don't do that" this sort of misunderstanding. So he [K.P.K. Menon] said, "I can't carry on with these people."[45]

Friction with the Japanese resulted in the arrest and imprisonment of both K.P.K. Menon and Mohan Singh at the end of 1942, while other major leaders of the Indian movement either resigned or were removed from office, including

[42] Ibid., pp. 178–87.

[43] Lebra, *Jungle Alliance*, p. 221n9; Statement by Field-Marshal Lord Wavell, 10 Dec. 1945, in Allen, *The End of the War in Asia*, p. 146. In her later *Japanese-Trained Armies in Southeast Asia* (pp. 25–6), Lebra claims that about half of the 45,000 Indian troops in Singapore at the time of the surrender volunteered after the Farrer Park rally, and others joined after the arrival of Subhas Chandra Bose.

[44] *Syonan Times*, 21 Aug. 2602.

[45] OHD, interview with K.M. Rengarajoo.

the chairman of the IIL in Singapore, S.C. Goho, and the chairman for Malaya, N. Raghavan. The INA collapsed, and those of its members who had been part of the British Army again became prisoners of war. These developments highlighted the IIL's lack of autonomy and increased the unhappiness felt by Malayan Indians.[46] Contributing to their unease was the fact that Jawaharlal Nehru was known to have said that Indians living outside of India should not interfere with Indian politics, and they were also well aware that an army of Indian liberation was incompatible with the non-violent stance of the Congress Party.

The leader of the IIL, Rash Behari Bose, struggled during this difficult period to keep the movement alive, but the Indian community lacked confidence in him. Some thirty years earlier Rash Behari Bose had settled in Japan after being forced to flee India as a result of his revolutionary activities. He had become a Japanese citizen, his wife was Japanese, and his son was an officer in the Imperial armed forces. His personal circumstances caused Indians in Malaya to question the sincerity of his commitment to India. Moreover, he was growing old, and suffered from tuberculosis. According to K.M. Rengarajoo,

> … he was not able to satisfy either side: Indian's side also he was not able to satisfy about their suggestions, demands and things like that. On the other hand, the Japanese people also felt it in such a way that this man is given a key position and he was not able to convince his own people. That was his position.[47]

The IIL found a new leader in Subhas Chandra Bose, a former president of the Congress Party who in January 1941 had left India for Germany to seek support for his struggle against British rule. In February 1943 he travelled by submarine to Southeast Asia, and in May went on to Tokyo where he met senior Japanese leaders. On 2 July 1943 he flew to Malaya together with Rash Behari Bose, and two days later assumed the Presidency of the IIL. Around the same time, Col. Toshio Yamamoto replaced Iwakuro, and the Iwakuro Kikan gave way to a higher level Hikari Kikan ("Light" Organization), which regulated the affairs of the IIL throughout the Japanese Empire. Yamamoto was replaced by Lt. General Saburo Isoda in 1944.[48]

---

[46] Fujiwara, *F. Kikan*, p. 246; Lebra, *Jungle Alliance*, pp. 94–8; Bose, *A Will for Freedom*, pp. 20–1. The *Penang Shimbun* announced N. Raghavan's resignation as President of the IIL owing to "ill health" on 25 Mar. 2603; he was succeeded by Dr M.K. Luksumeyah of Kuala Lumpur.

[47] OHD, interview with K.M. Rengarajoo. Rash Behari Bose died in January 1945.

[48] See Gerard H. Corr, *The War of the Springing Tigers*; Hugh Toye, *The Springing Tiger*; Supplementary Guide to JIFC (Indian) Activities, Malaya, issued by HQ Allied Land Forces, South East Asia Command, 16 Aug. 1945, WO203/2298.

The presence of Subhas Chandra Bose soon began to have positive effects. As a first step he re-established the Indian National Army, or Azad Hind Fauj. A large training camp opened at Seletar, in Singapore, on 3 September 1943, and additional training centres operated at Seremban, Kuala Lumpur and Ipoh. The centres could accommodate up to 10,000 men at one time and ran at close to full capacity during 1943, but by 1945 there were only 3,000 men undergoing training.

The INA had a women's section known as the Rani of Jhansi Regiment, named after a woman leader who died fighting the British during the Indian Mutiny of 1857. Its leader, Dr Swaminathan Lakshmi, said of the organization in August 1943:

> This new regiment when formed will be composed not only of women soldiers but also of others who may be employed as first aid nurses, cooks, orderlies or special staff all serving in the front line. The regiment will not work behind the lines but right in front. When we come into contact with the Indian Army on the other side, the very presence of Indian women armed for the freedom fight will, I am sure, have a very great effect on the British-Indian Army and the moral effect of their presence right on the front line will be very great for those of the Indian National Army fighting side by side with them. The battle cry of the Rani of Jhansi Regiment is "Rani Lakshmibai — die like her".[49]

After undergoing training, a member of the regiment gave Japan's Domei News Agency a statement that expressed both nationalist and feminist intentions: "We may be the softer and fairer sex but surely I protest against the word weaker. All sorts of epithets have been given to us by man in order to guard his own selfish interests. It is time we shattered this chain of man along with the chain of Indian slavery."[50]

The officer corps of the INA consisted of a Senior Wing whose members were selected from Indian Army POWs, and a junior wing recruited from the civilian population in Malaya. Officer training took place at Batu Pahat, Johore. There were also special courses for agents to be sent into India. British intelligence discovered the existence of infiltrators while interviewing men who claimed to have escaped from Malaya, and to deal with this activity the Combined Services

[49] Domei ELB, 16 Aug. 1943, FIR 12, 28 Aug. 1943, CO273/669/50744/7; *Syonan Sinbun*, 2 Aug. 2603. Peter Ward Fay, The Forgotten Army, is partly based on interviews with Dr Swaminathan Lakshmi.

[50] Statement by Janaki Davar, *Penang Shimbun*, 22 Feb. 2604. For a discussion of the Rani of Jhansi Regiment in the context of Indian feminism, see Carol Hills and Daniel C. Silverman, "Nationalism and Feminism in Late Colonial India: The Rani of Jhansi Regiment, 1943–1945", *Modern Asian Studies* 27, 4 (1993): 741–60.

Illus. 4.5 Subhas Chandra Bose arriving in Singapore.

Source: 20080000432-5302 Nirvan Thivy Collection, courtesy of National Archives of Singapore.

Illus. 4.6 Subhas Chandra Bose addressing members of the Indian National Army at a rally in Singapore.

Source: 20080000432-5297 Nirvan Thivy Collection, courtesy of National Archives of Singapore.

Detailed Intelligence Centre strengthened its language capabilities by recruiting specialists to translate and assess information in Asian languages.[51]

On 21 October 1943 Subhas Chandra Bose announced the formation of a Provisional Government of Free India (Azad Hind) with himself as Head of State, Prime Minister, and Minister of War and Foreign Affairs. Three days later he issued a declaration of war against Britain and the United States.[52] Following this step, the IIL called upon Indians in Malaya to donate funds to the movement based on assessed property values, following the precedent of the $50 million donation demanded of the Chinese. According to K.R. Menon:

> They were forced to give. There was no question of Indians keeping aloof, you know. Japanese were in power, Japanese were in power. So Indians go and ask, means they have to give. If they did not give ... You just tell them [the Japanese], "Well, we were able to get only so much." "What! So many Indians and you could not get! Who are the people who did not give?" Finished. The moment they see a Japanese with you, they will give out the whole thing in order to save their lives.[53]

An Indian who left Malaya in September 1943 told Allied interrogators that wealthy Indians were eager to convert their property into cash or other valuables that could be kept hidden, since they were "so pressed and persecuted for 'voluntary' contributions to Japanese or Indian 'National' funds they want to pose as property less".[54]

In 1944, when the IIL and INA were increasingly preoccupied with events in Burma, the Indian community in Singapore created an Indian Welfare Association, described as "a liaison organization separate from the Indian Independence League". Membership was voluntary, and the Association dealt with matters such as the food shortage and the supply of labour.[55]

---

[51] *Syonan Sinbun*, 9 July 2603; Domei ELB on 6 July 1943 and 16 July 1943, FIR 9, 17 July 1943, and FIR 13, 11 Sept. 1943, CO273/669/50744/7; Lebra, *Japanese-Trained Armies in Southeast Asia*, pp. 25–8; Supplementary Guide to JIFC (Indian) Activities (Malaya), WO203/3298; History of SEATIC, 12 Dec. 1946, WO203/6286.

[52] FIR 16, 23 Oct. 1943, FIR 17, 6 Nov. 1943, CO273/673/50744/7.

[53] OHD, interview with K.R. Menon.

[54] JICA/CBI, New Delhi, Report No. 8341, 5 Sept. 1944, NARA RG226 95618.

[55] *Syonan Shimbun*, 14 Apr. 2604.

Illus. 4.7 Members of the Provisional Government of Azad Hind. First row (left to right): Lieutenant Colonel Chatterjee, Lieutenant Colonel J.K. Bhonsle, Dr Lakshmi, Chandra Bose, A.M. Sahay and S.A. Ayer. Second row (left to right): Lieutenant Colonel Gulzara Singh, Lieutenant Colonel Shah Nawaz Khan, Lieutenant Colonel Aziz Ahmed, Lieutenant Colonel M Z Kiani, Lieutenant Colonel N.S. Bhagat, Lieutenant Colonel Ehsan Qadir, Lieutenant Colonel Loganathan.

Source: 20080000432-5299 Nirvan Thivy Collection, courtesy of National Archives of Singapore.

Japan and the Malay Community

Malay leaders fell into four distinct categories. One group consisted of the Sultans and the aristocracy, some of whom had displayed signs of sympathy with the Japanese cause before the war, although of necessity they all cooperated with the Japanese during the occupation. Religious leaders made up the second group, and the Japanese attempted to cultivate them, but gestures supporting Islam tended to be offset by insensitive behaviour on the part of soldiers and local officials. A third group of Malay leaders consisted of the men who worked for the Japanese civil administration, for the most part pre-war civil servants who had been ordered back to work by the Japanese. These officials, and the village headmen, had to carry out the odious task of recruiting forced labour, and explain and enforce other unpalatable Japanese policies. Some were assassinated by the

Malayan People's Anti-Japanese Army, and many lost the trust of the people they were expected to administer. The final group of Malay leaders came from pre-war nationalist organizations, particularly the Kesatuan Melayu Muda (KMM), and included Ibrahim Yaacob, Onan Haji Siraj and Ishak Haji Muhammad. The KMM, like a number of other disaffected groups in Southeast Asia, had dealings with the Japanese before the war.

Japanese officers later asserted that they cultivated Malay radicals to get support at the time of the invasion and made no promises regarding future political arrangements. For his part, Ibrahim Yaacob denied agreeing to provide active assistance and claimed only to have promised that the KMM would not resist the Japanese advance. At the start of the occupation some members of the KMM "swaggered about in the villages and in the government offices, throwing their weight around as if they were the government", but the Japanese paid little attention to Malay nationalists and in setting up their administration turned to pre-war civil servants and the aristocratic elite to staff government offices. The KMM was banned in June 1942, and both Ibrahim and Ishak joined the Propaganda Department where they were given jobs on a new Malay-language newspaper called *Berita Malai*.[56] Ibrahim later became commander of the Malay Volunteer Army (Giyu-Gun), with the rank of Lieutenant Colonel. In this capacity, he claimed to have come to an understanding with the MPAJA that his troops would try to avoid military engagements, and would at some future date defect, but communist sources do not confirm the existence of any such agreement.[57]

Religion was a sensitive issue for the Malays, and the new administration convened two important meetings shortly after the beginning of the occupation, one for local political leaders and the other for senior religious figures, to explain Japan's religious policies and attempt to overcome negative feelings aroused by incidents when Japanese soldiers had behaved improperly around mosques. The basic principle was that Muslims were free to practice their faith without hindrance. In April 1943 the Japanese sponsored a three-day religious conference in Singapore involving representatives from Sumatra and the peninsula, with the object, according to a Domei broadcast, of "bringing about closer cooperation between the Moslems residing in Malai and Sumatra", and of "rendering every support to attain complete and final victory in the war of Greater East Asia".[58] In July the Marquis Tokugawa proposed setting up a supreme Islamic religious

[56] Cheah, "The Japanese Occupation of Malaya", pp. 102–4.

[57] Cheah, *Red Star Over Malaya*, pp. 71–2.

[58] Domei ELB, 15 Mar. and 3 Apr. 1943, CO273/669/50744/7; the conference took place on 4–7 April, and participants' speeches are in MB Johor 37/2603.

council for Malaya, but the military administration rejected the idea. However, in September the authorities approved the creation of a Singapore religious committee embracing all faiths. In April 1944 the military administration in Perak lifted a ban on the state's Council of Chief Ulama, which had been the central body responsible for religion and Malay custom before the war, and other states followed this precedent. Between September and October 1944 religious councils were created in each of the five states that remained under Japanese rule following the transfer of the northern provinces to Thailand. The military administration also convened a conference of Islamic leaders at Kuala Kangsar in December 1944 to discuss issues of concern to Muslims.

These initiatives provided some reassurance, and at the official level relations were reasonably cordial toward the end of the occupation, but the Japanese lacked a coherent policy toward the Malay community, and their insistence that people bow in the direction of the Imperial Palace, their use of religious occasions to deliver propaganda, the inclusion of prayers to the Emperor and to Japanese soldiers killed during the war in mosque services, and the promotion of lotteries and other forms of gambling offended many Muslims. Moreover, for want of active support from the administration, officials concerned with religious affairs found it difficult to carry out their duties, and the observance of religious obligations became noticeably lax. It was, of course, impossible for Muslims in Malaya to make the pilgrimage to Mecca for the duration of the occupation.[59]

The associations developed for the Chinese and Indian communities had no parallel among the Malays until somewhat later in the occupation, although "Malay Committees" functioned in some areas immediately after the invasion, and a Malay Distress Relief Fund was created in the Kinta District during 1942.[60] In May 1943 representatives of the Selangor Malay community held discussions about the possible formation of a Malay association, following a Japanese suggestion that they set up a body similar to the Indian Independence League and the Oversea Chinese Association. Asked to choose between reviving the defunct Persatuan Melayu Selangor (Malay Association of Selangor), created

[59] Abu Talib Ahmad, "The Impact of the Japanese Occupation on the Malay-Muslim Population", pp. 30–2. A report on this conference entitled "Butir-Butir Mesyuarat Ugama Islam" is found in Kathi Besar Johor 257/2604. See also Itagaki, "Some Aspects of the Japanese Policy for Malaya", pp. 257–9, and Akashi, "Japanese Military Administration in Malaya", pp. 102–10. A group of pilgrims travelling to Mecca had reached Colombo when the invasion began, and were forced to return home without completing their journey. People dubbed them "Haji Colombo". Hairani Mohd Khalid, "Satu Tinjauan Am tentang Kehidupan Penduduk Mukim Relau, Kedah semasa Pendudukan Jepun".

[60] Stia Usaha, Jawatan Kuasa Melayu, Batu Gajah, Kenyataan, 19 Jan. 1942, Batu Gajah 1/2602; Minutes, Meetings of the Malay Distress Relief Fund, Batu Gajah 130/2602.

in June 1938, or forming a new organization, the meeting opted for the latter, and established a Malay Welfare Association, the Persekutuan Khidmat Orang Melayu (Malay-jin Hoko Kai). The definition of a "Malay" used by the body was taken from the Malay Reservations Enactment passed some thirty years earlier: "a person belonging to any Malayan race who habitually speaks the Malay language or any Malayan language and professes the Muslim religion." The government provided $3,000 to set up a fund for the organization to use in assisting destitute Malays living in the state, and in June 1944 the size of the fund was increased by requiring each Malay household in Selangor to contribute $1, with part of the proceeds going to the Malay Relief Fund and the rest to the Wounded Soldiers' Home in Tokyo.[61]

A similar association for Singapore was announced in December 1943, and in the other Malay states during 1944. All Malays automatically became members, and the leaders were drawn from younger and more radical elements in addition to the aristocrats and civil servants who were the usual Japanese contacts. When the Singapore branch held its inaugural meeting on 3 April 1944, two aristocrats—Tengku Abdul Kadir bin Asmad and Tengku Putera—became President and Vice-President, but other key positions went to members of the radical faction: Ibrahim Yaacob was Advisor, Onan Haji Siraj the Secretary-General, and Ishak Haji Mohammed a committee member.[62] In March 1944 the Domei News Agency announced the imminent creation of parallel Malay Women's Associations, and the Singapore group created a women's section at its first meeting.[63] In Pahang the Japanese Chief Officer in charge of the General

[61] Minutes mashuarat berkenaan dengan chadangan hendak mengadakan Jawatan-Kuasa bagi mengaturkan derma menolong orang2 Melayu Selangor, 8 May 2603; Mashuarat Ramai yang di-adakan di-Sultan Sulaiman Club 18.5.03 kerana Merundingkan Chadangan Hendak Menubohkan "Persatuan Melayu Selangor"; Rules of Malai-jin Selangor Hoko-Kai; Fund for the purpose of making a contribution …, 21 June 2604, Ulu Langat 92/2603. For information on the Persatuan Melayu Selangor, see Roff, *The Origins of Malay Nationalism*, pp. 237–41.

[62] Halinah Bamadhaj, "The Impact of the Japanese Occupation", p. 157; *Syonan Shimbun*, 16 May 2604. Ishak was growing disillusioned with Japanese rule. Around this time he fell out with Onan Haji Siraj and decided to resign his position as Editor-in-Chief of the *Malai Shimbun* newspaper and leave Singapore to live in the Malay agricultural colony on Bintan Island. He was quoted as saying: "I have reached the decision to cast aside my pen for the spade and to contribute towards the increased fighting power of Greater East Asia for the victorious conclusion of the war." Ibrahim Yaacob persuaded him to come back to Singapore, but after a short stay he returned to his home in Pahang and remained there for the duration of the occupation. Cheah, "The Japanese Occupation of Malaya", p. 109.

[63] FIR 19, 4 Dec. 1943; FIR 1, 15 Jan. 1944; FIR 6, 31 Mar. 1944; Domei ELB, 4 Apr. 1944, FIR 7, 15 Apr. 1944; Domei ELB, 29 Apr. 1944, FIR 8, 30 Apr. 1944, CO273/673/50744/7.

Department greeted the Malay Welfare Association with a marked lack of enthusiasm:

> The Malay Association is expected to help the Government and to work hard for the good of the Community and not to merely have tea parties and dinners. Some of the rules are not very good but all the same they have been passed.[64]

Japan and the Eurasian Community

The Eurasian population, which eventually also got its own welfare association, viewed the Japanese invasion with a good deal of trepidation, and could have drawn little comfort from a tongue-lashing delivered by the Chief of the Syonan Defence Headquarters at a Eurasian assembly on 3 March 1942. After a conventional introduction informing the group that people who cooperated with the Japanese would suffer no harm but that anyone who opposed them could expect severe punishment, he continued:

> Until now you were spoiled in circumstances of individualism and liberalism. You were used to an easy-going life of amusements, but you will soon see the real idea of mankind, the new conception of the New World....
>
> Facing these facts some of you complained to us regarding small and petty personal affairs. This is regrettable. Most of you belong to the educated class and you still continue your thoughts and actions as before, disobeying our orders. We must think of heavy punishment for you.
>
> Those who emphasize their rights and ideas, forgetting their duties and services, are an evil to the nation. To anyone who persists in continuing to have old ideas, consistently disobeying our orders, we must considering meting out severe punishment.

He went on to say that Eurasians who had served as military volunteers or worked in the Police Force or the "mischievous propaganda department" should "state so clearly and in detail", failing which they would be "severely punished". If the military authorities wished to commandeer anything belonging to Eurasians, they should not resist, and anyone who did would be "punished". Finally, he instructed Eurasians who had previously been employed in the electrical, water, engineering or other important departments to report for work, adding that anyone who failed to do so would be "severely punished".[65]

A story published in the press later the same month stated that in the past Eurasians had been dependent on their "blood relatives" the British, and

---

[64] Notes, Meeting of District Officers, 16 Aug. 2604, Temerloh 82/2602.

[65] "Nipponese Injunction to Local Eurasians", *Syonan Times*, 6 Mar. 2602, p. 3.

the majority "still clung to their old ideas of 'European respectability' and 'superiority'". The writer ("Charles Nell", a by-line that appeared frequently in the early days of the occupation) admonished those who thought in such ways: "There is no room in the New Order for 'superior people'. There are no 'superior' people in the New Order." Eurasians, he suggested, would have to abandon the pre-war system of "seeking favours and preferential treatment as a buffer community between the white and the coloured races", and adjust to earning a living as "labourers and tillers of the soil".[66]

Dr C.J. Paglar became President of the All-Malayan (Eurasian) Association of Syonan and President of the Eurasian Welfare Association, making him the de facto leader of the Eurasian community. A medical doctor who was instrumental in setting up the wartime Malacca Medical College, he had local roots and appears to have protected Eurasian interests during the occupation. Nevertheless, he was not well liked. George Bogaars, for example, said that his parents and their friends did not think highly of Paglar and others who "went out of their way to help the Japanese".[67] However, F.A.C. Oehlers, whose father served as vice president of the Eurasian Welfare Association, emphatically stated that both men accepted the positions under duress, and rejected the imputation that they were willing collaborators.[68]

Relations with the Japanese

The use of terror to intimidate the population abated with the re-establishment of civil administration and the formation of communal organizations, but it did not cease altogether. Sentries administered corporal punishment when passers-by did not bow to their satisfaction, and the *Kempeitai* treated people suspected of being in contact with anti-Japanese guerrilla organizations with great brutality. Black market activity or offenses such as listening to overseas radio stations could also result in severe punishment. The methods of torture that became the *Kempeitai* hallmark included beatings with a piece of wood—sometimes while the person was suspended from a rope, placing lighted cigarettes or heated pieces of iron on sensitive areas of the body, and pulling out fingernails. The *Kempeitai* made frequent use of the water torture, which involved pumping vast quantities of water into their victim, and then placing a board across the stomach and standing or jumping on it. One man who endured this treatment

---

[66] "Malayan Eurasians", *Syonan Times*, 24 Mar. 2602, p. 3.

[67] OHD, interview with George Bogaars. According to an intelligence report, Paglar had been struck off the medical register. Malaya under the Japanese, NARA RG220 128585.

[68] Oehlers, *That's How It Goes*, p. 92.

said afterwards that water came out of every opening of his body: "Words cannot convey the pain."[69]

The experience of Sybil Kathigasu, who was arrested in 1943 for supporting resistance activities, is one of the most horrifying, and the physical damage she suffered at Japanese hands caused her premature death in 1949.

> They seemed desirous of battering the truth out of my body. Each unsatisfactory answer I gave—and they were all unsatisfactory—was followed by a dose of intense physical pain, administered in varying quantities and in many different forms. Usually I was punched and slapped in the face, and beaten with sticks and heavy rattan canes. The places on which the blows were concentrated were those containing no vital nerve or organ so that no permanent injury resulted to the victim; in particular the outside surface of the upper arm, the thigh, and the calf were chosen.
>
> These parts of my body were soon solid bruises, the pain from which made it impossible to lie down and sleep with any sort of comfort. Sometimes as a change from the beatings other tortures were tried; it might be the water treatment or some other equally diabolical method of inflicting pain. It seemed to me that Kunichika was trying out every weapon in his armoury in an effort to make me talk. Under his supervision policemen, some of whom seemed to hate their task almost as much as I did, would run needles into my finger-tips below the nail, while my hand was held firmly, flat on the table; they heated iron bars in a charcoal brazier and applied them to my legs and back; they ran a stick between the second and third fingers of both my hands, squeezing the fingers together and holding them firmly in the air while two men hung from the ends of the cane, making a see-saw of my hands and tearing the flesh between my fingers; they thrust the rough ragged ends of canes into the hollows of my knees and twisted them until I screamed with pain. I used to find a certain relief by screaming and yelling at the top of my voice, and several times was spared further suffering by falling to the floor in a dead faint.[70]

Others experienced similar treatment. In Singapore Ng Seng Yong had two friends taken in by the *Kempeitai* for questioning, in the course of which "they had a thrashing of their life". They were picked up "because of certain unpleasant circumstances, I believe. But those days, it was nothing strange. Anything … anybody taken by the Japanese was nothing strange."[71] Those who were arrested by the ordinary police considered themselves fortunate. It was far worse to be arrested by the *Kempeitai*: "So once you are in you had it. Nobody leaves the

[69] Lee Kit Yeng, "Sook Ching dan Perkembangannya di Pulau Pinang"; the quotation is from a man called Mandur Salleh, and appears in Dobree, *Hujan Panas*, p. 124n1.

[70] Sybil Kathigasu, *No Dram of Mercy*, pp. 140–1.

[71] OHD, interview with Ng Seng Yong.

place without being beaten up. It's a question of how serious you are beaten up."[72] Roma Ryan, an Indian employed by the Telecommunications Department in Malaya, was suspected of listening to overseas radio broadcasts. His hands were tied behind him and he was beaten unconscious. Later, water was pumped into his stomach, he was doused with water and forced to stand naked beneath a fan, and he was beaten until the skin on his back was shredded. In the end he was taken before a judge, who concluded that the charges against him were groundless and dismissed the case. Over 40 years later, recounting the experience to a university student writing a class paper, the memory reduced him to tears.[73] Lawrence Manickam, a railway worker, was accused of the same offence, even though his Japanese boss had already fixed his radio set so that it could only receive local frequencies. He was beaten and had needles driven into the soles of his feet, and remained in detention for ten months despite the intervention of his employer on his behalf.[74] Although in general Malays received somewhat better treatment than other races under the Japanese regime, many suffered similar interrogations. Ahmad bin Daud and a friend worked selling oil in Penang, a job for which they did not have the necessary permit. They were betrayed by an informer, and one day the Japanese took them in for investigation. At the police station they were kicked, cut with a knife, and beaten into unconsciousness. They were finally released after their employer provided a guarantee for them, but fifty years later Ahmad still felt the effects of the beating he suffered. He and his friend fared better than two other young men from the same village, who were taken away by the Japanese and never heard of again.[75]

While the *Kempeitai* used fear as a tool to secure obedience to Japanese wishes, ordinary soldiers meted out harsh treatment on their own initiative, sometimes against the wishes of their superiors. Sentries were extremely powerful, and many people were slapped or suffered other indignities at roadside checkpoints. According to Yap Pheng Geck:

> I felt I could hold my own with the Japanese officials but with the sentries on the streets, I was like the others, completely at their mercy. The sentry was a law unto himself. Every Japanese sentry swaggered, enveloped in his self-importance. But the lowest ranking sentry was the worst of the lot.

[72] OHD, interview with Heng Chiang Ki.

[73] Mary Florence Meera Diridollou, "Semasa Pendudukan Jepun di Tanah Melayu Kaum India Tidak Terlepas daripada Kekejaman Jepun" [During the Japanese Occupation of Malaya, the Indian Community Did Not Escape Japanese Cruelty].

[74] Ibid.

[75] Hairani Mohd Khalid, "Satu Tinjauan Am tentang Kehidupan Penduduk Mukim Relau, Kedah semasa Pendudukan Jepun".

> Some of the military people at Oxley Rise and the civilian officials who used to call on me for one thing or another were not brutal. The brutality was in the streets, at the hands of the ordinary soldier and inside the MP Headquarters.[76]

A Japanese officer told Aisha Akbar's family that the first wave of Japanese forces consisted of "country bumpkins" who were meant to strike terror into the local population, something she says "they did admirably". When soldiers encountered people in the streets, they often demanded fountain pens or wristwatches.

> Some soldiers had as many as ten wristwatches on their arms. When they saw someone wearing a watch they liked, they demanded it. There was no question of refusing. Baby Lau was very fortunate; a Japanese sentry asked for the cheap, flashy watch he was wearing and in exchange gave him a far better one.[77]

Later a better educated class of Japanese arrived to fill posts as administrators, teachers and cultural officers. They were a considerable improvement over the combat troops, but people found many of them pompous, irascible and erratic.

> Often they asked you silly, naive questions which had to be treated seriously. You had to give them an answer but you could easily arouse their interest with some comments on some other subject, so that they became more interested in what you had to say rather than in interrogating you or beating you up.[78]

Japanese officers imposed corporal punishment on their own subordinates who committed mistakes. Aisha Akbar wrote, "We also noticed that if a Japanese soldier did anything wrong, no matter how slight the offence, his face was slapped brutally by his superior officer."[79] Fujiwara Iwaichi reprimanded two Japanese soldiers he found looting Tungku Abdul Rahman's residence in Kedah, and was told by their commander later the same day that the solders "felt shame for their misconduct and took their own lives to atone for their crime".[80] Junior officers who carried out a massacre at Alexandra Hospital shortly before the fall of Singapore were tried by their superior officers, and executed. In some cases, too, the Japanese came to the defence of the local population.

A number of memoirs report instances when Japanese officers provided testimonials on pieces of paper which, posted outside the door of a hosue,

---

[76] Yap, *Scholar, Banker, Gentleman Soldier*, p. 64.

[77] Aisha Akbar, *Aisha Bee at War*, p. 115.

[78] Yap, *Scholar, Banker, Gentleman Soldier*, p. 62.

[79] Aisha Akbar, *Aisha Bee at War*, p. 115.

[80] Fujiwara, *F. Kikan*, p. 81.

protected those inside. There was also an occasion in Johore when an Indian chief clerk made advances to a woman who was seeking work on his estate. She complained to the foreman, who ignored her. She then walked 19 miles to the town of Muar, carrying a young child, and reported the matter to the Japanese. They gave her a case of tinned milk, some biscuits and some sugar, and took her back to the estate, where they beat up the chief clerk, hurled him into a drain and then ordered him off the property.[81] In some cases sincere friendships developed between the two sides,[82] but local people had to behave circumspectly to avoid the suspicion that they were acting as informers, and the Japanese, too, seem to have found it necessary to be cautious. A Japanese lieutenant befriended Joan Hon's family, and one of her male relatives went for rides in his car: "… they would take routes to avoid the Kempetai for it would not do for an officer to be caught fraternising with the fallen." The officer became attracted to a girl living in the household and wrote a letter in Chinese asking her to marry him. "Seng Chew read it and was terrified and wept. In his position, he had the advantage and could force his attentions on her if she refused him." The girl escaped by fleeing to Penang.[83]

In time, people learned to adjust their behaviour to avoid getting into trouble with the Japanese. When Mary Lim's cousin sold her cakes in the streets of Singapore, sentries sometimes helped themselves and refused to pay. "But what my advice to him was, 'Don't pass by the Japanese.'"[84] George Bogaars, who was in his mid-teens during the occupation, said: "We treated the Japanese with a lot of kind of care because we didn't want to be slapped and beaten and all that. We didn't want to lose our heads and that kind of things. So I don't think we kind of love them really. At the same time I don't think there was a tremendous fear of them. But it was basically that if you could stay clear of them, if you didn't get on their wrong side, you're okay."[85]

* * *

[81] Selva Rani Raman, "Pendudukan Jepun di Panchor, Muar, Johor". The story was recounted by Rukkumani a/p Kuppureddy, who was the child accompanying her mother when she sought help from the Japanese.

[82] Lee Siow Mong says that he developed friendly relations with the Japanese owing to his Chinese scholarship and artistic interests. He did Chinese painting and calligraphy, and carved name seals for Japanese officers. *Words Cannot Equal Experience*, pp. 26–7.

[83] Joan Hon, *Relatively Speaking*, pp. 88–9.

[84] OHD, interview with Mary Lim.

[85] OHD, interview with George Bogaars.

In Malaya the Japanese had to deal with a diverse population. Before the invasion, Indians and Malays did not have strong feelings about the Japanese, but there was intense hostility within the Chinese community. For Japan, it was essential to deal with this situation quickly and effectively because their combat troops would be sent elsewhere immediately after the fall of Singapore, leaving behind a relatively weak garrison force. From this point of view there is a certain logic to the massacre of Chinese who had actively supported China's war against Japan, and some of the people informants identified during the screening operations fell into this group. Yet the victims included individuals who seem to have had no involvement in politics. Possibly the men carrying out the operation intended to use these killings to bludgeon the entire Chinese population into submission, but most of those who witnessed the screenings blame young and inexperienced soldiers. Certainly the consequence was widespread hatred among people who might otherwise have acquiesced in Japanese rule.

The use of ethnically-based organizations to handle certain aspects of the administration followed precedents established by earlier colonial governments, and was done for the same reasons. The Japanese formed a small enclave within the country, isolated by their inability to communicate in local languages, and by a racial ideology that conceived of the Japanese as a superior people. Lacking local knowledge, they needed the assistance of people who understood the languages and the societies and the psychology of the people of Malaya. It was a situation far removed from the ideals expressed by the Japanese regime, which envisioned a united Asia and urged people to abandon parochial concerns and think of themselves as members of an Asian community. This Asian identity was based on a shared opposition to the West, participation in a common political framework under the Japanese Emperor, involvement in Japanese culture and the use of the Japanese language as a lingua franca. The educational system and the government's propaganda organs, described in the following chapter, attempted to promote this Asian ideal, but the harsh treatment meted out to those suspected of disloyalty, and the example of Japanese soldiers and officials treating the local population as inferiors, largely negated Japanese propaganda efforts.

CHAPTER 5

Education and Propaganda

The Japanese sought to foster an Asian nationalism, mobilize support for the war, replace the materialism and individualism of the West with an Asian spiritualism, promote discipline, secure obedience and cooperation, and instill the Japanese spirit (*seishin*) in the population. For young people this was to be accomplished through the school system, while adults were bombarded with propaganda disseminated through newspapers and radio broadcasts, at public ceremonies, and as part of the campaign to get people to learn the Japanese language. People in Malaya saw much of this activity as specifically Japanese rather than Asian: the new spirit of Asia was the Japanese spirit, the prospective lingua franca for the region was the Japanese language, and people were to follow Japan's Imperial Way by giving complete loyalty to the Japanese Emperor. Their response was a heightened awareness of and pride in local cultural features which would manifest itself in post-war nationalist activity.

Education

The school system

A planning document prepared in August 1942 spelled out Japanese intentions regarding education in the occupied territories:

> The emphasis of native education shall be upon industrial technological instruction adapted to practical life and the vigorous cultivation of an atmosphere respectful of labor. At the same time an education conforming to the special character of each region and to local circumstances shall be implemented, but policies such as compulsory or universal education should not be devised. Schools beyond the existing precollege level shall be universally closed and, following an examination of the educational system and content, the reopening of those which are considered especially necessary shall be subject to the approval of the Supreme Commander.[1]

[1] Benda et al., Japanese *Military Administration in Indonesia*, Document no. 50 (Instructions of the Superintendent-General of Military Administration, 7 Aug. 1942), p. 192.

Primary school instruction was particularly important because it allowed "the minds of future generations of citizens of Malai [to be] trained from the start to follow the lines of Shin Chitsujo (New Order) and discard Western ideas and habits".[2] Secondary and tertiary institutions were closed, although some industrial and vocational training took place beyond the primary level, and eventually a teachers' training college and a medical faculty were allowed to conduct classes.

Vernacular primary schools began to resume operations in April 1942, although each state established its own guidelines regarding education, and practices varied from place to place. A high proportion of the country's Malay schools re-opened during 1942, but fewer Tamil and Chinese schools received government approval, and English schools were not allowed to function at all. Private schools, most of which had been operated by the Chinese or by Christian missions, also remained closed, and large numbers of teachers found themselves out of work. In July 1942 the Japanese introduced school fees, charging $2 per month for the first three years, $2.50 for years four and five, and $3 for years six and seven, but many people could not afford these amounts and they were lowered in December 1942. In July 1943 the Japanese introduced free education for some children, and this later became the general practice throughout the peninsula. By June 1943 about half of the primary schools in Malaya were back in operation, and enrolments were nearly 80 per cent of the pre-war level (233,977 compared with 294,008 before the occupation), but in 1944 the number of students attending classes fell sharply owing to a rise in the incidence of malaria and other diseases, and because children had to help their families grow food.[3]

A number of English-medium schools eventually re-opened as Japanese schools. In addition to learning the Japanese language, pupils attending these schools studied arithmetic, mathematics, physical geography, science, physiology and hygiene. The balance of their time was devoted to physical training, gardening, drawing, and handicrafts such as needlework, basket weaving and toy making. Until students could attain proficiency in Japanese, instruction was given using English and Malay, although most courses lacked textbooks because there were few written in an acceptable language or free of objectionable content.[4]

---

[2] *Syonan Sinbun*, 6 May 2603.

[3] Akashi, "Education and Indoctrination Policy", p. 4; FIR 19, 4 Dec. 1943, CO273/673/50744/7; *Syonan Shimbun*, 31 Dec. 2603. Free education was only introduced in Singapore at the beginning of 2604, and it took some time to implement the policy throughout the island. *Syonan Shimbun*, 4 Aug. 2604.

[4] Nippon Gakko, 16 Jan. 2603, Sel Kan 94/2603.

Malay schools received preferential treatment, and 721 out of 885 Malay schools throughout the country resumed operations during the first year of the occupation.[5] The objective of pre-war Malay education had been "to give a sound primary and practical education to boys who would remain on the land and find occupation in local agriculture or in work that did not require a knowledge of English", and the five-year curriculum had emphasized manual labour and practical skills.[6] In Selangor the Japanese left the curriculum unchanged except for the omission of religion and history. Students learned to read and write Malay using both the Arabic and Romanised script, and also studied composition, elementary arithmetic, geography, hygiene, drawing, handwork, gardening and physical training. For girls there were classes in lace-making, sewing and domestic science. However, shortages of materials made it impossible to teach batik making, book binding, net making, soap making and other crafts, and it was difficult to teach cookery or to maintain school gardens because looters had taken away utensils and tools. There was little in the way of organized games "as footballs could not be supplied". One major addition to the curriculum was the Japanese language, but at the end of 1942 the level of achievement was reported to be low.

> Nippon-go [Japanese language] in Malay schools is very poor because 85 schools have no Nippon-Jin [Japanese] teachers to teach the children or to help the teachers. In the middle of the year some schools managed to have Nippon officers or soldiers for a few months to teach the children but when they were transferred, the schools were left without Nippon-Jin teachers.
>
> Mostly books from which teachers can study by themselves are written in English and the Malay teachers find it difficult to learn from them as nearly all (though there are some who understand) have no knowledge of English.
>
> Many Malay schools are very far from towns and are very far from one to another so it is very hard for them to come to town where a class in Nippon-go is held. But in spite of these difficulties teachers have tried their best to study Nippon-go by themselves and to teach the children.[7]

Indian schools re-opened somewhat later than Malay schools. Selangor, for example, had 228 Indian schools in 1940 with a teaching staff of slightly more than 300. All remained closed until July 1942, and at the end of the year just 22 were operating, employing 71 teachers. During 1943 about three-quarters of the

[5] Akashi, "Education and Indoctrination Policy", p. 6.

[6] Inspector of Malay Schools, The Outline of the Education (Malay) in Selangor, from 1938–41, n.d., Sel Kan 94/2603.

[7] Report on Malay Gakko for the Year 2602, n.d., Sel Kan 94/2603.

Indian primary schools offered classes, but enrolments fell off sharply in 1944, apparently because many Indian men had been recruited as labourers on Japanese projects, and children had to help support their families. The curriculum was as before "with geography and history left out", and with pro-British and pro-American material removed from school readers.[8]

Chinese schools, which had been among the principal centres of anti-Japanese activity before the war, were a particular target of Japanese hostility. Most of the extensive network of private Chinese schools remained closed throughout the occupation, and for a time the Chinese language could not be taught. In October 1942 Wataru Watanabe issued a directive allowing private Chinese schools to operate subject to government approval, and permitted Chinese to be taught as a secondary language, a concession interpreted in Penang as allowing instruction in dialects rather than in Mandarin. In practice few private schools received approval, and a new "Education Policy Relative to the Malayan Chinese" issued in March 1944 ordered those that were operating to shut down. The ban on Chinese language instruction was also reimposed. Overall, there were 180 Chinese schools active in Malaya after the first year of occupation, compared with 1,369 before the war; in Singapore just 23 Chinese schools had reopened in April 1943, compared with 369 before the war, and enrolments were 18 per cent of pre-war levels. Textbooks posed a problem. The 1942 report on Chinese schools in Selangor observed that "the old text-books were not very suitable", and two sets of new textbooks were only approved for temporary use after they had been "corrected" by the state Inspector of Schools. In Penang, bookshops had to hand in Chinese books for censorship, and all books apart from dictionaries and geography textbooks were burned, destroying by one estimate around 200,000 volumes. As the occupation progressed, the Chinese increasingly rejected Japanese education, which was known in Penang as "slavery education" and seemed to have as its purpose the Nipponization of the population.[9]

In Singapore most Catholic mission schools re-opened in April 1942 as Municipal Schools, and those teaching missionaries who had avoided detention

---

[8] L.J. Rajah, Assistant Inspector of Indian Schools, Selangor, The Outline of the Education in Selangor, 1938–40, 12 Jan. 2603; Succinct Report on Indian Schools for the year 2601, 8 Jan. 2603; and Report on Indian Schools for the Year 2602, 13 Jan. 2603, Kel Kan 94/2603. See also the statistical appendices to Akashi, "Education and Indoctrination Policy".

[9] Akashi, "Education and Indoctrination Policy", pp. 6–8, 37; Akashi, "Military Administration in Malaya", p. 62; Inspector of Chinese Schools, Selangor, The Outline of the Education (Chinese) in Selangor, 2598 (1938) to 2602 (1941), 14 Jan. 2603, and Education Department (Chinese Section) AR 2602, 13 Jan. 2603, Sel Kan 94/2603; Shü and Chua (eds), *Malayan Chinese Resistance to Japan*, pp. 52–3.

because they came from neutral countries or nations allied with Japan were re-employed as public servants working for the Japanese. The Japanese apparently respected their abilities, and asked Brother Joseph Brophy, the Irish director of Saint Joseph's Institution, to prepare a plan for the school curriculum throughout Malaya during the next 20 years. As elsewhere, the emphasis in the reconstituted mission schools was on Japanese language and moral and physical training. Religious instruction was not permitted, and schools were given secular names. Enrolments were far below pre-war levels.[10] As of 1 April 1944 all public and private schools in Singapore had received new names that removed any designation of nationality, but the renamed schools were grouped into sections, the first three of which admitted mainly Malays, Indians and Chinese respectively, while admission to the fourth section was open.[11]

Higher education

A limited number of institutions offered instruction beyond the primary level. For government officials the Japanese created a "Leading Officers Training Institute", the Syonan Koa-Kunrenjo, which opened on 18 May 1942. A Radio Tokyo broadcast described this institution as an "Axis Promotion Training Camp" but its character was distinctly Japanese: "One of the main aims of the course is to give the cadets a complete course in Nippon-Go [Japanese language], develop a spiritual outlook, and a general Nippon education." It was attended by prospective civil servants, who followed a regimen similar to that used for newly drafted Japanese soldiers, including a heavy dose of physical exercise, strict discipline, and "a rigid training in moral discipline". Speaking at the opening ceremony, Wataru Watanabe told students they should be prepared to face many hardships, but that hardships "endured at the institute would later instil obedience in Malayans". Reviewing this programme, the *Syonan Times* praised the Japanese for showing trust in local men by giving them opportunities to enter public service, in contrast with the British policy of holding them back as long as possible. After completing a six-month course of study, graduates received positions in government departments.[12]

---

[10] Stephanie Kwok, "Extraordinary Lives", pp. 17–20.

[11] *Syonan Shimbun*, 16 Mar. 2604.

[12] *Syonan Times*, 22 May 2602; *Syonan Sinbun*, 29 Jan. 2603; Akashi, "Education and Indoctrination Policy", pp. 18–21; Akashi, "Japanese Cultural Policy", pp. 135–42. A Penang "Kunrensho" began its first course in October 2602, and another opened in Malacca on 1 Feb. 2603. See the *Penang Shimbun*, 3 Jan. and 17 Apr. 2603.

The Koto Kogyo Gakko, an institution teaching Civil and Electrical Engineering and Telecommunications, opened on 28 May 1942, and in 1943 and 1944 several other training programmes began operations, including a fisheries training school, a railway training school, a school for seamen, agricultural schools and various technical and vocational schools. The Higher Education College (Higher Normal School) for senior teaching staff and inspectors of schools offered a six-month program during which students were "imbibed with the Nippon spirit". A Medical College, which included dental and pharmaceutical departments, began operations in 1943, at first using the buildings of the former Tan Tock Seng hospital in Singapore. It later moved to Malacca, presumably as part of the effort to shift people away from the city and closer to food producing areas.[13] To prepare prospective students for the opening of the College, where all lectures would be conducted in Japanese, a Malay Cultural Institute (in Japanese, Marei Bunka Kenkyu-Jo; in Malay, Siasat Kebudayaan Melayu) opened in Singapore to teach the Japanese language along with Japanese and Malay culture. Classes were open to applicants from all races.[14]

Language instruction

Less than two weeks after Britain's surrender, the Japanese signalled their intention to introduce the Japanese language languate into Malaya once the period of reconstruction was past. As a first step, the Syonan Times suggested that shop signs and streets names should be replaced by "Nipponese signs and names as a material indication that Malaya is included in the new order of things".[15] The idea that Japanese could become an Asian lingua franca was pursued with some vigour. An article in the Syonan Times on 1 June 1942, the first day of Nippon-go [Japanese-language] Week, made this assertion:

> This country is now ruled by Nippon and Nippon-go takes its rightful place as the language of the people. In fact it must gain precedence over all other languages and be the language in the office and home.... It is very essential that every citizen learn Nipon-go both for his or her own personal advancement and as a duty to our rulers.[16]

---

[13] AR for 2602, Koto Kogyo Gakko, Sel Kan 94/2603; Domei ELB, 20 Mar. 1943, CO273/669/50744/7.

[14] *Syonan Times*, 4 Nov. 2602; *Syonan Times*, 25 Nov. 2602; FIR 16, 23 Oct. 1943, CO273/673/50744/7.

[15] *Syonan Times* 28 Feb. 2602 (1942).

[16] *Syonan Times*, 1 June Syowa 17 (1942, p. 3.

Illus. 5.1 Propaganda poster: Come! We study in a trade school so we can make and distribute the most airplanes in the world.

Source: Author's personal collection.

Nearly two years later, a propaganda summary prepared for the second anniversary of the birth of New Malai in Johore suggests that the Malayan population remained unpersuaded:

> The public should be urged to realize the fact that Nippon-Go is a popular and universal language of Dai Toa [the Great East]. Through this only they will be able to achieve Nippon Spirit and Culture. In addition this language will act as the only weapon that will sweep away the language of the enemy.[17]

The study of Japanese provided a "short-cut" to help people "absorb the best there is in Nippon culture and to grasp better the educational, financial and foreign policies which have enabled Nippon to become the great nation she is today".[18]

School teachers had to provide instruction in Japanese, and spent their free time studying the language. A report on the Japanese schools in Selangor prepared at the end of 1942 noted that "at the beginning the teachers found it difficult to teach Nippon-go [Japanese language] as they had not acquired the knowledge. They had to learn and teach."[19] The Inspector of Schools in Pahang told all primary school principals that they should set up Japanese language classes at night or at any other suitable time to train unemployed teachers. His letter noted that future appointments would require proficiency in Japanese, and that only Japanese-language instructors would be eligible to become primary school principals.[20] Language instruction was complicated by a shortage of teachers and textbooks, and by the fact that elementary textbooks teaching Japanese were generally written in English, which handicapped people not proficient in that language. In conformance with a set of guidelines laid down by the Headquarters of the Southern Expeditionary Forces in January 1942, basic instruction given to school children included no *kanji*, the Chinese characters used in writing some Japanese words, and was confined to renderings of the language in the *katakana* syllabary.[21] Language teachers, finding that Japanese songs were "quite alluring to the ear of the Asians" and "very popular

---

[17] Summary of propaganda to be executed during 2nd anniversary of birth of New Malai, MB Johor 6/2604.

[18] *Syonan Sinbun*, 23 June 2603. See also Akashi, "Japanese Cultural Policy", pp. 119–28.

[19] Nippon Gakko, 16 Jan. 2603, Sel Kan 94/2603.

[20] Inspector of Schools, Pahang, Teachers Nippon-Go Class, 6 Nov. 2602, Temerloh 82/2602.

[21] See Document 1 in the appendix to Akashi, "Education and Indoctrination Policy", p. 22. In the postal system people using *kanji* in addresses were required to show the pronunciation in *katakana*. Agreement concerning the Transfer to Thailand of the Postal Services of the Four Northern Malayan States, n.d., SUK Kedah 182/2486.

even from the oldest to the youngest", used them extensively as an instruction aid. People who studied Japanese during the war confirm the appeal of Japanese music, which included patriotic marches, children's songs and sentimental music about scenes in Japan (such as the beauty of Mount Fuji, or the blooming of the cherry blossoms). One man said that 50 years later he could still hum the tunes, and upon hearing the Kimigayo, the Japanese national anthem, he found the words running through his mind. School children receiving language instruction enlivened the proceedings, and terrified their parents, by turning Japanese syllables such as "*ka ki ku ke ko*" into phrases like "*kaki ku bengkok*" (Malay for "I have bow legs"), and "*Nippon-go*" into "Nippon, Go!"[22]

Illus. 5.2 The *Kimigayo*, the national anthem of Nippon. *Syonan Times*, 29 April 2602 (1942).

The words translate as follows:

Ki mi ga yo wa	The master's reign
Chi yo ni ya-chi yo ni	shall last 1,000 and 8,000 generations
Sazare ishi no	till the pebbles
Iwao to narite	becoming rocks
Koke no musu made	shall be covered with moss

Source: E. Papinot, *Historical and Geography Dictionary of Japan* (Rutland, VT and Tokyo: Charles E. Tuttle, 1972 [1st ed., Yokohama: Keely and Walsh, 1910].

[22] Interview with Lee Liang Hye, 16 Dec. 1994.

There was also language training for adults. A school called the Syonan Nippon Gakuen offered a three-month course that provided instruction in Japanese, including the use of *kanji*, along with lectures on the Japanese spirit and the Japanese way of life. Language lessons were available through the radio and the press, and the military administration opened adult education centres where the public could study Japanese. At the start of 1943 the Director of Education for Perak observed of students in a Japanese-language course in Ipoh:

> They are good in picking up the language, but some of them were backward in imbibing the Nippon Seishin. They came to me and asked for decisions on trivial matters, whereas they should have shown more initiative and cultivated the spirit of independence. This, I find, is a general weakness of the youth in Malai generally.[23]

He added that students must not think that Japanese was hard to learn, although much work was needed to master the language.

In fact people in Malaya found Japanese very difficult, and for adults, whose working days were occupied with their normal jobs and increasingly as time passed with home gardens, it was all but impossible to achieve proficiency. Efforts to popularize Japanese continued throughout the war years and much of the population learned at least basic phrases. However, a Japanese account notes that the language "was used only when necessary in daily conversation" and "was not widely used so much when the war ended".[24] A report on the Public Works Department in Perak said that in some sub-offices officers began using Romanised Malay in preparing files, but that English was the official language for correspondence, while a "hybrid of Malay, English and Japanese" was used in conversation.[25] Japanese visitors to post-war Malaya found people willing to produce what they remembered of the Japanese language, but were often aghast at the rude and harsh expressions that emerged, larded with words like *bakayaro* ("moron" but used as an all-purpose expression of anger or displeasure), reflecting the way many Japanese soldiers and administrators spoke to the local population during the occupation.[26]

---

23 Minutes, Meeting of District Officers, 22 and 23 Mar. 2602, P.T. Larut 106/2602.

24 JM 103, p. 44.

25 Notes on the Work Carried out by the Public Works department in the State of Perak during the Japanese Occupation 1942 to 1945 Inclusive, MSS. Ind. Ocn. S. 172.

26 A. Samad Ismail, "Peristiwa Sejarah Patut Diingati dan Dipelajari oleh Generasi Sekarang" ("Historical Events Should be Remembered and Studied by the Current Generation"), *Ketokohan dan Kewartawanan*, p. 331.

For administrative matters the use of Malay was temporarily permitted, and as an interim measure even English, because of the difficulty involved in arranging translations, but the administration told civil servants they must prepare for the time when Japanese would be the language of government.[27] In December 1942 the Governor of Selangor (S. Kikuchi) said in a speech that official correspondence would at some future date be written in Japanese, and he invited District Officers to express their views on this matter. The District Officer for Ulu Langat responded that few members of the administration knew written Japanese well and most were too busy to study it, so that insistence on the use of Japanese would force large numbers of civil servants to retire. "I suppose it is not the intention to encourage such a state of affairs as it is not conducive to the proper government of the country." As an alternative, he suggested that the administration recognize Malay as an official language.[28] Employees of the Public Works Department in Perak reported after the war that after a burst of enthusiasm for Romanized Malay, English became the official language for correspondence, while everyday conversations took place in a mixture of Malay, English and Japanese.[29]

In Kedah a government circular stated that officials should use Japanese after June 1943, but two months before this deadline the District Officer for Kulim warned that even though he and his colleagues were studying Japanese, they did not understand it very well owing to a shortage of dictionaries to explain meanings.[30] The transfer of the northern states to Thailand brought a shift there from the Japanese language to Thai. The Military Administrator for Kelantan wrote to the Chairman of the Montri Spa in August 1944 to say that in view of the fact that Thailand and Kelantan had "joined together as elder and younger [brothers]", and each side was learning the customs, tradition and language of the other, it would be appropriate to give bonuses to officials who became

[27] Minutes, Meeting of District Officers, 22 and 23 Mar. 2602, P.T. Larut 106/2602.

[28] DO Ulu Langat, Memorandum on Nippon-go as the Official language, 4 Jan. 2603, DO Ulu Langat 132/2602.

[29] Gardiner, "Notes on the Work carried out by the Public Works Department in the State of Perak during the Japanese Occupation", 3 Dec. 1945, MSS. Ind. Ocn. S. 172, Weston Library, Oxford University.

[30] Gun Cho Kulim to Gun Yakusho Kulim, 18 Apr. 2603, SUK Kedah 474/2602. The statement hedged the point with a characteristic series of qualifications: "… saya maalomkan banyak pegawai2 dudok belajar bahasa Nippon tetapi tiada berapa faham chukop halus tentang ma'ana2 hurop nippon oleh sebab tiada ada khamus yang boleh me[ne]rang ma'ana2-nya yang betol [… I inform you that many officials are studying Japanese but do not quite understand with sufficient refinement the meaning of Japanese letters because they do not have dictionaries which can explain the correct meanings."

Illus 5.3 Japanese class in Syonan.

The Syonan Nippon-go Gakko which is conducted by Gun Sendenhan (Nippon Army Propaganda Department) is attended by over 380 pupils. During the day these pupils work hard in various departments for the reconstruction of Syonan. Despite this they find time to attend a night school to study Nippon-go. They enjoy studying Nippon go!

Source: *The Syonan Times*, 22 May, Syowa 17 (1942), p. 4.

Illus. 5.4 Japanese language lessons, printed in the *Syonan Times*, 3 June 2602 (1942) and 21 Feb. 2603.

proficient in Thai. The state government responded by issuing a notice saying that as a sign of the good will existing between Thai and Malay officials, and in order to give those Malay officials who had studied Thai an opportunity to make use of what they had learned, the government would view it favourably if officials signed their names in Thai script on official documents. This practice would "indicate the manifestation of one's appreciation and good feelings".[31] The Thais also required that signs on shops and public buildings include Thai script, which had to be in bold letters and appear on the top line. The latter measure caused difficulties because paint was in short supply and there were very few sign painters able to work in Thai.[32]

Propaganda

Japanese propaganda

Japanese propaganda attacked Western exploitation of Asia and the West's lack of respect for Asian peoples and cultures, and portrayed Japan as the liberator and leader of a newly united Asia: "The East has taken up the challenge of the West and, with the victorious advance of the Nipponese Army, is realising its dreams of freedom. Freedom from White Domination; freedom from Injustice and Freedom from Oppression.... Nippon has shown the way to the liberation of the East...."[33] Newspapers criticized the British regime for following a policy of ethnic divide-and-rule,[34] and accused Britain and America of having sought to "subjugate the people of Asia to their will for all time" through "subtle intrigue", which "constantly set one Asiatic nation against another and fostered communal illwill among people enjoying a common heritage".[35] It was the duty of the people, and "an expression of thankfulness to the Nippon Empire", to eradicate "all the English-like easy and indolent life in the past" and "push forward the war time life under the spiritual and humanistic control

---

[31] Military Administrator of Kelantan to Chairman of the Council of Ministers of Kelantan [24 Aug. 1944, in Thai], and Kerajaan Kelantan, Pengidaran No. 21, 2487, Menuron tanda tangan dengan tulisan Thai, Kelantan Montri Spa 748/2487.

[32] Kelantan Montri Spa 665/2487. There was, of course, a further shift to Thai at the end of the war. The first government circular issued in Kelantan after the Japanese surrender told heads of departments to remove and destroy all Japanese and Thai posters found in government offices. Government of Kelantan, Circular No. 1 of 1945, 24 Sept. 1945, Kelantan Montri Spa 665/2487.

[33] "Nippon Has Shown East Way of Liberation", by Charles Nell, *Syonan Times*, 10 Mar. 2602.

[34] See, for example, *Syonan Times*, Saturday Supplement, 25 Apr. 2602.

[35] Opinion column on Imperial Rescript Day, *Syonan Sinbun*, 8 June 2603.

of the Nippon Empire".[36] People needed to eliminate "the habit and customs left behind by the haughty and cunning British", such as materialism and opportunism and individualism, and "proceed the work of reviving Oriental culture based on moral and spiritual principles and speedily cause the increase of racial consciousness and prosperity of Oriental races". To overcome the damage done by Western rule, Asia needed to emulate Japan and acquire the Japanese spirit. The *Syonan Times* asked rhetorically "why Nippon is the strongest nation in the world, nationally, and the most superior racially", and found the answer in the Nippon spirit, which "contains such great virtues as bravery, loyalty, propriety, faith, simplicity and self-sacrifice" and should be emulated by "every Asiatic not only to make them upright citizens but also to create a superior race in the time to come".[37] In Penang, the governor told people that while the island was noted for its scenic beauty, "in addition there must also be spiritual beauty to characterise it. For this, I am trying my best to implant the Nippon spirit here."[38] The Governor of Johore said that "morality should play an important part in the administration", and his intention was "to establish a moral civilisation".[39]

The Japanese hoped that local political sentiment could be turned to their benefit, but felt that since the population had been "under Western Yoke for over a century it would be difficult to eradicate the spirit of individualism forthwith".[40] Some Japanese considered the southern territories politically backward, and adopted a paternalistic attitude toward the local population. The Governor of Perak told a meeting of Penghulus that "the Government is just like a father to his children",[41] and the Director of the Industrial Bureau for Kelantan said that there should be no misunderstanding when the local population came into contact with Japanese officers "even if the latters' words and actions may appear a little harsh or unkind for in reality they only mean well—even a father may sometimes have to rebuke his son whom he loves more than anything else".[42] A post-war account written by Japanese officers who served in Malaya also invokes the image of the family:

---

36 *Syonan Times*, 25 Feb. 2602. See also Akashi, "Japanese Cultural Policies", p. 129.

37 "First Imperatives in New Order", by "Obara", and "New Order Calls for Self-Sacrifice", by "Spectator", *Syonan Times*, 14 Mar. 2602.

38 *Syonan Sinbun*, 23 June 2603.

39 His Excellency the Governor's Speech, n.d., MB Johor 209/2602.

40 Minutes, Penghulus' Conference, 16 Aug. 2604, Batu Gajah 11/2604.

41 Minutes, Penghulus' Conference, 27 Mar. 2604, Batu Gajah 11/2604.

42 Minutes, Meeting held at the Sangyo-Bu on 9th Ni-Gatsu, 2603 [9 Feb. 1943], DO Pasir Puteh 58/2603.

> The natives were instructed to trust the Japanese government to the fullest extent. As a whole they co-operated favorably and reacted as children, younger brothers or pupils to us and obeyed our army very willingly. Consequently our army took good care of them and except for a very few cases peace and harmony were restored.[43]

Along with concepts such as "Asia for the Asiatics" and Asian co-prosperity, the concept of *Hakkoichiu* ("Eight Corners of the World under One Roof"—the Japanese expression is given a number of different spellings and is explained in various ways in wartime materials) figured prominently in discussions of Asian unity.[44]

> ... Co-Prosperity can never be established without the spirit of "Hakke Ichiu" (Under one roof). The Government will guide the people by moral, according to the old Nipponese statesmanship saying if "We enjoy after hardship." [*sic*] This means that we face hardship and enjoy after. It is by this that the business of the Government will be carried on. I hope you will understand the meaning of this phrase and always work fast and show good example by carrying out the district administration by moral.[45]

In these exhortations, the Japanese evoked a pan-Asian identity: "we Nipponese administrative officers always have in our hearts the welfare of the natives who are also Asians like ourselves".[46] This idea was in some ways counter-productive, for many of Japan's local supporters considered, and had been encouraged to consider, Japan as a liberator who would free them to pursue their own national aspirations, and an Asian nationalism with a distinctly Japanese flavour was a poor substitute.

Propaganda directed toward the Muslim community presented Japan as the liberator of Muslims from Western domination and the protector of Islam, and emphasized that Japan followed a policy of religious tolerance. Responding to an Australian radio broadcast that accused Japan of planning to destroy Islam, the *Syonan Times* claimed that the Allies in their desperation were trying to find points of difference in order to "split the natural affinity which exists between the people of Nippon and other Asiatics", and said in response that on this particular point the Japanese armour was "absolutely impenetrable". "Religion is the one

---

[43] JM 103, p. 16.

[44] For a discussion of the background of Hakkoichiu and its connection with Japanese expansionist ideology, see Sato, *War, Nationalism and Peasants*, pp. 13–14.

[45] Speech of the Johore Industrial Administrator, Mr Mizuno, manuscript dated 8 Sept. 2602, MB Johor 209/2602. See also Akashi, "Japanese Cultural Policy in Malaya and Singapore, 1942–45", pp. 118, passim.

[46] Director of the Industrial Bureau for Kelantan, Minutes, Meeting held at the Sangyo-Bu on 9th Ni-Gatsu, 2603 (9 Feb. 1945). DO Pasir Puteh 58/2603.

field in which Nippon stands alone, unchallenged", practising a religion—Shintoism—that "is less dogmatic, less exclusive" than any other, and pursuing a goal of "universal harmony" in accordance with the idea of "Hakko-Itiu, of universal brotherhood".[47] An account of an interview with Imam Abdarashid Ebrahim, described as the patriarch of the Tokyo Mosque and "the respected patriarch of the Muslim world", compared Japan's crusade in Asia with that of the Prophet Mohammed: "Nippon's cause in Dai Toa Senso [the Great East Asian War] is a sacred one and, in its austerity, is comparable only to the war carried out against the infidels by Prophet Mohammed in the past."[48]

The administration expected civil servants to contribute to propaganda activity, or as the Governor of Perak termed it, "general enlightenment work":

> To attain the successful execution of this great war all the people must be made to know the object of this sacred war of emancipation. The people must be united and fully prepared to bear all hardships and difficulties that may arise on the march to victory. To obtain complete unity between the people, the people must understand each other. There must be mutual assistance. The Government must tell the people what they are aiming at and give advice accordingly. We want to enlighten the people in every way in our undertakings. By this enlightenment of the people we can expect better results.[49]

The propaganda machinery was also used to promote various Japanese campaigns, including efforts to increase food production, control diseases and recruit labour. The tenor of this activity can be seen from materials developed for an anti-malaria week in Negri Sembilan, when the government distributed leaflets containing what the *Syonan Sinbun* described as "select and clever slogans", such as "Prevention is Better than Cure", "Destroy the Mosquito, Prevent Malaria", "Cleanliness is next to Godliness" and "Clean Your Drains. Cover Water Receptacles. Keep Your Houses Tidy".[50]

The Japanese regime introduced ritual observances that served as a constant reminder of Japanese overlordship. One of the most common, and from the frequency with which it is mentioned one of the most galling, was a requirement that everyone bow upon passing a Japanese sentry. The Japanese explained that the sentries represented the Emperor, and that by paying respect to a sentry people paid respect to the Japanese throne.[51] Failure to bow to the satisfaction of

---

47 *Syonan Times*, 6 Aug. 2602.

48 Ibid., 7 Aug. 2603.

49 Minutes, Meeting of District Officers, 5 Nov. 2602, Batu Gajah 69/2602.

50 *Syonan Sinbun*, 3 July 2603.

51 E.J.H. Corner, *The Marquis*, p. 107.

the sentry resulted in the offender being slapped or otherwise punished on the spot. A newspaper columnist attempted to justify the practice by suggesting that it would be an insult to the Japanese army which had liberated Malaya if citizens were to walk past a sentry without acknowledging him, and "if a sentry allows a citizen to pass by him with his nose in the air and that 'I'm monarch of all I survey' look in his eyes, he would indeed be failing in his duty to the glorious army to which he belongs if he neglects to enforce respect for it." Why, he asked, did people who had readily saluted the British find it so difficult to respect a Japanese sentry? "It only shows a cheap and low mentality to consider it below one's dignity to acknowledge the superiority of one so obviously a superior."[52]

At schools and government offices, daily activities began with a ceremony that included hoisting the "national" flag (the *Hinomaru*), singing the "national" anthem (the *Kimigayo*) while facing the Imperial Palace and bowing deeply (*saikeirei*), and carrying out Radio Taiso exercises, performed to music broadcast over the radio. Regarding the *Hinomaru*, the following text was issued in both Malay and English to explain to the Malayan population the symbolism of their new national flag.

> The origin of the Hinomaru—the National flag dates far back to our Imperial Grand Sire, as started by Amaterus Omikami—the great Heavenly Goddess and it represents the Sun and the Hinomaru indicates the foundation of the Imperial Empire.
>
> The white texture of the flag around Hinomaru shows purity, cleanness as respected and exhibits the National trait of love of righteousness, fairness and peace. Moreover, its appearance displays harmony and the red colour signifies the true heart, light, valour and elevation and all these are the thoughts and representation of the National Trait.
>
> The red colour of Hinomaru is the colour of the rising Sun and as such it should always be remembered.[53]

The Malayan population celebrated Japanese holidays, now treated as national holidays, and participated in ceremonies related to the conduct of the war. On major ceremonial occasions people observed "*Kokyumin-Girei*", which consisted of paying homage to the Imperial family and offering a silent prayer for the spirits of the loyal dead. These observances concluded with the singing of the Kimigayo.[54] To commemorate the first anniversary of the British surrender and

---

[52] *Syonan Times*, Saturday Supplement, 25 Apr. 2602. The column containing these remarks appeared under the very British title "Cabbages and Kings".

[53] History and Knowledge of Hinomaru – The National Flag, MB Johore 26/2603. The document went on to state with great precision the proper dimensions of the flag, and to outline the way in which it was to be displayed.

[54] *Syonan Sinbun*, 17 Dec. 2602.

the establishment of *Shinsei Malai* (New Born Malai), celebrations were held between 9 and 15 February 1943. All businesses except for coffee shops and hotels were required to close on the 11th (*Kigensetsu*) and on the 15th (the date of the British surrender), and at 11 a.m. on those days the Japanese decreed that "all traffic *must* stop and every one *must* observe one minute of silence".[55] At the designated time, a signal was given by means of bells, drums and sirens mounted at mosques, temples, churches and public buildings. For the second anniversary, heads of departments were asked to turn out for ceremonial parades on the 11th and 15th. The organiser of this event in Batu Gajah said: "The attendance of Government employees at the parades has, in the past, been glaringly poor and I wish now to take the opportunity to convey to you the 'None-too-good' impression it has created on the Military Authority."[56] At "10 noon" everyone was to observe one minute of silence. "During this, every one must pray in silence for the souls of the glorious dead and offer thanks to the Imperial Forces." The third anniversary was celebrated in similar fashion.[57]

Illus. 5.5 Passengers on a Singapore trolley-bus observing a minute's silence in memory of Fleet Admiral Yamamoto Isoroku (d. 18 April 1943).

Source: *Syonan Sinbun*, 7 June 2603 (1943).

[55] Celebrations in Klang from 9 to 15 February 2603, 7 Feb. 2603, copy in DO Klang 303/1942 where the reverse side of the paper was used for correspondence.

[56] Organiser, Second Anniversary of Shinsei Malai, 8 Feb. 2604, Batu Gajah 38/2604.

[57] Celebration of Kigensetsu and the Second Anniversary of the fall of Singapore; Second Anniversary of Rebirth of Malaya, Programme for Celebration (Kuantan District), 10 Feb. 2604; Third Anniversary of the Re-birth of Malai, 14 Feb. 2605, DO Kuantan 49/2604.

The most important Japanese holiday, Tentyo Setsu, the celebration of the Emperor's birthday, took place on 29 April. The announcement of this occasion in 1942 read as follows:

> This is the biggest event in the Japanese Calendar of National Holidays. On this day we must pray for the long life and good health of our Emperor. On this day we must not only rejoice but we must also think of our country and make renewed efforts in the establishment of the New Order in the Greater Asia Co-prosperity Sphere, to the attainment of which we must all work harder.

In Perak the programme for the day commenced with bowing to the Governor, bowing very low to the Imperial Palace, observing one minute of silence to honour the war dead, and singing the Kimigayo. These activities were followed by speeches delivered by the Governor and representatives of the state's ethnic communities, performance of a march (the *Aikoku Koshin Kyoku*) and the awarding of prizes to those people "who rendered most help to the Japanese Authorities". At the close the crowd shouted "*Banzai*" three times.[58]

In December the country celebrated the anniversary of the Japanese invasion. On this occasion in 1944, the first order of business in Kuantan was to bow to the Imperial Palace. Next came the singing of the national song, a reading of the Imperial War Rescript, and a speech, after which the crowd shouted "*Banzai*" three times to the Emperor. A rally followed, which began with this pre-arranged exchange:

> After the greeting by the Chairman [the Governor of Pahang], Tuan Kundo will say "I wish to appoint a Master of Ceremony." The Indian representative will get up and say "I leave it to you". Then Tuan Kundo will ask the representative of the Chinese and the Malay Communities if they have any objection. They will say "No objection". Then Tuan Kundo will nominate Dato Mahmud as the Master of Ceremony.

The task of Dato' Mahmud, a respected District Officer from Kuantan, was to invite representatives from the Malay, Chinese, Indian and Japanese communities to give speeches, after which he told the audience:

> Now you have heard the speeches of the various Communities. You have already understood the significance of the day. In support of the burning enthusiasm in our hearts, should we not pass a resolution?

[58] Birthday of His Imperial Majesty the Emperor of Japan, and Private Secy to the Governor, Perak, Celebration of His Imperial Majesty the Emperor's Birthday, 27 Apr. 2602, Hutan Perak 56/2602.

Illus. 5.6 "Schoolchildren, proudly waving Hinomaru (Rising Sun) flags, marching towards the Syonan Gekiryo during Syonan's birthday celebrations of Tenno-Heika."

Source: *Syonan Times*, Saturday Supplement, 2 May Syowa 17 (1942).

Illus. 5.7 Cartoon on the occasion of the Emperor's birthday celebration.

Source: *Syonan Times*, 29 April 2602 (1942).

Everyone was then to say "No Objection", and the representatives of the four communities would read out their resolutions.[59] The following day, 9 December 1944, brought a further ceremony which included prayers for the dead, short addresses by communal leaders in praise of the dead, and the burning of incense by "the Authorities".[60]

A particularly sensitive observance took place on 7 July, the anniversary of the outbreak of war between Japan and China in 1937. Speaking on this occasion in 1943, a Japanese official in Kedah delivered a speech that blamed the whole affair on the animalistic character of the White Man, who wished to seize power in East Asia as he had done in Malaya and before that in India where human beings were forced to labour like cattle and horses. Chiang Kai-shek had not wanted to fight Japan, and the war grew out of a plot by an English adviser. Japan likewise did not wish to fight another Asian nation and responded with minimal force, but the Chinese had been listening to the devilish incitements of America and Britain for too long, and did not pay attention to Japan. Now, however, China's new nationalist government recognized that England and America were the enemies of China and of all Asians, and the lands formerly held by foreigners had been liberated by Japan and returned to China.[61] A newspaper editorial published a few months later spoke of Chiang Kai-shek as a "wayward younger brother" whose mistakes were being corrected by an elder brother, in the form of the troops of the National Government of China and of Japan. "It is a little family squabble which should have ended long ago in everybody's good but for Anglo-American interference."[62]

When combined with existing festivals, Malaya's new observances produced a large number of public holidays. Early in 1943 the *Syonan Sinbun* complained editorially that people were taking too much time off for religious festivals, and suggested that only "national" celebrations should be public holidays.[63] The four northern states transferred to Thailand in 1943 stopped observing Japanese holidays and began celebrating Thai festivals, giving them between 30 and 35 public holidays a year, not counting half a day (from midday on) during the entire fasting month.[64]

---

59 Meeting on 29 Nov. 2604, Tuan Shimada Presiding, DO Kuantan 315/2604.

60 Ireisai Ceremony, DO Kuantan 315/2604.

61 Salinan Uchapan Chokan Kakka pada Hari Ulangan Bangkit-nya Perkara China, 7 July 2603, SUK Kedah 196/2603.

62 *Syonan Sinbun*, 23 Nov. 2603.

63 Ibid., 21 Jan. 2603.

64 List of Public Holidays in 2486 and 2487 (1362 and 1363), SUK Kedah 47/2486.

Radio was a key medium for disseminating propaganda. Radio broadcasts typically began at 6 p.m. and lasted for five hours, presenting news in Japanese and in various local languages (Hindustani, Hokkien, Cantonese, Malay, English), Japanese language lessons, and music. The Japanese only permitted the use of medium wave radio receivers, and penalties for possessing a radio that could receive overseas broadcasts were severe. Nevertheless, some short-wave receivers escaped detection, and clandestine news sheets reproduced reports taken from the BBC and other Allied radio broadcasts. An escaped British prisoner of war reported that war news spread very quickly, and during a stay in Singapore lasting from late June till early September 1944 he learned of the capture of Saipan (July 1944) and the use of the V-1 rocket.[65] One of those who refused to surrender his shortwave radio was a teacher on the staff of St Francis' Institution at Malacca named P.G. Pamadasa. An informer reported him to the Japanese, and he was arrested and sentenced to death. The day before his execution Pamadasa prepared a final testament:

> I am writing this in my cell with manacled hands on the eve of my execution. I am no felon but a patriot condemned to death for listening to the B.B.C. news and telling it to pro-British friends. I did this for two years till I was betrayed. The Japanese Military Police tortured and finally sentenced me to be hanged.
>
> I helped to keep up the morale of our people and there are many to say so. Had I lived I would have been rewarded. I have no regrets. It is sweet to die for freedom.... I have always cherished British sportsmanship, justice and the Civil Service as the finest things in an imperfect world. I die for these.
>
> I die gladly for freedom. My enemies fail to conquer my soul. I forgive them for what they did to my poor frail body ... to my dear old boys, tell them their teacher died with a smile on his lips....[66]

It was some time before the Japanese turned their attention to the cinemas. There were, according to a newspaper article, 23,000 reels of American, English, Chinese, Malay and Indian films in the country when the invasion took place,[67] and for a year and a half people continued to watch Walt Disney's *Dumbo*, Eddie Albert in *On Your Toes*, Boris Karloff in *The Night Key*, Cary Grant and

---

[65] Conditions in Singapore in the late Summer of 1944: Summary of information obtained from interrogation of escaped British P.O.W., CO273/673/30744/7.

[66] Annual Report on Education in the Malayan Union for the period 1 April 1946 to 31 December 1946, p. 3. Mohamad Yusoff Hj Ahmad, who was in the same prison, wrote that the evening before he was hanged, Pamadasa "sang hymns beautifully from the condemned cell and all those who heard him cried". Mohamad Yusoff Haji Ahmad, *Decades of Change*, p. 254.

[67] *Penang Shimbun*, 26 Dec. 2602. A Japanese source places the number of seized reels of British and American films at more than 50,000. See Akashi, "Japanese Cultural Policy", p. 132.

Jean Arthur in *Only Angels Have Wings*, John Wayne in *Winds of the Wasteland*, Geraldine Fitzgerald in *A Child is Born* and John Howard in *Bulldog Drummond in Africa*. Among the Indian films was *Vimochanam*, which concerned "The Evils of High Drinking" ("Congress Intervened—and City Went Dry!"). As of 1 September 1943 the Japanese ordered cinemas to stop screening British and American productions, and to show "Nippon screen masterpieces" instead. The first offering in Singapore, *The Union Jack is Down*, dealt with the fall of Hong Kong. It was followed by *Donen Kokyogaku*, a film about a blind girl that showed "the joys and sorrows and turmoil of humanity". *On to Singapore*, "an unbiased and authentic" account of the war in Malaya, opened with a military unit advancing on bicycles toward Kuala Selangor, "singing lustily all the way 'Hashirei Hinomaru Ginrin Butai' (Advance Hinomaru Cyclists Corps)", and concluded with the British surrender. Another Japanese offering was entitled *Opium War* and featured Ichikawa Ennosuke playing anti-opium advocate Lim Chik Choo, and Suzuki Denmei playing Captain Elliot. In this film "the English merchant with his characteristic smoothness of tongue and gestures soon triumphed over the kind and unsuspecting Chinese"; had the Chinese realized that the English presence meant exploitation, the course of history would surely have been different. Cinemas not able to obtain Japanese films screened "second and third run Malai, Chinese and Indian films".[68]

Because music wielded "considerable influence on the sentiments of a people", the Japanese felt it "necessary that in the midst of a war the musical tastes of the public should be properly directed". Accordingly, in January 1943 the government imposed a ban on some 1,000 American and British "musical compositions", a list that included not only military or patriotic songs ("Wembley Military Tattoo", "Anchors Aweigh", "Colonel Bogey") but also love songs and jazz. Some British-American numbers, such as "Auld Lang Syne", "Home, Sweet Home" and "The Last Rose of Summer", had already been popularized in Japan and "well assimilated with Nippon sentiments", and escaped prohibition because they extolled desirable qualities such as comradeship and love of home. Other "light" music, including "Dinah", "Aloha Oe", "Kisses in the Dark", and the music of Stephen Foster, was deemed unacceptable, while jazz "even before the war was considered undesirable by true lovers of music".[69] A journalist in Singapore eloquently condemned Western music in the following passage:

[68] *Syonan Sinbun*, 13 Jan. 2603, 7 Apr. 2603, 1 Sept. 2603, 10 Sept. 2603, 24 Sept. 2603; *Penang Shimbun*, 12 Dec. 2602; *Perak Times*, 10 July 2603.

[69] *Perak Times*, 20 Jan. 2603; *Penang Shimbun*, 20 Oct. 2603.

Illus. 5.8 Advertisement for the Japanese film "On to Singapore".

Source: *Syonan Shimbun*, 19 Sept. 2603 (1943).

Illus. 5.9 Advertisement for the Japanese film "Hawaii-Malai Oki Kaisen" [The War at Sea from Hawaii to Malaya].

Source: *Syonan Shimbun*, 3 May 2603 (1943).

> When we retrospect and observe how we were in the past poisoned unknowingly by the demoralizing music of our enemies, we discover the most appalling things. Our arch-enemies America and Britain have utilized the sacred field of music in order to corrupt the minds and souls of the people of Greater East Asia, and thereby, aid in the achievement of their sinister designs to seize control of and to dominate East Asia.
>
> Our enemies, in an attempt to destroy the peoples of East Asia and as an anaesthetic agent to aid in the accomplishment of their world domination, had mixed a deadly potion into their hideous music. With various noisy and debased musical instruments, they created music without any great depth of feeling or artistic value and with the devilish utilization of it, they schemed to steal into our souls and poison us slowly and unknowingly from within.[70]

To replace Western music, the Japanese attempted to popularize the ancient music of East Asia. In 1943, following a recital of Nippon gramophone records that demonstrated the "charm and beauty of Nippon Songs and of Nippon interpretation of music", a writer for the *Penang Shimbun* enthused:

> With these examples of typical Nippon music to assist them local orchestra leaders will have no trouble in giving their public really good music. The going of Western tunes will indeed prove no great loss to the world of music when by comparison Nippon rhythm and harmony expresses so much more aptly the emotions and ideas of the peoples of East Asia.[71]

The Japanese placed the press in Malaya under the control of the Domei News Agency, which formed a syndicate of 12 Japanese newspaper companies to publish newspapers in Malaya and Sumatra.[72] This group published a number of English-language newspapers, and also newspapers in Malay, Tamil, Chinese and Japanese. Later all newspapers in Malaya came under a syndicate known as the Syonan Sinbun-kai.[73] According to the journalist A. Samad Ismail, who began his career during the occupation, the military administration viewed the press simply as a propaganda tool. It wasn't enough, he wrote some years after the war, for articles to laud Greater East Asian prosperity, nor was it enough to worship the Japanese spirit; praise had to be in accordance with the current line followed by the Propaganda Department, and was scrutinized by the Japanese

---

70 *Syonan Shimbun*, 15 Aug. 2604.

71 *Penang Shimbun*, 22 Oct. 2603.

72 The newspaper companies operating under Domei were the Hokkai Times, Kahoku Sinpo, Godo Sinbun, Koti Sinbun, Nisi Nippon Sinbun, Osaka Sinbun, Hokkoku Mainiti, Tyugoku Sinbun, Tokyo Sinbun, Tyubu Nippon, Kyoto Sinbun, Kobe Sinbun. *Syonan Times*, 21 Oct. 1942.

73 *Penang Shimbun*, 10 Mar. 2603.

to ensure that this was the case.[74] K.R. Menon worked for the *Indo Shimbunsha*, and when asked in a post-war interview what were the most interesting columns he responded:

> It's all the same old stuff.... Praising the Japanese you know, and praising their war efforts and running down the British and Americans. There was nothing interesting there, you see that. There was practically nothing interesting there. They were all very monotonous.

The English-language *Syonan Times*, he said, was "almost having the same tune. Almost the same tune facing the Japanese, and Japanese suffered and all those things. Nothing more than that. Japanese are the blessed people who've won the earth. They were the sons of God."[75]

Newspapers published a mix of local news and accounts of the war. The latter consisted of an unending parade of stories announcing Japanese and Axis triumphs ("Nippon Forces Sink, Damage Enemy Warships in Aleutians; Destroy 34 Planes in India", "Axis Air Forces Blast Enemy Targets in Mediterranean, Russia"), and forecasting the imminent collapse of those who opposed the Axis powers ("Allied Nations in Tight Corner"). Some stories supposedly emanated from prisoners of war, including one that quoted Lt. Gen. Arthur Percival ("The reason why I lost is simply because I did not have a chance, that is all.") and another which asserted that Lt. Gen. Lewis M. Heath had "unreservedly saluted the Imperial Nippon Forces as possessing superb daring, strategy and valour unprecedented in military annals".[76] A seaman who had been on the *Prince of Wales* when it was sunk by the Japanese was reported to have said: "The Pom-Pom guns, one of which I was manning, went into action, with a terrific fire, but the brave Nippon airmen, undaunted by the fire, attacked the ship from the right, left and right over us. Indeed, they attacked from every direction.... We were dismayed and unable to know what we should do."[77]

The emphasis later shifted from co-prosperity to "co-endurance",[78] and finally to the need to defend Malaya against possible Allied attacks. As early as July 1943, newspapers began urging the population to take part in air raid drills.

---

[74] A. Samad Ismail, *Ketokohan dan Kewartawanan*, p. 59.

[75] OHD, interview with K.R. Menon.

[76] The Percival quotation appeared in the *Syonan Times*, 25 Nov. 2602, and the report on Heath in the *Syonan Sinbun*, 16 Feb. 2603.

[77] *Syonan Times*, 28 July 2602.

[78] See, for example, the *Perak Times*, 1 Mar. 2603: "You have to realise the fact that any kind of happiness in the human world can only be attained through our constant effort and struggle ... your co-operation is in a sense required to be co-endurance."

> The exercises are being held, as we have explained, for the safety of the civil population, and the people are expected to show that they are grateful for the interest being taken in their welfare by the authorities by fully co-operating and diligently participating in the drills.[79]

In August 1943 the *Syonan Sinbun* carried a message from the Chief of the Propaganda Department saying that people should not feel concerned by the fact that the "enemy seems, at a glance, to have some partial advantage over us". Mentioning the German withdrawal from North Africa and "ups and downs of the war trend on the Eastern front", the statement said Japan's strategy was to remain on the defensive while preparing for the time when they would be able to crush the enemy.[80] The September armistice in Italy was "regretted", for it constituted a "betrayal of the Axis Powers", but it had been anticipated, and in any case involved only the southern part of Italy, which stuck out into the Mediterranean Sea and was vulnerable to attack, and the new development actually strengthened the Italian fascists who were entrenched in the natural fortress of the north and determined to prosecute the war.[81] The *Syonan Shimbun* portrayed the Allied invasion of the Philippines as a "golden chance" for Japan to wipe out the enemy,[82] and in an end-of-year summary explained Japan's retreat in the South Pacific by saying:

> It is noteworthy that, to maintain such isolated islands as Attu, Kiska, Guadalcanar [sic] and New Georgia indefinitely, only proves a nuisance and forms a vulnerable point in our strategic position. Upon conclusion of the object of restraining part of the enemy forces or subjecting his fighting power to attrition, which accounted for the temporary occupation of these islands as they played an important role strategically in this respect, any further occupation is entirely unnecessary. And yet the enemy had to pay a very high cost for his attack on them.[83]

There was a frenzy of excitement at the start of 1944 when the Japanese Army, supported by the INA, launched an attack along the eastern frontier of British India. When this offensive faltered and was repelled, the story quietly disappeared, although in November the INA spoke of a second offensive which would "seal off the dents made by the anti-Axis in the border regions of Burma".[84] Apparent

---

[79] *Syonan Sinbun*, 20 July 2603.

[80] Ibid., 21 Aug. 2603.

[81] Statement by the Chief of the Propaganda Department, Col. Koichi Okubo, *Syonan Sinbun*, 14 Sept. 2603.

[82] *Syonan Shimbun*, 24 Oct. 2604.

[83] Ibid., 8 Dec. 1943.

[84] Ibid., 24 Nov. 2604.

retreats in fact gave Japan strategic advantages by drawing the enemy into regions where the Japanese Army had its greatest strength.

> Of course, the enemy is only deluding himself if he thinks that the occupation by his forces of small islands in the wide Pacific ocean constitutes a significant success and is the key to final victory. The enemy will yet learn—and learn the lesson bitterly—that the small islands are all that his forces can occupy; the bigger, more strategic islands will stand out firmly as bulwarks in the defence of Greater East Asia. It is in an attempt against the stone-wall defence of these major islands that the enemy will take the plunge to his ultimate ruin and destruction.[85]

The *Syonan Shimbun* heralded 1945 as the "Year in Which Enemy will be Driven Out of Entire East Asia Area". It began with reports of B-29s shot down over the Japanese mainland, "sanguinary battles" in Burma, relentless attacks against the enemy fleet investing the Lingayan Gulf in northern Luzon, followed a few weeks later by a furious counter-attack against Allied forces that were by now "trapped in Manila", and Japanese successes against enemy attacks on Corregidor and Iwo Jima. "Body Crashing Pilots" from Japan's Special Attack Corps were carrying out a "bleeding" strategy that would lead to victory because every Japanese death caused "tens or even hundreds" of Allied deaths, or in the case of an attack on a battleship or aircraft carrier, over 1,000 Allied deaths. According to Lt. Col. Shozo Nakajima, spokesman for the Japanese forces in the Southern Regions, "on these lines, the 100,000,000 people of Nippon will fight with that same fighting spirit and can outnumber over 200,000,000 Anglo-Saxons. Herein lies the significance of our bleeding strategy."[86]

In March 1945 newspaper readers learned that enemy forces were "being cleverly lured nearer to [the] Nippon homeland", where they would be dealt a crushing blow, and in April that enemy troops were dying by the thousands on Okinawa.[87] In June the paper suggested that an enemy attack on Japan would prove a "divine opportunity to crush the enemy and turn the tide of war in Nippon's favour".[88] The following day brought an announcement that Singapore was to be evacuated because of the war situation.[89]

[85] Ibid., 20 Sept. 2604.

[86] Ibid., 10 Feb. 2605.

[87] Ibid., 17 Mar. 2605.

[88] Ibid., 29 June 2605.

[89] Ibid., 20 June 2605.

Stories such as these left little room for doubt that the war was going badly for Japan.

> ... in any war communique, it was always mentioned that they were withdrawing to a strategic line, new strategic lines. And from these ... even from the newspaper *Syonan Shimbun* ... we could read between the lines because they were all the time forming strategic lines.
>
> But if you had an atlas, you would see that they have been withdrawing all the time. Also there were a few people who had listened to radio New Delhi which would give their version of the results of the war or rather how the war was going on. That was how I knew that the Japanese were losing.[90]

People still had to exercise caution, despite the fact that the Japanese behaved less harshly than before. "Although inwardly happy, we dared not show it because we had suffered three years of Japanese cruelty. And none of us were going to run the risk of any untoward incident with the Japanese."[91]

Allied propaganda

The Allies disseminated propaganda in Malaya by means of radio broadcasts, leaflets dropped from aircraft, and statements spread by infiltrated agents. The plan for Malaya developed by Britain's Political Warfare Executive aimed to intensify discontent with Japanese rule, to strengthen the belief that Britain would return after the inevitable defeat of Japan by "Britain and the Allies", to encourage the Malayan population to welcome the British and to show that their return would bring a resumption of freedom and progress.[92] Specific points singled out for attention were Allied military and productive power, Allied successes in Europe, deteriorating conditions in Malaya and particularly rice shortages, Japanese domination of the administration and exploitation of natural resources, and problems caused by unemployment and inflation. There was an emphasis on "factual news", and material was presented in a conservative way because optimistic rumours were known to be circulating and the Allies wished to avoid saying anything that might induce a premature revolt.[93] British propaganda directed specifically toward the Malays highlighted sensitive issues such as Emperor worship and inconsistencies between Shintosim and Islam,

---

[90] OHD, interview with Lim Choo Sye.

[91] Ibid.

[92] Political Warfare Executive, Plan of Political Warfare for Malaya, 28 May 1945, HS1/114.

[93] "Psychological Warfare", Annexure 7 to Vice-Admiral The Earl Mountbatten of Burma, *Report to the Combined Chiefs of Staff by the Supreme Allied Commander South-East Asia 1943–1945*.

the wearing of peaked caps in place of traditional headgear, and pressure on women to dress in Japanese-style "*mompe*" trousers,[94] while propaganda for the Chinese and Indians focused on Britain's support for China and India, where the authorities were looking after the interests of relatives of people living in Malaya, and on the restoration of prosperity in business and industry following a British victory. As for British prestige, which had been dealt a severe blow by the Japanese conquest, the defeat of Japan was considered the best counter-propaganda. "There should be no question of any apologetic attitude although sympathy with the sufferings of the population is desirable." Finally, propaganda materials gave assurances that there would be no "unjustified reprisals", and emphasized that the British government was aware that some "compulsory co-operation with the Japanese is inevitable". The British would return to Malaya "in no spirit of vengeance against people who have been forced to conceal their loyalty to the Allied cause provided they have not deliberately assisted the enemy war effort or taken part in injuring or persecuting British or Allied prisoners or interned civilians or minority communities".[95]

US propaganda took a slightly different tack, playing down America's association with Great Britain and emphasizing cooperation with Australia, India and China, as well as the role of the United Nations. In preference to "British Malaya", US materials referred to Malaya or the Malay States, or Malaysia (which at the time was understood as referring to the Malay world of peninsular Malaya and the Netherlands Indies).[96] The Office of Strategic Services (OSS) developed propaganda for Southeast Asia, and an Implementation Study for Malaya prepared by the Morale Operations Branch of the OSS listed the following seven objectives:

---

[94] *Mompe* trousers featured in a Japanese effort to encourage women to play a greater role in the workforce. In Japan they were made from thick linen or wool, but in Malaya from the batik cloth used for sarongs. Ishak Haji Muhammad raised the matter after he visited Japan, where he found women discarding the kimono in favour of trousers (see the *Syonan Shimbun*, 15 Dec. 2603), and on 19 Feb. 2604 the *Syonan Shimbun* described *mompe* trousers as "trim" and "business-like", and declared that women found them "more practical and less cumbersome than the sarong for real wartime work".

[95] Political Warfare Executive, Plan of Political Warfare for Malaya, Aims and Objectives, HS1/114; Political Warfare for Malaya: (Proposed) Plan—July 1944, BMA 506/10; Plan of Political Warfare against Japan: Malaya Plan, CAB 119/51.

[96] Psychology Division, Divisional Report No. 47. (Originally prepared for the Foreign Information Service.) Social Conditions, Attitudes and Propaganda in British Malaya with Suggestions for American Orientation Toward the Malayans, BMA 522/00.

A. To harass, discredit and subvert the Japanese military and civilian personnel.
B. To discredit collaborationists.
C. To impede and eventually sabotage the Japanese military and economic plans.
D. To organize Chinese groups and native leaders so that they will passively resist the Japanese and at the right time take active means of resistance.
E. To create distrust and anxiety among Moslems as to Japanese intentions in regard to their religion.
F. To gather information.
G. To locate and facilitate the removal from the territory of natives (Malays and Chinese) suitable for training as agents.[97]

Materials for Southeast Asia included both white propaganda, consisting of true information, and black propaganda which included a degree of fabrication. Within the American intelligence community there was disagreement over the use of black propaganda, with opponents arguing that it might eventually discredit all Allied statements concerning the war,[98] but it featured prominently in materials disseminated in Southeast Asia. Typical of white propaganda was a leaflet that announced Germany's defeat in Europe and asserted that "Germany's Fate is Japan's Fate". Another item showed King Abdul Aziz Ibn Saud of Saudi Arabia seated alongside "his friend Mr Churchill", and listed Muslim countries that had declared war against "Japan and Germany, the enemies of Islam" (Turkey, Egypt, Iraq, Iran, Syria and the Lebanon in addition to Saudi Arabia). It called attention to the "great hardship and suffering" experienced by the people of Malaya because Muslims had been "unable to go on the Haj pilgrimage" since the Japanese invasion, and noted that the people of Kedah, Perlis, Kelantan and Trengganu had been "separated from their brother Moslems". There was also a leaflet which showed photographs of skeletal men said to be *Heiho* soldiers, and asked, "Where is the co-prosperity promised by the Japanese?"[99]

For black propaganda, the OSS Implementation Study offered a list of 38 "Rumour Themes" that could be directed at the local population (pigs had been slaughtered in mosques and Muslims had been forced to eat pork, the Japanese planned to confiscate all businesses, the Japanese were deriving handsome profits from lotteries and from the black market) and at Japanese serving in Southeast Asia (rations were to be cut, the southern army was to be abandoned when the

[97] MO Implementation Study – Malaya, NARA RG226 Entry 139 Box 131.

[98] Lawrence H. McDonald, "The OSS and Its Records", pp. 79, 83.

[99] Malayan Leaflets in NARA RG226 E144 Folder 1308.

big retreat began, conditions at home were bad).[100] The Morale Operations Branch used this material in developing two kinds of black radio scripts, one ostensibly emanating from an underground or freedom radio station located in Southeast Asia, the second made to seem as if the information came from official Japanese sources.[101] The latter spoke in glowing terms of Japanese military successes but carried the hidden message that these heroic efforts were necessary because of the overwhelming might of the Allied forces, and that Japan expected all Asians to fight and if necessary die on its behalf.[102] A radio script for Malaya released on 1 April 1945 provides an example of black propaganda. Its objectives were: "(1) to hint at the overwhelming military strength lined up against Japan; and (2) to carry war information from Europe, especially with regard to the Netherlands; and (3) to make it clear that Japan expects all Asiatics to shed blood to prevent Japanese defeat." The text read as follows:

> *War Review of the Week*: In China the great Japanese offensive has made smashing new gains all week. But the real center of the war has been in the Ryukyu Islands, just south of Japan. Here, over hundreds of miles of sea Japanese "body crashing" pilots and surface units have dealt heavy blows against the formidable Anglo-American naval armada. At least 20 enemy vessels are known sunk and dozens more damaged. Despite their losses, however, the enemy seems to be steadily increasing the scale of his attack. A Japanese military spokesman in Tokyo today, declared that Americans landing on Okinawa would find the same determined Japanese resistance they did on Iwo Jima.
>
> As the Pacific war draws closer to the homeland, all the nations of GEA [Greater East Asia] rose to join the battle [*sic*]. In French Indo China where all rebellious elements have by now been put down,

100 MO Implementation Study – Malaya, NARA RG226 Entry 139 Box 131. US efforts tended to focus on Sumatra, although items written in Malay for Sumatra could be readily understood in the peninsula. The author of Malay language propaganda was a Sumatran identified as "Careem". The OSS wanted to print materials specifically designed for Malaya in Jawi, Malay written with the Arabic script, but Careem was not proficient in Jawi, and it proved difficult to find an Arabic type-font in the Washington, DC, area. A Syrian newspaper in Washington had a set of Arabic type, but was considered a security risk.

101 NARA RG226 E144 Box 128 folder 1259.

102 In fact the Japanese were saying in Malaya that they themselves were willing to die. The Japanese residents of Singapore adopted a resolution saying that they would "defend Syonan to the last man" (*Syonan Shimbun*, 25 Sept. 2604), and the Governor of Perak told a meeting of District Officers in October 1944 (as recorded in the minutes of the meeting) that "for the sake of the continuation of the war and for the successful consummation of their Military Administration the Nippon-zin were ready to carry out the duties vested in them with a determination to die rather than fail, and asked the District Officers to do their best on their part." Minutes, Conference of District Officers, 4 Oct. 2604, PT Larut 161/2602.

> thousands of Annamese and Cambodians are eagerly enrolling in the Japanese army. Thousands of Thais, Bunnese and Indian soldiers—as well as Indonesians—are already fighting at the fronts, while throughout the Southern Regions the people are clamouring to join against the foe.
>
> Significant news also came from Europe this week. Despite seemingly overwhelming odds, Germany is still carrying on the fight for her homeland. The new advances of the British and America into Germany have produced one tragic result, however. According to neutral radio reports yesterday, the Germans have begun a complete withdrawal from the Netherlands.
>
> The war situation facing us is no doubt very serious, but Japanese leaders are still fully confident of victory, if all nations of GEA will sacrifice to their utmost to preserve the liberty Japan has brought them![103]

By this time Allied propaganda broadcasts sometimes contained "practically straight Japanese news, except with slight added emphasis on negative aspects". One script carries a remark that "It is hard to imagine how negative, defensive and phantastic Japanese propaganda is at present."[104]

* * *

The Japanese attempted to shape the character and thinking of the Malayan population, remaking people along lines that were presented as pan-Asian but were essentially Japanese. The educational and propaganda undertakings of the Japanese seem both audacious and naive: audacious in the scope of the changes they hoped to achieve, and naive in underestimating the tenacity with which the people of Malaya would cling to their values and way of life. Yet they were not without effect. People who passed through Japanese training programmes often claim to have derived considerable benefit from the discipline to which they were subjected, and post-war nationalists drew on some of the concepts and themes used by the Japanese, adapting them for their own purposes. However, post-war Southeast Asia turned away from the model of a united Asia, and pursued a strategy in which the former colonial territories became independent states, emphasizing their cultural distinctiveness and embarking on policies of "nation-building" to draw together the disparate groups living within their respective borders.

---

103 Project JN-27, Number 22A, against Radio Tokyo, NARA RG226 E144 Box 108. Iwo Jima was used as a point of reference in other broadcasts as well, since it called attention to a Japanese defeat.

104 Project JN-27, Number 19A, to be delivered in Malay, released 29 Mar. 1945, NARA RG226 E144 Box 10.

Education and propaganda largely affected literate and educated people living in the peninsula. For a great many of them, these irritants were of much less significance than the growing economic distress, and the difficulties they faced in securing food and clothing and other essential items, and it is to these matters that the discussion will now turn.

CHAPTER 6

The Economy

The Japanese spent most of 1942 consolidating their new regime, but in 1943 launched a series of economic innovations, some designed to overcome war-related shortages, and others marking the first steps toward restructuring the Malayan economy as part of the Greater East Asian Co-Prosperity Sphere. Overall, the tendency was toward centralization and government economic planning. By 1944, though, Japan had no further resources to invest in Malayan development, and the military administration became pre-occupied with the daunting task of trying to shore up Malaya's defences against an expected Allied invasion.

In the short-term Japan's economic plans called for securing natural resources from Southeast Asia and promoting self-sufficiency for territories within the region. Malaya played almost no role in supplying raw materials because, with the exception of bauxite, the peninsula produced very little that Japan needed to prosecute the war. The primary economic advantage Japan won with the conquest of Malaya was that the resources of the peninsula were no longer available to the Allies, but in other respects Malaya was far more of a burden than an asset. With respect to self-sufficiency, Malaya's agricultural and industrial output was far from adequate to meet local requirements, and during the occupation it had to supply both the civilian population and the Japanese military. Various stopgap measures were put into place, but the military received priority, and the people of Malaya found it difficult to satisfy many of their basic needs.

Economic Policy

The military administration spent the first months after the British surrender dealing with war damage and trying to overcome local shortages. It then began introducing a series of regulations that moved the country toward centralized economic planning, shifting Malaya "from a liberal economy to a planned economy" in order to promote economic reconstruction and increase fighting power.[1] A Five-Year Production Plan introduced in May 1943 regulated the

[1] Domei ELB, 9 Sept. 1943, BMA PS/410 Pt. 1.

disposition of more than twenty kinds of materials (among them iron ore, cement, soda, powder, paper and fibres) and established a Material Research Committee to investigate new uses for local resources. The following month brought a Five-Year Industrial Plan, and in September 1943 the administration created a Production Control Organ to assist heavy industries. The aim of these measures was to reduce the need to supply Malaya with manufactured goods from Japan or elsewhere in the Co-Prosperity Sphere by systematically developing local industry and ensuring that optimum use was made of existing equipment and facilities.[2]

On 7 August 1943 the Japanese introduced an "Ordinance for the Control of Important Things and Materials, etc." that was described as "the balance wheel of other regulations". This law was promulgated "for the purpose of increasing fighting power by means of controlling the supply of the demand for raw material and other goods necessary for the smooth operation of the Military Administration, as well as for the conservation of goods and their effective utilization". It dealt with "things and materials used in communication work, things and materials used in engineering and building operations, things and materials essential to life and other things and materials that are important for the purpose of carrying out the military administration", and stipulated that designated items could not be transferred, "lost", used as security or taken from one place to another without permission from the Military Administrator. It also empowered the government to requisition goods, industrial plant, equipment, land and buildings.[3]

In an effort to improve the supply of civilian goods, the government lifted restrictions on inland trade in 1943 and allowed free movement of goods in Malaya, Java and Sumatra, although permits were required to buy or sell a long list of products, including salt and sugar, petrol, soap, candles, toys, paper, camphor, fly paste, earthenware, glass wares, iron wares, cosmetics, medicines, bicycle spare parts, electrical products and empty bottles.[4] The easing of trade restrictions led

---

[2] Domei, 8 Sept. 1943, *NARA* RG165 Entry 77 Box 2417/14; Domei ELB, 9 Sept. 1943, BMA PS/410 Pt. 1; Malaya under the Japanese, NARA RG226 128585; FIR No. 11, 14 Aug. 1943, CO273/669/50744/7; Malaya: Japanese Military Domination (Administration), BMA PS/412.

[3] *Syonan Sinbun*, 9 Aug. 2603; Ordinance No. 13 of 2603, DO Temerloh 392/2603; *Penang Shimbun*, 21 Aug. 2603, 22 Aug. 2603, 24 Aug. 2603; Report of the Office of the [Kedah] Legal Adviser for the Year 2486, SUK Kedah 770/2487.

[4] Chief Officer-in-Charge, General Department to DO Temerloh, 8 June 2603, DO Temerloh 318/2603. Following the transfer to Thai control the local administrations of the northern states followed a similar procedure, with export permits issued by a Committee comprising the Food Controller, a Thai officer, and the Superintendent of Monopolies and Customs.

to price increases, and on 20 August the government issued regulations that established tight controls over "materials necessary for daily life", in the first instance rubber tyres and tubes, paper and stationery, medicines and textiles. All stocks of these items had to be reported, although the government insisted that such goods would not be seized, and that the purpose of the exercise was to help arrange for a fair distribution of scarce commodities.[5] On 10 September the military administration introduced a Price Control Ordinance that allowed the government to set price ceilings on goods sold within the country. Only designated merchants could sell controlled items, and they were required to display price lists for controlled goods in a prominent place, and to record transactions in ledgers along with evidence that sales were lawful (such as the number of a purchaser's Labour Pass Book, the number of a Purchasing Coupon or details of an official permit). The government required monthly reports on quantities of goods sold, prices and remaining stock.[6]

In Pahang three commodities distribution corporations were formed to handle controlled goods: the Kuala Lipis Commodities Corporation, the Pahang South-West Commodities Corporation, and the Pahang East Commodities Corporation. Committees of the Oversea Chinese Association set up these bodies, and District Officers served as advisers with instructions to supervise their activities. The state administration suggested that each corporation should have around 30 members, but in Temerloh alone more than 90 firms applied, and retailers not invited to the inaugural meeting submitted petitions appealing against being left out. Each of the Pahang corporations was allowed to accumulate a total fund of $50,000, and sold shares to members for $100 each, apportioned on the basis of past performance. Returns were based on fixed commissions, and the corporations were not supposed to earn profits in excess of the rates set. Members shared the profits or losses. To send a controlled commodity out of the state, traders had to obtain either a permit from the government or a sub-permit from one of the corporations, and corporations were authorized to confiscate any commodities exported without a permit.[7]

---

[5] The regulations imposing control over daily necessities were issued under the Ordinance for the Control of Important Things and Materials. *Syonan Sinbun*, 19 and 20 Aug. 2603; *Perak Times*, 20 and 22 Aug. 2603; Pahang State Order no. 1 Re: Sales System of Requisite Goods for Livelihood, Temerloh 392/2603; Notice issued by Shotaro Katyama, Governor of Selangor, *Malai Sinpo*, 21 Aug. 2603.

[6] Ordinance no. 16 (Price Control), 10 Sept. 2603, and Tokubetu-si Notice No. 268, *Syonan Sinbun*, 19 Sept. 2603.

[7] See Temerloh 481/2603, inter alia Regulations of the Pahang Temerloh District Commodities Distribution Corporation, and The Temerloh District Commodities Distributing Corporation Notice no. 1. See also DO Kuantan 191/2603 pt 1.

Controls became more stringent the following year. In May 1944 the Military Administration announced a scheme to speed up the acquisition of materials necessary for the welfare of the people. The ordinance covered 99 different articles divided into three categories. Foodstuffs such as vegetables, fruits, fresh fish, meat, eggs and rice could only be exported or imported with approval from the state governor. Another set of products, including lead, zinc, sulphur, charcoal, tyres, vegetable oils and electric light bulbs required authorization from the Chief of the Military Administration. According to a newspaper editorial, the new regulations were introduced because the supply of goods in the countries of the region had increased to such an extent that it was necessary to impose controls to ensure efficient use of shipping space.[8]

In addition to regulating business activity, the Japanese created associations and councils that dominated key industries. By the end of 1942 the Malayan administration had in place a Communications Bureau, a Postal Administration Bureau, a Public Facilities Bureau, a Broadcast Control Bureau, a Marine Affairs Bureau, a Railways Bureau and a Meteorological Bureau.[9] In the eyes of the Japanese, it was also "very important to have organisations of economic work", for example, of "farmers, fishermen and merchants".[10] In line with this idea, they established a number of business organizations, including a Mining Association, an Oil Council, a Forestry Council, a Maritime Association and a Rubber Association. With the creation of a Manufacturers Association for Malaya, in February 1944, the Japanese announced that the process of forming economic organizations was for the time being complete.[11]

The Japanese introduced similar organizations in Singapore, and by early 1944 staple foods such as rice, and supplementary foods (vegetables, fresh and dried fish, meat and cooking oil) were sold at authorized distributing stations. Locally-grown vegetables and grains other than rice had not yet been brought under control, and a report prepared early in 1944 said that ideally rationing of locally grown food would be entirely handled by 47 appointed distributing stations drawing supplies from the Syonan Vegetable and Fruit Rationing

---

[8] Malai Administration Ordinance No. 13, The Export and Import Ordinance, 20 May 2604, *Syonan Shimbun*, 10 May 2604; Appreciation of the Economic Position of Malaya under the Japanese, BMA COM/21.

[9] *Syonan Sinbun*, 15 Dec. 2602.

[10] Speech of the Industrial Administrator for Johore, Mr. Mizuno, MS dated 8 Sept. 2602, MB Johor 209/2602.

[11] Handbook of Japanese Industry in Japan and Occupied Areas, OSS Assemblage No. 43 Supplement No. 1, R&A No. 2280.I, 15 Dec. 1944; Domei ELB, from Tokyo, 14 Mar. 1944, FIR 5, 1-15 Mar. 1944, CO273/673/50744/7.

Association, but the report warned that "if this idea is attempted immediately, it might destroy the existing complicated collection and distribution system which is an intricate network, and create unease about food shortages".[12]

Wartime businesses could not import fresh supplies and survived on stocks brought in before the war. In the absence of imports, the pre-war structure of importers, wholesalers and retailers ceased to function, and surviving businesses all operated as retailers. Without wholesalers, retailers could only purchase supplies from other retailers, paying retail prices and re-selling to customers at higher prices, a situation that drove up prices.

To a great extent, Japan relied on private enterprise to carry out business activities in Malaya, although a small number of key operations, notably the production of quinine, the management of railroads and communications facilities, and the running of the petroleum industry, were kept under Army control. According to a Japanese account, "neither the system of synthetically developing a company nor the co-operative enterprises was employed since it was believed that the enterprisers could produce better results without the above systems."[13] "Enterprisers", who underwent screening by the Army before coming to Malaya, were generally businessmen from Japan, although smaller concerns sometimes employed managers recruited in the occupied territories. The Malayan Association of Japan was a major source of manpower, and some 500 of its members returned to the peninsula to join business firms or the civil administration. Private firms operated under strict controls, and an "on the spot auditing procedure" prevented enterprisers from earning excessive profits. Only income resulting from investments originating in Japan could be repatriated to Japan.[14]

Transport

Transport shortages lay behind many of the difficulties that plagued Malaya during the occupation, hampering internal trade, impeding plans for industrial expansion and making it difficult to obtain supplies from overseas sources. The administration adopted various expedients to overcome these limitations, but

---

[12] "Reorganizing Commercial Businesses in Syonan Municipality", Sept. 1944, prepared by Higuchi Goro and Nagamori Masaji, in *The Chōsabu Reports*, trans. and ed. Huff and Majima, Chapter 4.

[13] JM 103, p. 14.

[14] Ibid.; see also Political and Economic Changes Effected by the Japanese in Malaya, 1 Dec. 1943, OSS. R&A 1433.

transport remained a major obstacle to economic development and the conduct of the war.

Motor vehicles were scarce, and because civilian transport companies could not obtain petrol, local workshops re-engineered buses to operate on fuel derived from charcoal, using an apparatus that the *Syonan Times* described as follows:

> The device comprises four main components—a charcoal burning boiler, a gas generator and convertor, a gas accumulator and a discharger.
>
> The boiler has also a separate water tank attached to it, to regulate the heat. From the boiler the gas generated and is transferred through a pipe to the convertor which absorbs all sediment, [*sic*]. The "purified" gas is then transferred to a special tank, near the driver's seat, whence the gas finds its way to the "carburettor" and thence to the engine.

Illus. 6.1 A Singapore bus operated by charcoal gas.

Source: *Syonan Times*, 2 Aug. 2602 (1942).

Buses equipped with this device could carry 35 passengers at speeds of up to 35 miles per hour, and a picul (133⅓ pounds) of charcoal was sufficient to operate a bus for "a whole day and night" at a cost of 1 cent per mile.[15] Long distance bus services were unified under the Tokyo Kyuko Dentetsu Kabushiki Kaisha (Tokyo Express Tramcar Company),[16] and an otherwise sober report on the activities of the Kuala Lumpur Sanitary Board in 1942 heaped lavish praise on the new arrangement:

---

[15] *Syonan Times*, 2 Aug. Syowa 17 [1942]. See also AR, KL SB 2602, Sel Kan 108/2603.

[16] NARA RG226 L37542.

> With the elimination of [the existing bus companies] road services can be run on the most economical lines without any possibility of wasteful competitions which rival companies are bound to have. The travelling public can now rest assured that the Tokyo Kyuko Dentetsu Kaisha will provide the most convenient and comfortable transport at the most economical fares. The standard of passenger service will soon reach its zenith and it is the first time in the history of transport industry in this country that one company is controlling the whole system of road transport.[17]

In August 1943 the administration brought privately-owned motor vehicles, and spare parts, under the act for the control of essential materials in order to prevent the use of motor vehicles for non-essential purposes. People who wished to continue using their vehicles had to apply to the Military Administrator, and provide justification.[18]

Before the war the country had over 14,000 kilometres of asphalted roads. The Japanese constructed a new road along the east coast of the peninsula (see Maps 6.1 and 6.2), but maintenance of existing roads was poor.

> A report from Tokyo in September 1944 speaks of rocks "protruding like a file" from roads which were originally smooth. It was stated that it would be a great mistake to imagine that splendid roads stretched throughout Malaya.... A tyre which was good for more than 10,000 kilometres in Japan, was no longer usable after 8,500 kilometres in Malaya.[19]

Railway service resumed on the west coast by June 1942, but there were breaks in the line where bridges had been destroyed, and it was 1943 before a through service between Singapore and Bangkok was announced.[20] Track from branch lines, and also from the east coast line, was removed in 1943 and used for construction of a railway line linking the Thai and Burmese railway networks (see Map 6.2).

Shipping space was extremely tight. At the time of the invasion, the British scuttled or evacuated many of the ships operating in Malayan waters, and despite salvage operations by the Japanese Navy in the waters around Singapore, which by September 1942 claimed to have recovered 94 vessels, there was an acute shortage of shipping capacity.[21] A Japanese newspaper highlighted the issue of shipping in a story published in August 1943:

---

[17] AR, KL SB, 2602, Sel Kan 108/2603.

[18] *Perak Times*, 6 Sept. 2603.

[19] Malaya under the Japanese, NARA RG226 128585.

[20] Ibid.

[21] Malaya – Part II, 1 Oct. 1943, BMA 506/10.

Map 6.1 Roads and railways of Malaya, 1942

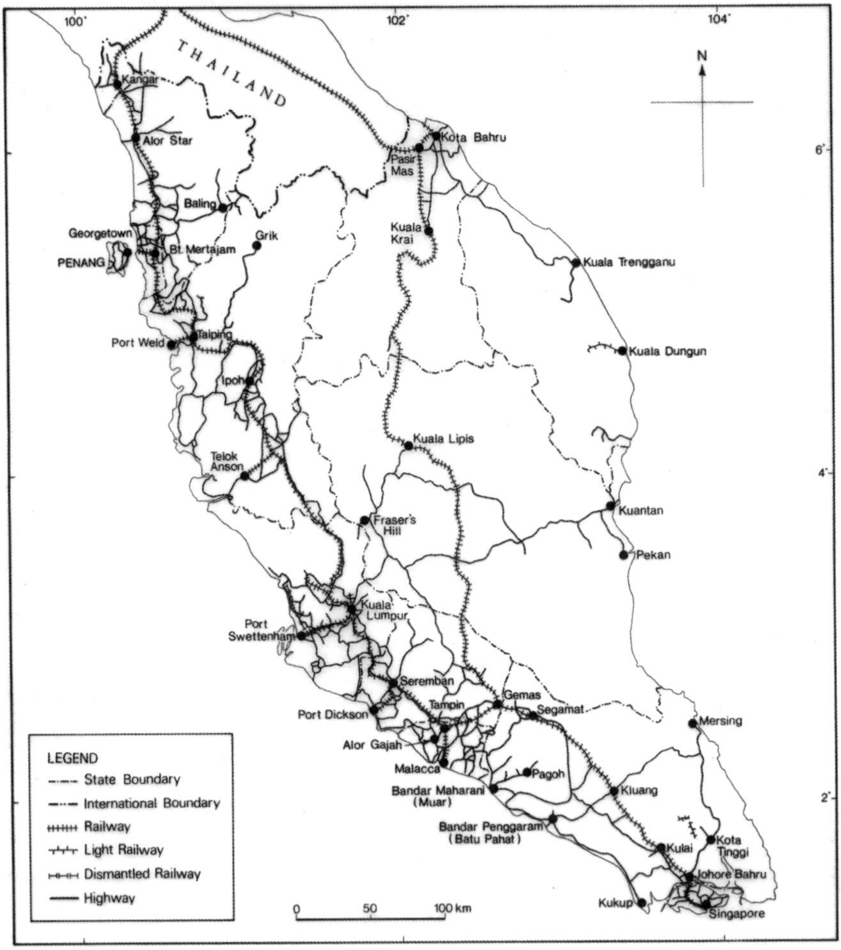

Map 6.2 Roads and railways of Malaya, 1945

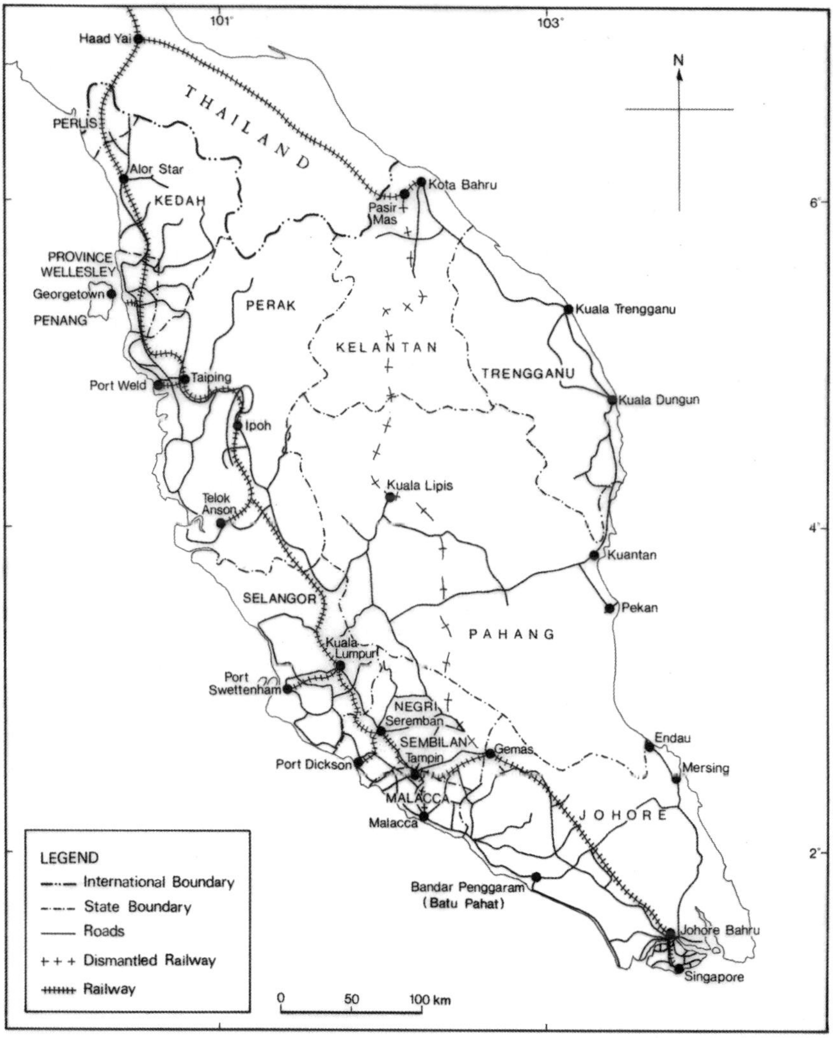

> Whatever one may say, the greatest worry of all is the question of shipping. If only we had ships, the greater part of our difficulties could easily be overcome, and most of our problems solved. Owing to lack of ships, we are obliged to make unnatural self-sufficiency plans and superfluous efforts become necessary. Again, as we haven't got the ships, the smooth flow of goods between the various regions of the Co-prosperity sphere is impossible, and instead of the unified construction of the Co-prosperity sphere as a whole, the various regions are being developed separately and independently. If only we had the ships, these problems would all be solved and remedied at once.[22]

On 20 March 1943 the military administration announced the creation of a Southern Regions Shipping Company that incorporated all Japanese shipping concerns in Singapore, and mobilized steamships and sailing vessels to carry goods within the Southern Regions.[23] In January 1944 a Malayan Marine Transport Association similarly united all local shipowners. This body handled shipping operations, and also regulated freight rates, charges for repairs and supplies, and the commissions, salaries and allowances paid within the industry. The Japanese Director General of the Southern Regions Shipping Company became director general of the association.[24]

To overcome the shortage of shipping space, Japan launched a major programme to build ships throughout the Co-Prosperity Sphere and ordered all districts in the Southern Regions to give the highest priority to this effort, which received some 30–40 per cent of the funds available for civilian enterprises in 1944. In Malaya, at least ten shipyards constructed vessels under this scheme, and the Japanese brought experienced shipbuilders from Canton to assist local artisans. Plans called for five standard types of vessels of various sizes, but the majority of those built were between 100 and 250 tons. Semi-diesel engines expected from Japan did not arrive, so some vessels were equipped with "hot-bulb engines"—oil-fueled motors in which the cylinder head was heated to a high temperature to ignite the fuel—and others with engines converted from other uses. However, the greater part of the output consisted of simple wooden ships equipped only with sails. It was announced in Singapore in July 1944

[22] *Mainichi Shimbun*, 23 Aug. 1943, quoted in Appreciation of Malaya: II – Post-Japanese Occupation, BMA 506/10.

[23] Domei ELB, 31 Mar. 1943, CO273/669/50744/7.

[24] Domei Japanese language broadcast, 25 Jan. 1944, and ELB 7 Feb. 1944, FIR 3, 15 Feb. 1944, CO273/673/50744/7. According to Malaya under the Japanese (NARA RG226 128585), the Malayan Marine Transport Association was founded in March, 1943.

that shipbuilding operations would concentrate on constructing lighters and simplified tugs, vessels of 10–15 tons for use along the coast.[25]

Many of the ships built under Japanese programmes during the occupation were poorly constructed.[26] According to a post-war account of the Kuantan shipyard,

> junks were turned out to ply up and down the coasts. Owing to incredible mistakes and to sabotage, no junk made two journeys; many sank in the Kuantan River without reaching the sea. Bolts holes were bored larger than the bolts; miscellaneous softwoods of different shrinkage were used in place of hardwoods.[27]

In Singapore, another post-war report noted that the Japanese established shipyards "in which they showed the Chinese craftsmen how junks should be built, thus trying to teach their grandmothers to suck eggs".

> I saw many of these vessels in different stages of construction and they were a source of great amusement to the Chinese. Any species of timber was good enough for the Japanese to use, all of it unseasoned, and many pieces with sapwood in them. Even very soft woods ... were employed and it was possible to see three or four different species in adjoining strakes, and all the seams gaping.[28]

Few cargo ships operated in Malayan waters during the latter part of the occupation. In August 1943, an intelligence source reported only one steamer but large numbers of wooden junks at Penang, most of them carrying cargoes to and from Burma. The captain of a vessel shelled and sunk in May 1944 told Allied interrogators that just three or four junks sailed regularly between Penang and Mergui, a port along Burma's Tenasserim coast, although he had heard that a larger number travelled between Singapore and Rangoon.[29] An Allied submarine commander patrolling in the Straits of Malacca in July and August 1944 found an "almost total lack of targets of any size", and speculated

---

[25] Appreciation of the Economic Position of Malaya under the Japanese, ca. 1944, BMA COM/213; Mitsui Bussan Kaisha to PWD Perak, 14 Dec. 2603, and to DO Dindings 16 Mar. 2604, Hutan Perak 140/2603. A description of a hot-bulb engine is found in NARA RG 457 SRDJ 35222. I am grateful to E. Bruce Reynolds for supplying me with this information. There was a suggestion at one point that Japan might construct ships out of crude rubber to transport commodities from SE Asia, and that upon arrival in Japan the ships would be broken up and the rubber used for other purposes. *Syonan Sinbun*, 6 Feb. 2603.

[26] Forest Department, Report for Jan. 1946, BMA DEPT/11/3.

[27] Position of the Pahang Forest Department at the time of the reoccupation and subsequently, Forests 30/1945.

[28] Situation Report on the Forest Department, Malaya, for September 1945, Forests 30/1945.

[29] NARA RG226 79807, RG226 78667.

that "the enemy is unwilling any longer to risk his shipping in our area and has probably constructed sufficient railways to take its place".[30]

The *Kumiai* System

Toward the end of 1942 the Japanese began trying to reduce wasteful competition by forming local companies into associations known as *kumiai*, groupings of firms in the same line of business which were given quasi-monopolies over certain types of wholesale and retail trade.[31] There were *kumiai* for fish, vegetables, rice, cloth, and many others items, and they became responsible for much of Malaya's internal trade and retailing.[32] The stated purpose was to control prices and increase economic efficiency, but the system did not achieve its objectives, and the monopolistic position enjoyed by *kumiai* allowed them to make exorbitant profits.

> ... in Malaya, Kumiais turned out to be a complete fiasco. They were a curse to the country. They did exactly the opposite of what they were expected to do. They became government-protected compartments of the Black Market. Instead of a fair distribution of commodities, there was the most haphazard inequality of distribution.
>
> Every Kumiai was nothing but a monopoly to fleece the public. As soon as a Kumiai for any particular commodity was formed, that commodity soon disappeared from the markets and became difficult to get. As a result, prices soared.[33]

Rising prices in 1944 led to strong criticism of the *kumiai*. A study of fish marketing in Perak gives some indication of the nature of the problem. Fishermen obtained advances from a group of financiers to whom they sold their catch. In the case of one good quality fish, *bawal tambak* (S. niger, a pomfret), the financiers paid the fishermen $200 per pikul (133⅓ lbs), and then sold the fish to the Dindings Fish Syndicate for $250 per pikul—a mark-up the Ipoh Price Control Board characterized as "very surprising" in view of the fact that the financiers were themselves members of the Syndicate. The Syndicate sold the fish to the *kumiai* at $400 per pikul, and the *kumiai* added $20 for short weight allowance, $12 for transport, and $2 for packing, and then marked up the price

---

30 "Appreciation of the Economic Position of Malaya under the Japanese", no author, n.d., BMA 506/30; HMS *Maidstone* Monthly General Letter, Aug. 1944, NARA RG226 XL2332.

31 AR, Department of Commerce and Industry, 2602, Sel Kan 26/2603. The department controlled bicycle tyres and tubes, fresh fish, and domestic animals and poultry. It also handled requests for permits to export non-food products from the state.

32 Lau and Barry, A Brief Review of Chinese Affairs, BMA ADM/8/1.

33 Chin Kee Onn, *Malaya Upside Down*, pp. 86–7.

by 10 per cent, before selling the fish to wholesale dealers in Ipoh for $486.20 per pikul. The wholesalers sold the fish to retailers for a profit of 10 per cent, and retailers then added on a profit margin that brought the retail price to $6 per kati ($600 per pikul), three times what the fishermen received. Raja Othman, the Kinta District Officer, summed up the results of this study by saying:

> We are forced to admit that things have been allowed to get out of hand and a bad state of affairs has been permitted to go unchecked for a long time. The Government cannot claim entire freedom of responsibility from blame for this unsatisfactory state of affairs.... We know it is discreditable for all concerned to admit but we are forced to admit that in no single instance has the so-called controlled price been observed either theoretically or practically.

He added, however, that it was necessary to proceed slowly, setting prices at levels close to those already prevailing because while high prices caused difficulties for consumers, drastic cuts would drive sellers away from legal markets.[34]

Japanese officials told district officers in Pahang that *kumiai* were not being properly run, and suggested that they deal with the matter, noting that local produce need not necessarily be sold to a *kumiai*.[35] In Perak the Ipoh Price Control Board proposed doing away with "broker *kumiais*" and replacing them with producer and consumer *kumiai* which could deal directly with each other,[36] but the head of the state Industrial Bureau, M. Watanabe, defended the *kumiai* system, claiming that it had brought about lower prices. He cited the case of the Perak Bussi Hyakyu Kumiai, which he credited with halving the price of sweet potatoes by collecting the product at its source for distribution in the town of Ipoh. When the District Officer of Batang Padang suggested that products such as tapioca and padi should be freed from control so that capitalists would invest in agriculture, Watanabe replied that abolishing price controls "would give capitalists the chance to manipulate the market in which event it would be found that prices of commodities would soar up even higher". In any case, he pointed out, the tapioca *kumiai* had been formed not just to market the product, but also to keep tapioca from being smuggled out of the state.[37]

---

[34] Interim Report of the Foodstuff Prices Control Board of Ipoh, Perak, n.d., Batu Gajah 57/2604. See also Notes on District Officers' Conference, 3 June 2604, Temerloh 82/2602, and Asst DO, Batu Gajah, Monthly Report for October 2604, Batu Gajah 84/2604.

[35] Notes, District Officers' Conference, 3 June 2604, DO Temerloh 82/2602.

[36] Notes, Meeting of Ipoh Price Control Board, 22 June 2604, Batu Gajah 57/2604.

[37] Minutes, Conference of District Officers, 4 Oct. 2604, PT Larut 161/2602.

Smuggling and the Black Market

Despite heavy penalties, a Black Market operated more or less openly in occupied Malaya. Unemployment forced many people to sell their personal belongings to raise funds, a practice which the Japanese allowed, and these private sales shaded into illicit trading in controlled goods. George Bogaars, whose father had lost his job, recalls that their family sold off the contents of their house in Singapore.

> Furniture ... I remember one day someone coming in and buying our sitting room furniture. My dad had to sell it ... And so we made shift, moved some things around.... And gradually things began diminishing. And I think most people ... did the same thing. The Japanese were buying most of it to furnish their own kind of living accommodation.[38]

People generally sold their belongings to middlemen: "You told him you had something and he came along and looked at it. Or you take it down and he looked at the thing."[39] Ng Seng Yong, who worked as a middleman during the occupation, described his activities as follows:

> Now, in a rough way of describing it, everyone is a broker. You start trying to sell things for one friend to another. You get the idea. One has to know a lot of friends.... And you just go from a friend to another.... So it's a question of walking. Sometimes you practically walked half a day trying to contact each other.[40]

According to Tan Cheng Hwee, brokers handled "anything, ranging from these measuring tapes up to gold".

> Normally, they don't care what goods you are selling, they will try and get a buyer for you. And usually, they have a buyer. Some people, they make a lot of money during this time. So they know that it's better to keep goods than money. We from the working class, we don't realise that one day, money may not be acceptable as a means of buying things. But these people know that once the Japanese go, their money goes with them.[41]

People who became rich working as black market traders were called "mushroom millionaires": they "were not really millionaires in the sense of doing proper type of business. Just a matter of being daring. And some were caught, some were beaten up, punished and all that. And some got [away] scot-free."[42]

---

[38] OHD, interview with George Bogaars.

[39] Ibid.

[40] OHD, interview with Ng Seng Yong.

[41] OHD, interview with Tan Cheng Hwee.

[42] OHD, interview with Heng Chiang Ki.

A shipment of Japanese goods reached Malaya in mid-1943 and was advertised with great fanfare as the solution to illicit trading. The *Syonan Sinbun* announced: "Systematic distribution of Nippon-made goods, which are being sold at prices within the reach of the poorest, will in due course close the Black Market altogether…." However, less than two weeks later the newspaper noted with "the greatest regret" that "certain types of Nippon goods, recently distributed to the public, are already said to have found their way to the Black Market".[43]

The black market in foodstuffs played a crucial part in maintaining the health and welfare of the Malayan population. Because police informers were active, black market traders preferred to sell to regular buyers, and black market rice, salt and sugar often reached the public through coffee shops, eating shops and roadside hawkers. These outlets were patronized by middle class people who had money to spend but lacked direct access to black market supplies.[44] By mid-1944 tighter controls and growing shortages had forced most coffee shops in Singapore to cease operations, while those that remained open offered only sugarless and milkless coffee. In smaller places, though, controls were lax. The District Officer for Batu Gajah reported late in the year that although no sugar had been released for general purchase, coffee shops and small eating stalls continued to find supplies. Responding to such reports, the government of Perak announced plans to shut all but a small number of coffee shops, and reduce by half the number of shops selling food.[45]

Some black market supplies came from authorized dealers who diverted rice or sugar intended for sale under the rationing system, but the primary source was smugglers who operated along the Malayan coasts. Karimun Island, in the Riau Archipelago, became a major transfer point for smuggled goods passing between Java, Sumatra and the peninsula, so much so that in March 1945 the Syonan Rice Import Kumiai set up a branch there to "smooth" the import of rice.[46] In Johore small sailboats entered the Batu Pahat River at night carrying "rice, sugar, flour, pigs, cigarettes, wine, brandy and opium", for the most part purchased from the former Netherlands Indies.[47] Further north, Ibrahim bin

---

[43] *Syonan Sinbun*, 15 July and 27 July 2603.

[44] Asst DO, Batu Gajah, Monthly Report for October 2604, Batu Gajah 84/2604. The number of casual sellers of foodstuffs increased by as much as 60 per cent.

[45] Conditions in Singapore in the late Summer of 1944: Summary of information obtained from interrogation of escaped British P.O.W., CO273/673/30744/7; Minutes, Conference of District Officers, 4 Oct. 2604, PT Larut 161/2602.

[46] Twang Peck Yang, "Indonesian Chinese Business Communities", pp. 72–3.

[47] Cheng Kok Peng, "A Brief Study of the Situation in Batu Pahat during the Japanese Occupation", p. 36.

Cheek patrolled the coastline near Sungei Udang in Perak in connection with his duties with the *Jikeidan*, and often encountered Thai or Burmese rice smugglers. Although he was obliged as a *Jikeidan* member to report these sightings, he also felt a responsibility to the people of the area, and allowed the smuggling to continue.[48] A Chinese boat captain interrogated by Allied intelligence early in 1945 reported that smugglers followed a regular circuit, collecting rice at Kantang, in southern Thailand, and selling it at Telok Anson in Lower Perak, where the black market price was higher than at Penang. Smugglers earned a profit of around 50 per cent on their cargoes, which were worth between 200,000 and 300,000 Japanese dollars. The captain said his own junk, which was 70 feet long and had a 16-foot beam, was too large to be used for smuggling, and he sold parboiled rice from Burma through official channels in Penang, each time making a profit of between 70,000 and 80,000 Japanese dollars.[49]

There was also a considerable amount of internal smuggling, with farmers or traders moving grain from producing areas to towns and other places where supplies were scarce and black market prices attractive. Farmers in the Krian District of Perak carried rice down the Kurau River, south along the coast to the Larut River, and inland to the town of Taiping, either evading or bribing guards stationed at the mouths of these rivers. Residents of Relau, in southern Kedah, carried rice, sago flour and cooking oil to Penang, travelling through the forest to avoid detection. They moistened the rice before selling it to increase its weight and get a better price.[50] On the east coast, rice was smuggled from Kelantan to Besut, in Trengganu, and from there was moved further south, going as far as Pahang. In principle all imports or exports had to be channelled through an official body and the Kelantan administration offered large rewards for information about smuggling activities, but with little success. According to the District Officer for Pasir Puteh, who was charged with stopping the traffic in rice, every village in the district had at least a few people who sent rice to Trengganu, and in areas near the Trengganu border such as Bukit Awang and Semerak nearly every resident was involved in the trade. Moreover, it was impossible to patrol the many jungle trails crossing the border. Although the District Officer suggested

[48] Interview with Ibrahim bin Cheek, in Siti Zubaidah bte Kassim, "Pengalaman Penduduk Sungai Acheh yang Bekerja Sebagai Jikeidan Jepun pada Waktu Pendudukan Jepun di Tanah Melayu".

[49] OSS, Advanced HQ, SEAC, Report of Interrogation of a twenty-eight-year-old Hokkien Chinese, conducted in Hokkien, 11 Jan. 1945, NARA RG226 112749.

[50] I was told about Krian when I lived in the area in 1973–74. Information on Relau was supplied by Awang bin Cha, who was in his late teens during the occupation. See Hairani Mohd Khalid, "Satu Tinjauan Am tentang Kehidupan Penduduk Mukim Relau, Kedah semasa Pendudukan Jepun".

sending additional policemen to the border area and intensifying efforts to locate rice collected for smuggling purposes, he referred to those involved in the trade as "*perais*", a word which is associated with people who are trying to eke out a living and suggests a certain sympathy with them.[51]

Japanese efforts to control illicit trading were desultory at best, and Japanese soldiers not only took bribes but in some cases actively participated in the black market. A Singapore businessman said that the biggest black market dealers were the Japanese themselves, especially the higher-ranking officers, who operated on the principle that "They can arrest you, you can't arrest them."[52] Lai Ping Khiong, who escaped from Malaya by travelling overland to China late in 1942, reported that corruption was universal among soldiers and civil servants, and that anything could be gotten from the military administration "if it is done the right way". There were recognized forms of payment to the Japanese in return for their assistance with smuggling, including gifts and particularly "introductions to the houses of entertainment", referring to gambling houses, which the Japanese were not supposed to patronize, nightclubs and brothels.[53] In the eyes of one Singapore businessman, such things did not even amount to corruption:

> During war years, if the authorities would like to have a few bags [of rice] free, if you are a trader, you would just give to them without charge. Little favours like that would help. I don't call it a bribe, but if somebody did a good turn to you, then if you have, you could spare, you might as well spare it. Otherwise, you may not be able to get your permits renewed.[54]

Goods were often carried past customs check-points with the assistance of Japanese (or in the northern states, Thai) military personnel, who claimed to be acting officially. The District Officer for Bentong, in Pahang, complained in June 1943 that scrap iron was being removed by army, navy and air force lorries, sometimes escorted by Japanese officers, and that the police did not dare to stop them. On one occasion when the police did detain a lorry, the driver

---

[51] Ketua Jajahan Pasir Puteh to Datok Menteri Kelantan, Perkara melarikan beras bawa' keluar negeri, 18 Dec. 2486, Pasir Puteh 25/2486; Notes of a Meeting on the padi problem at the office of the Vice President Montri Spa on 10 Jan. 2488, Pasir Puteh 83/2688. *Rais* is a variant of *kais*, a word found in the Malay expression *kais pagi makan pagi, kais petang makan petang* (scratch [like a chicken] in the morning, eat in the morning; scratch in the afternoon, eat in the afternoon—living from hand to mouth). See also "Pemberitahu" (announcement) issued by the Kelantan Sangyo-Bu Cho, 24 June 2602, and Keimubutyo Kelantan to Guntyo of various districts, 13 June 1943, Pasir Puteh 144/2603.

[52] OHD, interview with Heng Chiang Ki.

[53] Conditions in Malaya up to October 1942, based on information supplied by Lai Ping Khiong, former Secretary of the Bank of China in Singapore, HSI/114.

[54] OHD, interview with Jack Kim Boon Ng.

simply contacted the local military commander who gave instructions to release the vehicle.[55] Faced with situations such as these, the police prudently decided that responsibility for smuggling really lay with the Customs Department, but Customs officials fared no better. In July 1943 the officer on duty at Bentong reported that two lorries had passed his post at about 11 p.m. without halting: "*Kita orang ada panggil* 'Stop Stop' *tiga empat kali* [We shouted 'Stop Stop' three or four times]", but the driver paid no attention. To prevent such occurrences, the Customs officer obtained approval from the District Officer ("D.O.") to place obstacles in the road so lorries would have to stop, and for his pains was scolded by a Japanese officer. "He asked me 'Who asked you to do this?' I said 'D.O.' He said 'Ta Bore —Rain Kari Pukor-Ra'." The last phrase, properly *Ta' boleh—lain kali pukul-lah* ([you] cannot, next time [I] will beat [you]), makes fun of the Japanese officer's inability to pronounce the letter 'l'. In another incident a customs officer tried to stop a lorry carrying rice and was told by the driver that "he did not care for our instructions because the military … had permitted him to take".[56]

In Kedah, although duty became payable on imports and exports after the transfer of the state to Thai control, the Japanese ignored this requirement, and coupons issued by the Kedah government to be submitted when goods were exported on behalf of the military were rarely used. According to the Superintendent of Monopolies and Customs, Tunku Mohd Jewa: "Despite the efforts of the Customs Officers … in informing them [the Japanese] that Customs Duty must be paid … yet they paid no heed whatsoever to such demands and strongly insist upon exportation or importation as the case was." He added: "Such actions on their part indeed bring difficulty and even danger to the Customs Officers who are bent conscientiously in carrying out their duties."[57]

Some sense of the hazards faced by officers engaged in anti-smuggling activities is conveyed by the following account of an encounter that took place off the coast of Kedah on the night of 15 March 1943, a few months before the transfer of the state to Thai control. Six men responded to a report that two boats were lying off-shore waiting for a load of Kedah rice. On board the first boat they found three male Chinese and some sacks of rice. Two men remained with this boat, and the other four chased the second boat.

---

[55] DO Bentong to Financial Officer Pahang, 30 June 2603, DO Bentong 166/2603.

[56] The papers describing these events are in DO Bentong 170/2603.

[57] Superintendent Monopolies and Customs, Kedah to Under Secy to Govt, Kedah, 29 Dec. 2486, and Tengku Abdul Majid, Asst Supt Monopolies and Customs, South Syburi to Supt Monopolies and Customs, Syburi, 12 Dec. 2487, SUK Kedah 240/2486.

> We ordered it to stop and bring down the sail, at that moment I noticed two Thai Soldiers, fully equipped, standing on board; one of them pointing his rifle at my boat shouted to me in Thai. I was frightened and jumped into the sea clinging to the anchor-rope of my boat leaving Ismail, Saad and the Civilian to row back and during that time I managed by clinging and swimming to get back into the boat.
>
> Meanwhile the officers on board the first boat had been told it contained thirty sacks of rice destined for Pangkor Island off the coast of Perak to the south. Then another vessel arrived carrying four men, two of them Thai soldiers, who claimed the rice was theirs and was to be carried north into Thailand. The officers wanted to make an arrest but the soldiers said they could not, and took the customs officers back to their own boat, which returned to its base at Kuala Kedah.[58]

Manufacturing

Although exports of commodities such as tin, rubber and palm oil dominate Malaya's economic statistics, the colony had a substantial amount of industry that served demand within the peninsula and in neighbouring territories. In 1943 there were 53 soap factories, 30 mills extracting oil from coconuts, and factories producing oxygen, acetylene, carbonic acid gas, cigarettes, bricks and paint.[59] Japanese firms took over managements of factories producing materials with military uses, such as drums for oil and petrol, rubber products and ships.

Japan was unable to supply manufactured goods to Southeast Asia during the war, and had to promote industrial development within the region to meet local needs. The intention was to make the Southern Region as a whole, and ideally each sector within it, self-supporting. Wherever possible, existing plant was to be rebuilt or refitted, and if necessary machinery would be sent from Japan to set up new factories.

Although Malaya had deposits of iron ore, there was no local steel industry, in part because the soft coal mined in Malaya was unsuitable for use in smelting. When war requirements and shipping shortages made it impossible to obtain steel from Japan, the military administration developed an ambitious scheme to produce iron and steel locally. Japanese firms installed rolling mills along with open hearth and Bessemer steel converters, and in the absence of coking coal

[58] Tahuddin b, Md. Salleh, O.D.O. (Out Door Officer) 11, Kuala Kedah to Asst Supt Monopolies and Customs North Syburi, 18 Mar. 2487, and Ahmad b. Haji Md. Isa, O.D.O. Kuala Kedah to Asst Supt Monopolies and Customs North Syburi, 18 Mar. 2487, SUK Kedah 302/2487.

[59] Huff and Majima, *The Chōsabu Reports*, pp. 309–11, 315–20.

used charcoal made from mangrove trees as fuel. Most of the output from these operations went to the military.[60]

There were also plans for a chemical industry, which among other things was to produce explosives. The Japan Nitrogen Company began constructing a large factory in July 1943, but needed a full year to get the plant ready, and as of August 1945 had only produced 100 tons of carbide, while a facility to prepare ammonia remained unfinished. The Nippon Soda Company manufactured caustic soda, hydrochloric acid, bleaching powder and sulphur chloride in plants at Seremban and Johore Bahru. Work on these facilities started in February 1944, and production commenced in October, using sulphur from Java, salt from Java and from Port Dickson, and lime from Kuala Lumpur. Oxygen and carbonic oxide were produced by the Nippon Rikka Kokyo Kabushiki Kaisha in premises belonging to the Far East Oxygen and Acetylene Company in Penang and Singapore. Both plants had been disabled during the British retreat, but the Japanese repaired the Singapore factory in less than a month, and had the one in Penang operating by October 1942. Between June 1942 and August 1945 the firm produced 1.2 million cubic metres of oxygen and 35,000 kilograms of carbonic oxide. The Dai Nippon Toryo Kabushiki Kaisha took over the Malayan Paint Works in Singapore, and Nippon Yusai Kabushiki Kaisha built a new paint factory, also in Singapore, that began production in November 1944 using equipment transferred from Japan. During the ten months of its operation before the Japanese surrender, the Nippon Yusai plant produced 300 tons of paint, most of it for use on the hulls of ships.[61]

The Japanese also promoted light industry, encouraging local manufacture of a wide range of goods for daily use. A Tropical Products Exhibition, staged in Singapore in May 1943 and subsequently at towns throughout the peninsula, featured new products, existing products manufactured in new ways or put to new uses, and products that could be used in place of other products. Submissions for the show included paper, produced with pulp derived from local plants such as rubber trees and various kinds of grass, along with "cardboard, coir rope, oil, grease, ink, rubber oil, biscuits, footwear, disinfectants, wine, tooth brushes, earthenware, ironware, lighters, red palm oil emulsion, tooth powder, toilet and washing soap and perfumes". From Penang there was "fish liver oil, and ghee,

---

[60] Charcoal was normally produced in Malaya by burning wood in shallow pits covered with a thin layer of earth and decaying leaves, or in brick kilns. In both cases valuable by-products such as pyroligneous acid, acetic acid and other acids mixed with tar, were generally wasted, although at Batu Arang the colliery used a retort that allowed collection of by-products. Note on Charcoal Producing Methods in Malaya by Major Colin Marshall, CO273/667/50744/7.

[61] Summary of Economic Intelligence No. 134, WO203/2647.

margarine, vitamalt, red palm oil emulsion, tomato ketchup, vitamin powders, vinegar, lipstick, condensed milk and soap". Starting in mid-September 1943, a Self-Sufficiency Fair displayed similar goods at the Great World Amusement Park in Singapore. Machines were installed at the park to allow visitors "to see the actual manufacture of goods and to encourage them to manufacture them at home".[62] A further exhibition of new commodities took place in Singapore in February 1944, the purpose being to emphasize that while progress had been made, there was still room for further improvement. The exhibits also served to "encourage the maintenance of self-sufficiency in the various States in Malai".[63]

Local factories produced a soy sauce substitute made from coconut milk, peanuts, potatoes and starch. According to a press account, "The previous method employed was the Chinese, the disadvantages of which were unavoidable, and the Japanese method has many advantages of nutrition, taste and economy over the former." The disadvantages were not explained, but presumably had to do with difficulties in acquiring ingredients, which in the case of soy sauce were salt, soya beans and rice. Two soy sauce factories in Kelantan with a combined monthly production of 6,000 gallons required 2,720 gantangs (a unit of measure roughly equivalent to a gallon) of salt, 25 tons of soya beans and 11.6 tons of rice each month.[64]

Malaya's well-established match industry foundered early in the occupation when supplies of potassium chlorate for making match heads ran out. One of the two factories in Selangor closed in August 1942 after exhausting its stock of chemicals, while the other, the Elkayes Match Factory, managed to remain in operation until December. A match factory in Kelantan with a capacity of 90,000 boxes per month was also forced to stop production because it could not procure chemicals. Matches were in great demand on the black market, and the administration devised schemes for their rationing and distribution.[65]

---

[62] *Syonan Sinbun*, 8 June and 14 Aug. 2603; Pertunjokan Pendapat Baharu dan Barang2 yang di-perbuat dalam Tempoh Peperangan, 17 Mar. 2603, and 2nd Exhibition of New Commodities, DO Temerloh 116/2602; Domei News Agency release, 4 May 1943, FIR 19, 4 Dec. 1943, CO273/673/50744/7.

[63] *Syonan Shimbun*, 21 Dec. 2603.

[64] Memorandum of a discussion with the representatives of the Ministry of Commerce which took place at the Sangyo-Bu building on 27th Thoulakhom, 2486 [27 Oct. 1943], Pej. Menteri Kelantan 74/2482; FIR 4, 8 May 1943, NARA RG226 38483; NARA RG226 59688 contains translations of material that appeared in the Chinese-language *Syonan Daily* between 4 and 15 Sept. 1943.

[65] Memorandum of a discussion with the representatives of the Ministry of Commerce, 27th Thoulakhom, 2486 [27 Oct. 1943], Pej. Menteri Kelantan 74/2486; AR, Customs and Excise Department, 2602, Sel Kan 117/2603.

Map 6.3 Malaya's industrial facilities, ca. April 1944

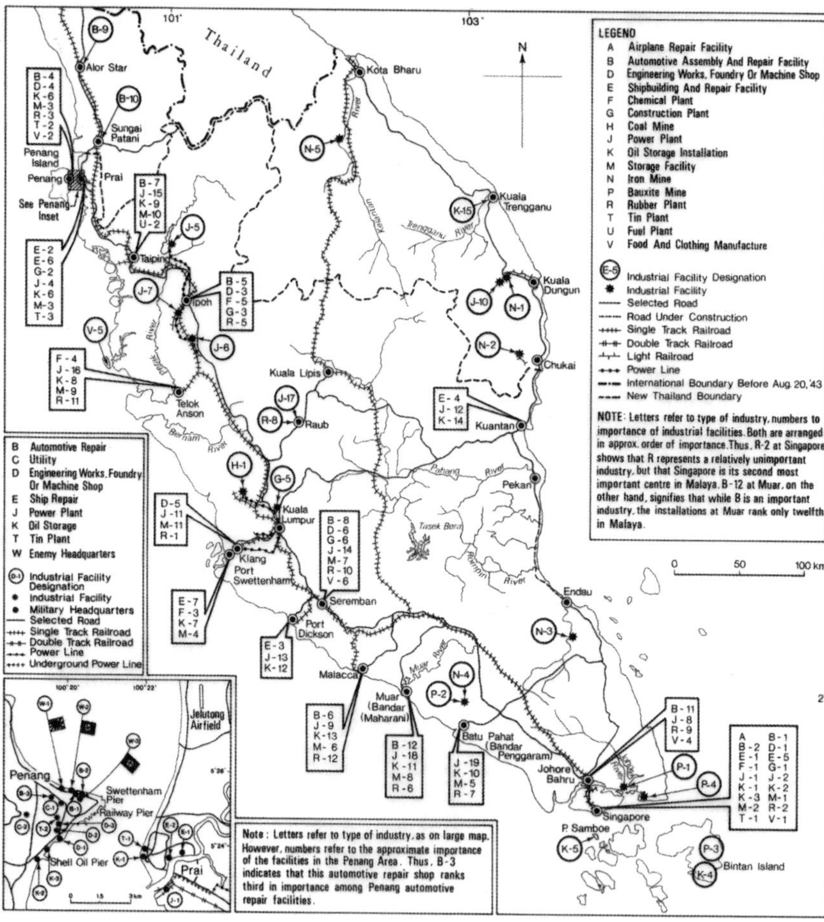

Map 6.4 Singapore's strategic facilities, ca. 1940

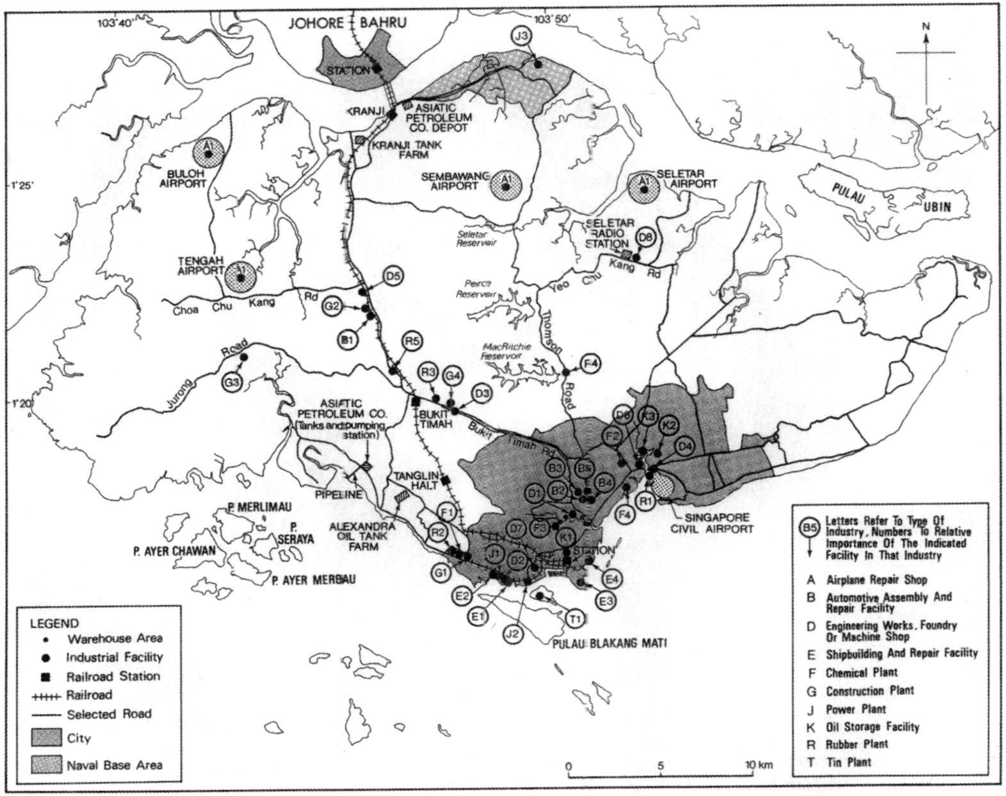

In 1943 Bentong District received 7,000 boxes of matches to be sold through retail rice dealers on the basis of one box per ration card. The District Officer said the 7,000 boxes would be useful, but observed that 11,317 rice cards had been issued in Bentong and asked for more matches, which proved unavailable.[66] In the absence of matches, people used various ingenious devices to light fires. One consisted of a water buffalo horn in which a hole had been drilled to hold wood dust which was rubbed with a piece of iron until it was hot enough to catch fire. Another was a tube in which a wire was placed with a bit of phosphorus at the end. A plug kept the tube airtight, but the phosphorus ignited when it was pulled out and exposed to the air.[67]

There was a considerable increase in cottage industry during the occupation, with people in villages making mats, coconut oil, coconut sugar, soap and other products for personal use and to sell at weekly fairs. The District Officer of Kuala Langat reported with satisfaction, "One will notice more women bringing in their produces for sale and also more women visiting the fair to make their purchases. The neighbouring estate labourers and Chinese peasants too bring in a fairly good amount of food-stuffs and vegetables for sale."[68] To make mats and other containers, people revived traditional techniques that had all but vanished with the introduction of imported manufactured goods under the British regime.

In 1940 Malaya consumed approximately 26,000 tons of soap. Nearly all of it (22,000 tons of detergent and 580 tons of toilet soap) was produced locally.[69] During the Occupation soap was in short supply because there was no caustic soda. In Perak the government introduced a new soap based on caustic potash (potassium hydroxide), which it marketed as "Perak Soap". Villagers made soap substitutes by burning coconut shells or pieces of wood and mixing the ash with palm oil and lime, and also by pounding together a mixture of leaves, flowers and cinnamon bark.[70] For toothpaste, people used salt or finely ground charcoal,

---

[66] Pahang Shu Chokan [Governor] to DO Bentong, 12 Jan. 2603; DO Bentong to Pahang Shu Chokan, 12 Jan. 2603, DO Bentong 18/2603.

[67] See Zainuddin bin H. Ahmad, "Pendudukan Jepun di Kampung Permatang Tuan Samad". I was shown the phosphorus lighter in Titi Serong, Perak in 1974.

[68] AR Kuala Langat, 2602, Sel Kan 32/2603.

[69] "An Overview of Important Industrial Factories in Syonan Municipality", by Gunsei Kanbu, General Department Research Office, March 1943, in *The Chosabu Reports*, trans. and ed. Huff and Majima, Chapter 6.

[70] *Perak Times*, 6 Jan. 2603; Chan Moi, "Kesan Pendudukan Jepun Terhadap Kaum Cina di Kawasan Kulai, Johor"; Lynley Ruth Gomez, "Satu Tinjauan Umum mengenai Keadaan Sosioekonomi di Tanah Melayu dan Sarawak pada Masa Pendudukan Jepun".

and for toothbrushes they chewed the end of certain kinds of branches until the fibres could serve as a brush.[71]

Wartime manufacturing had a makeshift quality to it. The products served as fairly satisfactory substitutes for unavailable imported goods, but were inferior in quality and would have been unsalable under normal circumstances. Discussing Japanese industrial undertakings in Selangor's Klang district, where there were two steel factories, a rubber oil refining factory, a pencil factory, a wood tanning factory, and a shipbuilding yard, the Asst District Officer, Raja Ayoub, said after the war:

> The Japanese were very secretive in their ways and in all enterprises undertaken by them, they did not want the local people to know. They kept everything to themselves and whenever they had anything to do with the Land Office they would only give the bare minimum of information and if more details were asked they usually gave the proverbial answer "military secret"—pronounced by them 'mi-li-ta-rrysee-kerr-etto'. When that reply was received it was advisable not to pursue the matter further, lest the enquirer might render himself liable to be suspected of trying to know more than he should know—a dangerous thing to do in those days.

According to Raja Ayoub:

> ... this office was not aware of the actual activities undertaken by these Japanese firms and whatever was known was mostly hearsay. However it can be said that no satisfactory work was done by any of them and at the time of the surrender these premises were entered upon and the trespassers did a good deal of looting. Of course, most of the machineries assembled by the Japanese were materials looted by them from the lawful owners during the period of occupation. All of these factories are no more intact.[72]

Despite the large number of items produced locally, industrial output remained far from adequate throughout the occupation period. According to a Japanese source:

> To cultivate the industries in the territory, it was necessary to import a great deal of equipments from Japan. If Japan sent these equipments her military supplies will be greatly hindered. In addition many valuable transportation days would be required. Under these circumstances it was inadvisable to send these equipments. Consequently the territory could not carry out the cultivation plan. Furthermore production of the necessary materials did not progress as expected due to various

[71] Aisha Akbar, *Aisha Bee at War*, p. 137.

[72] Investigation of Problems affecting Land arising out of Japanese Occupation, Anwer to Question No. 22 by Raja Ayoub, Asst DO Klang, 4 Apr. 1946, BMA Sel CA436/1945.

> unfavorable conditions. The daily livelihood of the inhabitants was gradually getting worse and they began to doubt our ability. Strictly speaking, the self-support of the army depended a great deal on the welfare of the inhabitants and the production and development of raw materials. From the standpoint of military administration industries for public welfare had first priority. However as the war situation began to grow worse public welfare became secondary due to the urgent demand of the operation army. Under this circumstance this was the most natural course to take.[73]

Labour

Unemployment was an immediate consequence of the Japanese invasion. Cut off from overseas markets, Malaya's estates and mines reduced production or stopped operations altogether, throwing their own labourers out of work, and also people employed in the ports and in the many industries that serviced the export sector. However, as the occupation progressed, the Japanese recruited large numbers of men and some women for military construction projects, both within Malaya and elsewhere, while others became farmers to avoid conscription, and by 1944 the country was experiencing a severe labour shortage. The Japanese responded to this situation by creating volunteer labour organizations, and ultimately by forcing male workers to abandon non-essential occupations.

Unemployment affected all levels of society. Large numbers of teachers and clerks lost their jobs, and the Japanese were not particularly sympathetic to their plight. The Governor of Perak said in late 1942:

> ... I would advise all these educated people who are jobless to go back to the land, where there is every prospect in growing foodstuffs and in rearing cattle and poultry. It is a most pitiable thing in this country that those "educated" people dislike manual labour. This state of mentality is most repugnant to our Nippon Seisin—Nipponese Fundamental Thought. We will have nothing to do with these people.[74]

Labourers on estates received rice in return for doing routine maintenance, but officials strongly encouraged them to grow food. They had a "golden opportunity" to become self-sufficient and would only have themselves to blame for their suffering if they did not seize this opportunity and "show themselves industrious".[75] The military administration was reluctant to acknowledge the existence of unemployment among able-bodied workers. According to

---

[73] JM 103, pp. 15–16.

[74] Minutes, Meeting of District Officers, 5 Nov. 2602, Batu Gajah 69/2602.

[75] AR, Sel Rubber Department, 2602, Sel Kan 111/2603.

the Labour Department in Selangor, a "majority of those who registered as unemployed were persons who had lost interest for work on estates and mines and those who through a declining state of health had drifted to a life of vagrancy".[76] In Perak, officials claimed there was no lack of work, just a need to redistribute labour, but in fact so many people had lost their jobs that Perak introduced a programme of public works to alleviate distress.[77]

The Japanese made extensive use of forced labour. As part of a campaign to discredit Europeans, the military administration organized teams of European prisoners of war to clean up the town areas immediately after the British surrender. In November 1942 the Japanese began work on a railway line to link the Thai and Burmese railway networks. The original plan called for the job to be completed by November 1943, and European POWs were sent to Thailand to provide labour for the project. The target date was later moved ahead to August, and in July, when it became apparent that this deadline could not be met, State Labour Offices in Malaya began enlisting workers to go to Thailand, operating through District Offices, the Public Works Department, rubber estates, mining companies, military contractors and communal organizations.[78] The administration told recruits that their period of service would be short and they would be able to return home when it was finished, a promise that was not fulfilled. Dependents of workers sent to Thailand received an allowance of $15 per month, plus a gratuity of $120 and a certificate of service if a labourer died, but the allowance was stopped if the labourer absconded. In Klang the initial call for recruits went out from the District Office to local branches of the Indian Independence League and the Oversea Chinese Association on 21 July 1943, and the first batch of 500 labourers left for Thailand on 17 August. In Perak the estates operated by the Ipoh branch of the Singapore Rubber Association supplied more than 8,000 workers in response to the first request. Both areas were immediately told to recruit several thousand additional labourers.[79] Estates in southern Kedah also provided large numbers of workers, and the District Officer for Kulim wrote the government in December 1943 to say that dependents of 3,000 Indians who had left for Thailand six months earlier had yet to receive a letter or news of any kind, and not a single person had returned, although workers

[76] AR, Sel Kosei Kyoku, 2602, Sel Kan 59/2603.

[77] DO Kuala Kangsar 168/2602; *Syonan Times*, 29 Oct. 2602.

[78] Kirby, *The War Against Japan*, vol. 2, pp. 427–8. Workers were also recruited in Burma.

[79] N.A. Appan for Controller of Labour, Perak, to DO Kinta, 17 July 2603, Batu Gajah 101/2603; correspondence in Klang 193/2603.

had been promised leave to visit their families every 50 days. The allowance for dependents also seems not to have been paid regularly.[80]

Illus. 6.2 Sign-up sheet for labourers going to work on the Thailand-Burma Railway.

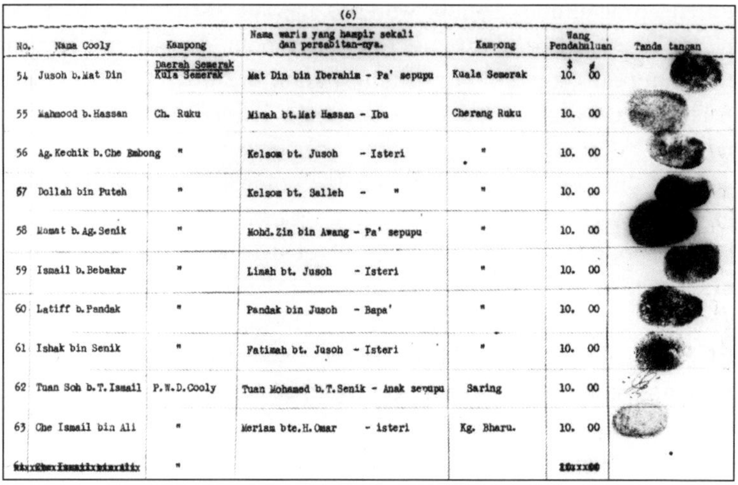

(6)

No.	Nama Cooly	Kampong	Nama waris yang hampir sekali dan persabitan-nya.	Kampong	Wang Pendahuluan	Tanda tangan
54	Jusoh b. Mat Din	Daerah Semerak Kula Semerak	Mat Din bin Iberahim - Pa' sepupu	Kuala Semerak	$ ¢ 10. 00	
55	Mahmood b. Hassan	Ch. Ruku	Minah bt. Mat Hassan - Ibu	Cherang Ruku	10. 00	
56	Ag. Kechik b. Che Embong	"	Kelsom bt. Jusoh - Isteri	"	10. 00	
57	Dollah bin Puteh	"	Kelsom bt. Salleh - "	"	10. 00	
58	Mamat b. Ag. Senik	"	Mohd. Zin bin Awang - Pa' sepupu	"	10. 00	
59	Ismail b. Bebakar	"	Limah bt. Jusoh - Isteri	"	10. 00	
60	Latiff b. Pandak	"	Pandak bin Jusoh - Bapa'	"	10. 00	
61	Ishak bin Senik	"	Fatimah bt. Jusoh - Isteri	"	10. 00	
62	Tuan Soh b. T. Ismail	P.W.D. Cooly	Tuan Mohamed b. T. Senik - Anak sepupu	Saring	10. 00	
63	Che Ismail bin Ali	"	Meriam bte. H. Omar - isteri	Kg. Bharu.	10. 00	
[illegible]		"			[illegible]	

Source: Arkib Negara Malaysia file Pasir Puteh 176/2603.

The railway began operations on 25 October 1943, but required considerable upkeep, and Allied bombing raids caused damage that had to be repaired. Malayan labourers lived in camps along the railway line doing maintenance work, and in February 1944 the Japanese told the Indian Independence League, the Oversea Chinese Association and the Penghulus that still more workers were needed ("Qualifications are not necessary").[81]

Some 20,000 labourers worked in southern Thailand to construct a railway line across the Isthmus of Kra. Work began on the Kra railway in June 1942. It was 92 km long, and opened on 10 Jan. 1944 with 150 engineers, 150 station workers, and 700 maintenance workers. The staff came from the Railway Bureau of the Malay Inspectorate of Military Administration. Labourers were

[80] DO Kulim to Under Secy Kerajaan Kedah, 27 Dec. 2486/29 Dec. 1362 (27 Dec. 1943), DO Kulim to Under Secy Saiburi (Kedah) Government, 8 Muharram 1363/4 Moreka Khom 2487 (4 Jan. 1944), SUK Kedah 4/2487.

[81] Correspondence between DO Klang, President of the Klang branch of the IIL, and the Chairman of the Klang branch of the OCA, Klang 193/2603.

also recruited March 1943 to build an airfield in Borneo, and in April 1944, to construct a Trans-Sumatran Railway.[82]

Working conditions on these projects were extremely harsh. Many of the labourers sent abroad died of malnutrition and disease, while those who managed to get home often needed hospital treatment for malaria, malnutrition and skin ulcers.[83] According to the 4th Railway Corps in Thailand, apart from prisoners of war Malaya sent approximately 75,000 workers, mostly Malays and Indians, to Thailand, and the death rate was nearly 38 per cent.[84] Figures supplied to interrogators in Malaya showed 73,500 workers—more than 1.3 per cent of the entire population—sent to Thailand, and a confirmed mortality rate of 30 per cent (see Table 6.1).

Table 6.1 Labourers transported from Malaya to work on the Thai-Burma and Kra railways (8 October 1945)

	Total supplied	*Deceased*	*Returned to Malaya*	*Deserted*	*Balance*
Malacca	4,573	2,022	881	311	1,359
Negri Sembilan	10,871	3,593	1,608	439	5,231
Selangor	15,755	6,009	3,478	960	5,308
Perak	19,187	6,263	3,388	1,231	8,305
Penang	2,892	889	436	169	1,398
Pahang	2,278	576	381	124	1,197
Kedah	12,074	3,550	1,390	819	6,315
Kelantan	4,795	1,504	497	609	2,185
Trengganu	1,077	84	210	–	783
Total	73,502	24,490	12,269	4,662	32,081

Source: Translation Report No. 75, 8 Oct. 1945, Sel CA250/1945.

Following the Japanese surrender, the Allies prepared assembly points at Kanchanaburi, Bangkok, Chumpon and Haadyai for systematic repatriation of labourers, and by 3 October 1945 had processed around 27,900 workers.[85]

[82] JM 167, p. 2.

[83] DO Larut, Labourers sent abroad during the Japanese Occupation Period, 8 Oct. 1945, Larut 26/1945; List Showing the Persons Taken to Siam by Japanese for Compulsory Labour Who Have Not Yet Returned to Pasir Puteh District, DO Pasir Puteh 369/1945; Report of the Selangor Medical Department for the Years 1941–46, RC Sel 296/1947.

[84] SEATIC Publication 246, "Burma-Siam Railway", 8 Oct. 1946, WO203/6325, pp. 6, 25.

[85] Information collected by Majors S.E. Chanier and A. Arbuthnott, C0537/1571.

Others, including some who had deserted from the worksites, eventually returned on their own. Teh bin Said, a Kelantanese who fled from the Burma railway and spent the balance of the occupation in the Malay-speaking area of southern Thailand, went home shortly after the Japanese surrender.[86] Selamat Hj Salleh from the Mukim of Gersik in Johore, who was recruited to work in Sumatra, deserted and hid in the interior of the island. When he finally managed to get back to Malaya in 1946, his family had already conducted a funeral ceremony for him.[87]

Forced labour was also used for projects within Malaya. For example, in September 1943 the Japanese needed workers to do earth work in Kuala Lumpur and Singapore; they assigned the Kinta District a quota of 200 men,[88] and Larut and Matang a slightly lower quota of 150 men in view of "the large number of labourers already taken out from your district for employment in Thailand". The District Officer for Larut was told to "do the needful", but people were less afraid of the Japanese than before, and when the Penghulu of Trong was asked to produce some candidates, he replied that no one wanted to go and work in those places. Larut did supply 75 Malay labourers for a project in Klang in September 1943, and the government requested 75 more later the same month. In December 1944, Larut sent 57 labourers to work on the Kedah aerodrome, and three months after the Japanese surrender the District Officer reported that no word had been received about this group since its departure.[89] To build an airfield near Kuala Pilah, in Negri Sembilan, the administration summoned 3,000 men from surrounding areas. They had to bring their own tools and cooking equipment, and collected rainwater or dug wells to get water for drinking and bathing.[90] In 1944, the Nippon Kogyo Kabushiki Kaisha issued a recruitment notice in 1944

---

[86] Yuszah Akmal bte Yusoff, "Teh bin Said, 1942–1945: Pengalaman Sebagai Buruh dan Pengalaman Melarikan Diri Dari Jepun di Burma" in *Pendudukan Jepun di Tanah Melayu, 1942–1945*, ed. Paul H. Kratoska and Abu Talib Ahmad, pp. 129–35.

[87] Ahmat Puat bin Moh. Basir, "Mukim Gersik Semasa Pemerintahan Jepun di Tanah Melayu, 1942–1945: Satu Tinjauan Mengenai Keadaan Ekonomi dan Sosial Penduduknya". The ceremony carried out by the family, *sembahyang ghaib*, is performed in cases where a person is believed dead but the body is missing, in contrast with *sembahyang jenazah*, used when the corpse is present.

[88] Controller of Labour Perak to DO Kinta, 16 Sept. 2603, Batu Gajah 101/2603.

[89] JM 103, p. 46; AR Kosei Kyoku, Sel, 2602, Sel Kan 59/2603; Controller of Labour Pk to DO L&M 16 Sept. 2603, and Penghulu Trong to DO Larut, 30 Sept. 2603, Larut 315/2603; DO Larut, Labourers sent abroad during the Japanese Occupation Period, 8 Oct. 1945, Larut 26/1945.

[90] Aripin b Othman, "Suatu Tinjauan Teoritis: Kehidupan Buruh (Paksa) Pembinaan Lapangan Terbang Zaman Jepun di Kuala Pilah, N. Sembilan".

for 1,700 labourers (including women and children) to go to the iron mines at Dungun in the state of Trengganu, where they were employed in "building shelters, lumbering, transporting, making charcoal and other odd-jobs".[91]

Many of the workers sent to construction sites contracted malaria, because earthworks created breeding places for mosquitoes, as did wells dug by the labourers. Reporting on a project that employed around 2,500 labourers in 1942 and 1943 to build a landing field at Port Swettenham, the state Medical Department said that three to four workers died of malaria or malnutrition every day.[92]

As Malaya's labour surplus turned into a labour shortage, the Japanese found it increasingly difficult to obtain workers. In 1943 the administration paid $1 per day with free food and lodging, but by 1945 the rate had increased to $20 per day with food and lodging, and there were few takers. Many estates closed down entirely, and the remnants of the estate workforce, often the wives and children of labourers recruited for Japanese projects, spent their time growing food.[93] In 1943 the Japanese tightened control over the country's workers through a newly formed Malai-Sumatra Labour Association. Singapore created a Labour Office in April to maintain a register of unemployed labourers, and Labour Departments in the various states in the peninsula acted as employment agencies, collecting names of people seeking work.[94] In August the Japanese established a Central Labour Control Committee and Regional Labour Control Committees, and in September they formed a committee for the allocation of manpower. With effect from 1 January 1944 all labourers in Singapore had to register with the Syonan Special Municipality, a measure that allowed the administration to keep track of around 150,000 workers.[95] Administrations in the peninsula introduced similar provisions and in June Selangor instructed businesses not to

---

[91] DO Larut, "Labourers sent abroad during the Japanese Occupation Period", 8 Oct. 1945, Larut 26/1945; Particulars regarding Recruitment of Labourers [for the Dungun Iron Mine], Klang 193/2603.

[92] Report of the Selangor Medical Department for the Years 1941–46, RC Sel 296/1947. In 1944 the military called for construction of over 2,000 air raid shelters in the Port Swettenham area. These structures also collected water and made the malaria situation in the area even worse.

[93] Controller of Labour Pk to DO Larut and Matang, 16 Sept. 2603, Larut 315/2603; correspondence in DO Bentong 238/2603.

[94] Rodo Jimu Kyoku Cho, Pahang to DO Temerloh, 21 Nov. 2604, Temerloh 73/2604.

[95] Broadcast from Tokyo in Japanese, 28 Dec. 1943, FIR No. 2, 16–31 Jan. 1944, CO273/673/50744/7; ELB, 28 Mar. 1943, OSS R&A Assemblage no. 45, Manpower in Japan and Occupied Areas, vol. II pt. III, 26 Aug. 1944; Malaya under the Japanese, NARA RG226 128585.

hire any person who did not have an Employee's Identity Book (*Romu Tetyo*), an order that must have been widely disregarded because the District Officer for Ulu Langat reported some four months later that he had not received a single application for this document.[96]

In December 1943 the Japanese began creating special organizations to meet the demand for labour. The first was a Labour Service Corps, the *Seicho*, that operated within the framework of the *Jikeidan*. There were branches throughout the country, and for every 250 inhabitants, 20 men aged 15 to 45 had to be designated as *Seicho* members. Government employees took part, as did members of the various communal associations. *Seicho* groups performed their assigned tasks, generally construction work or food cultivation, in their free time but on occasion the military mobilized the *Seicho* and forced people to work for longer periods.[97] This scheme mostly operated along ethnic lines, with the Malay Welfare Association creating a Free Labour Service Corps as a branch of the association, and the Oversea Chinese Association forming a Chinese Labour Service Corps, although the Syonan Sports Association also sponsored a labour service unit with 2,000 members.[98] Also in December, the Japanese administration in Perak formed an organization called the Kinrohoshitai, the object of which was "to get the people to take a keener interest in production of foodstuffs through their own effort and to hold manual labour in such dignity as it deserved in the scheme of life". Members, who worked on food production and on military construction projects, had to be between 18 and 45, and have good physiques.[99]

At the end of 1944, the worsening labour situation led the administration to obtain additional manpower for war-related activities by forcing some men to change jobs. In 1943 the *chosabu* team discussed the need to force certain residents of Singapore to change their occupations, but the researchers acknowledged that it was difficult to persuade Chinese traders or merchants to become workers. The report suggested "promoting awareness of the value of labour and its significance to the prosecution of a holy war", and providing

---

96 DO Ulu Langat to President Selangor Chinese Oversea Association, 28 Nov. 2604, Ulu Langat 139/2604.

97 Malaya under the Japanese, NARA RG226 128585; ELB, 23 Dec. 1943, 17 Jan. 1944, 1 Apr. 1944, OSS R&A Assemblage no. 45, Manpower in Japan and Occupied Areas; Syonan Shimbun, 19 Jan. 2604.

98 *Syonan Shimbun*, 4 Apr. and 10 Apr. 2604; Domei ELB, 7 Apr. 1944, FIR no. 7, 1–15 Apr. 1944, CO273/673/50744/7; Lau and Barry, A Brief Review of Chinese Affairs, BMA ADM/8/1.

99 Minutes, Conference of District Officers, 4 Oct. 2604, PT Larut 161/2602.

economic incentives by cutting rations and imposing strict price controls on businessmen who refused to comply.[100] Regulations introduced earlier regulating the occupations of male workers had been applied only in a limited way. On 30 December 1944 the Japanese began enforcing these provisions throughout the country, requiring men between the ages of fifteen and forty to abandon jobs "not having any bearing towards the war effort". According to the administration, "change of occupation should take place (a) towards food production (b) employment in war establishments and factories (c) in the production of essentials such as soap, paper making etc." A Change of Trade Ordinance set as a target the closing of 60 per cent of all shops in order to free employees to perform essential services. From 1 April 1945 men were in principle no longer allowed to work as porters, waiters, information clerks, janitors, launderers, touts, guides, salesmen, clerks, itinerant pedlars, hawkers, telephone operators, ticket collectors or elevator operators. Exceptions were made for those who were crippled or lame, those working at sea, and those who fell into other special categories.[101] Rigorously enforced, this law would have caused a great many businesses to close, but shopkeepers could avoid this fate by making substantial donations to the Oversea Chinese Association. Millions of dollars may have been collected in this way, but "what had been done with the money was only known to the association".[102]

The labour shortage also forced the Japanese to pay greater attention to female labour, and jobs vacated by male workers were often taken over by women. At the start of the occupation the Japanese had shown little interest in female workers, possibly because of the high levels of male unemployment, but in 1944 the newspapers began featuring stories about jobs done by women, and encouraging greater participation of women in the workforce. For example, a Miss Delia Lee, who worked as a typist in the Yokohama Specie Bank, was quoted as saying: "Today when labour service is essential, idleness is a sin. There are many opportunities for women to be of service today. The various schemes to make Malai self-sufficient in foodstuffs and other essential materials afford women the chance they lacked before."[103] Enforcement of the Change of Trade Ordinance greatly increased the importance of female workers. It also gave rise to

---

100 Huff and Majima, *The Chōsabu Reports*, p. 191.

101 Malaya under the Japanese, NARA RG226 128585.

102 Minutes, Penghulus' Conference, 16 Jan. 2605, Batu Gajah 11/2604; Lau and Barry, A Brief Review of Chinese Affairs, BMA ADM/8/1; Malaya under the Japanese, NARA RG226 128585.

103 *Syonan Shimbun*, 12 Jan. 2604. Additional articles in the same vein appeared on 15, 19, 20 and 25 Jan., and 19, 21, 23 and 28 Feb. 2604.

rumours that women were to be forced to take over jobs formerly done by men, a suggestion the *Syonan Shimbun* took pains to rebut:

> The authorities wish it to be clearly understood, however, that they are not compelling women to work or putting into effect any ordinance for mobilization of female labour power. The authorities respect the many religious and racial customs prevailing in this city and they will not compel women to work unless they voluntarily wish to do so.[104]

Illus. 6.3 "Syonan girls are working as typists, messengers, and telephone operators in the office of the Asahi Newspaper, recently established here. They are working as hard as soldiers on the battlefield. 'Yuki Tiran', who speaks good Nippon-go, is seen in the foreground. She pleasantly informed me: 'At night I attend a Niippon-go school. I am happy to learn Nippon-go'!"

Source: *Syonan Times*, 30 May 2602 (1942). Sketch by Kikuo.

104 *Syonan Shimbun*, 12 Feb. 2605; the original was set entirely in capital letters.

Medicines and Health Care

Immediately after the fall of Singapore, much of the British staff of the Health Department were interned, although the Japanese left some staff members of the General Hospital at liberty to move patients from the General Hospital to the Mental Hospital compound, and to bury the dead. The Japanese selected several Europeans, including Dr F.V. Jagues, Sidney Dent, Prof B.A.R. Cater, H. Lander, and the Rural Health Officer Dr W.L. Blakemore, and ordered them to create an organization to control public health in rural Singapore. Jagues and Dent were interned before the end of 1942, but the other three men remained free until until 10 June 1943, at which point they were interned at Changi.[105]

After the invasion, medicines and hospital supplies rapidly became scarce.[106] As early as July 1942 the Labour Inspector for Kelantan complained that estate workers were suffering from diseases such as malaria, pneumonia, dysentery, diarrhoea and ulcers, and that drugs to treat these illnesses were no longer available.[107] In Klang the venereal disease clinic and the travelling dispensary halted operations for the same reason.[108] However, when the British reoccupied Penang, they discovered that the storerooms at the General Hospital contained enough medicines left over from 1941 to meet the hospital's needs for a full year, supplies that inexplicably had been withheld from the public.[109] Chinese medicines remained available to a limited extent, but many ingredients came from inaccessible overseas sources and practitioners could not prepare mixtures without a complete pharmacopoeia. Stocks of ingredients existed in major centres such as Penang and Singapore, but the Japanese placed these under strict controls, and supplies could not be sent elsewhere without a special permit.[110]

Vaccines for typhoid, paratyphoid A and B, cholera and dysentery were prepared at the Institute for Medical Research in Kuala Lumpur, but their success rate was lower than before the war. In Kedah the government gave innoculations to 13,710 children in 1944 but just 5,762 were successful, and the programme was suspended during the last four months of the year.[111] Although

---

105 Faris, Report on the Working of the Government Health Department – Singapore, Part III, and Boeki-ka cho, Syonan Rural Health Unit, MSS. Ind. Ocn. S. 135.

106 Report of the Selangor Medical Department for the Years 1941–46, RC Sel 296/1947.

107 Labour Inspector, Kel, to Depy Controller of Labour, Kel, 27 July 2602, Somubu Kelantan 22A/2602.

108 AR Klang, 2602, Sel Kan 61/2603.

109 See Appendix 9 to T.J.N. Hilken's report on Proceedings at Penang, WO203/2675.

110 Tai Tiee Seng to DO Larut, ca. May 1943, Larut 177/2603.

111 Report of the Health Officer, Selangor East, for the Year 2602, Ulu Langat 216/2602; Medical Department Annual Report of the State of Syburi for 2487, SUK Kedah 119/2487.

official authorization was required to obtain vaccines, controls were ineffective and the preparations found their way onto the black market.[112] In Singapore the Japanese carried out compulsory vaccination against smallpox and typhus, and required those who cooked or served food to be inoculated against cholera.

Quinine and atebrin were used to treat malaria. By March 1943 quinine could only be purchased with a doctor's certificate, and doctors were required to maintain records of the quinine sulphate they used or sold. The officer in charge of coconut estates in Selangor routinely requested 63 bottles of quinine tablets (containing 500 tablets each) per month for workers on the properties operated by the Agriculture Department, but he increased the order to 250 bottles in November 1943 owing to the rising number of malaria cases. The next month he was told that supplies had run out.[113] In 1944 limited amounts of quinine remained available in Perak for distribution through Penghulus, who were instructed to keep the drug from falling into the hands of "non-cooperators".[114] In Kuala Lumpur during 1944 quinine sulphate sold on the black market for about $500 per pound, and quinine bi-hydrochloride for $900 per pound. Japanese troops received supplies through military channels, and their malaria rate was low owing to prophylactic doses of quinine and the use of mosquito nets and anti-mosquito creams.[115]

Folk medications replaced unavailable imported drugs, and the Kedah State Medical Report for 1944 noted that the following had been found effective: "Mangosteen skin (Carcinia Mangostena), Akar Seruntun (Tinospora Crispa), Daun Gelenggang Besar (Casiasciata), Gambir, Garlic, Batu Kawi [manganese] and Rice Bran."[116] Akar Seruntun is a root used as a diuretic and a tonic; Daun Gelenggang Besar refers to the leaves of the Gelenggang plant, known locally as ringworm bush, which were used to treat prickly-heat and shingles; rice bran is a source of Vitamin B and was used to treat beri-beri. For beri-beri people also consumed water in which ginger and mung beans had been boiled, or a "Vitamin Mixture" known as "Mist, vitamin B", made by soaking pineapple skin, potato peelings and bran. Headaches could be treated with a paste made from garlic and a certain type of leaf, cuts were bathed in rice wine, and tropical ulcers were smeared with an ointment made by mixing camphor with coconut

112 Interrogation of a Captain in the Indian Medical Service, age 30, who left Malaya in August 1944 and was captured in May 1945. NARA RG226 XL10702.

113 See correspondence in A.D. Sel Estates 115/2602.

114 Gyoseika Tyo, Perak to DO Kinta, 11 Mar. 2604, Batu Gajah Land Office 28/2604.

115 Malaya under the Japanese, NARA RG226 128585; Interrogation of a Captain in the Indian Medical Service, NARA RG226 XL10702.

116 AR for 2487, Medical Dept of the State of Syburi, SUK Kedah 119/2487.

oil and red onions. Such preparations were not always effective. One Chinese man treated a cut on his leg with a poultice made of pineapple and overripe banana, and the wound turned blue, began to give off a rotten smell and became infested with maggots.[117]

Local officials involved in health care continued working after the British evacuation, and under the Japanese were incorporated into the civil medical administration. In Singapore the General Hospital and the Alexandra Military Hospital were taken over by the Japanese military, while civilians used the Tan Tock Seng Hospital, the St Andrew's hospital in Chinatown, and the Kandang Kerbau Hospital. Military authorities in Kuala Lumpur also took control of the General Hospital, and appropriated hospital buildings elsewhere, leaving only the Malay Hospital at Kampong Baru, renamed the "First Civil Hospital", for civilians. A Second Civil Hospital opened in June, using the Tung Shin and Chinese Maternity Hospital buildings on Pudu Road. Inmates of the decrepit wards returned in May 1942, but these wards were shut down in November 1943, with about half of the inmates transferred to Serendah Hospital, and the other half given no alternative accommodation. The Japanese made a number of changes to arrangements for health care during 1943. A new department known as the Eiseika became responsible for the tasks of the pre-war Medical Department and of the Sanitary Boards, which were now abolished, and greater numbers of Japanese staff were now assigned to medical offices, replacing trained and experienced local staff. Labour was in increasingly short supply, with some department employees leaving to join the Indian National Army, and others sent away to Thailand or to work for Japanese firms. Moreover, low wages created difficulties for staff, who had to find "ways of augmenting their pay and the Kuala Lumpur Health Office became a bazaar where things of all sorts could be bought". In 1945, members of the Health Office staff were directed to cultivate a garden at the golf club, and to dig air raid shelters. "Health work for all practical purposes ceased."[118]

---

[117] He Wen-Lit, *Syonan Interlude*, pp. 158, 180–1; Lynley Ruth Gomez, "Satu Tinjauan Umum mengenai Keadaan Sosioekonomi di Tanah Melayu dan Sarawak pada Masa Pendudukan Jepun"; Ahmat Puat bin Moh. Basir, "Mukim Gersik Semasa Pemerintahan Jepun di Tanah Melayu, 1942–1945".

[118] T.J. Danaraj, *Memoirs of a Doctor*, p. 98; He Wen-lit, *Syonan Interlude*, pp. 102–10; Report of the Selangor Medical Department for the Years 1941–46, RC Sel 296/1947; DO Ulu Langat, Report on the Administration of the District on the lines indicated by His Excellency the Governor of Selangor, 7 June 2603, Ulu Langat 216/2602.

Cloth

Textile shortages caused a great deal of distress during the occupation. In 1938 Malaya consumed some 88 million yards of imported cotton cloth, around 16 yards for every person in the country.[119] Following the Japanese invasion, cloth imports ceased and the small domestic handloom industry foundered owing to shortages of dyes and yarn.

In September 1943, in connection with the order imposing restrictions on sales of materials necessary for daily life, the government placed limits on the distribution of textiles (including cloth and ready-made foreign clothes), allowing these items to be sold only to holders of "Textile Goods Distribution Cards". These cards were distributed through communal associations such as the Oversea Chinese Association, the Indian Independence League, and the Malay Welfare Association. Rules put into force under this order stipulated that only distributors appointed by the government could handle textiles, and all other dealers had to sell their stocks to authorized distributors for 10 per cent less than the retail price fixed by the government. The government used the pre-war market price times three as a standard for setting maximum retail prices. Chinese, Malay and Indian *kumiai* established branches in each district, and the government instructed authorized dealers to join the *kumiai* for their own race.[120] According to a letter written after the war by a group of traders seeking redress, the following developments ensued:

> In the year 1943 the Japanese ordered the formation of an Indian Textile Kumiai (association). Out of this, only a few merchants were appointed authorised cloth dealers. And those appointments were made in rather a strange manner. Having no sense of justice, the Japanese gave no preference to old established firms or the size of the firms, in permitting them to become authorised dealers, but those who could dance to their tune and curry favour with them, were appointed authorised dealers. Some cloth dealers whose businesses had been established in the Jap regime, and who knew nothing about cloth business, but who had influence both in the association and with the Japs and with the Indian Independence League were appointed authorised cloth dealers. Some of these dealers whose stocks amounted only to about fifty or sixty yards of cloth became authorised dealers and thousands of yards of cloth were supplied to them from stocks seized from old established firms carrying large stocks.
>
> The cloths were to be sold for coupons, but the public suffered terribly because the merchants hid the good cloths from public view and sold them at black market prices, charging the public more than the

---

[119] Malaya imported nearly 115 million yards of cotton textiles in 1938, and re-exported 26.5 million yards.

[120] *Perak Times*, 27 Sept. 2603.

> authorised prices. As for the non-authorised dealers, their cloth stocks were kept sealed for a long time, rendering the capital involved useless to the dealer. A large part of such cloth stocks were removed by the association only about one or two months before the Japs surrendered to the Allied Nations and distributed them among the favoured ones who already possessed large stocks. They were paid the value of the cloths at a time when the Jap currency value was at its lowest, making the cash received useless as capital for the merchants concerned— adding more difficulty to the merchants.[121]

The letter appended a list of 27 authorized cloth dealers in Kuala Lumpur, identifying two firms as book sellers, one as a flower seller and one as a provision store.

In Perak the basic cloth ration was 1 yard per person per year, and 3 yards of khaki cloth for labourers; people getting married were entitled to 6 yards, and families with new babies got 1.5 yards. Supplies were insufficient to maintain even this low standard. Larut, with a population of 138,099, received 28,986 coupons for the first quarter of 1944, while in June 1944 the Kinta District, with 400,000 residents, received 40,000 coupons.[122] Under these circumstances, cloth was distributed to "those *really in need* of clothing", as certified by a Penghulu or Ketua Kampong.[123] In certain parts of the country, particularly in rural areas, the shortage of clothing became so acute that some families had only one usable sarong, which had to be shared between husband and wife.[124] In Kedah the people of Kuala Nerang and Kuala Terap were "almost naked",[125] and in Perak the District Officer for Larut wrote in December 1943: "Two years have since elapsed, since the outbreak of the Dai Toa Senso [Great East Asian War] and almost all the clothings whatever the people had, have now been totally worn out. I know personally that most of the Kampong People who are farmers and coolies, have at present almost nothing decent to wear."[126] There was no cloth to carry out Muslim burial rites, which required wrapping the corpse in a white cloth, and by the end of the occupation mats woven from *mengkuang* (a

121 C.H. Kizar Mohamed & Co., M.P.M. Deen, and A.A. Mohamed Shariff Co. to CCAO Kuala Lumpur, 20 Sept. 1945, Sel CA105/1945.

122 Minutes, Conference of District Officers, 4 Oct. 2604, PT Larut 161/2602; Minutes, Penghulus' Conference, 27 June 2604, Batu Gajah 11/2604.

123 Minutes, Penghulus' Conference, 27 Oct. 2603, Batu Gajah 104/2602. Emphasis in original.

124 PAO Syburi to Secy to Govt Syburi, 28 June 2487, Kedah Sec 615/2487.

125 DO, Padang Terap to Und Secy to Govt, Syburi, 8 Aug. 2487; Che Merican, O.C.P.D. Kuala Nerang to O.S.P.C. Alor Star, 6 Aug. 2487, SUK Kedah 234/2486.

126 DO Larut to Sangyobu-Syoko Kacho, Perak, 31 Dec. 2603, Larut 329/2603.

type of screw-pine) or other leaves, normally laid on the floors of nouses, were being used in place of cloth as burial shrouds.[127]

In 1944 the Japanese launched a Three-Year Self-Sufficiency Plan for textiles which called for the transfer of "several tens of thousands" of idle spindles from Japan to Southeast Asia, with Malaya scheduled to receive 20,000 spinning machines. Companies throughout the peninsula, organized into a Malayan Fibres Council, were to grow fibre-producing plants such as cotton, kapok, hemp, ramie, flax and jute, and collect the fibres for sale to spinners. Other sources of fibre included banana skins and banana stems, biduri (Calotropis procera and Calotropis gigantea), leaves of castor-oil plants, pineapple leaves, and the fibrous bark of a large tree known in Malaya as "*kayu terap*" (Artocarpus elastica), which was normally used to make houses walls, rice bin liners and fishing nets.[128]

Pineapple fibres, extracted by scraping leaves with a piece of glass or with coconut shell, became the usual substitute for cotton thread,[129] but experiments carried out by the Department of Rural Industries and Development in Kedah to examine the feasibility of weaving pineapple fibre into cloth proved unsuccessful because the cloth was rough and uneven, and also expensive.[130] Silk was another alternative, and a school of sericulture conducted training courses in Singapore for students who were to be posted to worm farms planned in various parts of Malaya. Silkworms traditionally fed on mulberry leaves, but the Japanese claimed they could thrive equally well on a diet of tapioca and castor-oil leaves.

---

[127] Minutes, Penghulus' Conference, 27 Oct. 2603, Batu Gajah 104/2602; Minutes, Penghulus' Conference, 27 June 2605, Batu Gajah 11/2604; Ahmat Puat bin Moh. Basir, "Mukim Gersik Semasa Pemerintahan Jepun di Tanah Melayu 1942–1945: Satu Tinjauan Mengenai Keadaan Ekonomi dan Sosial Penduduknya".

[128] *Syonan Shimbun*, 8 Feb. and 25 Feb. 2604. Farms that supplied hemp and cotton received a special issue of plain cloth. In Negri Sembilan a large factory equipped with Japanese machinery was planned at Seremban to produce "about the same quantity as the pre-war consumption of fibre manufactured goods". FIR no. 11, 14 Aug. 1943, CO273/669/50744/7. See also FIR no. 4, 16–29 Feb. 1944, CO273/673/50744/7. The Perak administration produced a pamphlet on ramie cultivation, but noted that in the absence of local experiments it provided information on methods used in Taiwan. *Cho-Ma (Ramie or China Grass)*, Perak Shu Seicho, Ju-Ichi Gatsu [Nov.] 2603, Batu Gajah 141/2603.

[129] Jaafar bin Hamzah, "The Malays in Tasek Gelugur during the Japanese Occupation", Malaysia in History 21, 2 (Dec. 1978): 61; Jam binti Yaakob, quoted in Hairani Mohd. Khalid," Satu Tinjauan Am tentang Kehidupan Penduduk Mukim Relau, Kedah semasa Pendudukan Jepun", also mentions this point. She concludes by saying, with nicely muted sarcasm, "… pandai sungguh Jepun ajar orang kita [the Japanese were very clever at teaching us things]".

[130] AR, Department of Rural Industries and Development Kedah, 2486, and AR, Dept of Rural Industries and Development, 2487 (1362 A.H.), SUK Kedah 101/2487.

In connection with this scheme people living at Tasek Gelugur, near Penang, planted castor-oil plants that continued to flourish many years after the war ended, but they received no silkworms.[131]

To protect fibre-yielding plants and foodcrops from attacks by insects, the Japanese encouraged use of a natural insecticide prepared from the root of the Derris plant, known in Malaya as tuba-root, which contains a toxic substance called rotenone. The Malays used pounded tuba root to poison fish, and research had been underway since the nineteenth century into the possible utilization of this substance in insecticides for plants. Japan was an active participant in this effort and had accounted for between 15 and 30 per cent of Malaya's tuba exports before the war.[132]

Textile shortages were never overcome, and cloth prices rose to phenomenal levels during the last year of the occupation. In June 1944 material for women's sarongs sold for between $80 and $150 per yard in Kulim, and for men's sarongs the price was $125–$140 per yard. Silk sarees, on the other hand, were much cheaper at $45. A mosquito net sold for $250, about what a labourer earned in a year and a half before the war.[133] In May 1945, clothing in Singapore sold for more than 250 times pre-war levels, while cotton cloth was quoted in Selangor at prices ranging from $300 to $1,000 per yard at the end of August 1945.[134] Prices for Kota Star District, in Kedah, are shown in Table 6.2.

Table 6.2 Cloth prices in Kota Star, Kedah ($)

	Pre-war	*ca. Aug. 1944*	*1 Feb. 1945*
Sarong (each)	1.80	25.00	1,000.00
Silk (per yard)	0.75	5.00	300.00
Chintz (per yard)	0.24	4.00	250.00
Trousers (pair)	4.00	60.00	700.00

Source: District Office Kota Star, Annual Report for 2487, 28 Feb. 2488 [28 Feb. 1945], Kedah Sec 208/2488.

131 Appreciation of the Economic Position of Malaya under the Japanese, BMA COM/21; Domei ELB, 23 Feb. 1944, FIR 3, 16–29 Feb. 1944, 16 and 20 Mar. 1944, FIR 4,16–31 Mar. 1944, CO273/673/50744/7; Jaafar bin Hamzah, "The Malays in Tasek Gelugur", p. 61; *Syonan Shimbun*, 24 Feb. 2604.

132 Sangyobu-Nomu-Kacho Perak to DO Kinta, 5 Mar. 2603, Batu Gajah 40/2603; Burkill, *A Dictionary of Economic Products*, pp. 795–805. The Japanese also used tuba in medicines, and to disinfect bunks on steamships.

133 Price List of Piece Goods, Kulim, 16 June 2487, SUK Kedah 234/2486.

134 Sliding Scale of Values of the Japanese Dollar Throughout the Period of Occupation, CO852/726/3; Sel CA340/1945 has lists of market prices in Selangor.

The Cost of Living

On the first of February 1942, some two weeks prior to the British surrender, the Commander of the Japanese Army issued a decree intended to prevent profiteering:

> I. The prices of goods in each district of Malaya shall be kept at the prices that precede the outbreak of the Great Oriental Asiatic War. Any article cannot be dealt in with a higher price than the above-prescribed.
>
> II. Every market or shop shall put up a price-list of the goods to show prices with a most easy way to see.
>
> III. Any person who violated the above two provisions or trades in cunning business, who hides or hoards goods hesitating to sell, shall be liable to the extreme penalty of the military law.
>
> For the interest of every one and all in Malaya, I proclaim the above regulations. Never disobey.[135]

This decree notwithstanding, prices soon began to rise. According to the officer who was in charge of the Selangor Customs Department:

> As soon as transport facilities were restored under the present regime, there was much speculation in the local markets and stocks of all varieties of goods were being freely transferred from place to place where better prices prevailed. There was a serious danger to the State arising from this speculation, since it would not only raise the prices of commodities locally, but most of the goods would have been exported.[136]

The Japanese responded to this situation by banning the export of essential commodities, restricting inter-state trade and controlling imports. These measures produced a semblance of economic normality by the middle of 1942, but there was widespread unemployment, and the absence of a market for rubber and tin caused considerable hardship. A former civil servant wrote some four months after the British surrender:

> With what money I had in hand in January last I have pulled on till the end of April and am now eking out an existence by selling my household furniture piece by piece, through charities, and hard labour by selling odd eatables at streets, lanes and toddy shops.[137]

---

135 Decree by Commander of the Dai-Nippon Imperial Army, 1 Feb. 2602, CLR Batu Pahat 4.2602.

136 AR, Customs and Excise Department, 2602, Sel Kan 117/2603.

137 *Malay Mail* (*New Order*), 9 June 2602, Sel Kan 35/2602.

The Governor of Perak described the "profiteering in and hoarding of essential commodities which are prevalent in the streets" as acts of "disloyalty to the Government". Addressing the District Officers of his state, he said,

> To check this ... I took drastic measures, as you are all aware. I cannot allow those avaricious people who are making exorbitant profits at the expense of the public, to continue their unfair business. I request you to keep a close watch over these people and to see to it that every member of the public live helping one another. You must also take every means to check the illicit exportation of these commodities from the State, which is coupled with object of profiteering elsewhere at the expense of the fellow-citizens of this State.[138]

When prices did not come down, newspaper editorials inveighed against high prices and the pervasive illicit trading.

> The prices of all foodstuffs are controlled, and ceilings fixed that will ensure reasonable margins for both producers and middlemen. That these price ceilings are being so openly ignored—a visit to our markets is enough to convince anyone of this—seems to point to manipulations on the part of certain distributors who obtain supplies at controlled prices and who do not observe price ceilings in selling to retailers.[139]

By the end of 1943 the combination of inflation, shortages and rising transport costs had pushed the cost of everyday requirements to extremely high levels, as illustrated by the market prices for Kedah in Table 6.3.

Table 6.3 Market prices in Kedah[a]

	Pre-war	*July 1943*	*Nov. 1943*
Curry spices	0.12	3.20	5.60
Turmeric	0.14	1.70	1.90
Cinnamon	0.40	0.55	0.90
Long beans	0.04	0.15	0.30
Brinjal	0.04	0.15	0.24
Fresh chilli	0.20	0.50	1.20
Pineapple (each)	0.06	0.30	0.45

Note: [a] $ per kati (1⅓) pounds unless otherwise indicated.

Source: SUK Kedah 109/2486.

138 Minutes, Meeting of District Officers, 5 Nov. 2602, Batu Gajah 69/2602.

139 *Syonan Sinbun*, 27 July 2603.

Evaluating figures such as these, a report on weekly fairs in Kedah offered the following observation:

> ... it may be stated that although the valuation of capital used in these fairs is large yet it does not mean the prosperity and business have been multiplied twenty times since pre-war. The serious fluctuation of prices elsewhere also affects the goods sold at the fairs, as evidenced by the fact that before the war one may obtain 10 "restali" bananas for 15 cts. now they fetch about $4.00.[140]

In 1944 government supplemented the salaries of civil servants by paying "high cost of living" allowances, set at between $3 and $5 per month in January and doubled in October, as well as family allowances, which at the end of 1944 amounted to $4 per family member up to a maximum of $20.[141] However, 30 per cent of these allowances had to be held as savings, and the amounts were deducted from salaries and paid directly into the Yokohama Specie Bank.[142] Even with such benefits, civil servants and others with fixed incomes faced serious difficulties as prices continued to rise. According to a report prepared early in 1945:

> All the Government servants are hard-hit as their salaries are nowhere compared with the high cost of living. They have been forced to sell almost all their little jewelleries and clothing for over a year in order to meet the daily expenses. Now they have practically nothing to sell but to depend on their salaries during these very trying days.[143]

During the final year of the occupation large amounts of currency flooded onto the market and prices reached very high levels, a process that is reflected in the price list for Kedah's Kota Star District shown in Table 6.4. There were comparable increases elsewhere in the country, with mutton selling in Klang for $250 a kati at the end of August 1945, and ten chicken eggs offered for sale there for $90, a bargain compared to Rawang where ten chicken eggs cost $220. Burmese rice commanded anywhere from $50 to $100 per kati (1⅓ pounds).[144] Price movements in Singapore followed a similar pattern, as shown by the Cost of Living Indices in Table 6.5.

---

[140] AR, Department of Rural Industries and Development (Year beginning 19 Oct. 2486, ending 31 Dec. 2486 [19 Oct. 1943–31 Dec. 1943]), SUK Kedah 101/2487.

[141] Gyoseika Circulars dated 11 Jan. and 1 Oct. 2604, Batu Gajah 10/2604. Salary bands were $59 and under, $60–189, $190 and above, so the allowances amounted to slightly more than a 10 per cent supplement at the lower end of the scale.

[142] Gunsei Kanbu Circular No. 302, Ulu Langat 31/2604.

[143] DO Kota Star, AR for 2487, 28 Feb. 2488 [28 Feb. 1945], SUK Kedah 208/2488.

[144] See lists of market prices in Sel CA340/1945.

Table 6.4 Food prices in Kota Star, Kedah[a]

	Pre-war	*ca. Aug. 1944*	*1 Feb. 1945*
Rice (per gantang)	0.18	6.00	24.00
Salt	0.02	3.00	6.00
Sugar	0.08	12.00	28.00
Coffee	0.20	14.00	22.00
Chillies	0.16	12.00	50.00
Coriander	0.12	10.00	25.00
Onions	0.08	5.00	12.00
Coconut (each)	0.02	0.45	2.30
Coconut oil (per tin)	2.40	85.00	315.00
Cucumber	0.04	0.50	2.50
Cabbage	0.03	0.40	3.00
Bean sprouts	0.02	0.20	2.00
Eggplant (brinjal)	0.03	0.30	3.50
Fish			
Siakap (sea perch)	0.30	5.00	18.00
Bawal (pomfret)	0.26	5.00	18.00
Temenong (horse-mackerel)	0.05	0.50	5.00
Taniban (sardine)	0.02	0.25	3.00
Beef	0.26	3.00	10.00
Mutton	0.32	4.00	15.00

Note: [a] $ per kati of 1⅓ pounds unless otherwise indicated
Source: District Office Kota Star, Annual Report for 2487, 28 Feb. 2488 [28 Feb. 1945], Kedah Sec 208/2488.

Many people took to the streets to earn a living. In Kuala Lumpur the administration issued 5,160 licences to roadside hawkers in 1942, about six times the pre-war level, and also increased the number of licences for street stalls. Tricycle rickshaws, or "trishaws", provided some employment, although initially the number of licences was restricted "to prevent friction between rickshaw and tricycle pullers and to keep the public peace". Before the war, trishaws were regarded as a novelty in Malaya, but they became a major form of transport during the occupation. In Penang there were about 100 trishaws registered at the beginning of 1942, and around 2,500 one year later, when they may have outnumbered rickshaws.[145] The incidence of prostitution appears to have risen as well, and in July 1943 the administration required that prostitutes—defined as "any female who indiscriminately consorts with men for hire"—purchase licences.[146]

Table 6.5 Singapore cost of living indices, 1942–45

(Dec. 1941 = 100)

	Foodstuffs	*Tobacco*	*Light, fuel, water*	*Transport*	*Clothing*	*Rent*	*Weighted cost-of-living*
1942							
Feb.						100.0	
Mar.						105.1	
Apr.						110.4	
May						116.0	
June						121.9	
July	204.2	240.0	122.5	199.0	240.2	128.0	195.1
Aug.						134.6	
Sept.						141.5	
Oct.						148.6	
Nov.	267.7	388.0	141.8	261.0	393.4	156.2	259.6
Dec.						164.1	
1943							
Jan.	342.3	328.0	139.2	384.4	430.6	172.4	319.3
Feb.	350.0	328.0	141.0	350.2	529.2	181.1	328.0
Mar.	325.2	400.0	152.1	361.7	615.1	190.3	321.6
Apr.	330.0	304.0	172.8	384.2	668.2	200.0	329.2
May	339.8	328.0	172.8	412.6	824.9	210.1	346.1
June	393.2	419.2	263.1	610.2	1,175.7	220.8	420.1
July	428.3	544.0	362.5	672.5	1,347.7	232.0	466.1
Aug.	493.0	563.2	420.5	700.7	1,646.3	243.8	527.2
Sept.	540.9	568.0	390.8	638.3	1,673.6	256.2	556.5
Oct.	614.7	640.0	368.9	576.3	1,701.5	269.2	603.7
Nov.	698.9	720.0	330.2	576.3	1,729.7	282.8	660.3
Dec.	843.6	736.0	345.7	655.3	1,758.4	297.2	762.1

145 AR, KL SB, 2602, Sel Kan 108/2603; Penang Shimbun, 24 Jan. 2603.

146 *Perak Times*, 31 July 2603.

Table 6.5 *(cont'd)*

	Foodstuffs	*Tobacco*	*Light, fuel, water*	*Transport*	*Clothing*	*Rent*	*Weighted cost-of-living*
1944							
Jan.	1,014.8	856.0	381.8	1,022.7	1,787.6	312.3	912.8
Feb.	1,498.4	1,096.0	388.3	1,163.7	1,817.3	328.2	1,211.0
Mar.	2,022.4	2,018.0	394.7	1,243.1	1,847.5	344.8	1,490.0
Apr.	2,722.8	2,122.0	562.5	1,389.8	2,045.2	362.3	1,929.0
May	2,903.3	2,184.0	639.9	1,615.9	2,459.3	380.7	2,047.0
June	2,761.0	2,888.0	724.5	1,672.2	3,214.5	400.0	2,121.0
July	2,932.1	3,296.0	724.5	1,898.3	5,144.8	420.4	2,343.0
Aug.	3,702.6	3,520.0	731.0	2,011.2	6,448.6	441.7	2,813.0
Sept.	4,157.6	3,728.0	821.3	2,350.5	8,016.7	464.0	3,171.0
Oct.	4,322.6	4,984.0	1,066.5	2,632.9	9,039.9	487.6	3,410.0
Nov.	4,964.6	5,008.0	1,337.4	2,971.5	10,217.2	512.4	3,867.0
Dec.	5,648.8	4,864.0	1,736.2	2,971.5	11,629.5	538.4	4,310.0
1945							
Jan.	6,753.6	6,570.0	1,943.9	3,672.5	13,102.4	565.7	5,094.0
Feb.	8,001.3	6,960.0	1,943.9	4,350.2	14,287.7	594.4	5,864.0
Mar.	10,532.9	6,496.0	2,266.5	5,141.4	18,701.8	624.6	7,341.0
Apr.	12,275.6	8,928.0	2,911.6	6,946.9	20,679.7	656.3	8,600.0
May	16,000.6	11,248.0	6,160.0	7,288.1	25,765.9	689.6	10,980.0

Source: Sliding Scale of Values of the Japanese Dollar throughout the Period of Occupation, CO852/726/3.

There was also a general increase in crime. The Kajang police report for 1942 indicated that theft had become a serious problem:

> The New Administration first issued the correct order to the inhabitants of Selangor to surrender their arms, and the honest people obeyed this willingly. But there were others who did not and they with the arms left behind by the defeated British soldiers gave opportunity for those dishonest persons to commit crimes [*sic*]. Robberies were rampant and the Police could do little to suppress these as they were not issued with arms. However Military aids were available and the robberies and communistic activities were mostly dealt by them.[147]

[147] AR, Kajang Police District, 2602, Ulu Langat 216/2602.

In Ulu Langat the court docket for 1942 was dominated by "thefts, dishonestly retaining stolen property, suspected stolen property and profiteering".[148] By 1943 the pattern of crime seems to have changed somewhat. Speaking in June, the Chief Justice of Selangor enumerated several types of crime which were becoming increasingly prevalent: theft of telegraph and telephone wires, thefts of military and government property by gangs of thieves both at night and in broad daylight, purchasing or retaining stolen property, and offenses against economic control.[149] Punishments for criminals included flogging in serious cases, and local officials contended that this practice helped keep the situation under control. However, in some respects the Government response to crime seems to have been remarkably relaxed. The District Officer for Kuala Langat suggested that petty thefts were caused more "by want of food than by avarice",[150] and a conference of District Officers in Perak in 1944 made light of the matter:

> As for thefts, His Excellency [the Governor] said that even the food crops in his own garden were being stolen (laughter). This was unavoidable and the only way to prevent that, His Excellency said, was to improve the morale of the inhabitants or something in that direction.[151]

The *Jikeidan* instituted night watch arrangements but faced several difficulties, not least a lack of fuel for lamps. Kerosene was difficult to obtain, and coconut oil was a controlled substance and also in very short supply.[152]

A number of institutions, some of them financed privately and others at least partly by public funds, offered aid to people who were impoverished. In Selangor these included an Old Women's Home, a Catholic Convent Orphanage, and the Government Choultry for Indian Labourers, which had operated since 1914 and provided assistance to the unemployed, orphans and convalescents.[153] In 1942, Pahang offered financial relief to the destitute amounting to 15 cents per day for a single person, 25 cents for a couple and 10 cents for each additional family member, paid for a maximum of six months. Those eligible were the unemployed, the old and weak, the sick, people not suited for any work and families with no income. Able-bodied males could not receive benefits.[154]

---

[148] AR Ulu Langat, 2602, Sel Kan 33/2603.

[149] Summary of Speech of S. Masuyama, Chief Justice of the Selangor Supreme Court, 17 June 2603, DO Ulu Langat 132/2602.

[150] AR Kuala Langat, 2602, Sel Kan 32/2603.

[151] Minutes, Conference of District Officers, 4 Oct. 2604, PT Larut 161/2602.

[152] DO Larut to DO Kinta, 7 June 2603, Larut 21/2603.

[153] AR Kosei Kyoku, Sel, 2602, Sel Kan 59/2603.

[154] Extract from Note of DO Conference 19.10.2602, and Pahang Financial Dept to DO Temerloh, 27 Aug. 2602, DO Temerloh 222/2602.

Retired civil servants faced a particularly difficult situation because the Japanese said they were not responsible for the past services of former employees of the British administration, and refused to pay their pensions.[155] In Johore, where some 1,100 people had been receiving special and superannuation allowances, a report on relief for destitutes said the situation of pensioners was "most pitiable":

> The majority of them are old and infirm and past their days of usefulness. They have no private means and depend for their living entirely on their pensions which they have now ceased to draw.

Some were able and willing to work, but the administration had a large pool of younger retrenched officers available and there seemed to be little prospect of helping pensioners by re-employing them. The local administrative staff suggested, in a document that seems to have been worded very carefully, that the government might do something to assist this group:

> We admit that it is a difficult matter for the Government to consider and if it is possible we would suggest granting the pensioners a reduced rate of pension even less than what the Government officers are now receiving as compared with their previous emoluments. This will enable the pensioners to have something to rely on for their subsistence while life lasts.[156]

By 1945 poverty was so widespread that charitable institutions could no longer cope with the situation. Japanese officials noted an alarming increase in the number of vagrants found in most towns and villages, and complained of the nuisance caused by beggars and destitute people. The head of propaganda activities in Perak suggested that poor people should be picked up and given work if they were able-bodied, and if not they should go to the Destitutes' Home or the hospital. In Larut a general round-up took place on 26 May, netting 62 people who were sent to detention homes "to be cared for with funds from the respective communities". Of those detained, 14 were Malays, and the President of the Malai Kosei Kyokai (the Welfare Association) for Larut and Matang appealed to the government to provide "at least a bag of rice" each month to feed them. A further round-up was carried out on 2 June 1945.[157]

* * *

---

[155] Minutes, Meeting of District Officers, 22 and 23 Mar. 2602, PT Larut 106/2602.

[156] Paper in MB Johore 215/2602.

[157] Senden Katyo Pk to DO Larut & Matang, 10 May 2605, DO Larut to Senden Katyo Pk, 2 June 2605, Mohamed Haniff Sulaiman to DO Larut, 29 May 2605, DO Larut to Somubu Gyoseika Tyo, 16 Aug. 2605, DO Larut 62/2605.

Japanese efforts to impose central control over the economy received little support from the local population, and were impeded by corruption and inefficiency. Yet even without these difficulties, it seems unlikely that the economic situation could have been improved under wartime conditions. Malaya had been an integral part of a larger economic system, a fragment of the British Empire, and lacked the capacity to operate in isolation. It had a limited range of raw materials, minimal industrial capacity, and modest levels of food production. The plantation and mining industries, and international trade, lay at the heart of the pre-war economy, and the collapse of these sectors affected nearly the entire population. Even under the best of circumstances it would have been a slow and arduous task to remake the Malayan economy, and the Japanese were simultaneously administering other territories in the region which faced similar breakdowns in their local economies, and attempting to prosecute a war that was going against them.

Japan's long-term policies called for a restructuring of the pre-war economic system to utilize Malaya's economic resources within its own imperial system. Although the government attempted to lay the groundwork for future development along these lines, the occupation was primarily a time of expedients developed to overcome short-term difficulties. The economic plans outlined above, and the currency and banking arrangements described in the next chapter, were part of a systematic attempt to restructure the economy, but in the latter part of the occupation the economy became increasingly distorted as the government struggled to cope with the growing crisis caused by shortages of essential goods, inflation, labour difficulties and inadequate food supplies.

CHAPTER 7

Currency and Banking

The Japanese adopted prudent monetary policies. To deal with inflation, they immediately took steps to reduce the amount of money in circulation, and for about two years enjoyed reasonable success in managing Malaya's currency. Banks resumed operations and provided financing for industrial projects designed to restore and reshape the Malayan economy, but these enterprises had little vitality, and when the local economy failed to generate revenue, the administration eventually resorted to printing money to meet expenses, and the military did the same. The government adopted various expedients to withdraw some of this money from circulation, among them forced savings campaigns, lotteries and licensed gambling, but it could not prevent rempant inflation, and by the end of the occupation the currency retained very little purchasing power.

Currency

Between 1938 and the end of 1941 the gross currency note circulation in Malaya increased from $105 million to $220 million, reflecting a surge in sales of rubber and tin to build stockpiles abroad following Japan's attack on China, payments to labourers engaged in military construction projects, and expenditure connected with the large and growing numbers of military personnel stationed in Malaya (see Table 7.1). With the Japanese invasion, additional cash went into circulation as departing British employers paid wages and bonuses, and as the local population withdrew funds from the banks.

Normally about 3 per cent of Malaya's total currency issue was in the form of coin. This figure rose to 14 per cent in 1938, and remained around 12 per cent at the end of 1940, but large quantities had been hoarded, exported or melted down, and employers found it difficult to obtain coins to pay day labour. To overcome this problem, the government issued small denomination currency notes, down to the level of 1 cent.[1]

[1] R.E. Turnbull (SOI, Finance) to Pedler (CO), 4 Sept. 1944, CO852/586/16.

Table 7.1 Currency note circulation in Malaya[a]

	Gross circulation	*Active circulation*
31 Dec. 1938	105,300,000	73,054,913
31 Dec. 1939	126,215,000	92,529,745
31 Dec. 1940	164,579,000	120,617,228
31 Dec. 1941	220,000,000[b]	n.a.

Notes: [a] Gross circulation includes money held by government treasuries and banks; active circulation omits this money and is notionally the amount of money in the hands of the general population.

[b] After it was withdrawn from circulation and demonetized in 1948, the pre-invasion note issue was put at $238,804,963. Gurney to S of S no. 675 (Conf.), 9 June 1949, CO852/677/7.

Source: W.D. Godsall, *Report on the Working of the Malayan Currency Commission for the Period 1st January, 1941 to 31st December, 1946* (Singapore: Government Printers, 1948), p. 4; W.D. Godsall, *Report of the Commissioners of Currency, Malaya for the Period 1st January, 1948 to 31st December, 1948*, p. 8.

When the loss of Malaya seemed imminent, the British administration took steps to prevent currency and other things of value from falling into Japanese hands. Bearer bonds were called in, converted to registered stock, and then destroyed. Of a total issue of $105 million, $104 million was processed in this way. The government invited people to hand over valuables (such as jewels and stamp collections) to the Treasury, and sent items worth $4 million to Australia for safe-keeping. In Singapore the government burned stocks of currency notes worth $75 million, and shipped an additional $39 million to India. Banks sent currency held in their own vaults that was surplus to their immediate requirements to the Currency Commissioners for destruction, and on 14 February the Currency Commissioners destroyed surplus currency on behalf of Malayan banks, advising the Crown Agents of the sums to be credited to each of them. Finally, stocks of coins were dumped into the sea.[2]

The Japanese plan for regulating the currency of occupied territories included the following provisions:

1. The currency in the respective areas will be changed to currency with the Japanese "yen" on the background.
2. The international value of the currency will be decided on the basis of Japanese yen and the exchange rate to Japanese yen will be determined by the economic conditions of the respective areas.

---

[2] Note by H. Weisberg, Financial Secretary for the Straits Settlements, in Ag HC for UK, Canberra, to S of S for Dominion Affairs, 27 Nov. 1945, CO852/856/17.

3. International economy will be settled by Japanese yen in Tokyo and a synthetic clearing system with Japan as its nucleus will be firmly established.
4. Monetary systems suitable to the new situation will be established in each area for the purpose of reorganizing the circulation of money and the controlling of exchange.
5. In enforcing the above directives the order, method, time, etc. will be decided after considering the relationship between the various situations such as military affairs, politics and economy without hindering the economic development of the territory concerned.[3]

Japanese troops involved in the invasion of Malaya carried unnumbered military yen (denominated in dollars and printed in English). These notes were declared legal tender on 23 February 1942 and valued at par with the Straits dollar, although the pre-war value of the yen had been half that of the Straits dollar (1 shilling and twopence compared with 2 shillings and fourpence). The Chinese press issued the following announcement concerning currency arrangements:

> It is hereby notified that the currencies to be used in Malaya are first, Military Yen Notes used by the Imperial Japanese Government (those notes having denominations in Chinese characters cannot be used) and second, Local currency. At the present time both currencies will have the same value in use.
>
> Outside of the two currencies, no other currency should be either used or retained.
>
> Anyone counterfeiting or in any way altering Military notes or Local currency, or spreading rumours to the detriment of the use of Military notes, will, if apprehended, be severely dealt with according to military law. Tremble and obey this notice.[4]

The next day brought a further notification:

1. Military notes are issued by the Imperial Government of Japan, which takes full responsibility for them, and accordingly they are of absolutely reliable [sic], and may be freely used without concern, according to their face value.
2. Recipients of Military notes may use them for all payments.

---

[3] JM 103, p. 18.

[4] Malaya under the Japanese, NARA RG226 128585; translation of a Concordance of Military Regulations published in Chinese by the *Shonan Daily*, 15 June 1943, NARA RG226 63840. The English version worded the first point slightly differently: "The sole currency in Malaya shall be the Military Dollar Notes issued by the Government of Nippon. The Straits Currency Notes, however, shall be for the time being allowed their circulation with the equal parity to the military notes." *The Good Citizen's Guide*, published by the *Syonan Sinbun* (English edition), Apr. 2603, p. 9.

3. If any individual plots against or in any way causes damage to military notes (such as refusal to accept the same or in the releasing of slanderous rumour) such shall be accounted as equivalent to enemy activity and will receive severe punishment.[5]

A statement issued in Johore put the first point more simply: "The military notes used by the Nippon Army, being issued by the Government of Nippon, have great force of credit and never fail their value."[6] At the end of May the newspapers published a notice stating that it was "entirely illegal" for members of the public to hold or circulate foreign currencies, and that anyone who did so would face severe punishment.[7]

Shortly after the start of the occupation, as much as $285 million may have been circulating in Malaya, but within half a year the new regime brought the figure down by about 50 per cent.[8] Pre-war British notes remained legal tender but they quickly disappeared from open circulation because their use suggested a lack of faith in the Japanese regime, although they commanded a premium on the black market.[9] Forced donations, including contributions to the massive $50 million "gift" demanded from the Chinese community—an amount equivalent to half of the entire note issue of British Malaya in 1938 and nearly a quarter of the gross circulation at the end of 1941—also accounted for substantial amounts of currency. Other devices the Japanese used to control inflation included savings campaigns, lotteries and licensed gambling, thought to have a particular appeal for the Chinese. "Even though their desires, such as horse racing, lotteries or the opening of gambling houses, are not in accord with

---

[5] Concordance of Military Regulations published by the *Shonan Daily*, NARA RG226 63840.

[6] Decree issued by the Commander of the Dai-Nippon Army, n.d., CLR Batu Pahat 4/2602.

[7] Concordance of Military Regulations published by the *Shonan Daily*, NARA RG226 63840. The notice appeared on 28 May 2602.

[8] Japanese Finance in Malaya, BMA PS/412. A handwritten note at the end of the report indicates that it was prepared by H. Wakefield, 8 Dec. 1944. A second document in the same file, entitled Financial Control, contains similar information but provides additional details. Cf. Interim Report on Wages by the Joint Wages Commission, Appendix J. The *Syonan Times* reported on 19 May 2602 that "The British over-issue of $200,000,000 is now being recovered smoothly through the joint offices of the Yokohama Specie Bank and the Bank of Taiwan and the Chinese banks, and there are no signs of apparent inflation."

[9] BMA(M) to SACSEA, n.d., CO537/1376. Kwa Siew Tee, in Sliding Scale of Values of the Japanese Dollar throughout the Period of Occupation (Registrar of Malayan Statistics, 11 Aug. 1947), CO852/726/3. Japanese military yen that came into government hands was not re-issued. Minutes, Meeting of District Officers, 22 and 23 Mar. 2602, P.T. Larut 106/2602.

the Japanese sense of morality, they should be permitted."[10] Some 300 gambling houses operated in Singapore alone, and amusement parks such as the Great World and the New World became "veritable gambling centres".[11]

Illus. 7.1 "Syonan's open-air theatres are full of joyful people. Children are frequent visitors to these shows and they are usually accompanied by Nippon soldiers who love the company of children very much. That is why the children proudly throw out their chests for they are glad to be with the Nippon soldiers. It is such a transformation from the fire of war some two and a half months ago for everybody is happy now."

Source: *Syonan Times*, 2 May 2602 (1942) Saturday supplement.

---

[10] JM 167, p. 17.

[11] Lau and Barry, A Brief Review of Chinese Affairs, BMA ADM/8/1.

A government lottery (the Konan Saiken) was launched in July 1942 with tickets costing $1 each, and continued operating till August 1945. The top prize was $50,000, and initially there were 2,507 prizes worth a total of $139,500, although a new category of 50,000 $1 prizes was added later.[12] District Officers sold tickets directly and also through communal organizations, and were under considerable pressure to find buyers. In 1944 the number of tickets issued for each draw increased. The allocation for Bentong rose from 1,000 to 2,400, and the District Officer wrote to the local branches of the Oversea Chinese Association and the Indian Independence League to seek their "assistance and co-operation in disposing of these tickets". The General Secretary of the Bentong Sub-Branch of the Indian Independence League replied that his organization would take more tickets only if unsold tickets could be sent back, because otherwise the officer in charge would have to bear the cost. He was told that unsold tickets could not be returned.[13] Banks also ran lotteries in connection with Savings Campaigns, and in July 1945 the Oversea Chinese Association received permission to organize a lottery, the stated purposes being to absorb money and check inflation, to meet the general demand for public amusement, and to raise funds for the association's benevolent fund.[14]

During the first year of the occupation, residents of Malaya could only send exchange remittances to Japan, but in April 1943 the Syonan Military Administration extended this arrangement to include Sumatra, Burma, Java, North Borneo and occupied China. The various currencies within the Southeast Asian area ("the Malay dollar, the Sumatra and Java guilder and the Burmese rupee") had been assigned the same value, which precluded the possibility of currency speculation. For a time, all exchange business had to pass through Japanese banks, but in August 1943 the administration permitted 34 Chinese remittance houses to resume operations as a way of promoting trade within the southern regions, thus allowing the Chinese to increase their contribution to the war effort.[15]

---

[12] Financial Officer to DO Bentong, 6 Jan. 2604, DO Bentong 85/2603.

[13] General Secy IIL Bentong Sub-Branch to DO Bentong, 8 Feb. 2604, DO Bentong 84/2603; DO Bentong to General Secy IIL, 16 Feb. 2604, DO Bentong 85/2603.

[14] Pahang Shu Seicho to DO Bentong, 25 July 2605, DO Bentong 85/2605.

[15] Domei ELB, 31 Mar. 1943, CO273/669/50744/7; Kang Jew Koon, "The Chinese in Singapore during the Japanese Occupation", p. 27.

Illus. 7.2 Front and back view of a lottery ticket issued during Japanese Occupation.

興南彩券(第七回)發行十月十五日四十万枚・賞金一等一本五万圓・前後賞二本一千圓・二等一本二万圓・三等三本一万圓・四等四本五千圓・五等八本一千圓・六等二十本五百圓・七等二百本百圓・八等千二百本五十圓・九等二千本十圓・計三千四百三十九本二十四万圓・抽籤十二月四日於昭南公會堂・賞金支拂十二月九日ヨリ昭和十九年一月三十一日ニ至ル間・南方開發金庫昭南支金庫ニ於テ各州ハ同代理店（横濱正金銀行）ニ於テ行フ・期間後ハ支拂ラナサズ・

Hadiah pertama $50,000 (Ticket yang ber-nombor terlibeh dahulu dan yang ter kemedian nombor hadiah pertama, sabaniak $1,000 menjadi sago hati = $2,000). Hadiah ke 2 — 1 ticket = $20,000. Hadiah ke 3 — 3 ticket, satu $10,000 = $30,000. Hadiah ke 4 — 4 ticket, satu $5,000 = $20,000 Hadiah ke 5 — 8 ticket, satu $1,000 = $8,000. Hadiah ke 6 — 20 ticket, satu 500 = $10,000. Hadiah ke 7 — 200 ticket, satu $100 = $20,000. Hadiah ke 8 — 1,200 ticket, satu $50 = $60,000. Hadiah ke 9 — 2,000 ticket, satu $10 = 20,000. Chabutan akan diadakan di Syonan Kokaido pada 4 hari bulan December, 2603, terbuka kepada am. Bayaran hadiah di Nanpo Kaihatsu Kinko, Syonan, dan Yokohama Specie Bank di Malai wakil Nanpo Kaihatsu Kinko diantara 9 hari bulan December, 2603 dan 31 hari bulan January, 2604 lewat dari itu tidak di ra-aikan.

Source: 19980005535-0110 Chew Chang Lang Collection, courtesy of National Archives of Singapore.

Illus. 7.3 Lottery advertisement.

Source: *Syonan Sinbun*, 10 April 2603 (1943).

In 1944 and 1945 the value of the occupation currency declined sharply, in large part because of the Japanese practice of issuing fresh currency notes to meet their expenses at a time when little economic activity was taking place.[16] The military administration in Malaya printed notes worth at least $4,000 million, and setting aside the $900 million held in reserve, the active circulation

[16] See, for example, the discussion by R.E. Turnbull (SOI, Finance) in Draft memorandum on Malayan currency for the Advisory Council, 10 Nov. 1943, CO852/510/24, and HQ BMA(M) Penin Div to SACSEA, n.d., CO852/541/4.

rose to at least 30 times pre-occupation levels.[17] One Japanese account suggests that the currency issue was justified by "the development of natural resources, billeting of large number of troops, and the position of Singapore as the center of political, economy, and communications [*sic*]", and offers the following explanation for inflation:

> The inhabitants of that area [Malaya and Singapore] lacked thriftiness and the Chinese speculated by buying. This caused the inflation in the southern region and also caused the shortage of food. Great attention was given to its counter-plan. The fundamental plan was to increase the supply of imported food, local food and import the daily necessities. In addition to this, various other plans were executed to absorb the currency. The various plans could not be executed due to the critical situation of the war. The war then ended.[18]

In the final month of the war, the Japanese printed still more currency that may have brought the note issue as high as $5,000 million. In Singapore alone a stockpile of banknotes worth $1,200 million was created in August 1945 against the possibility that the city might be cut off from the Southern Regions Development Bank during military operations, and the military used some of this money to settle outstanding accounts. However, the military also released significant quantities of textiles and other rationed goods in August 1945 to absorb as much of the wartime currency as possible, arranging sales through the black market. Owing to practices such as this, it is impossible to get a reliable overall picture of the currency situation during this period.[19]

Banks

The Yokohama Specie Bank and the Bank of Taiwan operated in Malaya before the war, and both reopened in March 1942, with the former serving as the Military Administration Cash Office. They were joined in June by the Japanese Kanan Bank.[20] On 30 March 1942, the Japanese created a Southern Regions Development Bank that served as a central bank for conquered territories in Southeast Asia, financing economic activities and regulating the circulation of money. The Southern Regions Development Bank, which had its main office in Tokyo, was capitalized at 100,000,000 yen and the Japanese government

---

[17] JM 103, p. 18; Malaya – Part II, BMA(M) 506/10. All metal coinage disappeared during the occupation years, and banknotes down to 1 cent were in use.

[18] JM 103, p. 46.

[19] Notes on the Southern Regions Development Bank (Nanpo Ginko), 15 Oct. 1945, WO203/4190.

[20] Malaya – Part II, BMA(M) 506/10.

was the sole investor, utilizing a military expense account to supply it with funds. The Malayan branch began operations in Singapore in July 1942, taking over the functions of the Military Administration Cash Office, and assuming responsibility for exchange control, industrial finance and development activities. The bank was authorized to sell bonds worth up to ten times its level of capitalization, and was expected to support the local currency. From 1 April 1943 it began issuing currency to replace the military scrip, manufacturing banknotes to make it self-supporting.[21]

During 1942 the Southern Regions Development Bank concentrated on funding the exploitation of natural resources in Southeast Asia to serve the war effort, but in 1943 it became increasingly involved in the development of industry. In Malaya the amount of long-term credit the bank made available for industrial enterprises rose from $6 million at the end of 1942 to $80 million at the end of September 1943. Loans were offered for "mining, transportation, shipbuilding, agriculture and forestry, electric power, warehousing, marine products, iron and machinery manufacturing, communications, civil engineering, chemical manufacturing and foodstuffs production".[22]

Immediately after taking control of Malaya, the Japanese administration closed all banks and blocked use of their funds. According to an officer with the Oversea Chinese Banking Corporation, the Yokohama Specie Bank and the Bank of Taiwan "did not meet with success, due probably to the majority of the Chinese being unwilling to transact business with them", and the Japanese then required Chinese and Indian banks to resume operations, providing them with loans for the purpose but compelling directors of the Chinese banks to execute "a joint and several guarantee pledging all their personal possessions to the Japanese bank".[23] Business was conducted under a "blocked account" arrangement under which all existing accounts were frozen. Customers opened new accounts, and the banks later transferred blocked credits to these new accounts.[24] Five Chinese banks (OCBC, Sze Hai Tong, United Chinese Bank, Ban Hin Lee Bank and Lee Wah Bank) re-opened in April 1942, followed on 1 June by the China and Southern Bank, and on 1 September by the Kwong Yik

[21] JM 103, p. 18; Malaya – Part II, BMA(M) 506/10; Political and Economic Changes Effected by the Japanese in Malaya, 1 Dec. 1943, OSS R&A No. 1433.

[22] *Syonan Sinbun*, 1 Jan. 2603; Domei ELB, 18 Oct. 1943, FIR 16, 23 Oct. 1943, CO273/673/50744/7.

[23] Memorandum prepared by CHL, probably Chew Hock Leong, of the OCBC, 8 June 1946, CO85/726/1.

[24] Yap, *Scholar, Banker, Gentleman Soldier*, p. 62.

Bank. Taiwanese agents monitored their activities on behalf of the Japanese.[25] Three Indian banks (the Indian Bank, the Indian Overseas Bank and the Oriental Bank of Malaya) began operations a short while later. All banks operating in Malaya took part in a Malayan Banking Association, and agreed to offer standard rates of interest amounting to 3 per cent on fixed deposits and 2 per cent on normal savings accounts.[26]

The Japanese used local banks to encourage trade and to put new currency into circulation. However, the administration also imposed restrictions on loans and at various times required the banks to place cash in fixed deposit accounts with the Yokohama Specie Bank. Most of these funds were returned to the banks in late August or early September 1945 in occupation currency, which immediately became valueless when the British demonetized wartime currency.[27]

Deposits in savings accounts had fallen to a very low level when the occupation began ($30 million against $450 million before the war). The Japanese military administration felt that the low level of savings contributed to inflation,[28] and staged campaigns encouraging people to deposit money in savings accounts. Voluntary programmes had little impact, and the *Syonan Sinbun* complained in September 1943 that "people still remain non-cooperative in depositing their money in banks or post office savings banks. Neglect of this important practice is a vice for money held in the hand only invites the attention of the covetous and of thieves and robbers."[29] Early in 1944 the Japanese introduced a forced savings campaign "to withdraw from circulation surplus money and thereby stabilise the price of commodities".[30] On the second anniversary of the British surrender a savings fund was created to which Japanese officers were required to contribute 5 per cent of their monthly salaries, local civil servants 3 per cent, and menial staff 50 cents per month.[31] The Banking Association set up a Savings Encouragement

[25] This point is made in Kang Jew Koon, "The Chinese in Singapore during the Japanese Occupation", p. 25, based on a Force 136 Intelligence Report held by the Singapore Chinese Chamber of Commerce.

[26] Daily Digest of World Broadcasts, 16 Aug. 1943, CO273/669/50744/7; HR 13, 11 Sept. 1943, CO273/669/50744/7. The association was initially a Malai-Sumatra Banking Association.

[27] Memorandum prepared by CHL of the OCBC, 8 June 1946, CO852/726/1.

[28] The $30 million figure is taken from a Domei News Agency report dated 27 June 1942, and reported in Review of the Foreign Press no. 150 (20 Aug. 1942), p. 264, CO852/356/7.

[29] Quoted in Japanese Finance in Malaya, BMA PS/412.

[30] Minutes, Penghulus Conference, 27 Sept. 2604, Batu Gajah 11/2604.

[31] Celebration of Kigensetsu and the Second Anniversary of the fall of Singapore; Second Anniversary of Rebirth of Malaya. Programme for Celebration (Kuantan District), 10 Feb. 2604, DO Kuantan 49/2604.

Section to handle the anticipated influx of deposits, and deductions began in February 1944. Other devices to promote savings included requirements that people not in government service make a monthly deposit of at least $1 for every gantang of rationed rice they received, that land owners deposit $10 per month for every acre of land they held, that owners of bicycles deposit $2 per month per bicycle, owners of bullock carts and goods vehicles deposit $100 per vehicle per month, and owners of private cars deposit $300 per vehicle per month.[32]

The banks also offered Fixed Deposit accounts, and used lotteries and bonuses to attract depositors.[33] The Sultan of Selangor declared that Malays in hs state "must co-operate" with one such scheme, and established quotas to be met in each district. The Secretary to the Sultan told the District Officer of Ulu Selangor that to meet his $500 quota he should draw up a list of Malays in "good financial position", apportion the deposit among them, and "having done that, explain the position to them" and collect the money. A subsequent letter noted that "as the matter was urgent", the Sultan had advanced the $500 and this money had been deposited in the bank in the name of the Acting District Officer ("The deposit might have been made in the name of the President of the Malai Kosei Kyokai [the Welfare Association], but the thing had to be done in such a hurry that there was no time to think properly"). The Acting District Officer was asked to reimburse the Sultan as soon as possible.[34] In connection with a 1945 campaign, which had as its purpose "counteracting inflation and ... stabilising the living conditions of the people", the Penang branch of the Oversea Chinese Association issued a letter saying that it was "very anxious" for people to "come forward and show their loyalty to, and appreciation of the kind treatment of the Government by voluntarily helping in this worthy cause". Reflecting the political atmosphere of 1945, the letter added that "any amount deposited for this campaign will be solely credited to the depositor and does not in any way represent a donation or contribution to the Government".[35] In June 1945 new rules issued in Pahang

---

[32] Kuala Lumpur Banking Association to District Officers, 7 Oct. 2604, and Kuala Lumpur Banking Association, Speeches and Talks during Savings Week Campaign, n.d., Ulu Langat 32/2604; Pahang Syo Somubucho to DOs etc., n.d., and Somubu Cho to DO Temerloh 19.10.19 (an error for 19.10.2604), DO Temerloh 398/2603; *Syonan Shimbun*, 29 Jan. 2604.

[33] On 8 Feb. 2694 the *Syonan Shimbun* announced a "Fixed Deposit with Bonus" scheme with a $10,000 prize. See also *Syonan Shimbun*, 10 Feb. 2604.

[34] Secretary to H.H. the Sultan of Selangor to DO Ulu Langat, 10 Nov. 2604; Hamzah b. Abdullah to Abdullah, 16.12.2604, Ulu Langat 92/2603.

[35] Somubu Cho, Sangyobu Cho, Pahang Shu Seicho to DO Kuantan, 23 Dec. 2604, DO Kuantan 346/2604; Penang Oversea Chinese Association to Chop Kwong Wah Cheong, 17 Feb. 2605, copy provided by Chow Siew Heng, whose father was the proprietor of this business.

Illus. 7.4 Poster advertising a fixed deposit campaign conducted by the Malai Banking Association.

Source: Arkib Negara Malaysia file Temerloh 85/2604.

required that whenever a piece of land or a house was sold, the seller had to place half of the purchase price in a bank on a "fixed deposit for a period of two or three years". A sale could not be registered without proof that the deposit had been made.[36] These initiatives produced a substantial increase in savings, which rose from $164 million at the end of August 1943 to $407 million at the end of February 1945, approaching pre-war levels but in depreciated currency.[37]

Before the occupation, British and Chinese banks dominated the banking industry in Malaya, although American, Dutch, French, Belgian and Japanese banks also operated in Singapore, and government Post Office Savings Banks were found throughout the peninsula. The major British banks were the Chartered Bank, with offices in nine cities throughout Malaya, the Hongkong and Shanghai Bank, in eight locations, and the Mercantile Bank of India, also in eight locations.

In March 1943 the Japanese administration began liquidation proceedings against twelve foreign banks, and demanded immediate repayment of all loans, overdrafts and other money owed to them. The banks liquidated were: Hongkong and Shanghai Bank, Chartered Bank, Thos. Cook & Sons, Banque de l'Indochine, American Express Co., Mercantile Bank of India, National City Bank of New York, Bank of China, Nederlandsche Handel-Maatschappij, Nederlandsch-Indische Handelbank, Kwangtung Provincial Bank and the Eastern Bank.[38] More than a year later, in October 1944, depositors received payments against their accounts, getting the first $100 in full, and 20 per cent of amounts over $100. The official notice concerning the refund policy pointed out that the amounts payable by foreign banks to depositors were very large compared to the assets that the banks held in Malaya, adding that depositors should be grateful to be allowed to withdraw even a portion of their money, and consider permission to do so "an act of grace".[39] Those receiving payments were instructed to place the money with approved banks because "the present

---

[36] Regulations regarding Savings in connection with Transactions on Immovable Property, and Minute dated 15 June 2605, DO Kuantan 165/2605.

[37] FIR 15, 9 Oct. 1943, CO273/673/50744/7; BMA DCCAO 188/45.

[38] *Syonan Shimbun*, 29 Nov. 2604; a Concordance of Military Regulations, Japanese Proclamations in Malaya (BMA COM/26) also lists the "Straits Settlements Currency Bureau", presumably the Board of Commissioners of Currency. The lists in the *Penang Shimbun* (19 Mar. 2602) included the Singapore Government Treasury, which may refer to the same thing.

[39] Extract from Malai Gunseikan Kokuji no. 52, in Notice to the Depositors of the Enemy Banks under Liquidation, Temerloh 259/2604; *Syonan Shimbun*, 30 Sept. 2604.

distress was due to there being too much money in the country which had given rise to inflation".[40]

The Post Office Savings Bank and the People's Bank

The Japanese re-opened the Malayan Post Office Savings Bank (renamed the Nippon Government Post Office Savings Bank) on 1 September 1942 for withdrawals, and in December the Bank began accepting deposits at all post offices. Government officials earning more than $100 per month were instructed to open accounts, and the administration asked for a list of all those who had done so. The minimum deposit was $1 (later reduced to 50 cents), with a limit of $2,000 per year, and no more than $5,000 could be held in any one account. Interest was paid at the rate of three per cent per annum. Occupation period withdrawals through the Japanese Bank from accounts held with the pre-war British Post Office Savings Bank amounted to around $3 million.[41]

Illus. 7.5 Rules of the Nippon Government Post Office Savings Bank.

NIPPON GOVERNMENT POST OFFICE SAVINGS BANK OF MALAYA.

Be thrifty and learn to save money. Any Post Office will keep your money for safety.

DEPOSITS.

$1 to $5,000 with a maximum of $2,000 in any one year.

WITHDRAWALS.

Repayment of deposits can be obtained in two ways.

(a) Up to $25 on demand at any Post Office, provided that not more than one such payment may be made within any period of seven days.

(b) Any amount on application to the Superintendent, Savings Bank, Syonan (forms of application obtainable at all Post Offices).

INTEREST.

3 per cent per annum (i.e. 3 cents for $1 per calendar year) on every complete dollar standing to the credit of a depositor.

Source: Arkib Negara Malaysia file Klang 543/2602 (1942).

[40] Minutes of a Conference of DOs held at Ipoh, 4 Oct. 2604, PT Larut 161/2602. See also Note from The Malai Banking Association, Syonan, *Syonan Shimbun*, 29 Sept. 2604.

[41] AR, Postal Department of Selangor, 2602, Sel Kan 28/2603; The Good Citizen's Guide, pp. 178–9; Asst Controller of Posts, Pahang to Pahang DOs, 25 Aug. 2603, Bentong 207/2603; FIR 15, 9 Oct. 1943, CO273/673/50744/7; Fed Sec 3090 Pt V/1948; Kedah Circular 25/2602, 3 Dec. 2602, SUK Kedah 502/2602.

Savings in the Dai Nippon Government Post Office Savings Bank rose sharply in the final year of the occupation. Deposits amounted to $250,000 on 31 December 1942, but reached $16.5 million on 31 December 1944, and $42 million by the time of the Japanese surrender. At the end of the occupation the average account held $81, twice the level at the end of 1944.[42] The Bank had no assets after the war, and these deposits were wiped out.

The People's Bank or People's Treasury (Shomin Ginko) was a government scheme to assist the "Middle class and other small traders and factory owners; farmers in general, owners of rubber estates, mines and works, and generally all people of modest means" by displacing moneylenders and pawnbrokers as a source of capital for small businessmen. The scheme originated in June 1942 in Penang, where loans were initially given to people who wanted to establish cottage industries or replenish stocks of goods in their shops, and later to farmers and fishermen as well. People's Bank subsequently opened throughout Malaya, operating under the auspices of the Yokohama Specie Bank but using funds provided by the government.[43] In places where there was no Yokohama Specie Bank office, District Officers handled operations for the People's Bank in addition to their other duties. Applicants for loans had to have "steady employment or regular income", and "good reasons and reasonable prospects" for extending their business. Bankrupts were ineligible, and loans were refused to applicants who were unemployed, had no regular income, or were seeking funds for purposes considered "wasteful, unsatisfactory, or injurious to the applicant or to the public welfare". A loan could be granted to someone "who wants to get married but is without money", or "to meet other extraordinary expenses arising from unforeseen circumstances not brought about by careless or intemperate living".[44] However, the manager of the Ipoh office of the Yokohama Specie Bank, who described himself as "a government employee entrusted with the management of the Peoples' Bank", told District Officers the regulations did not have to be strictly observed:

[42] Withdrawals from Savings Bank during Occupation, Fed Sec 3090 Pt V/1948.

[43] *Penang Shimbun*, 11 May 2603; *Syonan Shimbun*, 31 May 2604. An announcement regarding the Malayan-wide scheme appears in the *Syonan Times*, 30 July 2602.

[44] Syonan Tokubetu-Si Notice no. 108, *Syonan Times*, 28 Aug. 2602; Good Citizen's Guide, pp. 179–80; Cuttings from the Malay Mail (New Order), 8 Sept. 2602 and the *Syonan Times*, 9 Sept. 2602, Sel Kan 169/2602; Statement by Y. Uneme, Manager of the Yokohama Specie Bank, Ipoh, Minutes, Meeting of District Officers, 18 Feb. 2603, Batu Gajah 69/2602. See also Managing Director of the People's Bank, Johore Bahru to Commissioner of Lands and Mines, Johore, CLR JB 11/2603.

> … one thing which I have to stress is that the purpose of granting loans being as already explained, to assist the people, a too rigid observance of the rules will sometimes lead to results utterly contrary to our expectation. This is a very important point to bear in mind and I hope all of you gentlemen will use your best effort, discretion and judgment so that the results achieved may be satisfactory to all concerned.[45]

District Officers had full discretion in making recommendations, and were to "satisfy themselves on the bona fides of the applicant rather than be restricted by formalities".[46]

In Singapore, where a People's Treasury opened on 1 September 1942, loans ranged from $50 to $300 and had to be secured by two guarantors or by a caveat against title deeds. The loans were repayable in monthly instalments over a maximum period of two years and interest was assessed at 5 per cent per annum on the outstanding balance. Most borrowers used their loans to settle debts, although some were for trade, industrial purposes, and personal or domestic use. Some 60 per cent of the initial loans went for "unproductive purposes", and the administration hoped that in future the balance would be reversed.[47]

With the end of the war, the People's Bank ceased operations, and in some places the Japanese destroyed bank records. In Lower Perak alone outstanding loans exceeded $73,000, but they were in Japanese currency, which was declared valueless after the war, and in any case the British administration had no jurisdiction to collect these loans. The question of what to do about caveats lodged to secure loans was not resolved until 1949, but ultimately they were removed and the loans were written off. In the words of a post-war District Officer of Lower Perak, borrowers "got away with it".[48]

* * *

[45] Statement by Y. Uneme, Manager of the Yokohama Specie Bank, Ipoh, Minutes, Meeting of District Officers, 18 Feb. 2603, Batu Gajah 69/2602. See also Pk Regulation no. 2 of 2602, The People's Bank of Perak (Loans) Regulations, issued 15 Oct. 2602 by T. Kubota, Governor of Perak, CEP 197/1946.

[46] Statement by the Governor, Minutes, Meeting of District Officers, 18 Feb. 2603, Batu Gajah 69/2602.

[47] The People's Bank of Perak (Loans) Regulations, Regulation no. 2 of 2602, published in the *Perak Times*, 21 Oct. 2602, Sel Kan 160/2602; Report by the General Managers (Yokohama Specie Bank Ltd., Ipoh) on the working of the People's Bank of Perak for the period 1 November to 31 December 2602, 19 Jan. 2603, CEP 197/1946; *Penang Shimbun*, 26 Nov. 2603.

[48] Commssioner of Lands to Financial Secy, F of M, 9 Sept. 1949, CEP 197/1946.

Japan's failure to keep Malayan currency stable was a consequence of the faltering economy. The collapse of Malaya's export industries cost the country the greater part of its income and threw large numbers of people out of work. New industries absorbed only a limited part of the labour force, and the Japanese encouraged people to support themselves through subsistence agriculture, and alter recruited workers for military construction projects. Neither activity generated income, and with trade and primary production at a standstill, the administration lacked sources of revenue to meet expenses. Printing money to make payments inevitably caused inflation, and the government's forced savings campaigns and other expedients to withdraw money from circulation failed to overcome this problem. By the end of the occupation the currency had declined dramatically in value, although fear of Japanese reprisals forced people to continue accepting it. When the war ended, banks had accumulated vast quantities of currenty that was nearly impossible to invest.

CHAPTER 8

The Estate and Mining Industries

During the 1930s Malaya was the world's largest producer of tin, and the second largest producer of rubber. More than half a million people worked directly in mining or on estates and smallholdings, and many others earned their livelihoods providing services that supported these industries. Moreover, export duties collected on rubber and tin accounted for a substantial proportion of government revenues. Malayan production greatly exceeded Japan's modest requirements, and the Deputy Chief of the Military Administration of Malaya announced in March 1942 that production of both rubber and tin would temporarily be restricted.[1] For the duration of the war both industries languished, selling most of their output in the small domestic market, with severe consequences for the country.

The Rubber Industry[2]

In 1941, an exceptionally good year owing to stockpiling by countries preparing for war, territories in Southeast Asia exported approximately 1.3 million tons of rubber, about 85 per cent of the rubber entering the world market. Malaya alone produced more than 547,000 tons of rubber in 1940. However, the occupation left the country isolated from its major buyers, and Japan's wartime requirements were just 70–80,000 tons per year. Japan seized around 150,000

---

[1] Monitored radio broadcast 14 Mar. 1942, CO273/669/50744/7.

[2] General information on the working of the rubber industry during the Japanese Occupation is taken from a post-war interview with T. Okamoto, who was in charge of rubber collection and export for the Malai Gomu Kanri Kumiai. Information on the Fred Waterhouse Company came from the company's Chief Storekeeper, Goh Hee Lye, and interned Japanese civilians (including S. Kuroyanagi, the Japanese manager of Fred Waterhouse Ltd, and T. Kihara, who was in charge of accounts for the Chuo Gomu Kogyo Kabushiki Kaisha. See Malaya – Japanese Penetration of the Rubber Manufacturing Industry, 12 Oct. 1945, NARA RG226 XL23029. This report was compiled by Don Frank, and was given an F-2 evaluation, indicating that the reliability of the source could not be judged, but that the information was probably correct. Frank said the Japanese he interviewed were all "extremely, even embarrassingly, cooperative".

tons of rubber during its advance into Southeast Asia, including 143,000 tons in Malaya and the Netherlands Indies, and if, as is thought, this rubber was sent to Japan, it could have met the country's needs for two years.[3] In 1944 Japanese rubber imports apparently fell to about 35,000 tons, and some of this rubber came from Indochina and Thailand rather than Malaya. Germany needed 40,000 tons per year, but shipments to Europe had to go by submarine and involved blockade running; in 1944 German imports sof rubber from Southeast Asia amounted to just 5,000 tons (see Table 8.1).

Malaya had 3⅓ million acres of rubber land, with 3 million acres in active production. Two-thirds of this area consisted of estates, and the balance was made up of smallholdings—defined in Malaya as landholdings of less than 100 acres. Rubber was planted mainly on the west coast of the peninsula, with Johore, Malacca, Negri Sembilan, Selangor, Perak and Kedah accounting for more than 87 per cent of Malaya's rubber lands (see Map 6.3). The distribution of rubber holdings by state is shown in Table 8.2. It is difficult to estimate the capacity of the Malayan rubber industry because production during the latter part of the 1930s was limited under the terms of the International Rubber Restriction Scheme. Between 1935 and 1941, output averaged 442,000 tons per year.[4] Estimates of Malaya's wartime production are shown in Table 8.3.

---

[3] The figures in this paragraph were developed by the OSS and can be found in The Rubber Industry of Southeast Asia: An Estimate of Present Conditions and Anticipated Capabilities, 16 Dec. 1944, OSS, R&A No. 2589. The report contains the following explanation of the statistics it presents relating to the wartime rubber industry:

> The discussion and the conclusions are based upon (1) a quantity of Japanese claims of what they have done with rubber in Southeast Asia, tested against (2) known pre-war conditions, (3) scattered reports from inexperienced observers who have been in the area since Japanese occupation, (4) intercepted messages, (5) estimates prepared by other United Nations organizations, and (6) guarded reports from French official and journalistic sources. The statistical estimates of production, stock piles, and exports presented are logically developed from fragmentary factual information, and their possible margin of error in some cases is wide. (p. 1)

Another wartime report notes that Japan's own estimates of rubber requirements had never been more than 85,000 tons, and that production in Indochina and Thailand amounted to about 110,000 tons, making it unlikely that a further 500,000 tons from Malaya could be absorbed. R.U. Byatt, Ministry of Economic Warfare, Malaya's Food Position, 2 Feb. 1942, HSI/114.

[4] *Malayan Trade Statistics, 1938*; Malaya – Part I, BMA 506/10.

Map 8.1 Land utilization in Malaya

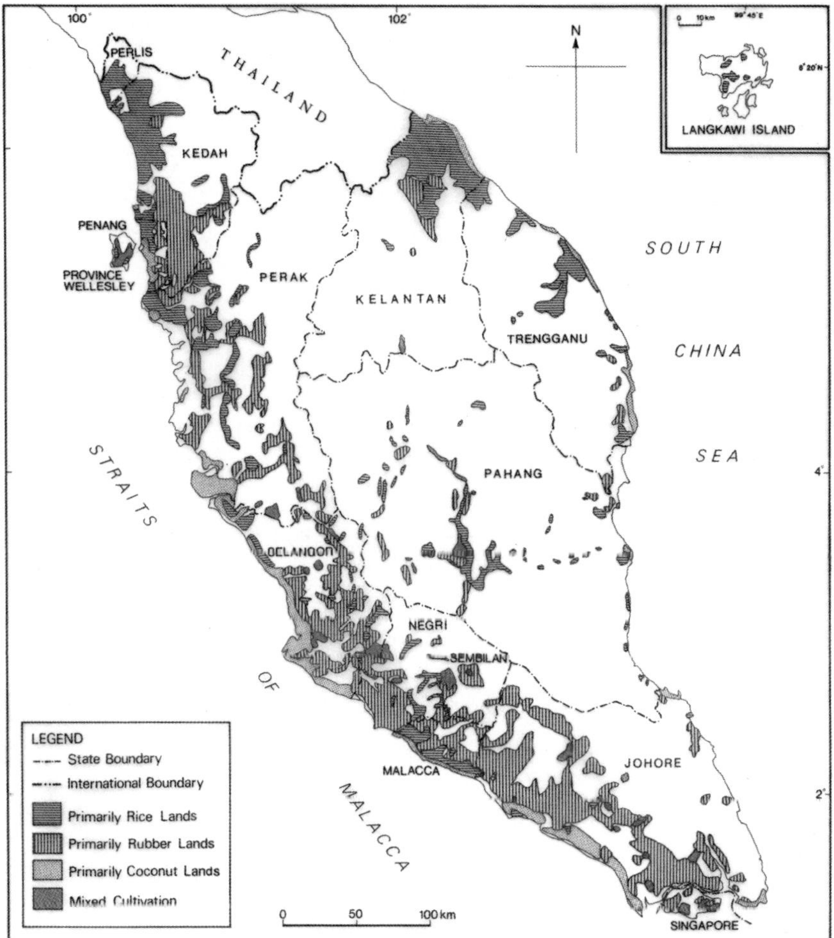

Table 8.1 OSS estimates of rubber exports from Southeast Asia, 1942–44 (*metric tons*)

To	*1942*	*1943*	*1944*
Japan and Inner Zone	177,000	65,500	36,050
China	3,000	8,200	3,100
Germany	40,000	47,000	5,000
Total	220,000	120,700	44,150

Source: OSS, R&A no. 2589, The Rubber Industry of Southeast Asia: An Estimate of Present Conditions and Anticipated Capabilities, 16 Dec. 1944, p. 4.

Table 8.2 Rubber land in Malaya, 1938

Territory	*Area (acres)*	%
Johore	890,000	27.2
Kedah	302,000	9.2
Trengganu	43,000	1.3
Kelantan	92,000	2.8
Perlis	5,500	0.2
UMS Total	1,332,000	40.6
Perak	563,000	17.2
Selangor	496,000	15.1
Negri Sembilan	381,000	11.6
Pahang	173,000	5.3
FMS Total	1,613,000	49.2
Singapore	53,000	1.6
Malacca	194,000	5.9
Penang	18,000	0.6
Province Wellesley	68,000	2.1
SS Total	333,000	10.2
Total	3,278,000	

Source: *Annual Report on the Departments of Agriculture, Malaya, for the Year 1938*, p. 3.

Table 8.3 Estimated Malayan rubber production, 1942–44 (*metric tons*)

	Pre-war average (1935–41)	*1942*	*1943*	*1944*
Production	442,000	109,000	97,900	136,500
Export	434,384	81,500	26,500	15,000
Domestic consumption	n.a.	n.a.	38,400	88,000

Source: OSS, R&A No, 2589, The Rubber Industry of Southeast Asia: An Estimate of Present Conditions and Anticipated Capabilities, 16 Dec. 1944, pp. 6, 10. The OSS described consumption figures for 1943 and 1944 as "highly speculative".

Although Japan could not absorb Malaya's large rubber output, the Japanese saw rubber as an important asset for post-war economic development. The military administration announced in 1942 that rubber acreage was to be reduced to allow for expansion of food production, but it reversed this policy the following year and thereafter made efforts to maintain the productive capacity of the industry. Use of rubber in domestic manufacturing and for fuel production absorbed some local production, but with exports negligible, demand remained far below pre-war levels.[5]

Only Japanese companies that had been involved in the industry before December 1941 were permitted to handle Malayan rubber during the occupation. These firms took over the operation of enemy estates occupying 1,727,575 acres of land, 79 per cent of which was planted with rubber, although ownership remained with the Japanese Custodian of Enemy Property. To oversee the rubber industry, the Military Administration Department created a syndicate of 18 Japanese rubber firms, which operated as the Singapore Rubber Association (Syonan Gomu Kumiai).[6] Founded on 1 May 1942, the Association had branch offices in the Malay Peninsula at Johore Baru (Southern District), Kuala Lumpur (Middle District) and Ipoh (Northern District), and in Sumatra at Medan and Palembang. A Producing Department decided which estates should operate, restored factories, gathered statistics, ran tapping operations and delivered rubber for processing, while a Business Department handled the selection and baling of rubber, organized local markets, purchased rubber from smallholders, and sent rubber sheet to manufacturers in Singapore and Penang. Member companies supplied manpower but did not invest capital in the Association, which was funded by loans from the Southern Regions Development Bank. In Selangor the Association, with some 50,000 workers on the 250 rubber estates under its supervision, was the single largest employer of labour.

The Singapore Rubber Association bought rubber sheet for 20 cents a pound (compared with a price of 36 cents a pound before the war) and sold rubber at prices calculated to force independent producers out of business. It failed to make a profit, and in 1943 the Japanese reorganized production and marketing arrangements. A Rubber Industry Supervision Plan introduced in June of that year left some 40 per cent of the enemy owned estates in the hands of private firms, and gave the rest to the Military Administration. At the end of October, the Singapore Rubber Association was dissolved and replaced by a Malay Rubber Management Association (Malai Gomu Kanri Kumiai, or MGKK), which

---

[5] The Rubber Industry of Southeast Asia: An Estimate of Present Conditions and Anticipated Capabilities, 18 Dec. 1944, OSS, R&A no. 2589, pp. iii, 9, 27, 69; Malaya – Part II, BMA 506/10.

[6] Much of the detail in the following paragraphs is derived from Translation Report no. 81, No. 3 Mobile Section S.E.A.T.I.C., Main HQ 34 Ind Corps, S.E.A.C., 9 Oct. 1945, BMA ADM/9/27, and Summary of Economic Intelligence, no. 130 (15 Oct. 1945), BMA DEPT/18/7. See also Minutes, Meeting of District Officers, 5 Nov. 2602, Batu Gajah 69/2602; Extract from Recent Press References to the British Empire, Summary no. 34, 21 Sept. 1942, BMA PS/410 part I.

became an affiliate of the Japan Rubber Importers Association. Singapore was again the site of the headquarters, and the Singapore office was responsible for Johore, Singapore, and Riau. A branch office in Kuala Lumpur took charge of Selangor, Negri Sembilan, Malacca and Pahang, and another in Taiping handled Penang, Province Wellesley and Perak. Estates sold crude rubber to the parent body, which set prices and compensated members for any losses at the end of each financial period. The purchase of rubber from independent producers was handled by authorized firms that were subject to MGKK regulations and sold the rubber they acquired to the Association. Estates controlled by the MGKK continued operations until March 1945, working under a quota set by the military which they failed to meet. For example, in the fiscal year ending in March 1945 the quota was 52,000 tons, but MGKK estates supplied just 30,789 tons. The government held the price at 20 cents a pound until April 1945, when it was doubled in an effort to overcome shortages.[7]

The estates and smallholdings that continued to operate found it difficult to obtain equipment and chemicals. On many estates the British had destroyed machinery, smokehouses, coagulating tanks and other processing equipment before withdrawing, and these items could not easily be replaced. However, the greatest impediment to rubber production was a severe shortage of acid to process raw latex. Formic and acetic acid, the usual coagulants, were all but unavailable and prohibitively expensive, with a large jar of acetic acid reportedly selling for $250 in September 1943. Producers tried a variety of substitutes, including wood acid (a by-product of charcoal manufacturing), urine, pineapple juice and toddy—an alcoholic drink made from the sap of the coconut palm. Toddy, which is obtained by tapping the inflorescence of palm trees, begins to ferment as soon as it is exposed to air and remains drinkable only for a few hours. For rubber production, the liquid was allowed to stand for four to five days until it assumed a "muddy transparent" appearance, at which point it was ready for use.[8] In Selangor, where the Agriculture Department rented several thousand trees from coconut estates (at a rate of 25–50 cents per month per tree) to obtain

[7] See correspondence in DO Temerloh 125/2602, and Akashi, "Military Administration in Malaya", p. 60. Akashi observes that the formation of the MGKK reflected a wish on the part of the bureaucrats to increase their control over the industry, but it resulted in inefficiency and confusion.

[8] Sel Rubber Department, AR for 2602, Sel Kan 111/2603; JICA/CBI Report no. 8341, 5 Sept. 1944, NARA RG226 95618.

toddy, the state Rubber Department claimed that rubber sheet produced using toddy was as good as that made in the conventional way.[9]

Smallholders found their incomes severely reduced because of the fall in demand, and without acetic acid it was all but impossible for them to produce rubber sheet of saleable quality. For a brief period early in the occupation they sold rubber through local officials, who were issued temporary permits allowing them to act as buyers, but rubber production soon fell off sharply. In May 1942 a Pahang official reported that nearly all rubber had been left unattended owing to "the non-existence of rubber price", and that smallholders had no interest in replanting or in acquiring bud-stock.[10] The following month the administration renewed the licences of pre-war rubber dealers, who began purchasing smallholder rubber at prices fixed by the government,[11] but at the end of April 1943 the Syonan Military Administrator advised private rubber dealers to stop buying rubber, and when the licences expired on 15 June they were not renewed. Fresh licences became available in August, but attracted little interest.[12]

Rubber manufacturing

Singapore's rubber factories[13] suffered relatively little damage during the invasion and soon resumed operations. In the 1930s production consisted largely of tyres and shoes, but during the occupation they turned out a wide range of new products, ranging from furniture and sanitary fittings to solid bicycle tyres. The latter were made of smoked rubber sheet with a wire cable or rope base, and people referred to them as "dead tyres". Rubber was also used to produce rubberized coconut fibres for stuffing cushions and mattresses, to make condoms, rubber gloves and erasers, and to prepare a latex compound used as an adhesive agent in making plywood.[14]

The Yokohama Rubber Manufacturing Company operated the Singapore Rubber Works (formerly a Dutch-owned company) and a much smaller Singapore firm called the Nanyang Manufacturing Company, along with the former

[9] Agriculture Department, Sel (Estates) 66A/2602; Sel Rubber Department, AR for 2602, Sel Kan 111/2603.

[10] Malay Agricultural Officer for South Pahang Circle, Monthly Report for May 2602, DO Temerloh 103/2602.

[11] Chief Officer, Rubber Department, AR for 2602, Sel Kan 111/2603.

[12] See correspondence in DO Temerloh 125/2602.

[13] Some of the most important were operated by the Tan Kah Kee Rubber Company, the Lee Rubber Company, the Firestone and Goodyear companies, and the Singapore Rubber Works.

[14] Abridged Report on the Work in 2602 of the Rubber Research Institute of Malai, pp. 20–1, Sel Kan 43/2603. Domei reported in January 1944 that solid tyres were "immensely popular". Poobalan George Rajamani, untitled paper.

Wilkinson Process Rubber Company, a British company in Kuala Lumpur. The factories produced rubber hoses, belts, rubber shoes, tyres, condoms and Bakelite goods. There were ample supplies of crude rubber and as of early 1943 a year's supply of chemicals. Much of the output went to the military.[15]

Rubber enterprises in Singapore operated at a loss throughout the war. The Japanese managers responsible for these firms blamed their lack of profitability on wartime conditions, particularly the Allied naval blockade, and on instructions issued by the Military Administration Department that showed little concern for business considerations. Other difficulties included a shortage of experienced technical management, the activities of black market traders and the inability of the government to control prices. Moreover, because production was carried out in premises that formerly belonged to British or American firms, expansion or alteration of the factories required approval from the Custodian of Enemy Property.

A detailed report on the wartime operations of the Fred Waterhouse Company, a Singapore rubber manufacturer, provides useful details on the rubber business during the occupation. Located along Bukit Timah Road, the Waterhouse plant had employed some 225 persons before the war to mill low quality smoked sheet into smoked blanket crepe for sale to Goodyear in Malaya, and to prepare rubber for shipment to Europe. At the beginning of the occupation the company's premises were taken over for about a month by an Army unit, which removed all finished products and shipped them out of the country. On 1 May the plant resumed operations as part of the Singapore Rubber Association, and in 1943 it was taken over by the Chuo Gomu Kogyo Kabushiki Kaisha (Central Rubber Industry Company), a newly-formed Kobe firm that had taken over the business of the Dunlop Rubber Company of Japan, and in addition to the Singapore facility operated the former Bata Shoe Company at Klang in Malaya and factories in Sumatra. This firm obtained capital by borrowing from Japanese banks at rates of 4.5 to 5 per cent, and used the funds to order machinery from Japan, but transport shortages impeded its expansion plans, as did difficulties in procuring adequate rice rations for the workforce, and the plant operated far below maximum capacity. Under its new management, the Waterhouse factory manufactured Dunlop products, including a line of cushions known as "Dunlop Pillows" used for chairs and in cars and other motor vehicles. It also produced hygienic sacks, icebags (used by the air force as in-flight urinals), balloons, solid bicycle tyres and machinery belts,

[15] "An Overview of Important Industrial Factories in Syonan Municipality", by Gunsei Kanbu, General Department Research Office, March 1943, in *The Chosabu Reports*, trans. and ed. Huff and Majima, Chapter 6.

retreaded old tyres and did waterproofing. Many of the company's products were substitutes for unavailable items, such as engine fan belts made from old airplane tyres and smoked rubber sheet. The company supplied the military, in particular the Tsukasa Unit, which handled air force supplies for the Southern Region, and in principle was entitled to make a 20 per cent profit. However, the plant reported substantial losses.[16]

The Japanese did not operate a central military buying office. The Army, Navy, Air Force, and Municipal Government arranged purchases under separate agreements with private factories, and Allied investigators found indications that Army contracts involved "personal arrangements" with plant managers. As an example, the Yokohama Rubber Company sold hygienic sacks for 8½ cents each while the Central Rubber Industry Company sold them for 15 cents, but the Air Force "inexplicably" stopped buying these items from the Yokohama Rubber Company and bought them from the latter firm.[17]

Rubber oil[18]

Rubber oil and products distilled from rubber oil were used widely in occupied Malaya, particularly to operate civilian vehicles. Pre-war attempts to derive fuel from rubber had been unsuccessful because samples of rubber-based gasoline had low octane ratings and high levels of resin, which could not be removed by conventional refining. During the occupation, the Rubber Research Institute in Kuala Lumpur renewed the attempt to develop a gum-free gasoline. The *Syonan Times* reported in May 1942 that experiments had shown that scrap rubber could be used to make machine oil, paints, medines to treat skin ailments such as athlete's foot and ringworm, and that high octane gasoline would be produced in the future.[19] In his annual report for 2602 (1942), the officer in charge of the Selangor Rubber Department, K.S. Pillay, claimed to have succeeded in producing a gasoline that was "absolutely colourless and water-clear", and with

[16] Malaya – Japanese Penetration of the Rubber Manufacturing Industry, NARA RG226 XL23029; Summary of Economic Intelligence no. 132, 29 Oct. 1945, WO208/1532. The data in this source were obtained from Japanese sources, but the author of the report indicated that many records had been destroyed. The information was considered "reasonably accurate".

[17] Malaya – Japanese Penetration of the Rubber Manufacturing Industry, NARA RG226 XL23029.

[18] The main sources of information used in developing this account of rubber oil are: AR on the Rubber Oil Factory for 2602, Sel Agr Dept AR 2602, Sel Kan 111/2603; Summary of Economic Intelligence no. 130, BMA DEPT/18/7; Extract from Far Eastern Weekly Intelligence Summary no. 9 for the week ending 26 Feb. 1943, CO273/669/50744/7.

[19] *The Syonan Times*, 14 May Syowa 17 (1942), p. 2.

the "unsaturated Hydrocarbons which gradually polymerises [*sic*] resulting in the formation of gum which is very detrimental to automobiles and other engines ... completely ... removed or converted into saturated compounds". He added, somewhat extravagantly, "It gives more mileage to the gallon, possesses more pulling power and is in no way inferior to the mineral petrol."[20]

In reality, rubber-based products had to be mixed with those made from mineral oils to be of any use. Rubber petrol was mixed with gasoline at a ratio of 1:1 or 1:2, while rubber oil used as a lubricant was mixed with mineral oil at a ratio of 3:7. Even then rubber oil products rapidly fouled engines, and vehicles using them required frequent cleaning.[21] The secretary of Ishihara Industries, Tojo Takumi, commented in an interview that appeared in the *Asahi Weekly* magazine in February 1943:

> We experimented with rubber to produce gasoline, but it is rather complicated. Crude oil resembling Diesel oil comes out from the first dry distillation of rubber and gasoline substitute comes out from the second distillation. However, within this gasoline substitute, there are rubber particles which are rather difficult to eliminate. When used in vehicles the rubber particles will be a hindrance and will stop the pistons in the cylinders. It is difficult to eliminate these rubber particles.[22]

The largest rubber oil factory in Malaya was located on the Wardieburn estate in Selangor, but the technology involved was simple and factories producing rubber oil sprang up on many other rubber estates and in various towns. The Wardieburn plant, officially opened on 11 December 1942, had 32 furnaces on which retorts holding 200 pounds of rubber each were placed. The rubber was heated, and the resulting vapours were passed through water-cooled condensers to produce oil. Separators removed water from the oil, which was then transferred to a pair of 15,000 gallon reservoirs to await further processing. Operating two shifts a day, the factory had the capacity to produce over 30,000 gallons per month. The output during the first month was 31,511 gallons of oil, which was sold without further refining at 90 cents per gallon for anti-malarial use, since at that stage the state had sufficient gasoline but anti-malarial oil was

---

[20] AR on the Rubber Oil Factory for 2602, Sel Agr Dept AR 2602, Sel Kan 111/2603. Similar remarks appear in newspaper reports. See, e.g., *Syonan Times*, 23 Aug. 2602.

[21] Summary of Economic Intelligence no. 134, WO203/2647; Monthly returns from DO Larut to Sangyobu Noen Kacho, Perak, and Perak Shu Chokan to Perak DOs, 31 Jan. 2604, DO Larut 138/2603.

[22] Article entitled "The Magnificent Reconstruction of Malaya", published in *Shukan Asahi* magazine, 21 Feb. 1943, ATIS Current Translation no. 122, 31 May 1944, NARA RG165 Box 286 Entry 79.

"wanted urgently".[23] With carefully controlled heating the rubber left a residue that resembled bitumen; "overheating gives hard charred remains … while under heating leaves a highly viscous substance which will not harden on cooling or exposure".[24] By weight, the yield of rubber oil was 35 per cent: 5 per cent for gasoline for motore, 20 per cent diesel oil, and 10 per cent fuel oil.[25]

Rubber oil could also be made using very simple equipment in the villages. Haji Che Man bin Muhammad, who lived in Kedah, owned a small lorry which he used to carry produce into town to sell at the market. To obtain oil for this vehicle, he heated scrap rubber in a large pot that was sealed except for a hole to which he had attached a piece of bamboo. The vapours liquified in the bamboo, and he collected the output in a bottle.[26]

The distillation process involved heating rubber oil to produce a gas that was passed repeatedly through cold water, yielding in succession first a benzine substitute, then heavy oil, and finally anti-malarial oils. The proportions were: benzine substitute, 30 per cent; heavy oil, 20 per cent; anti-malarial oil, 50 per cent.[27] According to the officer in charge of the Rubber Department, the anti-malarial oil produced in this way had "a good spread and larvicidal properties and compares favourably and perhaps better than the usual mineral anti malarial oil".[28] The Chairman of the Ulu Selangor Sanitary Board, who used it, said, "The effect of this Oil is not as good as the previous one but nevertheless it is a great boon at this time particularly to be able to get it at all."[29]

Prices for rubber oil became very high toward the end of the occupation. In Kedah it sold for $160 per gallon in July 1945, and manufacturers were refusing to quote firm prices because of the volatility of the market.[30]

---

[23] AR on the Rubber Oil Factory for 2602, Sel Agr Dept AR 2602, Sel Kan 111/2603.

[24] Kedah State Engineer, Interim Report on the Distillation of Rubber Oil, 4 Jan. 2487, SUK Kedah 21/2487.

[25] OSS, R&A no. 2589, The Rubber Industry of Southeast Asia, 16 Dec. 1944, p. 3n2.

[26] Hairani Mohd Khalid, "Satu Tinjauan Am tentang Kehidupan Penduduk Mukim Relau, Kedah semasa Pendudukan Jepun".

[27] An experimental still in Kedah produced six grades of oil. Kedah State Engineer, Interim Report on the Distillation of Rubber Oil, 4 Jan. 2487, SUK Kedah 21/2487.

[28] AR on the Rubber Oil Factory for 2602, Sel Agr Dept AR 2602, Sel Kan 111/2603.

[29] Ulu Sel SB, AR 2602, Sel Kan 108/2603.

[30] Secy General to Military Commissioner Syburi, 13 June 2488, SUK Kedah 431/2488.

Other Commercial Cultivation

Enemy estates planted with oil palm, coconuts and tea resumed operations in Selangor under the Agriculture Department in March 1942, and a newly organized Research Branch of the department launched an effort to develop additional uses for palm oil. Among other things, it encouraged production of soap, grease, a diesel oil substitute, and a nutritional supplement known as Red Medical Palm Oil. In October oil palm plantations were handed over to the Syowa Rubber Company, although the Agriculture Department continued to operate its soap factory and production reached 2,200 bars a day by the end of the year.[31] Attempts to use palm oil as a substitute for diesel oil produced unsatisfactory results: "The experiments proved that it could be used as a substitute by big engines only and that it was inferior to diesel oil in ignition value (flash point). Besides extra work is entailed in preheating the palm oil before combustion."[32]

Malaya produced 75,000 tons of copra, or dried coconut flesh, annually before the war. In Selangor smallholders resumed processing copra in July 1942, but prices were very low until November, when oil mills started operating. Coconut flesh was also used as food, and the sap of the coconut palm was boiled down to make palm sugar, which for many people replaced imported sugar during the occupation.[33] As a food product and a source of oil, coconuts were subject to trade restrictions, and a lively black market developed. In February 1944 the Perak government announced new regulations to stop the illegal export of copra from the state, made necessary by "the selfishness of some people who think only of making a large profit for themselves". Owners of coconut trees were now required to sell half of their monthly output of copra to the government at set prices for processing in oil mills under government control. People could process oil at home for personal use only if they obtained a written permit, and only up to a limit of one kati (1⅓ pounds) per person per month. Such oil was strictly not to be sold. Similarly, copra, copra cake, and the refuse from making oil were to be used as far as possible within the villages, and could not be removed from the districts where they were produced. Informers were promised bonuses for reporting people who violated these rules.[34]

---

31 AR, Oil Palm Estates, 2602, 27 Feb. 2603, AR Sel Agr Dept, 2603, Sel Kan 111/2603; AR Tekisan Kanri Kyoku, Sel, Showa 17 Nen (2602), Sel Kan 113/2603.

32 AR Sel Mines Dept, 2602, Sel Kan 107/2603; Far Eastern Bureau/Malaya under the Japanese, NARA RG226 128585.

33 AR, Sel Agri Dept, 2602, Sel Kan 111/2603; Burkill, *Economic Products of the Malay Peninsula*, vol. 1, pp. 618–19.

34 Sangyobu Rin-Enka (Koen), Perak, 23 Feb. 2604, Larut 60/2604.

There was some adulteration of coconut oil, and the State Surgeon for Kedah reported treating cases of acute gastroenteritis involving "fever, vomiting, diarrhoea, and collapse" caused by consumption of coconut oil mixed with rubber oil. Intended for use in lamps, this mixture was sold by some dealers as pure coconut oil, and if consumed produced symptoms which were "most alarming and distressing". Although no deaths had occurred, the State Surgeon said the practice amounted to "an attempt at wholesale poisoning of the inhabitants of this country". Unless the coconut oil was heavily adulterated, the deception was difficult to detect by visual examination. "I think the public will be safe in assuming all coconut oils that crackle loudly producing an irritating and nauseating vapour which catches the throat on heating, are adulterated."[35]

Timber was cut in Malaya before the war on a systematic basis by sawmills operating under the control of the Forest Department, which also supervised a replanting programme that had raised the quantity of usable timber from 16 tons per acre to 200 tons per acre by increasing the density of economically valuable species.[36] During the occupation the timber industry remained under government controls, and the Military Administration formed a Forestry Association in 1943 to handle lumbering and charcoal production. The capacity of the industry was 24,350 tons per month, 5,000 tons less than before the war owing to damage to sawmills, but actual production appears to have been far below this figure.[37] In Kedah the government cancelled all agreements with private contractors and assigned all forest reserves to Japanese timber firms and their agents. Thai administration apparently assigned rights to some areas to more than one bidder, causing considerable friction among the Japanese companies involved. All firms were supposed to obtain permits from the Forest Office and pay royalties to the Kedah government, but three Japanese companies refused to follow these procedures, and instructed Forest Department staff members to stay away from their working areas.[38]

There was widespread felling of reserved forests to open land for food production, although in some places this process turned into a disguised form of land grabbing, and resulted in the planting of non-food crops such as tobacco,

---

[35] Kedah State Surgeon to Under Secty to Govt, 18 Dec. and 30 Dec. 2486, SUK Kedah 206/2486.

[36] BMA Advisory Council, Perak, Meeting of 7 Mar. 1946, Sel CA 335/1945.

[37] Summary of Economic Intelligence No. 134, WO203/2647.

[38] S.O. III, Forests, Region I to Director of Forests, 9 Feb. 1946, Forests 30/1945. The companies concerned were Toyo Kozan, a mining company which was gathering firewood, Ando Han, a general military contractor, and Nichinan, a charcoal maker.

coffee and rubber.[39] At least 12,526 acres (43 per cent) of forest undergoing regeneration, and 31,289 acres (24 per cent) of completely regenerated forest were destroyed for foodcrop cultivation.[40]

Shipyards consumed great quantities of timber, and Japan's effort to build wooden ships led to increased felling of trees. When the war ended there were large numbers of logs lying in or near forest areas, although much of this wood had no commercial value. The rivers of Pahang were "choked with logs", and teak logs brought from Burma lay buried in 14 feet of mud at a huge timber dump near Penang.[41]

Overall, Malayan forests suffered extensive damage during the occupation from indiscriminate cutting and from the release of land for food cultivation. Forest officers attempted to maintain pre-war standards and pursue a rational programme of land use, but had little success. In Negri Sembilan, the field staff could not control Chinese timber cutters, "who treated them with contempt", and the Food Production Board overruled attempts by the State Forest Officer in Selangor to prevent the destruction of valuable forests.[42] In the words of a Japanese who served in the Selangor Forest Department, "*Kitapunya tanggan tiada chukop kuat manahan soldier*" [Our hands are not strong enough to restrain the soldiers].[43]

Minerals

Tin

Perak and Selangor accounted for more than 90 per cent of Malaya's output of tin. The major producing areas were the Kinta, Batang Padang and Larut districts in Perak, and the Ulu Selangor District and the Ampang area near Kuala Lumpur in Selangor (see Map 8.2). As of March 1941 there were 123 mining companies in Malaya operating a total of 1,016 mines. Capital investment amounted to £18.5 million, with about £1 million from foreign sources and

---

[39] Forest Department, Report for Jan. 1946, BMA DEPT/11/3.

[40] T.A. Strong, Director of Forestry, Malayan Union, "Report on Forest Administration in the Malayan Union for 1947", p. 1.

[41] S.O. III, Forests, Region I to Director of Forests, 9 Feb. 1946; Position of the Pahang Forest Department at the time of the reoccupation and subsequently; State Forest officer, Pk to Dir of Forests, BMA, 15 Feb. 1946, Forests 30/1945.

[42] OIC Forests, BMA, NS and Malacca to Dir. of Forests, BMA, 6 Feb. 1946; State Forest Officer, Sel, Report on the Forest Department, Sel, 11 Feb. 1946, Forests 30/1945.

[43] K. Kubo, cited in Extra Asst Conservator of Forests, Organisation of the Forest Department in Selangor under the Japanese Regime, 1942–45, 26 Sept. 1945, Forests 30/1945.

the rest equally divided between British and "local" (including local European) investors. Just 860 mines used heavy equipment, including 73 with bucket dredges. Dredges were operated by European-owned mines, and accounted for between half and two-thirds of the total output. About 100,000 labourers were directly employed in mining tin, and substantial numbers of people earned their livelihoods by transporting and smelting ore or providing related services.[44]

Map 8.2 Principal mining regions of Malaya

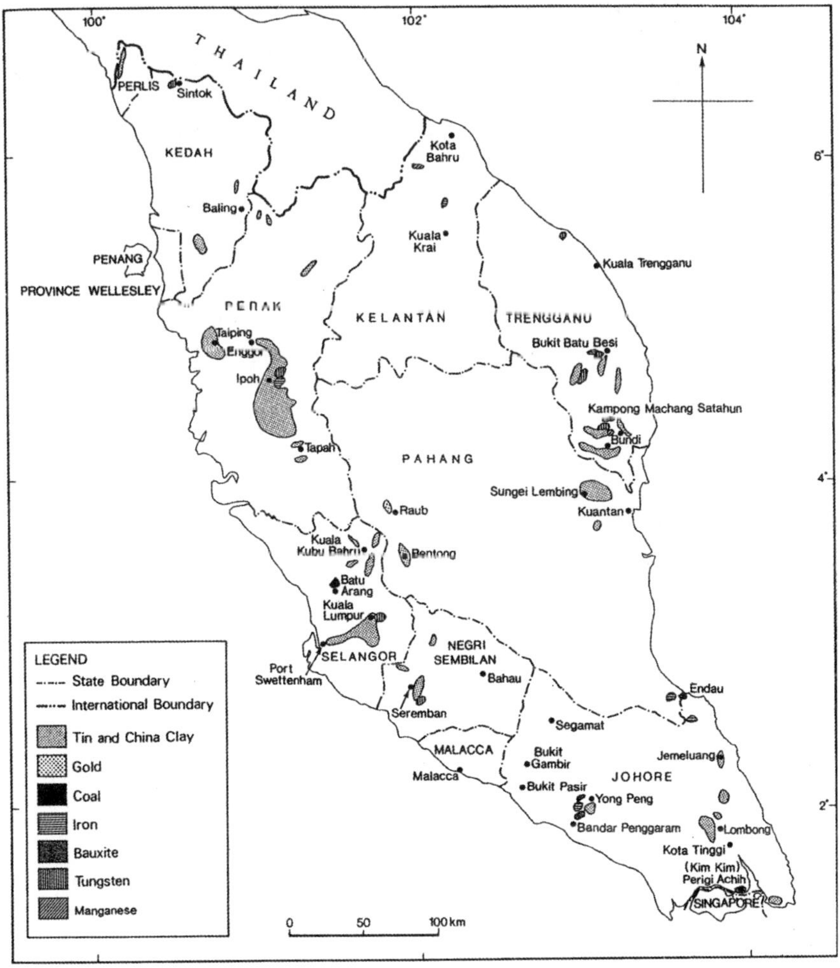

---

44 Malaya – Part I, BMA 506/10; An Outline of the Measures Now Receiving Consideration, CO852/623/5.

Britain's scorched earth policy targeted tin mining operations. Of 42 dredges in Selangor, 29 were sunk in the course of the British withdrawal, and "almost all the vital parts of the machineries were damaged". By the end of 1942 most of the sunken dredges had been refloated, and 14 were operating while another 10 were undergoing restoration. However, the industry faced many obstacles in carrying out repairs:

> Not only were materials scarce but also the prices demanded for such materials as were available were very high. In cases where materials were not available, they were taken either from the irreparable or partly dismantled dredges. In this connection it might be mentioned that but for the hearty co-operation extended by the local factories in casting spare parts the work on these dredges would not have been finished so rapidly.[45]

Shortages of diesel fuel and petrol, and of oil and grease for lubrication made it difficult to operate even those mines where the equipment remained in working order. By the end of 1942, the stocks of pre-war lubricants held by the mining industry had largely been exhausted, and the Chief Inspector of Mines in Selangor reported that if further supplies could not be found the dredges would have to cease operations, throwing thousands of miners out of work. His own requirements were 15 tons of yellow grease each month, and Japanese mining companies also needed substantial quantities. The Department of Agriculture made grease at its soap factory, but as of January 1943 the output was just five tons per month and the quality was unsatisfactory. The mining industry required grease that would not melt under high temperatures and could withstand pressures of several tons, and during 1943 the Agriculture Department began trying to produce a vegetable-based grease that would meet these requirements. Initial samples had an unsatisfactorily low sliding point of 75°C, but by April the Department had achieved a palm oil product with a melting point of 120°C, and one of the principal Japanese mining companies, the Nippon Kogyo Kabushiki Kaisha, declared it adequate.[46]

As with rubber, Malayan tin production far exceeded Japan's requirements, which intelligence estimates placed at around 10–12,000 tons per year. Malaya alone produced 83,000 tons in 1940, and Japan also had access to tin from Thailand and Indochina. Throughout the occupation Malayan tin production remained far below pre-war levels, and the situation steadily deteriorated. Tables 8.4 and 8.5 chart the decline in output and in the number of mines operating between 1940 and 1945. As tin production fell, idle mining equipment was

---

[45] AR Sel Mines Dept, 2602, Sel Kan 107/2603.

[46] Ibid.

transferred to other industries, and in some cases was broken up for use in shipbuilding.[47]

Table 8.4 Malayan tin production (*tons*)

	Production
1937	77,542
1938	43,247
1939	47,416
1940	83,000
1941	79,400
1942	15,700
1943	26,000
1944	9,400
1945	3,100

Source: Yip Yat Hoong, *The Development of the Tin Mining Industry of Malaya*, pp. 281, 295.

Table 8.5 Number of mines operating and producing in Malaya

	Dredging	*Gravel pump*	*Hydrau-licing*	*Opencast*	*Misc.*	*Small workings without machinery*	*Total*
1939	73	538	33	20	10	220	894
1940	72	722	34	22	9	151	1,021
Sept. 1941	74	668	31	17	10	123	933
1946	18	102	23	1	6	60	216

Source: Annual Report on the Administration of the Mines Department and on the Mining Industry of the Malayan Union for 1946, p. 8.

Other minerals

In addition to tin, Malaya produced gold, iron ore, manganese, bauxite, monazite and fluorspar (see Map 8.2). There was also some wolframite, used to make tungsten, but reserves were nearly exhausted before the invasion. Gold was found in several areas of the peninsula but only mined on a significant scale by the Raub Australian Gold Mining Company in Pahang. The Raub mine was a

[47] D.A.D.C.A. Selangor (Mines & Geological Survey), Statement of Periodical Reports on the Activities of the Mines and Geological Survey for the Period 1 October to 31 October 1945. Sel CA283/1945.

lode formation that yielded about 40,000 ounces per year.[48] With the exception of gold and tin, pre-war mineral extraction was dominated by Japanese firms, which operated mines in Johore, Kelantan and Trengganu (see Table 8.6).

Table 8.6 Mineral production in pre-war Malaya

	Mines	*Production (tons p.a.)*	*Ore quality (%)*
Iron Ore	Trengganu (Dungun and	1,000,000	62
	Machang Satahan mines)	150,000	46–50
	Kelantan (Temangan mine)	200,000	
	Johore	700,000	56–60
	(Sri Medan and Iizuka mines)		
Manganese	Trengganu (Machang Satahan mine)	25,000	25–30
	Kelantan (Temangan mine)	9,000	45
Bauxite	Johore (Bukit Pasir and Kimkim mines)	55,000	
Tungsten	Perak (Kramat Pulai)	400	

Source: Malaya – Part I, BMA 506/10.

Malaya had two bauxite mines in Johore, one near Batu Pahat and the other at the Kim Kim River along the Straits of Johore, both operated by the Ishihara Sangyo Kaisha. There were also bauxite mines on Bintan Island in the Riau archipelago, just south of Singapore, which were superior to those in Johore, and the Furukawa Kogyo Kabushiki Kaisha took over these mines following the Dutch surrender. During the occupation Bintan was administered from Singapore.[49] The Japanese prioritized bauxite production and intensified mining operations. In 1944 Johore and Bintan supplied Japan with 650,000 tons of bauxite, about 80 per cent of its total supply.[50] However, Allied attacks made it impossible to ship ore to Japan in 1945, and in March the Military Administration in Singapore halted mining operations. Bauxite shipments to Japan during the occupation amounted to 1,600,000 metric tons (see Table 8.7).

[48] China Station Colonial Intelligence Report (vol. III): Malaya (June 1941), WO252/900; Malaya – Part I, BMA506/10.

[49] Summary of Economic Intelligence no. 132, WO208/1532.

[50] JM 167, p. 19; NARA RG226 22025.

Table 8.7 Bauxite production, 1942–March 1945 (*metric tons*)

	Mined (1942–45)	*Ore stocks (Sept. 1945)*	*Ore shipped to Japan*
Johore			
1. Bukit Pasir	180,000	30,000	150,000
2. Bukit Seberang	170,000	70,000	100,000
3. Bukit Simon	45,450	42,000	3,450
Bintan	1,519,000	169,000	1,350,000
Total	1,914,450	311,000	1,603,450

Source: Summary of Economic Intelligence no. 132, 29 Oct. 1945, WO208/1532, p. 5.

The quality of the iron and manganese ores found in Malaya was poor, and before the war the mines were of little interest except to the Japanese, who had few alternative sources of supply. Japanese companies operated iron mines at Batu Pahat and Endau in Johore, at Kemaman and Dungun in Trengganu, and in Kelantan, and these facilities accounted for about one-third of Japan's pre-war iron imports. The same sites produced manganese ore, and Japan imported 320,000 tons from Malaya in 1936.[51]

The iron mines were opencast. Mine operators used compressors for drilling, and moved the ore on light railways to riverside wharves where it was loaded onto lighters. Apart from the Sri Medan Mine near Batu Pahat, Malaya's iron mines escaped damage in the British scorched earth campaign.[52] During the Occupation private firms operating under the control of the Military Administration handled mining operations, using loans provided by the Southern Regions Development Bank. However, the mining companies were unable to procure equipment from Japan, and considered locally-produced machinery unsatisfactory. They also faced labour shortages, and found it difficult to obtain supplies of rice for their workers. Throughout the Occupation the mines never managed to operate at pre-war capacity, and shipments of ore to Japan fell far short of expectations. For the fiscal year ending in March 1943, just 104,750 of a planned 350,000 tons of iron ore went to Japan, and 13,558 tons out of

[51] Japanese firms involved in manganese production were Ishihara Sangyo Koshi, Nippon Mining Co., and Nanyo Kogyo Koshi. See FIR 8 May 1943, NARA KG226 38483.

[52] OSS Planning Group, Implementation Study for Strategic Services Activity in the SEAC: Malaya, 3 July 1944, NARA OSS RG226 E136 folder 650; Japan Section, E.R.D., "Malaya – Japanese Economic Gains", 8/1/42, WO208/1527.

a planned 27,000 tons of manganese ore.[53] Wartime production of iron ore is shown in Table 8.8.

Table 8.8 Iron ore production in Malaya, 1942–45 (*tons*)

	Output
1942	90,780
1943	48,360
1944	10,450
1945	13,380

Source: Annual Report on the Administration of the Mines Department and on the Mining Industry of the Malayan Union for 1946, p. 25.

Coal

The Batu Arang coalfield in Selangor, operated by Malayan Collieries, was the only site in the Malay Peninsula where coal was mined commercially. The mines produced a high-grade lignite that was used by the Malayan railway system, and by tin mines and other local industries to fire boilers. Because it had "the unfortunate characteristic of being liable to spontaneous combustion",[54] the coal could not be carried on steamships, and its composition was unsuitable for metallurgical furnaces. Production amounted to about 600,000 tons per annum.

Table 8.9 Coal production in Malaya, 1942–45 (*tons*)

	Output
1942	244,590
1943	489,440
1944	409,100
1945	202,900

Source: Annual Report on the Administration of the Mines Department and on the Mining Industry of the Malayan Union for 1946, p. 24.

The British flooded the Batu Arang mines during the evacuation, causing serious damage. Under the Japanese, the Mitsubishi Kogyo Kabushiki Kaisha operated the Batu Arang facility, and despite guerrilla activity in the vicinity

---

53 Summary of Economic Intelligence no. 132, WO208/1532.

54 FIR 4, 29 Feb. 1944, CO273/673/50744/7.

exploited it intensively. During 1942, two of the six underground mines (the West Mine and the North Mine) were pumped out, cleaned and retimbered, while shale stripping took place in six of the eleven opencast pits. Output during 1942 was 244,590 tons of coal, compared with 781,509 tons in 1940 and 584,655 tons in 1941.[55] Production during the occupation is shown in Table 8.9. The forested area around the mine provided building materials and supports for the underground mining operations, while waste wood was converted into charcoal, and the surface clay removed from the coal beds was used to manufacture bricks. In 1944, intelligence reports indicated that shipments of machinery destined for Batu Arang had reached Kuala Lumpur, and that the Japanese planned to increase the output of coal, but production declined in 1945.[56]

* * *

It is a commonplace of historical writing on Malaya that the peninsula was an inviting target first for the British, and later for the Japanese, because of the reserves of tin and the rich plantation lands found there, yet in both instances there is substantial evidence to support the idea that the peninsula's strategic location rather than its natural resources accounted for foreign intervention. Had Japan been successful in the war, Malayan tin and rubber could ultimately have benefitted industry within the Greater East Asian Co-Prosperity Sphere, but during the war Japan could not absorb Malaya's production of these commodities. Without access to overseas markets, Malaya's economy was crippled for the duration of the occupation, and the collapse of the rubber and tin industries brought unemployment and widespread economic distress.

---

[55] AR Mines Dept, Sel, 2602, Sel Kan 107/2603.

[56] Article entitled "The Magnificent Reconstruction of Malaya", 21 Feb. 1943, ATIS Current Translations no. 122, 31 May 1944, NARA RG165 Box 286 Entry 79; China Station Colonial Intelligence Report (vol. III): Malaya (June 1941), WO252/900; Malaya – Part I, BMA506/10.

CHAPTER 9

Rationing and Food Production

The most important factor in gaining the support of the Malayan population, according to one Japanese account, was not the ideals associated with Greater East Asia but stability, and the key to that was food.[1] The Japanese achieved a precarious stability, but food shortages plagued Japanese administrations throughout Southeast Asia, particularly in food deficit areas such as Malaya. Before the war, Malaya imported around two-thirds of its annual rice requirements, but very little imported rice reached the peninsula during the occupation, and much of the population was forced to subsist on the limited quantities of rice and vegetables produced locally. The Japanese brought shipments of rice into Singapore but expected each state in the peninsula, and even districts within the states, to become self-sufficient with regard to food, and called upon the rural population to help meet the needs of people living in towns and cities. Campaigns to promote the cultivation of foodcrops succeeded in averting starvation, but many people survived on a nutritionally inadequate diet of starchy roots such as tapioca and sweet potatoes.

Before the war, Malaya imported rice from Burma, Thailand and Vietnam, countries that accounted for about two-thirds of world rice exports. Japanese figures indicated that in 1941 Malaya imported 50,000 tons of rice per month. In 1942 the figure fell to 42,000 tons, and by March 1943 it was 34,000 tons. To make up for the shortfall, the Japanese brought in around 4,000 tons of alternative foods each month, including maize, soybeans, dried tapioca and tapioca flour. A report on food supplies prepared in 1944 observed that poorer people relied almost exclusively on rice substitutes, and sold their rice rations on the black market. The report also indicated that the regulatory bodies had "little understanding of economic realities" and introducted regulation "on an ad hoc basis". There was no systematic policy, and the situation was aggravated by a

[1] JM 167, p. 14.

lack of cooperation between the Department of Industry and the Department of Police Administration.[2]

The commercial rice industries of Cochinchina and Thailand survived Japan's entry into Southeast Asia unscathed, but in Burma the infrastructure suffered serious damage from fighting and from the British scorched earth policy. Because the three territories could no longer sell rice to South Asia and Europe, they had ample capacity to supply Southeast Asia's requirements, but the shortage of transport and fuel made it impossible to move large quantities of rice within the region. Production declined in exporting territories as crops failed to find a market. The Japanese calculated that rice production in Burma fell from 7 million tons before the war to less than 2 million tons in 1943, which was insufficient to supply local requirements of around 3 million tons.[3] As supplies dried up, regional trading networks, which were largely in Chinese hands, either ceased to operate or became part of the black market. The latter was an important source of food for Malaya during the occupation, but it is impossible to gauge how much rice reached Malaya through illicit channels.

Rice Supplies in Pre-war Malaya

As a result of government efforts to promote rice cultivation, domestic production in Malaya more than doubled during the 1930s, from 160,000 tons to more than 330,000 tons, but the increase did not even keep pace with growing demand, and imports rose from 590,000 to 635,000 tons during the same period.[4] In 1940 the average Malayan diet provided approximately 2,500 calories per person per day, more than half of which came from imported foodstuffs (see Table 9.1). The principal imports apart from rice were wheat and other cereals, pulses and sugar. Imported foods of animal origin (which included more than 100 million eggs, over 1 million cases of condensed milk, and 1.2 million pounds of dried milk) made a negligible contribution to nutrition.[5]

---

[2] Huff and Majima, *The Chōsabu Reports*, pp. 369, 374, 377.

[3] Ibid., p. 430.

[4] Malayan Agricultural Statistics, 1949, Tables 30 and 31.

[5] The Dietary and Nutritional Conditions on Singapore Island before, during and after the Japanese Occupation, Report on the Conference on Nutrition sponsored by the Special Commissioner in South East Asia (May 1946), Appendix M, p. 53.

Table 9.1 Estimate of calories in the average Malayan diet, ca. 1940

	Calories per day
Imported foodstuffs	1,400
Locally-grown rice	560
Roots, bananas etc.	202
Fish, meat etc.	100
Garden vegetables	50
Oil	250
Total	2,562

Source: Colonial Office Food and Nutrition Survey, p. 2, BMA DEPT 9/4.

States such as Johore, Perak and Selangor, where large immigrant populations worked in mines and on estates, had long depended on imported rice, but by the 1930s the same was true of the predominantly rural states on the east coast of the peninsula. Kelantan, for example, with a population of 400,000, had about 200,000 acres of rice land and under optimum conditions could be self-sufficient, but in most years a certain amount of land was left uncultivated (in 1940 planting was done on approximately 88 per cent of the state's rice land) and yields were highly variable. A padi census carried out in Kelantan during 1943 showed the state producing just 40,000 tons of rice to meet an estimated consumption of 70,000 tons.[6] In Pahang, with 220,000 people, just 29 per cent of the population was self-supporting, and only the district of Temerloh was self-sufficient in agricultural production. During the occupation, Pahang produced 17,500 tons and consumed 28,000 tons of rice each year, and even rice farmers fell short of meeting their own requirements.[7] Kedah and Perlis, the one part of Malaya which had a significant rice industry before the occupation, produced modest surpluses but faced local shortages because of Japanese requisitioning.

[6] Kel Governor's Office 5/2486; Memorandum of a discussion with the representatives of the Ministry of the Ministry of Commerce which took place at the Sangyo-Bu building on 27th Thoulakhom 2486 [27 Oct. 1943], Pej. Menteri Kelantan 74/2486.

[7] T. Tojyo, Chief Officer-in-charge, Industrial and Engineering Departments, Agricultural Office, Pahang, to DO Temerloh, 1 Sept. 2602, and T. Tojyo to District Officers, 12 Sept 2602, DO Temerloh 207/2602; Conference of Pahang DOs 4.6.2603, DO Temerloh 82/2602; Census Regarding Surplus/Deficit of Rice in Each in Each District, Pahang, after Present Padi Harvest, 2602, encl. in Asst Agricultural Officer, Pahang, to DOs, 20 Nov. 2602, DO Temerloh 285/2602; H.G.R. Leonard (BR Pahang) to Ch Secy, FMS, 14 Mar. 1933, Sel Sec Gl13/1933.

Table 9.2 Monthly rice quota supplied by Mitsubishi Shōji Corporation to Malayan states, August 1942–April 1944

	Aug.–Nov. 1942	*Feb.–Mar. 1944*	*Apr. 1944*
Syonan	11,000	4,400	5,000
Johore	7,000	5,136	1,050
Malacca	2,000	624	560
Negri Sembilan	2,000	504	300
Selangor	8,000	1,687	1,430
Perak	7,000	2,000	850
Penang	3,000	1,520	1,220
Pahang	1,500	352	90
Total	41,500	16,223	10,500

Source: Huff and Majima, *The Chōsabu Reports*, Table 11.5, p. 444.

The Rationing System

Rationing in Singapore

The food shortage was particularly acute on the island of Singapore, where there was a large urban population and very little local food production. The Japanese Military Administration seized all stocks of rice, sugar, salt, flour and milk, allocating a portion of these supplies to the Food Control Department (the Syokuryo Ka) for distribution to the public and reserving the rest for military use.[8] Separate trading associations handled wholesale distribution of rice, sugar and salt until July 1943, when these bodies merged to form a Food Supply Office (Syokuryo Kanri Syo) under the Head of the Municipal Economic Bureau, with the Food Controller as his deputy. The responsibilities of the Food Supply Office included financing the operations of a Rice Importation Association and arranging for distribution of the rice brought into Singapore.

The Mitsubishi Shoji Corporation was responsible for acquiring and importing rice in Thailand on behalf of the military administration and bringing it to Singapore. In March 1942, the Japanese Food Controller arranged with Tan Keng Kor [Tan Keng Kow 陳肯構], the Managing Director of Tan Guan Lee & Co. and President of the Thailand Traders Association, to form a Syonan Rice and Paddy Distributing Association. The Association delivered rice to wholesalers, who resold the grain to shopkeepers and others holding Retail Permits. Initial supplies came from Harbour Board warehouses where the British Food Control Department had maintained its stockpile, and when this source was exhausted

[8] Except where otherwise indicated, the description of wartime food control in Singapore is taken from Food Control Department (Syokuryo Ka), WO203/4499.

the Association obtained rice from the Mitsui Shoji Kaisha stores. Nine "Special Retailers" appointed by the government handled all wholesale rice sales from 1 April until the end of July 1942, supplying a group of 1,953 retailers who had been registered rice traders before the war. The Special Retailers also took charge of sales of sugar and salt.

During the dry season on the east coast, a Bangkok firm called Ban Hong & Co. shipped rice from Bangkok to Singgora, and the Syonan Rice Import Association brought it from there to Singapore. During the monsoon season on the east coast, ships could not use Singgora and had to load cargoes on the west coast. Of the rice acquired in this way, 45 per cent was allocated to the Military Administration for distribution as Special Rations. Distribution of the balance was left to the State or Municipality where the vessels originated. On 16 May 1944, the intelligence unit of the Seventh Area Army, the Nami Kikan, began purchasing unregulated rice in southern Thailand and selling it in Singapore. On 6 August, the Syonan Rice Import Association took over responsibility for all sales of rice, including the grain acquired by the Nami Kikan, and on 20 September the Nami Kikan stopped buying rice and transferred the boats it had been using to the Association.[9]

Outside these arrangements, Chinese traders in the Malay States could apply for authorization to purchase unregulated rice in southern Thailand and Kedah, and in fiscal year 1943 brought 15.5 million tons of rice into the Malay states. Free, or black, market prices were substantially higher than the price set for rationed rice, and as a result sales to buyers making unregulated purchases disrupted official arrangements for rice purchases in Southern Thailand and Kedah.

By 1944, competition from unregulated rice buyers was disrupting official rice purchases in Thailand proper and in Kedah. Rice sold on the black market for as much as $1,800 per 100 kg, in contrast with an official price of $12–$16 per kg, and the large sums of money flowing from Malaya into Thailand were causing economic disruption. The Japanese administration prohibited importation of unregulated rice with effect from 20 March 1944, and created a Syonan Rice Import Association in May of that year to take charge of military-controlled imports of rice meant for civilian consumption. The association registered around 138 vessels ranging from 5 to 100 tons, with a total tonnage of 4,540, to handle the rice trade. The new arrangement had only a slight effect on the black market. Businesses dealing in unregulated rice simply shifted operations to islands in the Riau Archipelago and black market prices went up.[10] The Japanese faced an intractable situation; they were unable to provide sufficient

[9] Huff and Majima, *The Chōsabu Reports*, p. 451–2.

[10] Ibid., pp. 36, 450–5.

controlled rice through the official rationing system, and the people of Malaya and Singapore needed unregulated rice to survive.

Although rice was a rationed commodity, at first the only controls were entries in registers kept by the retailers. Members of the public could purchase rice without a permit and at government controlled prices, but had to provide details about their families and sign for purchases. A notice issued on 15 May 1942 required retail traders to submit returns with the signatures of all consumers buying rice from them, but instructed them "Not to refuse to sell to anyone who wants to buy rice provided the sale is limited to one week's ration, i.e. 5 katties to a person."[11] Some rice was also distributed outside the household rationing system through the Bussi Haikyu Kumiai. This grain went to manufacturers, and to people who for various reasons held Special Permits, Japanese residents among them.

Under a revised rationing system that came into effect on 1 August, residents holding identification certificates (Ankyosyo) received Rice Purchasing Cards. These cards recorded family details, while the fact that a Purchasing Card had been issued was noted on the Ankyosyo. The government then instructed retailers to sell rice only to persons registered with them and only on production of a Purchasing Card, and abolished the system of Special Retailers.[12] In an effort to tighten control, new Rice and Provision cards were issued to Singapore residents in August 1943. Each card now had to include the name and address of the household head, his or her Census Card Number (indicating the appropriate Police Division, Section Number, Ward Number, Team Number and Household Number), the number of adult males, adult females, and children under the age of ten in the household, and the retailer from whom they drew rations.[13] A post-war account suggests that this attempt to eliminate leakage in the system was not entirely successful: "Though the Census Card System might be said to be an effective method for a thorough check-up of the City's population, yet its effectiveness gradually became lessened by the multifarious forms in which corruption was practised both by the A.P. [Auxiliary Police] personnel and the police itself." The Auxiliary Police in particular drew on "persons of the uneducated class and even from undesirable type of persons, who were naturally prone to take advantage of their positions to practise corruption and intimidation rather than giving sympathetic help and advice to people under their charge".[14]

---

[11] *Syonan Times*, 15 May and 22 May 2602.

[12] Syonan Tokubetu-Si Notice no. 47, *Syonan Times*, 5 Aug. 2602.

[13] *Syonan Sinbun*, 31 July 2603.

[14] Lau and Barry, A Brief Review of Chinese Affairs, BMA ADM/8/1.

Illus. 9.1 Peace Living Certificate issued during the Japanese Occupation. Residents had to show this certificate to get a ration card.

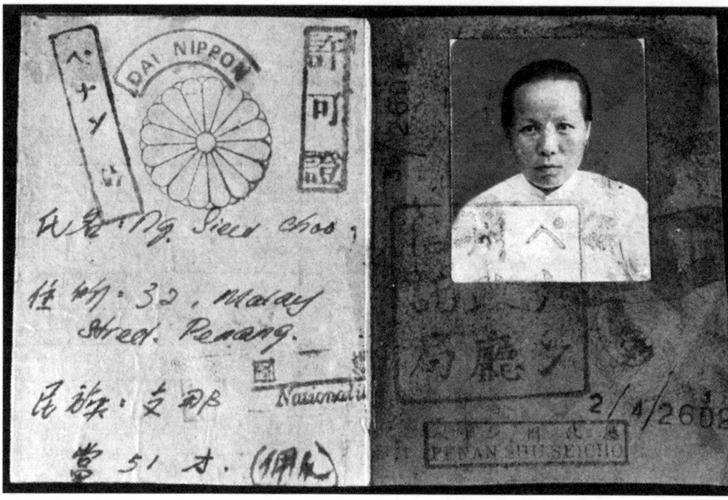

Source: 19980005536-0018 Chew Chang Lang Collection, courtesy of National Archives of Singapore.

Illus. 9.2 Wartime ration card.

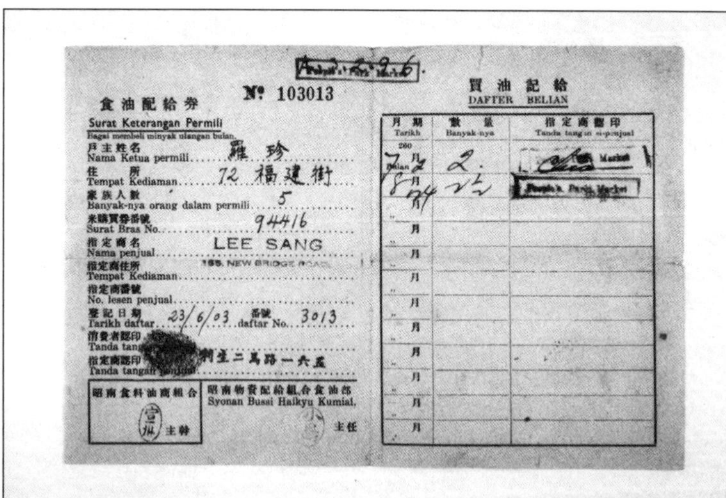

Source: 19980005130-0047 Loh Tek Cheong Collection, courtesy of National Archives of Singapore.

Singapore had 1,957 restaurants, cafeterias and cold drink shops in 1943, and more than 6,500 licenced hawkers selling cooked food, along with a large number without licences. Fruit and vegetables were sold through 47 ration stations, and 2,756 hawkers held licences to operate in what the Japanese termed "the uncontrolled greengroceries sector". Restaurants received limited food rations but hawkers got none at all. Because of the rationing system, public markets were closed, and hawkers turned to diverted private rations and black market purchases for supplies. The Japanese administration wanted to bring the situation under control, but many labourers in Singapore had no cooking facilities and depended on hawkers for their food, so those selling cooked food could not simply be shut down. A 1943 report suggested providing rationed food to hawkers and relocating them to fixed locations in the former public markets, which were no longer operating.[15]

The Japanese authorities also adjusted the distribution system during 1943, reducing the number of authorized retailers to 1,004 and dividing them into teams of 10 traders each, with one member selected as Head and made responsible for handling orders and instructions for the team as a whole. In mid-1944 a Private Rice Importers Association was formed to encourage civilian importation of rice by junks. A new category known as "Private Importer's Rice" was introduced, and the Food Control Department used rice obtained in this way to supplement supplies provided by the Military Administration. Japanese approval of private rice imports generated a flurry of activity. Ng Seng Yong became involved when a friend approached him with a proposal to take a marine diesel engine out of storage and build a wooden boat to bring rice to Singapore from Songkhla, in southern Thailand. They spent about two months working on the boat along Singapore's Beach Road. "Most of us were doing boat construction and everyone was rushing to get this rice which the Japanese Government permitted to let the public import from this Songkhla."[16] Wooden junks cost several thousand dollars to build, but people who owned them could become wealthy. "A junk ... it's like owning six ships during peace time."[17] In October 1944 the Japanese created a Rice Transportation Association to bring in rice on behalf of the government. The Head of the Municipal Economic Bureau and the Food Controller handled the affairs of the Association, although it was technically a private corporation.

---

[15] Huff and Majima, *The Chōsabu Reports*, pp. 178, 189–9, Table 4.8.

[16] OHD, interview with Ng Seng Yong.

[17] OHD, interview with Jack Kim Boon Ng.

The amount of rice and other foodstuffs distributed on the ration varied according to availability. The quantities of rice the Military Administration Department allocated to Singapore throughout the occupation are shown in Table 9.3.

Table 9.3 Monthly rice allocations to the Singapore municipality (× *1000 kg*)

Period beginning	*Quantity*
Sept. 1942	11,000
Dec. 1942	12,500
Apr. 1943	9,000
Aug. 1943	7,600
Oct. 1943	5,500
Feb. 1944	4,400
Apr. 1944	5,050
Nov. 1944	5,250

Source: "Food Control Department (Syokuryo Ka)", WO203/4499.

Table 9.4 shows official rations for Singapore, but announced quantities were not always available. Average pre-war rice consumption for Malaya was around one pound (0.75 kati) per day, although the figure was somewhat lower in cities and towns.

One Singapore resident summed up the situation by saying that people were very hungry, but that basic items remained available:

> Rice, as far as rice is concerned, we are so close to Thailand, and we get regular supplies. And it's controlled by the government. You could buy higher quality rice from the traders who owned junks and brought them down from Thailand to sell in the open market. There were shortages in others, for example, lard. Most families do not take [consume] lard at that time. They either take coconut oil, peanut oil, red palm oil as substitutes to what they have been taking before. Meat, there are shortages. You can't get beef around like what we get now. Chicken, not so much, once in a week during festive seasons and you may have to pay a high price for it. Fish, some. And whatever it is, the food that we take every day, is more or less unbalanced. We are full in the tummy but we lack of good substance.[18]

[18] OHD, interview with Jack Kim Boon Ng.

Table 9.4 Wartime food rations in Singapore (*1 kati = 1⅓ pounds*)

10.3.42–15.11.42	20 katis rice per person per month. Japanese 20 katis.
16.11.42–31.1.43	17 katis rice per person per month. 1 kati soya beans per person per month.
1.2.43–1.9.43	14 katis rice per person per month.
7.3.43	Sale of tapioca and soya bean bread.
1.9.43–31.10.43	12 katis rice per person per month. Japanese 14 katis.
1.11.43–10.2.44	Male 12 katis rice, female 9 katis, children (under 10) 6 katis. Essential military factory workers 5 katis extra per month. Japanese 14 katis.
11.2.44 onwards	Male 8 katis rice, female 6 katis, children 4 katis. Essential workers: heavy labour 11 katis; ordinarily 7 katis extra per month. Japanese 12 katis.
15.2.44	Tapioca noodles sold to public at 1 kati per card at all markets.
17.4.44	Distribution of tapioca flour bread through retailers at 6 cents a loaf. Daily ration: 1–3 persons 1 loaf, 4–6 persons 2 loaves, 7–9 persons 3 loaves, and so on.
20.4.44	As a result of the confusion at the markets, sale of tapioca noodles entrusted to Heads of Wards who in turn sold to Heads of Teams and then to householders (1–5 persons 1 kati, 6–10 persons 2 katis, and so on, every 3 days). Municipal and Government employees given 7 katis rice extra per month.
May 1944	5 katis extra rice to every essential worker from Private Importers Stock (1 month only).
Nov. 1944	1 kati rice, 1½ katis rice flour and½ kati beans from Private Importers Stock at $2.80 per kati all round.
July 1944	Ration to Japanese increased to 19 katis rice and 2 katis of pulot (glutinous rice) or bee hoon (rice noodles) per head.
Dec. 1944	Supply to public of bread and tapioca noodles stopped, but Municipal and Government servants continued getting bread ration at 6 cents a loaf per head as tiffin. Sale of 5 katis of rice and cereals to public from Private Importers Stock.
May 1945	Bread supply to above stopped.

Source: Most of this ration list is from a document entitled Food Control Department (Syokuryo Ka), WO203/4499; additional details are from Summary of Economic Intelligence no. 130, 15 Oct. 1945, BMA DEPT/18/7.

Table 9.5 Reported imports of rice into Malaya

Imported from	*1942*		*1943*		*1944*		*1945*	
	Source A	*Source B*	*Source A*	*Source B*	*Source A*	*Source B*	*Source A*	*Source B*
Burma	30,000	220,022	10,000	55,877	–	5,687	–	–
Thailand	150,000	134,262	200,000	149,753	100,000	55,430	35,000	12,280
Indochina	100,000	3,547	160,000	18,061	50,000	32,985	5,000	54,583
Java	–	16,894	–	5,086	–	–	30,000	–
Total	280,000	374,715	370,000	228,777	150,000	94,102	70,0000	66,863

Sources: Personal communication from Aiko Kurasawa Figures in Source A are based on documents collected by Col. Fumio Mori of the Southern Army, while those under Source B are drawn from documents from Matsuo Kumura, an official in the Department of General Affairs at Kuala Kangsar from May 1944 until the end of the war, and published in Marai wo Kataru Kai (ed.), *Marai no Kaiso* (Tokyo, 1976), p. 113.

Illus. 9.3 Advertisement for red palm oil, used as a nutritional supplement.

Source: *Syonan Times*, 24 Nov. 2602 (1942).

Rationing in the Malay States

In the Malay Peninsula the Japanese administration classified rice as a prohibited good, and dealers had to declare their stocks or face severe punishment. The export or import of rice, including movement between states, required government approval, and some agricultural districts were excluded from the rationing system in order to force residents to grow more rice or alternative foodcrops.[19] Apart from local production, limited quantities of rice were imported into Malaya; different sources report wildly divergent quantities, but the amount was clearly far below the level of pre-war imports, which averaged 580,000 tons per year between 1935 and 1940 (see Table 9.5).

Retail rice sales were handled by Rice Distribution Guilds until March 1942, when a Food Control Office took over this responsibility. By April rationing was being put into effect. At first the ration was a generous 36 katis per month (about 48 pounds) for males over the age of 12, and the price of rationed rice was fixed at 7 cents per kati (1⅓ pounds). As supplies dwindled the ration was reduced, and people who could afford to do so supplemented their diets with black market purchases.[20]

State administrations issued ration cards in August 1942 to people holding residence certificates, and, to provide a check on the system, lodged copies of Census Cards with the police and with local branches of the Auxiliary Police. Essential workers received special rations through two Chinese firms, and a small number of people held "individual consumption permits" exempting them from the rationing system.[21] As in Singapore, various groups, including manufacturers and Japanese civilians, obtained supplies through the Bussi Haikyu Kumiai. There were three categories of consumers: General Purchasers (including restaurants and other commercial outlets), Private Purchasers, and Self-Supporters. Self-Supporters were rice farmers who were required to surrender their Private Purchasers Cards and subsist on the padi they themselves produced. It appears that ever larger numbers of people were forced into this category as the occupation progressed. Table 9.6 shows the change in the Bentong District of Pahang.[22]

---

19 "Malaya, Part G: Exploitation of Material Resources", PS/412/pt II; BMA DEPT 9/4.

20 Notice concerning Rice Rationing, 12 Apr. 2602, found in DO Klang 303/1942 (where the reverse of the paper was used for correspondence); Malaya, Part G: Exploitation of Material Resources, BMA PS/412 Pt II; see also BMA DEPT 9/4.

21 *Malai Sinpo*, 31 Aug. 2603.

22 This point is discussed in DO Bentong 78/2603, inter alia Area Supply Officer Bentong to Food Controller Pahang, 23 Mar. 2603.

Table 9.6 Rationing in Bentong District, Pahang

	Population	*Private purchasers' cards*	*Food crop cultivators' cards*
July 1944	33,687	7,936	3,906
July 1945	35,640	1,534	13,229

Source: Area Supply Officer Bentong to Food Controller Pahang, 14 Aug. 2604 and 13 Aug. 2605, DO Bentong 78/2603.

While some people were excluded from the rationing system, others managed to draw extra rations. In Kelantan the Census Department found that after the transfer to Thai rule, people only reported births and new arrivals "and not a single death".[23] In Selangor Private Purchaser's Cards covering about 900,000 people had been issued by March 1943, although the Food Control Department estimated the population of the state at around 700,000, and the Census Department produced figures indicating a population of 687,690. The state Food Controller undertook a verification exercise, requiring District Officers and Penghulus to issue certificates confirming the particulars recorded on Private Purchaser's Cards, with similar action to be taken in cities and towns by the police Department and Self-Protection Corps, but corruption to some extent nullified the value of this exercise.[24]

Government employees received rations at reduced prices through their respective offices, an arrangement that forced government departments to do extra record keeping and take steps to ensure that recipients got only the amounts to which they were entitled. In Selangor the Food Controller initially handled these arrangements, but in July 1942 the task was transferred to the Selangor state administration, which collected applications from heads of departments and distributed supplies. The change brought a sudden increase in the number of persons supplied, and the Food Controller suggested that government servants should only be allowed to obtain rice for themselves and their immediate dependents, "so that the ordinary trader would not be deprived of his possible clientele".[25]

---

[23] Scheme of Rice Rationing to the Public, Pej. Pelajaran Kelantan 119/2487.

[24] Food Controller, Sel to Financial Officer, Sel, 27 Mar. 2603, DO Klang 133/2603. In 1941 the Selangor population was estimated to be 701,552; the 1947 census gives a figure of 710,788. Similar exercises took place in other states as well. See, for example, the Penang Shimbun of 10 Jan. 2604, which described a system for renewal of ration cards that gave people drawing excess ration a "last chance to rectify mistakes".

[25] Selangor Syuseityo Kanbo Circulars no. 8A and 12 of 2602, Sel Kan 2/2602. This message was sent to heads of departments in a government circular, though oddly enough only after a full month's delay.

As the rice situation worsened, the government began issuing less than the announced ration. In Penang at the end of December 1942 people were receiving 60 per cent of the stated amount, and in Malacca residents got one-third or one-fourth of the published figure. The District Officer for Ulu Langat observed in June 1943 that the amount of rice released by the Food Control Department in his area had been about one-third of the announced ration for some time, and said this state of affairs encouraged the black market.[26] Later in 1943 the government stopped giving rations to people living outside of urban areas, except in the case of government employees. In Kinta the District Officer (Raja Omar) spoke at some length to justify this policy, and warned "against being discontented, growsing at the Govt, or in any way cause discontent among the populace [*sic*]".

> The District Officer requested all concerned to make the position clear to the raayats [the people]. As responsible officers, Penghulus and Ketuas should give full explanation and satisfaction to the kampong people as regards the rice rationing step taken by the Govt. He has done his best to obtain rice for them not by asking for more but for permission to share with the country people the quantity released for the town but was not successful. However as it was a policy already fixed by the Govt, he urged them to make the best out of the situation and to give the matter their deep consideration. The Govt, by stopping rice supply for the country people does not mean that it desires to add further troubles and difficulties on the citizens. On the other hand the Govt, has always at heart the best of intentions as regards the welfare of the State by having all the essential departments, the medical, the police etc, and the Nipponese officers administering the Govt, are men of ripe experience and far sighted. Therefore every policy that is passed has received their full consideration. We must always remember that we are living under war conditions and every policy of the Govt, has a much deeper object in view than we could comprehend. Nippon has good intentions for every one be he Malay, Chinese or Indian.... As the Sangyobu Tyo has explained ... rice is not the principle food and urged on the raayats to take to rice substitutes, sweet potatoes, tapioca, ragi etc.[27]

These arrangements created difficulties for large numbers of people who worked in the towns but lived outside the town limits. Many of them had neither the

[26] Ahmed Meah Baba Ahmad, Suka Duka di Georgetown, p. 75; Akashi, "The Japanese Occupation of Melaka", p. 335; DO Ulu Langat, Report on the Administration of the District on the lines indicated by His Excellency the Governor of Selangor, 7 June 2603, Ulu Langat 216/2602.

[27] Minutes, Kinta Penghulus' Conference, 27 Nov. 2603, DO Batu Gajah 104/2602.

time nor a suitable place to plant food, and the policy caused an influx of people into already crowded urban areas.[28]

Foodcrop Cultivation

Vegetables

With the supply of imported rice inadequate to meet the needs of the population, local food production became a major preoccupation of the Japanese. A three-year Food Sufficiency Plan called for large increases in local foodcrops, and a widely publicized Grow More Food campaign encouraged people to plant vegetables, root crops and dry rice. The Governor of Malacca, Ken Tsurumi, told local leaders in June 1942 that the state had large areas suitable for cultivation which were not being utilized, and that landowners who failed to cultivate foodcrops might have their holdings confiscated. Repeating this threat some months later, Tsurumi said, "This is rather a drastic measure but without it, we cannot hope to carry out our plan to increase rice production."[29] In July he established a Padi Cultivation Encouragement Fund that provided interest-free loans to rice farmers, repayable after the rice harvest in cash or in kind. In Perak the Governor told state officials in July 1942 that food cultivation had to be increased until Malaya produced at least 70 per cent of its requirements, as opposed to around 30 per cent before the war, and that people must change their eating habits and consume local products such as maize, tapioca and sago flour rather than depend on imported foodstuffs. As these items were fresh, the Governor said, they were healthier than food imported from distant places.[30] The Perak administration made plans to double the area planted with foodcrops,[31] while in Negri Sembilan the government offered grants of land along with free seeds to prospective cultivators who were willing to help clear new food growing areas, and devised a compulsory scheme requiring that each *mukim* (sub-district) in the state develop 150 acres of land, and each estate 100 acres, for food cultivation.[32] In Pahang, where vegetable prices shot up to very high levels at the

---

[28] Memorandum by Area Supply Officer, Larut and Matang, 8 July 2604, in DO Larut 398/2603; Investigation of Problems affecting land arising out of Japanese Occupation, reply by Raja Ayoub, ADO Klang, to question no. 21, 8 Feb. 1946, BMA Sel CA436/1945.

[29] Malay Mail, 26 June 2602. Tsurumi remarked that the British had issued similar warnings in the past, but "as they themselves knew, these warnings were usually mere threats that had no action behind them". *Syonan Times*, 5 Nov. 2602.

[30] Minutes, Meeting of District Officers, 6 and 7 July 2602, Baru Gajah 69/2602.

[31] Plan to Increase Foodcrops – List of Acreages and Foodcrops, Larut 236/2603.

[32] Malay Mail (New Order), 10 July 2602; *Syonan Times*, 4 Nov. 2602.

start of the occupation, local production of maize, tapioca and sweet potatoes was sufficient by May 1942 to bring market prices down by about two-thirds, but food supplies remained inadequate, and the Governor suggested that people reduce food consumption by eating two meals a day instead of three.[33] In fact some rural Malays regularly did consume just two rice-based meals a day before the war, supplementing this diet by snacks of Malay cakes made from rice flour.[34]

To provide space for food cultivation the government released land from forest reserves, authorized tree cutting on rubber estates and smallholdings located near cities or main roads, and in some places instructed farmers to remove rubber from smallholdings. For example, farmers in Kelantan cultivated rubber on about 61,000 acres of land,[35] and in November 1942 the government told them to cut their rubber trees and plant foodcrops. The farmers met these orders with passive resistance. The Director of the Industrial Bureau complained in February 1943 that in Kota Bharu District very little had been done to comply with the order, and told local headmen that people "should be made to understand that they must not grudge the small loss they have to sustain by the cutting down of their rubber trees for they can never expect the price of the rubber to be so good as before again". Lest anyone think the policy might change in future, he added: "When the Government had decided to [do] anything the determination will be carried out to the finish however difficult it is, and from this it follows that any scheme or project of the Government should not be trifled with, for once fixed it must remain permanent."[36] In May a large number of rubber trees still remained uncut, and the government issued a further order that all rubber trees apart from those under the control of the Singapore Rubber Association and oddly enough, those that provided shelter for houses, were to be cut by the end of the month, after which time the government would inspect the land and consider what should be done in cases of non-compliance. This order produced a flurry of appeals from landholders who claimed they already had enough land to grow food, and that they were too old to cut the trees themselves and too poor to hire someone to do the job for them. A number of landholders said that rather than cut the rubber they would prefer to return their

---

33 Malay Agricultural Officer Pahang South, Report for May 2602, 10 June 2602, DO Temerloh 103/2602; Conference of District Officers, 19 Oct. 2602, DO Temerloh 82/2602.

34 Note to Che Sheriff, 16 May 2602, SUK Kedah 155/2602.

35 The area under rubber is taken from Memorandum of a discussion with the representatives of the Ministry of Commerce which took place at the Sangyo-Bu building on 27 Thoulakhom, 2486 [27 Oct. 1943], Pej. Menteri Kelantan 74/2486.

36 Minutes, Meeting held at the Sangyo-Bu on 9th Ni-Gatsu, 2603 [9 Feb. 2603], DO Pasir Puteh 58/2603.

rubber-bearing land to the government. On 27 May the administration did an about-turn on the issue, issuing a clarification of the original order that said it was not intended to apply to healthy rubber trees, but only to those that were old or unproductive.[37]

Even more controversial was a policy allowing non-Malays to occupy land in Malay Reservations. In Selangor the Governor authorized District Officers to issue Temporary Occupation Licences for Malay Reservation land to non-Malays,[38] and in December 1942 proposed revoking or amending the Malay Reservations Enactment to free more land for food cultivation by non-Malays. When Malay officials expressed near unanimous opposition to this suggestion, the District Officer of Ulu Langat wrote this strongly worded defence of the law:

> When the then government of the Federated Malay States decreed that there should be reservations for Malays, it was not merely indulging a whim. After proper consideration, the then Government had made up its mind that the welfare of the country demanded that there should be provision for the growth of its indigenous race. The burden of proving that such a policy is unsound rests on the non-Malay persons who wish to occupy the reserved lands.
>
> In short, I would state that the Malay Reservation is a statutory fort built by the former regime to protect the Malays against the incessant economic attacks by the wealthy non-Malays from outside. If this fort designed about 30 years ago is dismantled, the Malay posterity may have to go [to] the Museum to see a Malay Kampong. Before the proposal is pushed further, I would suggest that His Highness the Sultan be consulted. He would, I feel sure be able to give a valuable advice on this matter.[39]

The sole District Officer who supported the change argued that "the purport of the Malay Reservations Enactment is not to help the Malays but to exploit them. The selling value of the Malay Reservation land is very much low when compared with lands outside it. Besides, land owners will be at a great disadvantage to raise money, when they are in need, under security of their

---

[37] Syu Tyo Kan, Kelantan, Pembri-tahu darihal members eh kan tanah2 belukar dan menebang pokok2 getah, 10.5.2603, Minute dated 21 May 2603 reporting on a Penggawa's meeting held 20 May 2603, Peringatan dated 27 May 2603, Pemberitahu from the DU Ulu Kelantan, n.d., DO Ulu Kelantan 86/2603.

[38] Legal Adviser, Selangor, Circular to District Officers concerning Malay Reservations, 15 Sept. 2602, Ulu Langat 144/2602.

[39] DO Ulu Langat, Memorandum on the Malay Reservation Enactment, 28 Dec. 2602, Ulu Langat 132/2602.

titles." But even he was only willing to support revocations of reservations in areas under "virgin jungle".[40]

Food production occasionally ran afoul of military requirements. For example, in 1943 the military authorities demanded that all vegetation be cleared alongside certain roads up to a depth of 300 feet on each side, an order that resulted in the destruction of many vegetable plots. In another case a village headman complained that 88 families had been forced to abandon their gardens, which were near an airfield, and would be unable to harvest the crops they had planted. The District Officer responded that the instructions came from the military authorities and nothing could be done about it. Yet another order called for the grouping together of people living in scattered houses, and this too disrupted food cultivation.[41]

Root crops and particularly tapioca became the staple food of the population. In 1944 the Malay author A. Samad Ismail published an account of an expedition to the Geylang Serai area of Singapore in search of tapioca that began by saying:

> These days everyone loves tapioca; it is carried under the arm, on top of the head, on the shoulders; nothing is talked about except tapioca; in the kitchen, in the tram, at wedding ceremonies—absorbed with tapioca, tapioca and tapioca; until dreams too are sometimes about tapioca.[42]

The tapioca plant grew readily from cuttings and flourished in a wide variety of soil conditions, though it rapidly depleted soil fertility. Two varieties of tapioca (Manihot utilissima, in Malay *ubi kayu*) were grown for human consumption in Malaya, but one contained large amounts of hydrocyanic acid and was hazardous unless the roots were processed by being cut into thin slices and soaked in water to draw out the acid. It was generally used to make pearl tapioca and flour. The other variety, though also containing small quantities of acid, required no special processing for human consumption.[43] Tapioca roots were generally boiled, but for variety people steamed tapioca in banana leaves, made it into cakes, prepared dumplings of tapioca and coconut, and deep fried it. Tapioca which had been allowed to become overripe and was starting to ferment could be dried in the sun, pounded into flour, mixed with water, steamed and then eaten with shredded coconut. As a special treat for wedding dinners, shredded tapioca was

---

[40] S. Ramasamy, Note: Proposal to revoke or amend the Malay Reservations Enactment, 14 Go-gatu 2603 [14 May 1943], DO Ulu Langat 132/2602.

[41] Minutes, Kinta Penghulus' Conference, 27 Nov. 2603, DO Batu Gajah 104/2602.

[42] A. Samad Ismail, "Ubi Kayu", *Semangat Asia*, Sangatsu Syowa 19, 2604 (Mar. 1944), reprinted in Arena Wati, *Cherpen Zaman Jepun*, pp. 184–9.

[43] Col. Williams, Memo on Tapioca, n.d., BMA DEPT/12/4.

prepared with jackfruit cooked in coconut milk and young papaya fried in oil.[44] Tapioca bread was made by combining tapioca with coconut, a bit of sugar and salt, and a cup of water, and steaming the mixture for two hours.[45] The leaves could also be boiled and eaten. Nutritionally, tapioca provided bulk but it consisted mainly of starch, and if eaten without sufficient quantities of vegetables or fish did not provide an adequate diet.[46]

Illus. 9.4 Grow more food poster.

Source: Arkib Negara Malaysia file Temerloh 318/2603.

The Japanese published a Malayan recipe book that showed how to prepare dishes using tapioca and other local food substitutes, and beginning in March,

[44] Ahmat Puat bin Moh. Basir, "Mukim Gersik Semasa Pemerintahan Jepun di Tanah Melayu, 1942–1945". The list of dishes made from tapioca does not translate easily into English. The original passage reads as follows: "Untuk mengelakkan rasa jemu, penduduk kampung juga telah mempelbagaikan makanan daripada ubi kayu. Antara makanan yang diperbuat daripada ubi kayu itu ialah lepat, ubi sagat yang dikukus, bengkang, ondeh-ondeh dan kerepek. Ubi Kayu juga diperam sehingga busuk seterusnya dijemur dan ditumbuk menjadi tepung—dibancuh dengan air, dikukus dan kemudiannya dimakan dengan kelapa parut.... Biasanya hidangan istimewa yang disajikan semasa majlis [perkahwinan] ialah ubi kayu sagat berlaukkan nangka masak lemak dan betek muda masak tumis."

[45] *Perak Times*, 29 July 2603.

[46] "Malaya", BMA PS/412; Burkill, *A Dictionary of Economic Products*, vol. 2, pp. 1434–43.

1943, supplemented rice rations with issues of tapioca and tapioca noodles, and bread made of various ingredients in place of wheat flour.[47] According to one Singapore resident, the bread was "like rubber".

> It was just like our eraser. When you throw it, it can bounce. It was made of millet and I don't know what it was..., After the first time I've eaten it, I don't want to go and get my bread again. It was so awful.[48]

Another reluctant consumer said, "It's made of jagong, maize you know. It was just like rubber. You bite, you pull, the thing stretches. Terrible!"[49] But eat it people did.

> Even the bread, when we buy, there is a left-over, there is no such thing as throwing it away. We used to slice it into small pieces, and baked it in the sun, keep it. So whenever one needs to eat, just fry it with the oil, palm oil or whatever, coconut oil. Coconut oil also hard to get, just to eat like that.[50]

People raised chickens and ducks, even in town areas, to get meat to go along with their bread and tapioca, but did not feed them grain which could be used by humans.

> And then as people are concerned, they keep these fowls, those who got fowls, every evening used to carry candle light, used to go to the drain, look for cockroaches. We got not enough to eat, we have to look something in order to feed the chickens, we used to go down the drains and look for cockroaches. And then we put them in the bottles. And the next morning you feed them. Because by feeding cockroaches to these chicken, they grow very fast.[51]

In 1943 the administration called for a 10 per cent increase in the production of dry rice, sweet potatoes, tapioca, maize and ragi, and for an additional 20 per cent increase the following year. The Governor of Perak delivered these words of encouragement to a Conference of District Officers in July 1943:

> You already know that to increase the production of foodstuffs is the primary function of the state. It is the most important problem for assuring the people's living and securing of public peace. I know you have made some effort to encourage food planting. But I hope you will give your special attention here after....

---

47 Summary of Economic Intelligence no. 130, BMA DEPT 18/7.

48 OHD, interview with Mdm Chu Shuen Choo (Mrs Gay Wan Guay).

49 OHD, interview with Heng Chiang Ki.

50 OHD, interview with Lee Tian Soo.

51 Ibid. Malayan cockroaches are about 2 inches long.

> As far as I can gather, most of the farmers in your districts do not understand thoroughly the meaning of the Greater East Asia War and, therefore, their attitude towards the agricultural problem is almost the same as it was before the war.
>
> ...
>
> You ought to explain to the farmers the real meaning of the present war and make them recognize the importance of the production of more foodstuffs. Because they have the same idea as in the past, they carry on neglecting the planting of rice, tapioca, ragi, etc. The occurrence of a shortage of foodstuffs at the present time is entirely due to their fault. But those who have the responsibility of instructing them may also be blamed. You have land, heat, light and water, but you do not do your own planting. Now, during wartime, how is it possible to get what you want from other places?
>
> If you had recognized the importance of food-planting one year ago and all the people had been instructed to undertake it, although we may not get sufficient rice to eat, we ought yet to have plenty of other foodstuffs as substitutes. What has happened today is solely due to insufficient recognition of the importance of the matter and lack of effort in the past.[52]

The Governor gave District Officers six months to remedy the situation, and cautioned them that the supply of food would then be reduced. "If we still go on supplying those idlers with food, that means we encourage them to idle away their time and retain their British and American corruptive thoughts. The only consequence will be that our fighting strength will be impaired."[53]

In Pahang the Governor made a similar declaration, telling a conference of District Officers that after one and a half years the state was far from achieving self-sufficiency, and warning that in future the administration would probably stop supplying food, and those living in rural areas would then need to grow enough not only for themselves but also for the urban population. He said local officials should limit access to rations in order to force people to increase food production. "Town people should be given ration only 10% and 90% not to be given, get them all to plant." "Neglect to supply to people." And finally, "Distribution of daily necessities direct to people should not be given to useless people."[54]

During the occupation, the area planted with root crops increased from 63,000 acres to 245,000 acres, and the area planted with bananas rose from 45,000 to

---

[52] *Perak Times*, 24 July 2603.

[53] DO Larut, Circular Letter, 28 Aug. 2603, Larut 236/2603.

[54] Minutes, Meeting of Senior Agricultural and Irrigation Staff at Kuala Lipis on 29 and 30 July 2604, DO Temerloh 197/2604.

82,000 acres (see Table 11.15 for detailed figures). Production, however, was little more than double the pre-war level (see Table 9.7).[55] Pineapple cultivation declined because canning factories in Johore were destroyed during the Japanese invasion, and land planted with pineapples was converted to other crops.[56]

Table 9.7 Production of selected foodcrops in the Malay Peninsula (*tons*)

	Dec. 1939	*Dec. 1945*
Root crops	185,500	396,000
Bananas	140,000	314,000
Maize	1,800	3,000
Ragi	100	5,000
Groundnuts	1,500	1,500
Sugar	1,000	10,000

Source: Colonial Office Food and Nutrition Survey, p. 9. BMA DEPT 9/4.

Locally produced root crops, bananas, maize, ragi, groundnuts and sugar were sufficient to provide an average of 208 calories per person per day before the war, and 520 calories per person per day at the end of 1945. The minimum emergency dietary scale proposed for Malaya upon reoccupation was 1,700 calories per day, about two-thirds of the pre-war level of 2,500 calories per day. A post-war British study calculated that imports and domestic sources combined would provide an average of 1,295 calories per person in 1946, a figure which suggests that domestic food production during the occupation was far from adequate.[57]

Cultivation of vegetables and dry rice contributed to the country's food supply, but the practice of using human waste as fertilizer spread disease. Peter Wee, who spent the occupation helping his parents grow green vegetables in the Tampines area of Singapore, said he and his brother were responsible for collecting the fertilizer:

[55] Colonial Office Food and Nutrition Survey, p. 9, BMA DEPT 9/4; further details are found in MU 6078/1946.

[56] Additional details on this subject are found in Colonial Office Food and Nutrition Survey, BMA DEPT 9/4, and in MU6078/1946. Concerning pineapples, see Speech of the Industrial Administrator, Mr Mizuno, MS dtd 8 Sept. 2602, MB Johor 209/2602.

[57] Report of the Young Working Party, BT 25/75/SLA; Colonial Office Food and Nutrition Survey, BMA DEPT 9/4.

> Every day, carrying a bucket between the two of us, we would go to the manure pit and scoop up a bucketful of rich manure. It was horribly smelly, naturally, but we soon grew accustomed to it. With the bucket of manure suspended on a pole slung between our shoulders we would walk amidst the rows of vegetables following our parents as they poured fertilizer around the bottom of each plant.[58]

Newspapers warned against this practice, pointing out that human excrement could cause typhoid, dysentery and cholera, and was full of hookworm and roundworm eggs. The Japanese urged farmers to prepare compost from human waste mixed with vegetable matter, as the heat generated during the composting process would render the material harmless, but this advice was often not followed.[59]

Many of the settlers who moved into the country to grow food had little or no experience of farming. Malay villagers taught them the essentials of rural life: how to plant rice, how to catch fish and game, how to build houses, how to keep wild animals away and so on. Life in the jungle could be lonely—"It was as though we lived in a world that was separated from the outside world"—and while the arrangement had the advantage of removing people from Japanese scrutiny, settlers were often ill as a result of their poor diets and attacks of malaria, and no treatment was available.[60]

Inexperienced farmers caused environmental damage. In principle it was necessary to obtain Land Office approval before occupying a parcel of land, but these procedures were not always followed and people planted foodcrops in places on steep slopes or along river banks.[61] A report on Ulu Langat written in April 1945 noted that:

> Owing to the clearing out of high areas for planting of Foodcrops during the present emergency, soil erosion has been observed to be responsible for the increasing higher beds of the Langat and Semenyih River. As a result of the silting out of the river beds, the District has experienced very frequent and destructive floods even at slight showers causing severe damage to Foodcrops especially Wet Padi which are planted along valleys of the District.[62]

---

[58] Peter H.L. Wee, *From Farm and Kampong*, p. 22.

[59] See the *Perak Times*, 25 May 2603.

[60] Leong Lai Wan, "Masyarakat Cina di Sungkai semasa Pendudukan Jepun". These points were discussed in interviews with Leong Chow Ming, the person quoted, Chin Yew Peng and Ong Sent Keat.

[61] Minutes, Penghulus' Conference, 27 June 2604, Batu Gajah 11/2604.

[62] Monthly Report by Nomu Han, Ulu Langat (Futsuri), April 2605, DO Ulu Langat 71/2605.

Land Officers complained, but given the pressing need to produce more food it was rare for squatters to be relocated for ecological reasons, and by the end of the occupation erosion caused by indiscriminate planting was silting up rivers, streams and irrigation canals in many areas. Even land offered by the administration expressly for planting food was sometimes poorly suited for the purpose. When the Perak Forest Department released 720 acres of land for food crops in March 1943, a meeting of local officials observed that "only 200 acres of this area would be suitable for planting, the balance being too steep".[63]

Vegetable plots also created breeding sites for mosquitoes and contributed to a serious malaria problem. In Klang the Chairman of the Sanitary Board, while praising the local population for growing foodcrops to meet their everyday needs, commented in 1942 that "planting foodstuff indiscriminately in the heart of the town by everyone and sundry require better control, as otherwise mosquito nuisance is likely to be highly prevalent". The incidence of malaria had more than doubled since 1939, although the District Officer said that given the circumstances the figure could be considered low.[64] In 1944 the Klang Sanitary Board again warned: "The enthusiasm in growing foodstuffs has resulted in the opening of many dangerous breeding places. Planting foodstuffs indiscriminately in the heart of the town has led to a lot of mosquito nuisance."[65]

Rice

More than 60 per cent of the Malayan rice crop came from the four states in northern Malaya that were transferred to Thailand in 1943. The southern part of the peninsula had substantial plantation industries but produced relatively little rice, and contained few areas suitable for large-scale rice cultivation. The most extreme case was Johore, with a large area planted with rubber (over 27 per cent of the Malayan total) but just 1 per cent of Malaya's rice crop (see Table 9.8).

The Japanese attached great importance to rice production. They attempted to increase yields by introducing new cultivation techniques, sent soldier-farmers who had rice growing experience into rural areas to offer advice, and tried to ensure that planting and weeding were done systematically and followed a timetable. In Kedah the government opened a school where young men spent three months studying with a Japanese agricultural specialist. Malayan cultivation practices the Japanese sought to correct included:

---

[63] Minutes, 3rd Penghulus' Conference, 25 Mar. 2603, Batu Gajah 104/2602.

[64] AR, Klang Sanitary Board, 2602, Sel Kan 108/2603; AR Klang 2602, Sel Kan 61/2603.

[65] AR, Klang Sanitary Board, 2604, DO Klang 7/2605.

Table 9.8 Malayan rice production, 1939–40 season

	Area (acres)	%	*Production (tons)*	%
Federated Malay States				
Perak	107,910	13.7	49,275	14.9
Selangor	7,420	1.0	3,365	1.0
Negri Sembilan	29,850	3.8	12,205	3.7
Pahang	41,130	5.2	12,575	3.8
Total	186,310	23.7	77,420	23.4
Straits Settlements				
Province Wellesley	34,160	4.4	16,960	5.1
Malacca	30,710	3.9	1,950	0.6
Penang	3,290	0.4	7,800	2.4
Singapore	nil	–	nil	–
Total	68,160	8.7	26,710	8.1
Unfederated Malay States				
Johore	14,690	1.9	3,400	1.0
Kedah	264,820	33.7	133,270	40.2
Perlis	41,080	5.2	18,670	5.6
Kelantan	163,940	20.9	61,215	18.5
Trengganu	46,450	5.9	10,630	3.2
Total	530,980	67.6	227,185	68.6
Grand Total	785,450		331,315	

Source: *Malayan Agricultural Statistics*, 1940, Table 27.

- Using seedlings over one month old for transplanting.
- Scraping the surface of the soil to a depth of 2 or 3 inches rather than turning over the earth to a depth of at least 8 inches.
- Transplanting seedlings too far apart.
- Putting too many seedlings in a single hole.
- Planting seedlings too deep, a practice that impeded the growth of the plant and early development of tillers.

Farmers were advised to use some 60 per cent more seeds per acre, to reduce the distance between transplanted rice seedlings from 15 to 8 or 10 inches, and to put 3–4 seedlings in each hole, since the land was not very fertile and closer planting would mean more uniform production of tillers—the rice-bearing shoots sent up by the roots of rice plants. The Japanese discouraged the practice of harvesting fully ripened grain because rice then tended to fall off the stalk as it was handled, wasting food and attracting rats, and recommended that farmers harvest their crops as soon as the grain began to turn yellow.[66]

Another measure was double-cropping, and to facilitate this the Japanese introduced padi from Taiwan that had short growing seasons.[67] A Malay-language pamphlet supplying planting information for Taiwanese rice instructed farmers to prepare a nursery that was "10.76 sq ft (1m^2)" with rows "9.84 inches (25 cm)" apart, and warned that water on the field immediately after transplanting should be "approximately 3.936 inches (10 cm)", and after that should be held at "approximately 1.968 inches (5 cm)". For Malay farmers, who were unacquainted with the metric system, these instructions must have been less than enlightening.[68]

Planting of Taiwan varieties began on an experimental basis in 1943, and initial results were not encouraging. Sample plots in Perlis started well but were then attacked by disease ("leaf spot which turned the leaves yellow then scorched-like") and pests (grasshoppers and caterpillars ate the leaves, borers ate the stems, bugs sucked away the white substance in the young seeds and rats ate what the insects left). Schoolboys spent the season picking insects off the plants and salvaged a portion of the crop, which then proved very difficult to thresh. The new varieties gave a yield of 103 gantangs per acre, compared with 338 gantangs per acre for local varieties, and left the soil so depleted that heavy fertilization was required for further plantings.[69] The results were equally bad in Larut, possibly because the water was excessively deep, and there too the plants were attacked by pests. In Kelantan the official handling the programme blamed farmers when the crop did not meet expectations, saying they allowed weeds to grow freely and failed to control water levels. Despite such uniformly poor results, the administration continued to promote the new varieties until

---

66 Programme of Meeting in Connection with Plan for Increasing Wet Padi and Other Foodcrops, to be held 12 July 2603; AO Larut, Matang and Selama, to DO Larut, 24 Aug. 2603; Sangyobu-Nomu-Kacho, Perak, to District Officers, 24 June 2603, Do Larut 236/2603; *Syonan Sinbun*, 2 Sept. 2603.

67 Pure strains introduced in the Krian and Lower Perak Districts were Ryushu, Peipihun, Gosisai and Tai-Riuban, while hybrid strains were Kanan 2, Taichu 65 and Taichu 176. Van Thean Kee, "Cultivation of Taiwan Padi in Perak", pp. 121–2.

68 *Horaimai dan Taiwan Zairaimai* (Ipoh: Perak Shu Seicho, 2603), p. 1; copy in DO Larut 114/2603. Another source shows two sub-varieties for Horai (Taichu and Kanan Ni Go), and three for Zairai (Ryusyu, Bimihon and Gokisai). Experiments were also conducted on a dry rice from Japan called Hakkakuso. See Padi Taiwan, Pasir Puteh 143/2603.

69 Commissioner of Lands and Mines, Perlis, Brief Report on Trials of Padi (Taiwan) by the Japanese in Perlis, 1945 (date unclear), BMA Perlis 43/1945.

the end of the occupation.[70] Evaluating Taiwan varieties after the war, a British expert said they were unsuccessful because the short straw required better water control than was possible in Malaya, the seedlings needed extensive care and fertilization, and the young plants seemed particularly vulnerable to damage by rats. More importantly, the Taiwan varieties were highly susceptible to padi blast disease, previously not found in Malaya, and the post-war administration quickly stopped their use.[71]

To increase the amount of rice available for the military and for urban areas, the Japanese limited the quantities that farmers could keep for their own consumption, and required them to sell any surpluses to the government. People had to bring their padi to a collection point, and those travelling long distances received an allowance of 50 cents per mile for each picul (133⅓ lb.) of padi transported.[72] In Kelantan the ration of 90 gantangs per year for rice growers was thought very low, and state officials said that "not in any circumstances may be the Farmers share be reduced and that on the other hand there is justification for increase".[73] When announcing an even lower ration for Pahang, the Governor acknowledged that it was insufficient, but said that "planters have to sacrifice for the urban population".[74] Table 9.9 shows quantities farmers were allowed to retain in five states. People who sold padi to the government were rewarded by being allowed to purchase commodities such as cloth, matches, sugar, salt, tobacco and coconut oil at concessionary rates.

The forced sale of rice was not well received. In Larut the Penghulus reported that farmers had no excess padi. Pressed by the Senior Economic Officer, the District Officer tried again, with the same results. It was difficult, he said, for Penghulus to obtain correct figures "as the cultivators were apt not to disclose same when figures were collected last harvest, probably with the sole intention of keeping back more padi for themselves. This was mainly the

---

[70] Programme of Meeting in Connection with Plan for Increasing Wet Padi and other Foodcrops, Table II; Twice Planting with Taiwan Padi, DO Larut 236/2603; Ketua Pejabat Tanaman, Kelantan to DO Pasir Puteh, 10 June 2603, Pasir Puteh 145/2603.

[71] F. Burnet, Director of Agriculture, to SCAOs, 17 Jan. 1946, RC Malacca 76/1946.

[72] Selangor Order No. 8, Purchase of Rice Grain by Government, 8 Jan. 2604, Ulu Langat 27/2604; *Perak Times*, 13 Mar. 2603.

[73] Notes of a Meeting at the Office of the Vice President Montri Spa on 10 Jan. 2488; Notes of a Meeting at the Office of the Vice President Montri Spa on 23 Feb. 2488 on the Purchase of Padi, DO Pasir Puteh 83/2488.

[74] Notes on Pahang District Officers' Conference 9 Oct. 2603, DO Temerloh 82/2602; Plan for Food Campaign for Showa 19, Batu Gajah 62/2604; Notice to Padi Planters issued by the Food Controller, Perak, 26 May 2602, Larut 173/2602; AO Kinta and Parit to Taiwan Takushoku Kabushiki Kaisha, Ipoh, 21 Feb. 2604, Batu Gajah 26/2604.

Table 9.9 Rice ration for male rice farmers

States	*Gantangs of padi per annum*
Perak (Mar. 1943)	180
Pahang (Oct. 1943)	60
Kelantan (1945)	90
Selangor (Jan. 1944)	72
Kedah	130

Source: Minute Mashuarat Penghulu2 Jajahan Selama, 23 Mar. 2603, DO Larut 145/2602; Notes of Meetings at the Office of the Vice-President Montri Spa on 10.1.2488 and 23.2.2488 regarding the Purchase of Padi, DO Pasir Puteh 83/2488; Selangor Order No. 8, Purchase of Rice Grain by Government, 8 Jan. 2604, Ulu Langat 27/2604; Tunku Ismail bin Tunku Yahaya, "Notes on Padi Discussion", SUK KED 9/2488. In most cases women and children were allocated 2/3 and 1/3 of the adult male ration respectively.

cause of the frightfully low figures."[75] He was undoubtedly correct. In Penang, Haji Muhammad bin Daud was expected to give two-thirds of his crop to the Japanese and the remaining one-third could not be processed without approval, but he had a large family to feed and hid grain in his field.[76] Penang farmers also hid rice above the rafters of their houses,[77] while farmers in Larut, with the connivance of local officials, dug holes in the fields and hid grain there during the dry season. Farmers at Kuala Pilah in Negri Sembilan also buried rice in their fields, and in addition constructed small granaries near the edge of the jungle.[78] In Tasek Gelugor they stuffed pillows with grain, and placed other reserves in the jungle. People anticipated that more draconian measures lay ahead, although the Agricultural Officer responsible for Kinta and Parit tried to allay their fears by telling local officials, "No one need necessarily be alarmed and the false rumours that the Govt, would take over all padi should be scorched as entirely false and without foundation."[79]

[75] Larut 173/2602; Minute, ADO Larut to DO Larut, 5 Feb. 2603, DO Larut 250/2602.

[76] Abdul Malek bin Samsuri, "Pendudukan Jepun di Balik Pulau, Pulau Pinang", Jaafar bin Hamzah, "The Malays in Tasek Gelugur", p. 59.

[77] Rohaini bte Kamsan, "Keadaan Kehidupan Masyarakat Luar Bandar Melayu Pulau Pinang dimasa Pendudukan Jepun Secara Am", p. 99.

[78] Interview with Haji Ishak Sharie of Kampung Pinang, Kamunting, Taiping, in Rozita bt Nordin, "Pentadbiran Tradisional Peringkat Daerah di Zaman Pendudukan Jepun di Tanah Melayu, 1942–45"; Aripin b Othman, "Suatu Tinjauan Teoritis: Kehidupan Buruh (Paksa) Pembinaan Lapangan Terbang Zaman Jepun di Kuala Pilah, N. Sembilan"; Jaafar bin Hamzah, "The Malays in Tasek Gelugar", p. 59.

[79] Minutes, Penghulus' Conference, 26 Jan. 2602, Batu Gajah 104/2602.

In April 1944 the Selangor government announced that it was taking over all stocks of dry padi to use for seed, and would compensate farmers by giving them an equal portion of other kinds of padi plus 10 per cent. Penalties for violating the order to hand over dry rice were imprisonment for up to ten years, or a fine not exceeding $100,000.[80] The government also restricted the preparation of "kampong rice", done by individuals who pounded padi in mortars to remove the husks. Normally such rice was consumed within the villages, but high black market prices had led people to pound rice for commercial sale as well, and the Japanese began insisting that people obtain permission before processing rice in this way. Farmers evaded the restriction by pounding padi at night, muffling the sound by padding the mortar with old cloth.[81]

Despite, or in some cases because of, Japanese programmes, the size of the Malayan rice harvest fell from about 335,000 tons in 1939/40 to 227,000 tons in 1945/6 (see Table 11.14). There were a number of reasons for this decline, including low prices paid for rice sold to the government, the fear that crops would be confiscated, relocation of population, recruitment of forced labour, and the deterioration of irrigation facilities. Officials in Kelantan blamed a poor rice crop in 1944 on the fact that farmers had been forced to participate in military construction projects during the planting season and could not attend to their fields.[82] There was also a reduction of the area planted with wet rice (see Table 9.10), particularly in the commercial rice-growing districts of northwestern Malaya, where irrigation systems were poorly maintained. The area planted with dry rice increased, but wet rice produced substantially more grain per acre than dry (for the period covered by Table 9.10, 912 lb. per acre compared with 460 lb. for dry rice), and much of the increase in dry rice represented planting on marginal land by inexperienced cultivators. In the southern part of the peninsula, the states that were not transferred to Thailand, there was an increase in the area planted with wet rice but a decline in yields per acre, reflecting attempts to grow rice on unsuitable soils (see Tables 9.11 and 9.12).

---

80 Norin Ka-Nomu Han Selangor to DOs, 4 Mar. and 1 Apr. 2604, DO Klang 22/2604.

81 Minutes on SUK Kedah 146/2487; Zainuddin bin H. Ahmad, in his essay "Pendudukan Jepun di Kampung Permatang Tuan Samad", relates how Chinese rice buyers came to the village at night on bicycles to buy rice for sale in Butterworth and Penang. The farmers used the money they earned to purchase sugar and other goods on the black market.

82 AR, Drainage and Irrigation Department, Kelantan 19 Oct. 1943 to 10 Oct. 1944, DID MP 6/1945.

Table 9.10 Areas planted with rice in Malaya (*acres*)

	Wet rice	*Dry rice*	*Total*
1936/37	693,550	46,490	740,040
1937/38	681,410	44,550	725,960
1938/39	700,270	46,450	746,720
1939/40	721,580	63,870	785,450
1940/41	742,600	77,880	820,480
1945/46	684,010	105,640	789,650

Source: R.G. Heath, *Malayan Agricultural Statistics 1949* (Kuala Lumpur: Department of Agriculture, Federation of Malaya, 1951), Table 30.

Table 9.11 Areas planted with wet rice in selected states (*acres*)

	Late 1930s	*1945*
Perak	99,000	110,000
Selangor	21,500	47,000
Negri Sembilan	35,000	36,000
Pahang	40,000	50,000
Malacca	32,000	33,294
Penang/Province Wellesley	37,200	45,000

Source: Figures for the 1930s are from Malaya – Part I, BMA 506/10; figures for 1945 are taken from Translation Report No. 77, No. 3 Mobile Section SEATIC, Main HQ 34 Ind Corps, SEAC, 9 Oct. 1945, BMA ADM/9/27.

Table 9.12 Average rice productivity for Perak (*tons/acre*)

	Productivity
1938–39	0.707
1939–40	0.643
1940–41	0.412
1941–42	0.484
1942–43	0.468

Source: "Programme of Meeting in Connection with Plan for Increasing Wet Padi and Other Foodcrops" to be held 12 July 2603, DO Larut 236/2603.

Table 9.13 Causes of deaths registered in Singapore (*all races*)

	1940	*1941*	*1942*	*1943*	*1944*	*1945*	*1946*
Malaria	360	273	1,036	680	1,891	2,767	608
Dysentery	256	394	2,248	460	2,777	1,720	171
Influenza	249	264	609	292	596	556	183
Tuberculosis	1,928	1,791	2,172	2,282	3,324	2,764	1,976
Leprosy	14	14	26	53	87	31	7
"Fever"	888	882	1,982	1,722	3,659	3,288	1,321
Beri-Beri	607	636	2,817	2,009	6,749	6,683	786
Heart disease	527	536	963	560	1,056	750	516
Bronchitis	397	473	1,086	728	1,062	609	373
Pneumonia	1,440	1,432	2,383	2,097	4,249	2,379	1,519
Diarrhoea/ enteritis	1,029	1,183	1,954	1,285	1,713	1,022	703
Infantile convulsions	1,850	1,769	4,280	3,166	4,572	3,118	1,571
Old age or senility	925	1,062	2,174	1,220	2,250	2,285	1,101
Other	5,235	5,269	6,103	5,382	8,766	7,358	4,452
Total	15,705	15,978	29,833	21,936	42,751	35,330	15,287

Source: Colony of Singapore, Annual Report on the Registration of Births and Deaths for the Years 1940–47, Appendix I: Principal Causes of Deaths Registered in Singapore. It is unclear why death rates dipped in 1943.

Malnutrition

The food shortage caused malnutrition and contributed to a substantial rise in the number of deaths caused by disease during the occupation. Illnesses such as beri-beri were directly related to inadequate diets, but poor nutrition also left the population susceptible to other ailments (see Table 9.13). Information on the Malay States is less detailed, but shows a similar pattern (see Table 9.14).

Table 9.14 Deaths recorded in the Malay states

1940	*1941*	*1942*	*1943*	*1944*	*1945*	*1946*
92,491	63,436	99,257	123,282	146,476	110,112	105,040

Note: Records for 1941 and 1945 were incomplete in some states.

Source: Malayan Union, Report on the Registration of Births and Deaths for the Year 1941 to 1946. Kuala Lumpur: Government Press, 1948.

Relocation Schemes

In 1943 the administration announced plans to move people from towns and cities to rural areas where they could grow their own food. Through a detailed search of wartime newspapers, the Japanese scholar Hara Fujio identified more than 30 resettlement schemes for the Chinese population. Most were straightforward efforts to increase food production, although three sites (New Nanyang Village and Kuala Kubu Baru New Village in Selangor, and a new village for residents of Lenggong in Perak) involved forced resettlement of people suspected of aiding the communist guerrillas.[83] In Singapore plans called for relocating some 300,000 residents, around 40 per cent of the population of the island, mostly to Endau, a Chinese settlement in northeastern Johore ("New Syonan"), and Bahau, a Roman Catholic colony in Negri Sembilan ("Fuji Village"). In each resettlement area there was a place of worship, a school, a hospital, a kindergarten and an assembly hall, and colonists were to receive 3–4 acres of land along with construction materials, tools and sufficient food to sustain them until they became self-supporting. Certain lands were also set aside for collective farming. The Oversea Chinese Association, the Indian Independence League, the Eurasian Welfare Association and the Catholic Church handled the arrangements, soliciting private donations to fund the projects.[84] There were fewer schemes for Malays, but in Singapore the Malay Welfare Association set up a colony at Bintan Island, and planned another for Karimun Island. The government established additional settlements in the Riau Archipelago, which fell under the jurisdiction of the Singapore municipality, at Bintan Island for Indian families. A camp housing around 1,200 Chinese from Penang was located at the Bertram Estate in Province Wellesley.[85]

The Endau scheme ("New Syonan", known by the Chinese as Xing Lou) was an autonomous zone where Japanese law was not enforced and Chinese settlers administered their own affairs without interference from Japanese officials, although informers were known to be active and people had to be circumspect in what they said. Moreover, the forests and mountains surrounding the site offered many hiding places. One former resident of Endau, when asked about agricultural practices, responded, "Do you think that we really go there to cultivate the lands?"[86] Funds came from the Oversea Chinese Association

83 Hara, "The Japanese Occupation of Malaya and the Chinese Community", pp. 54–7, 76–9.

84 Appreciation of the Economic Position of Malaya under the Japanese, BMA COM/21; also see NARA RG226 E110 F288; FIR 19, 4 Dec. 1943, CO273/673/50744/7.

85 *Syonan Shimbun*, 8 Aug. 2604; "Intelligence Objectives for 'Zipper'", Resettlement Projects, RG226 E110 f 288.

86 OHD, interview with Chan Yim Lam.

and were raised through a levy on Chinese shopkeepers, who contributed sums ranging from $4,000 to $15,000. The area occupied by the Endau scheme included several hundred acres of Malay-owned land where the British administration had planned to establish a Malay Reservation. In October 1943, the Japanese forced the Malay residents to move out and incorporated their lands in the relocation scheme.

Illus. 9.5 Map of the Endau resettlement area.

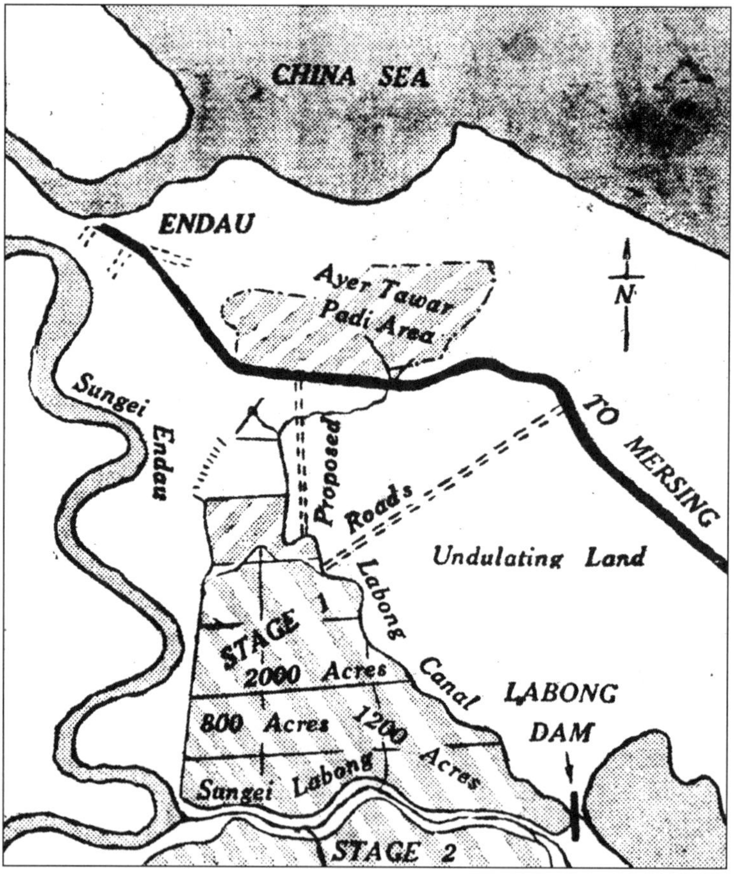

Source: Syonan Sinbun, 8 Dec. 2603 (1943).

The first batch of 200 Chinese settlers left Singapore for Endau on 21 December 1943 to establish a model farm, and by the end of 1944 some 12,000 people were recorded as living there. Every household received two acres of dry land to plant vegetables, and one acre of wet rice land. However, the settlers knew nothing about growing rice, and very few made use of their rice fields.[87] Some were well off and hired assistants to work on their plots, or simply purchased food from Malays living in the vicinity, but everyone, rich and poor alike, was expected to go to the fields and work. According to Yap Pheng Geck:

> It was an unusual sight indeed to see elegantly dressed women in floral-pattern clothes with permed hair and manicured fingernails, wearing broad-brimmed coolie hats and carrying changkuls and wicker baskets, trudging along jungle paths to cultivate the land.[88]

Tan Kim Ock, who did not have sufficient money to hire assistance, has recorded his feelings on being taken for the first time to the parcel of land he had been allotted: "When I saw the land, I was near to tears. Why? The plot was a wood. The trees had all been chopped down and were lying in a messy heap.... The trees were tall and huge and the heap was about two storeys high." He asked what he should do about the trees, and the official who had taken him to the place replied, "That is your problem. Our duty is just to allot you this land. How you intend to clear it is your business."[89] Chu Shuen Choo and her husband faced a similar heap of timber. After living for a time in the barracks, they cleared enough space to construct a house, and she rented a bullock cart to go see the Japanese in charge of the sawmill and get planks. She explained in an interview for the Singapore Oral History unit what happened after she told him how much she wanted:

> The Japanese he looked and then he came up....
>
> "You want so much you want to go and sell black market. You need a small house, no need for so much. I give you half." The Japanese were very sharp. They know that you were going to sell black market. You need only half that amount to build a nice house for yourself.
>
> I said, "I don't think so. I need the full amount. I know because I ask my friends. They told me to get all these. So I need all these tons."
>
> He said, "No. You want, I give you half. Otherwise you don't get the planks. I know you are going to black market the planks."
>
> So I said, "If you don't give me the planks, I can't build my house. I'm going to sit down here one whole day." My gosh! I can tell you I was

---

87 Lau and Barry, A Brief Review of Chinese Affairs, BMA ADM 8/1; AO Mersing to Ag RC Joh, 28 May 1946, and Ag RC Joh to Ch Secy MU, 5 June 1946, RC Johor 428/1946; Domei ELB, FIR 2, 31 Jan. 1944, CO273/673/50744/7; Shü and Chua (eds), *Malayan Chinese Resistance to Japan*, pp. 43–4 of the English-language section. Chan Yim Lam, who worked in the Land Section, notes that some migrants were unable to endure conditions in Endau and returned to Singapore. He suggests that the actual population of the Endau settlement was around 10,000. See OHD, interview with Chan Yim Lam.

88 Yap, *Scholar, Banker, Gentleman Soldier*, p. 69. A changkul is a heavy tool similar to a hoe.

89 OHD, interview with Tan Kim Ock.

> quaking. I was so frightened. But I was acting very brave. So I waited. He went into his office. I couldn't care less. Then he came out again. Something in Japanese, he said, "Ah, still there! Chop head off." I can tell you that feeling I can still imagine how I felt at that time. "Chop head, alright, no house. I sit here till you give me I build house otherwise cannot build."
>
> He said, "You can build that house, can build that house, enough half. ..."
>
> "No," I said, "I sit here till I get my planks."
>
> Then he came and made a threatening gesture. My god! I can tell you I was so frightened. I still remember the fright I got. But I was very determined to get it. So I knew the psychology of the Japanese. They liked people who are very brave. I said, "Chop, chop, never mind." I said, "No house same also." I said, "I got baby." I said, "Two, one boy, one girl. No house, no 'makan' [food]. Must have house."
>
> So he said, he looked at me and he said, "I come out once more then I am going to chop off your head."
>
> I sat down there quaking for dear life. He came out actually and wanted to more or less frightened me. He said, "Ai ya!" He spoke in Japanese. "Give her, give her what she wants, give her, give her." My gosh! I was so relieved. I said, "Quick, quick, quick." I told the man, "Quick. He's going to give me how many tons of these. You look for me, see how many tons. You just carry for me, put in the bullock-cart and please carry for me." Then I thank him very much. He looked at me, gave me a look and said, "I know you're going to black market," that sort of look....
>
> Then I took the plank, I went to Endau, I sold the other half black market. I took the rest home to build my house.[90]

Bahau formed part of a scheme of agricultural settlements announced in February 1944 for Negri Sembilan, which involved cultivation of a vast area lying between Gemas and the Pahang border to supply food for as many as 1 million people.[91] Four sites covering 150,000 acres were slated for development. The first, containing 100,000 acres, was in the Gemas-Bahau area. The second, along the Muar River, covered 20,000 acres including 7,000 acres already cleared and settled by 1,000 families from Negri Sembilan and some 200 Catholics from Singapore. The third and fourth included an additional 30,000 acres. The four sites were linked by the Gemas-Kuala Lipis railway line. Before the war, one of the earliest large Japanese rubber undertakings, the Taisho Estate, was in the vicinity of Rompin, about midway between Gemas and Bahau, and

---

[90] OHD, interview with Mdm Chu Shuen Choo (Mrs Gay Wan Guay).

[91] Appreciation of the Economic Position of Malaya under the Japanese, BMA COM/21; Far Eastern Weekly Intelligence Summary no. 57 for the week ending 11 Feb. 1944, F367/367/61, F0371/41732.

the Japanese may have selected this area because they had detailed information about local conditions.[92]

The Bahau Roman Catholic colony, settled by Eurasians and Chinese from Singapore, occupied 8,500 acres of land in a forest reserve near the town of Bahau. The first batch of settlers left Singapore on 28 December 1943 and by July 1945 the "Fuji-Go Reclamation Area" reported a population of 5,167 colonists. F.A.C. Oehlers, who moved to Bahau as part of a group of settlers that left Singapore on 14 February 1944, said "One could be forgiven for thinking that the site might have been delivertely chosen to eliminate Eurasians." The Japanese promoted Bahau as a "Land of Plenty", but his group of settlers found huts made of palm leaves and "an area riddled with large trunks of fallen trees lying haphazardly, surrounded by dense *blukar* [brush].[93]

On 12 April 1944 the Domei news service announced that Pope Pius XII had sent a message through the Bishop of Malacca blessing the scheme. In connection with this settlement the Japanese proposed to dam the Muar River and dig a canal about 5 miles long to provide irrigation water for 500 acres of land. Settlers began constructing a timber dam and excavated part of the main canal, a difficult task because the cutting at some points was more than 20 feet deep. The project was abandoned after the war, and the Technical Assistant for the Drainage and Irrigation Department told British officers that he had advised against the project, but had been overruled by his Japanese superior.[94]

The settlement was divided into two parts, the Bahau Catholic Colony in Mukim VI, which was predominantly Eurasian, and a settlement in Mukim V where the population consisted mainly of Chinese Catholics. Settlers suffered severe bouts of malaria, and infant mortality was extremely high. By 1945 the health of the colony appears to have improved to some degree, and the Secretary for Mukim VI commented in July: "Women suddenly snatched away from lives of ease and the amenities of town life transported into a primitive world with all the attendant hard work and the malaria too had, we suppose, much

[92] *Syonan Shimbun*, 12 Jan. 2604; Far Eastern Weekly Intelligence Summary no. 57 for week ending 11 Feb. 1944, F367/367/61, F0371/4172 (1944); FIR 1, 15 Jan. 1944, CO273/673/50744/7; Japanese Telegraph Service in English for Europe, 13 Jan. 1944, CO273/673/50744/7. The Taisho Estate was acquired by a British company many years before the war.

[93] Oehlers, *That's How It Goes*, pp. 105-46; quotations are from pp. 105 and 114.

[94] *Syonan Shimbun*, 29 Dec. 2603; Domei ELB, 29 Dec. 1943, FIR 21, 31 Dec. 1943; Domei ELB, 21 and 22 Apr. 1944, FIR 8, 30 Apr. 1944; Domei ELB, 12 Apr. 1944, FIR 7, 1–15 Apr. 1944, CO273/673/50744/7; S.O.1 (Irrigation) to Col. S.C.A.O. Works, Peninsula, "Report on Visit to Negri Sembilan 23rd and 24th November, 1945", n.d., DID MP 38/1945.

to do with the unfortunate number of infant deaths."[95] Conditions, however, remained poor. Tapioca and sweet potatoes were the main crops and some of the produce was exported to Singapore. Factories in Bahau made tapioca chips, with tapioca flour as a by-product, and manufactured flat *kway teow* noodles out of tapioca. Tapioca was the staple food in the settlement, but settlers also grew fruits and vegetables, and sugar cane. Reports prepared just before the end of the occupation speak of damage to tapioca, banana, papaya and maize plants caused by intermittent episodes of drought and excessively wet weather, and of a mysterious disease that was killing the chickens, which had "granule-like cysts embedded in the intestinal walls". Chickens were also laying eggs with soft shells, tapioca plants were being attacked by a fungus, and fruit trees had been badly damaged by insects.[96]

Illus. 9.6 Settlers leaving for the Bahau resettlement area.

Source: *Syonan Sinbun*, 30 Dec. 2603 (1943).

[95] "Report on the Catholic Colony Mukim VI for the Senden Ka, Seremban for July, 2605", and Kochi Ka, Negri Sembilan, "Monthly Report for July 2605. Fuji Go Reclamation Area", DID MP 72/1945.

[96] "Report on the Catholic Colony Mukim VI for the Senden Ka, Seremban for July 2605", and Agricultural Officer, Mukim 5, "Agricultural Report for the Month of July, 2605", 2 Aug. 2605, DID MP 72/1945.

At the end of June 1945, the government announced a plan to evacuate residents of Singapore to places where they could get food more readily, and be safe from air raids. People who had relatives in the peninsula, or in Java or Sumatra, were encouraged to go stay with them, and those who did not were sent to the agricultural colonies. Putting the most favourable interpretation on the situation, the Japanese pointed out that the British had not given local people a chance to evacuate at the end of 1941, but that they by contrast were "acting like a parent toward his children—having in mind only the safeguarding and protection of local citizens".[97] Newspapers published a series of stories painting a rosy picture of life up-country, where there was comfortable housing and adequate food, and warned that Singapore was "likely to become a big battlefield".

> By dragging the enemy to the shores of Syonan and then dealing him a crushing blow we will greatly contribute to the decisive battle to be fought on the Nippon mainland or its vicinity.... Should Syonan become a battlefield, we can assume that a most intensive and ferocious battle will take place.[98]

Singapore's "First Trainload of Happy Evacuees", carrying 298 people, left the city on 16 July, and apparently took 4 days to reach Perak, a distance of less than 400 miles.[99]

* * *

Japanese campaigns to promote food production averted famine in Malaya, but food shortages were a pervasive problem and overshadowed Japanese efforts in all other spheres of activity. The soil and terrain of the peninsula are poorly suited for growing rice, and because of inadequate transport foodstuffs that were produced could be carried to urban areas only with great difficulty. Administrative failures contributed to shortages as well, particularly in irrigation areas where poor maintenance caused a decline in wet rice production. The black market gave some relief, but many people were unable to afford supplies from this source, and even those who could found it difficult to maintain an adequate diet. In Singapore the controlled price for rice was $150 per picul (133.3 pounds), but there were reports of rice being sold for as much as $1,000 or $1,200 per picul there and in southern Johor. Food shortages worsened as the Occupation progressed, and agricultural colonies represented a desperate attempt to avert starvation, although

---

[97] *Syonan Shimbun*, 30 June 2605.

[98] Ibid., 7 July 2605.

[99] Ibid., 17 July and 21 July 2605.

many settlers saw them simply as a way to escape the attentions of the Japanese. Delegates at a preliminary surrender conference held in Rangoon on 26 August 1945 reportedly told Allied officials that food stocks in the occupied territories were "either non-existent or so small that they had no idea how they could have fed the subject population if the war had continued any longer".[100]

[100] Kirby, *The War Against Japan*, vol. 5, p. 239; Ministry of Economic Warfare, "Survey of Economic Developments in the Far East in the 6 Months ending 31st December 1944", p. 34, FO 837/386.

CHAPTER 10

The End of the Occupation

The Japanese Estimation of Allied Plans

By the end of 1943 the Japanese were preparing to resist an Allied invasion. The 29th Army based its movements on the assumption that the Allies would first attack Japanese installations in the Andaman and Nicobar Islands, and then establish a forward base in Sumatra or on Phuket Island. Strong installations in Kedah and the presence of Japanese forces along both sides of the Straits of Malacca appeared to preclude the possibility of an Allied assault in the southern peninsula, and the invasion seemed likely to take place along the northwest coast of Malaya. To build up defences in this region, the 29th Army transferred all but two companies of the 18th Independent Garrison Unit, which had been involved in suppression of communist activity in Johore, to southern Thailand in June 1944, and began constructing defensive works around Gurun, Kedah, where the hilly jungle terrain appeared to offer a chance to halt an Allied force moving southward. To minimize damage from bombing raids, the Japanese prepared underground stores for weapons and ammunition, dispersed or concealed barracks and warehouses, and reinforced the walls of factories manufacturing military equipment. Although there was some resistance to these measures (the need "was immediately understood by those units which had bitter experiences, but it took a long time to convince the other units of the advisability of this line of thought"), Allied air raids on Nicobar in August 1944 seem to have silenced the opposition. The following months brought increased Allied pressure on the Andaman and Nicobar Islands, and by the end of 1944 many of the troops there had been cut off.[1]

The military situation changed significantly in 1944 and 1945. Early in 1944 the Japanese attempted to forestall an Allied attack on Burma by launching a

[1] JM 167, pp. 5, 21–6. The Southern Army thought Allied naval forces were inadequate to attack Malaya from the Indian Ocean, and considered an invasion overland through Burma far more likely. JM 24, p. 65.

pre-emptive assault against Imphal, in the state of Manipur in eastern India. Fighting lasted for almost three months, but the offensive was repelled and Japanese defences in western Burma began to crumble. In this sector the Allies devoted the balance of the year to restoring overland communications between India and China. The Americans commenced their assault on the Philippines in August, and an American invasion force landed on Leyte on 20 October. A Japanese counterattack failed, and by the end of 1944 links between Japan and Southeast Asia were all but severed, leaving the Southern Army able to defend only "areas of great importance".[2] American forces invaded Luzon on 9 January 1945, and Manila was in US hands by the end of February.

Allied troops began attacking Japanese positions in central and lower Burma early in 1945. Mandalay was re-occupied on 21 March, and the defection of the Burmese National Army from the Japanese cause at the end of March seriously disrupted Japanese defences, allowing the Allies to capture Rangoon in early May. The offensive in Burma opened up the possibility of an attack on the Kra Isthmus to cut the link between Japanese forces in Malaya and in Burma, and forced the Japanese to strengthen their defences in southern Thailand. The 12th and 18th Independent Garrison Units in Malaya were converted into a new 94th Division, which was divided into three regiments, one posted in Southern Thailand, a second in Northern Malaya and a third in Southern Malaya. The Japanese also reassigned the 37th Division from Java to Johore, where with effect from 21 June 1945 it was placed under the command of the 7th Area Army in Singapore, and sent the 70th Independent Mixed Brigade from Indochina to reinforce the 29th Army. Beyond these measures, the Southern Army could offer no further assistance. A British report on the 94th Division notes that the formation had no operational experience and little training, was poorly equipped, and consisted of men who were relatively old to be involved in combat.[3] Officers of Japan's 29th Army shared this assessment of the quality of the troops at their disposal for defending Malaya:

> Early in 1945 the defensive training of the units stationed in Malaya was exceedingly lax. Training was old fashioned without going one step beyond the traditional tactics. Moreover, the officers' ability in tactical command was helplessly low because of their intellectual deterioration. In view of these circumstances, the army commander issued new instructions concerning training and new procedures for the tactical direction of the

[2] JM 103, pp. 3, 13.

[3] The Japanese Plan for the Defence of Malaya, WO208/1555.

> Burma Army, the text of which he had written himself, but his officers were in such a deplorable condition that they could not understand even these instructions.[4]

The main body of INA troops accompanied the Japanese to Burma. Around 85 per cent of this INA expeditionary force consisted of trained soldiers from the British Indian Army captured at the time of the Japanese invasion of Malaya. The Allied advance into Burma caught the INA in retreat, and by April INA surrenders were becoming "an administrative embarrassment to the Allies". INA losses at this stage may have been as high as 20,000 men killed, captured or surrendered, and a further 6,000 INA troops capitulated when Rangoon fell on 3 May 1945. The INA could still muster an army of between 16 and 20,000 men in Malaya, but about three-quarters of these soldiers were Tamils who had been recruited and trained locally, and had no combat experience.[5] Poorly equipped and considered unreliable by the Japanese, they were assigned the task of acting as a delaying force in front of the main Japanese positions, and were also expected to protect the flanks and rear areas. In addition, the INA had to help maintain control of Indian civilians.[6]

On 9 March 1945 the commander of the 29th Army received orders to "step up operational preparations in the Malaya Peninsula and, at the same time, secure the communications channels which run through Malaya by destroying the invading enemy". Whether or not these measures succeeded, they would "at least defend the outer perimeter of Singapore by securing the strategic areas of the southern Malay Peninsula".[7] The Japanese felt that their forces were too weak to contest an Allied landing, and decided instead to defend strong points in the peninsula. However, while they hoped to exploit their supposed superiority in jungle warfare and stop the Allies in the area around Gurun, Kedah, the Japanese recognized that the invading force would enjoy naval and air supremacy, and would be able to use the same tactics that Japan had employed in 1941–42, with the same outcome. "It was self evident, from the example of the British-Indian Army at the beginning of the Pacific War, that, if our forces conducted gradual southward advance they would be chased into Singapore

---

4 JM 167, p. 35.

5 HQ, Allied Land Forces, SEAC, "Supplementary Guide to JIFC (Indian) Activities (Malaya)", 16 Aug. 1945, WO203/2298. The fiasco in Burma caused a decline in the influence of the Hikari Kikan, which the Japanese began calling "Chicken-Butai". By the end of the war, its responsibilities were limited to arranging supplies and foodstuffs for the INA.

6 Kirby, *The Surrender of Japan*, pp. 71–5; The Japanese Plan for the Defence of Malaya, WO208/1555; JM 167, pp. 39–40.

7 JM 167, pp. 18, 21–3.

without inflicting any losses upon the enemy."[8] The Japanese established further defences between Taiping and Ipoh, and to the west of Kuala Lumpur, an important area that was particularly susceptible to attack because the coast nearby was suitable for military landings. However, to man the defences in the south fully, the Japanese would have to move troops down from positions in the north, a precarious undertaking given that the only lines of communication were a single road and a single railway line, both extremely vulnerable to air attacks. Japanese planners assumed that the invasion would take place around the end of 1945, when the weather would be most favourable, and their defensive preparations would have been complete by the end of September. In fact the attack was planned for early September, and would have been directed against southern Malaya. An Allied assessment of Japan's defensive plan suggests that it would have delayed the invading force but could not have prevented the Allies from recapturing Malaya.[9]

False intelligence disseminated by the Allies misled the Japanese concerning the strength and intentions of Allied forces. A post-war account based on recollections and notes of Lt. Gen. Masuzo Fujimura and Lt. Gen. Naokazu Kawahara, former Chiefs of Staff of the 29th Army, states that there were "increasing indications that the British-Indian Army in Burma would try to occupy Thailand at a single stroke by appeasing the Thai Army, cutting its communications with the Malay area at the narrow neck of the peninsula and dispatching parachute units, rather than by advancing directly against Thailand across the steep pass bordering Burma and Thailand".[10] This appreciation at least partly reflects a deception plan produced by the "D" Division of SACSEA Headquarters, the agency responsible for disinformation. Plan Sceptical, the last of a series of such plans, suggested that the Allies were preparing an airborne assault on Bangkok combined with movement of land forces into Thailand. Deception also caused the Japanese to over-estimate the strength of the Allied forces. A report on the activities of "D" Division notes that the Supreme Allied Commander's manpower resources were relatively insubstantial when he took over his command, but "the imaginary forces of which he simultaneously assumed control were both numerous and well-found". The Japanese General Staff had a "fantastic misconception" of Allied strength and came to believe that a huge force was waiting in India to attack their western perimeter. It was their estimation of the expected size of the Allied assault that caused Japanese commanders to decide against defending the beachhead. In other respects the exact

[8] Ibid., p. 39.

[9] The Japanese Plan for the Defence of Malaya, WO208/1555. See also JM 167, p. 33.

[10] JM 167, p. 43.

influence of Allied deception plans is difficult to gauge. Although the "credulity of the Japanese Intelligence Staff left nothing to be desired, and they were well prepared to swallow the most outrageous and implausible fabrications", their inefficiency and "the arbitrary distribution of alarmist Intelligence appreciations conjur[ed] up so many bogeys that the particular apparition sponsored by 'D' Division tended to become merely one among many". Moreover, senior Japanese officers seem to have disregarded much of the intelligence they received.[11]

Along with their military preparations the Japanese attempted to increase popular support for their regime, particularly among the Chinese. In keeping with the army's overall policy of "threatening and conciliating" the Chinese, restrictions on economic activities were eased. The Japanese were aware that while the Chinese "pretended to be obedient", they "harbored complaints and dissatisfactions", and the new policy was designed to produce a more cooperative attitude.

> Toward this end, the Army decided to hold a rally in Kuala Lumpur for the influential Chinese leaders who represented the entire Chinese population of Malaya. This was the Army's biggest change in policy since the outbreak of the war. The Army's purpose was to permit the Chinese residents to express their wishes to the Army regarding business and to comply with their requests as much as possible. In reply to the Army's inquiries before the rally, the Chinese stated that they wanted the rally and the names of those attending to be kept secret. The Army concluded that they made such a request because they guessed how the war was actually going and because it was characteristic of the Chinese to want to act purely in their own interests. The Army accepted their demands and decided not to publish their names. Thus the rally was held at the detached house of the former British Governor on 10 March, Army Day. At first the Army feared that many would not attend the rally, but almost all attended. The program proceeded in an amicable atmosphere and the meeting was satisfactory to both sponsor and guests.[12]

---

[11] Secret Supplement to Report to the Combined Chiefs of Staffby the Supreme Allied Commander South-East Asia 1943–46, Annexure T, "D Division in S.E.A.C.", WO203/6381. Deception in SEAC was less extensive than in the Mediterranean Theatre, owing to limited resources and perpetual uncertainty about what operations were going to be carried out. "It is impossible, or at least highly dangerous, to attempt to tell a lie until you know what the truth is going to be; and as time went on the frequency with which the notional or feint objectives proposed for the Supreme Allied Commander by 'D' Division were later forced to become his actual objectives became something of an embarrassment."

[12] JM 167, p. 42.

Clearly key figures in the Chinese community felt it expedient to maintain the appearance of cooperation with the Japanese, but the request for secrecy makes it plain that the Chinese had no confidence in Japan's future prospects.

Resistance Forces and Clandestine Operations

Working under the cover of the Ministry of Economic Warfare, the Oriental Mission of Britain's Special Operations Executive (SOE) began creating an organization to carry out special operations in Malaya as early as July 1941. These arrangements were not reported to the Governor and the G.O.C. Malaya until September, and both objected to the scheme, Shenton Thomas because it implied that at least part of Malaya was likely to be occupied, and Percival because it impinged on military plans and arrangements for which he bore sole responsibility. Percival's specific objections were that the scheme was unworkable because it envisioned having individual Europeans working with Asian groups in occupied territories where Europeans seemed unlikely to be able move about freely. He also complained that it made demands on an already small pool of European manpower, and that recruitment among the Asian population would indicate that Britain felt the enemy might enter the country, and would have adverse effects. He may have misunderstood the nature of the Oriental Mission's proposals, because he proceeded to suggest the creation of an organization doing almost exactly what the Oriental Mission had in mind. However, the Oriental Mission also felt that Percival was piqued because he had not been consulted earlier, and that both he and the Governor underestimated the intelligence of the local population, which was already aware of the possibility that Japan might invade the country.[13]

An Internal Report on the Far Eastern Mission presented a very harsh judgement on the leadership of its Singapore headquarters, suggesting that while they had been burdened with an unworkable Charter, members of staff had failed to set up an effective organization, had failed to recruit the Asian personnel who would be essential to the success of clandestine activities, and had failed to develop detailed plans or distribute stores. The report concluded that apart from issuing propaganda and carrying out a tin-denial scheme, the Mission had achieved "little or nothing".[14]

Discussions of "stay-behind" parties in October and November did not achieve any clear result, but following the Japanese invasion the Oriental Mission

[13] Percival to Governor, SS, 3 Oct. 1941; Memorandum for Lieut Col Warren, 11 Oct. 1941; Notes on Meeting with H.E. and G.O.C., in HSI/226.

[14] Report on Far Eastern Mission, 17 Dec. 1941, HS1/222.

received authorization to set up bases in occupied territory. Training began at once, and the first group was in place by the end of the second week of January. The eighth and last European party moved into position some 16 miles northeast of Johore Bahru on 29 January, making a total of 41 trained Europeans in place behind enemy lines. The Oriental Mission expected stay behind parties to remain in the field for three months, and then either slip back into Singapore or go to Sumatra, using escape routes especially set up for this purpose, but the speed of the Japanese advance and the collapse of Singapore made it impossible for European parties to operate as planned. Some members of the stay-behind parties reached Sumatra, but they were quickly captured and interned. Most of those who remained in the peninsula were also soon caught.[15]

On 19 December 1941, the Malayan Communist Party (MCP) offered to help the British fight the Japanese, and the Oriental Mission immediately created a training programme for Chinese guerrillas under the direction of two Chinese-speaking officers, R.N. Broome from the Chinese Protectorate, and J.L.H. Davis of the FMS Police force. Between 21 December and 30 January, a total of 165 recruits, most of them 17 to 20 years of age, went through the course. Each man was expected to enlist approximately 5 to 10 followers, and the Oriental Mission set up supply dumps with appropriate quantities of arms and food. The first of these was created on 5 January 1942 about 20 miles north of Kuala Lumpur, and the rest were sited further south. Several parties went into Malaya, with the last, consisting of 58 men, entering Johore on 30 January. In contrast with Europeans, who had to remain concealed in the jungle, the Chinese could appear in public and resume normal activities while preparing to act. In January 1942 the Oriental Mission also recruited and trained a small

[15] O.M. Operations in Malaya, April 1942, HS1/226. One beneficiary of the SOE escape routes was Peter Dobree, who would later return to set up a Malay guerrilla organization. Fleeing the peninsula in a small boat, Dobree and his party landed on an island in the Straits of Malacca, and were directed to the town of Rengat near the mouth of the Indragiri River in Sumatra, where they obtained assistance. See Dobree, *Hujan Panas Bawa Bencana*, p. 11. *Leftenan Nor: Pahlawan Gerila*, by Abdul Aziz bin Zakaria, recounts the experiences of Lieut. Nor bin Abdul Rani, a member of Dobree's organization. Probably the best-known member of a stay-behind party is F. Spencer Chapman, whose book *The Jungle is Neutral* describes his experiences during the three and a half years he spent in occupied Malaya. Another man who survived behind Japanese lines was Robert Chrystal, whose experiences are recounted in Dennis Holman, *The Green Torture*. See also Richard Gough, *SOE Singapore*, and John Cross, *Red Jungle*. H.D. Noone, who worked with the aboriginal population of Malaya before the war and was married to a woman from this community, went into the jungle on his own at the time of the Japanese invasion. He apparently died or was killed in 1943. MU7246/1946 contains statements by Chrystal and by J.K. Creer, also part of a stay-behind party, concerning Noone's disappearance.

number of Kuomintang (KMT) members, largely in response to concerns that by favouring the communists they might prejudice operations in China. Most KMT trainees lived in cities or towns, and their training was designed with the expectation that they would operate in urban environments. However, the course was not scheduled to begin until 21 January and little had been accomplished by the time the Japanese entered Singapore.[16]

When the Japanese reached the Straits of Johore, it became impossible to send any more groups into the peninsula, and many of the men still in training joined Dalforce and participated in the defence of Singapore. After the surrender, some of the survivors escaped to the peninsula and joined the armed resistance movement. Broome and Davis left Singapore for Sumatra on 4 February, but briefly re-entered Malaya behind Japanese lines and collected information about clashes between guerrilla forces and the Japanese before sailing to Ceylon on board a coastal trading prahu. Both men returned to Malaya in 1943 to help organize resistance forces. Some soldiers caught behind Japanese lines and a few members of the stay-behind parties, around 70 men in all, managed to join MPAJA units, but most of them succumbed to disease in the course of the occupation.

The guerrilla movement created by the MCP, the Malayan People's Anti-Japanese Army or MPAJA, drew on a civilian body called the Malayan People's Anti-Japanese Union for food and financial support. Organization of the resistance movement made considerable progress for several months, but suffered a severe setback on 1 September 1942 when the Japanese ambushed a meeting of MCP leaders at Batu Caves, killing many key figures. This attack was a result of the duplicity of Lai Tek, the MCP secretary general, who was secretly working as a Japanese agent. His betrayal was not discovered until after the war, and he retained his position throughout the occupation, seriously weakening the resistance effort.[17] The MPAJA was divided into eight regiments, based in Selangor, Negri Sembilan, North Johore, South Johore, Perak, West Pahang, East Pahang and Kedah, although coordination was difficult and these groups generally operated autonomously. By July 1945 the MPAJA was reported to have grown to around 10,000 members, mostly working-class Chinese with a smattering of intellectuals and non-Chinese.

---

[16] Brief for SAC, Malaya Resistance Movement, 26 July 1945, and The Kuomintang Guerillas in Malaya, 18 June 1945, WO203/5553. See also Shü and Chua, *Malayan Chinese Resistance to Japan*, pp. 74–5 of the English-langauge section. F. Spencer Chapman briefly helped with the instruction of stay-behind parties before beginning his own activities behind enemy lines.

[17] Sources of information on Lai Tek and the MPAJA include Hara, "The Japanese Occupation of Malaya and the Chinese Community"; Chapman, *The Jungle is Neutral*; Akashi, "The Anti-Japanese Movement in Perak during the Japanese Occupation, 1941–45"; and Cheah, *Red Star Over Malaya*, ch. 3.

On the Allied side three agencies conducted clandestine operations in Southeast Asia: Britain's SOE, the British Secret Intelligence Service (SIS), and the American Office of Strategic Services (OSS). SIS, known as the Inter-Service Liaison Department, lost nearly all of its Malayan network at the time of the Japanese invasion, and during the war was responsible for developing long-term intelligence, particularly with respect to Malaya. The OSS concentrated on Burma and Indonesia but carried out some clandestine work in the peninsula, and monitored the activity of the British agencies. The principal organization active in Malaya was the SOE, which in cooperation with the Chinese government maintained a network of operatives known as Force 136, whose task was to collect intelligence and to arm and train the MPAJA.[18]

As a nucleus for Force 136, the SOE drew on a group of some 2,000 Chinese seamen who had been in India when the war broke out, and were organized by the Overseas Department of KMT Central Headquarters into the Wartime Work Force of the Stranded Chinese Seamen in India. They were joined by additional personnel sent from China, and by residents of Malaya who were outside the peninsula when it fell.[19] The first Force 136 reconnaissance party to reach Malaya was led by J.H.L. Davis and consisted primarily of Chinese agents. The group landed in May 1943 and joined the Fifth Regiment of the Anti-Japanese Army in Perak.[20] Their presence was noted in a curious Japanese press statement published on 9 August 1943, which said that the Allies lacked the strength to attack Malaya, but warned that the country might face air raids, submarine bombardments, or the "landing of a small group of soldiers in an out-of-the-way place from craft in pursuit of certain aims".[21] Richard Broome joined Davis in September, but there was then a long hiatus before further personnel arrived. A party landed by submarine on 21 September 1944 and joined MPAJA forces in Johore, and additional groups that entered the country

[18] For an account of Force 136 activities in Malaya see Ian Trenowden, *Operations Most Secret SOE*.

[19] See Shü and Chua (eds), *Malayan Chinese Resistance to Japan*, p. 70 of the English-language section. The Work Force of the Stranded Chinese Seamen in India was led by Lim Bo Seng and Chuang Hui Tsuan. Lim Bo Seng was later captured in Malaya, and died in Japanese custody. See Akashi, "The Anti-Japanese Movement in Perak", pp. 100–5.

[20] For details on these activities, see Memorandum by Head of Malayan Country Section, Force 136 on Resistance Forces in Malaya on the Eve of the Japanese Capitulation, WO203/5767; Chapman, *The Jungle is Neutral*; Cheah, *Red Star Over Malaya*.

[21] *Syonan Sinbun*, 9 Aug. 2603.

between March and June 1945 established contact with all but one of the six remaining MPAJA regiments.[22]

During 1944 and 1945 the S.O.E. stepped up efforts to prepare the MPAJA to take part in fighting after Allied forces landed in the Malay Peninsula. Plans called for creating 35 patrols, each 100 strong, to disrupt Japanese communications while the landing took place. In March 1944 the S.O.E. got its first long-range Mark VI Liberator aircraft capable of flying from Calcutta to Malaya and back, a journey of more than 3,000 miles. There were just four sorties to Malaya in 1944 but 494 in 1945, of which 216 were considered successful. Because Japanese aircraft no longer controlled the skies over Malaya, supplies and men could be dropped by parachute during daylight hours. By the time of the Japanese surrender, Force 136 had dropped more than 300 officers and men in Malaya, along with equipment for 47 wireless telegraph stations and large quantities of weapons and ammunition.[23]

Malays had taken part in the fighting during the Japanese invasion as members of the Malay Regiment and the FMS Volunteer Force, which included a number of low-ranking civil servants.[24] Because the MPAJA was a communist-dominated Chinese organization with very little Malay participation, the SOE considered it desirable to create a parallel Malay organization so that the Chinese would not be able to claim sole credit for resisting the Japanese. In December 1944 a Malay party led by Lt. Col. P.G. Dobree, who had been with Malayan Department of Agriculture before the war, launched Operation Hebrides, making a parachute drop into Upper Perak where they developed an intelligence network and a guerrilla force called the Askar Melayu Setia (Loyal Malay Force). A second Malay party under Major G.A. Hasler arrived on 26 February 1945 and set up a similar organization, the Anak Melayu Setia, in Kedah, while in March a third party under J.D. Richardson made contact with

[22] The exception was the 7th Regiment in East Pahang, one of the strongest of the MPAJA units, which included a number of men hostile to the return of the British. Spencer Chapman describes the post-war situation in the area in a report dated 25 Oct. 1945, HS1/120. This group sheltered an English brother and sister, Vin and Nona Baker, during the occupation, and Nona Baker supplied Chapman with some of the material for his report. Her own experiences are recorded in *Pai Naa: The Story of an Englishwoman's Survival in the Malayan Jungle*, by Dorothy Thatcher and Robert Cross.

[23] "Secret Operations in Japanee Occupied Malaya", 4 Sept. 1945, and "Air Supply – Far East", HS1/333

[24] Abu Talib Ahmad, "The Impact of the Japanese Occupation on the Malay-Muslim Population", pp. 9–11; Leo Tin Boon, "Force 136: The Malayan Episode", pp. 55–69.

a Pahang resistance group called Wataniah, which had been created by Yeop Mahidin bin Mohamed Shariff.[25]

A KMT guerrilla organization with about 260 members also operated in northern Malaya, calling itself the Overseas Chinese Anti-Japanese Army, but the Malay guerrillas and the MPAJA considered these men unreliable, more a collection of bandits than a guerrilla force, and there were a number of clashes between the two Chinese groups. When the war ended, the Overseas Chinese Anti-Japanese Army controlled the upper portion of the Perak River Valley. Richard Broome contacted this group after the war to persuade them to come out of the jungle and surrender their arms, but not all did so. The group was strongly anti-communist, and H.J. Barnard, who became head of Perak's Criminal Investigation Department in 1947, later negotiated an arrangement with the its leader, Leong Yew Koh, under which OCAJA personnel joined the Special Constabulary and fought against communist forces during the Malayan Emergency.[26]

By August 1945 Force 136 had placed nearly 200 men in Malaya, including a number of British officers,[27] and had sent more than 1,000 flights over the country to supply the guerrillas, dropping at least 2,000 rifles (by one account 5,000 rifles) and more than 700 tons of equipment, including grenades and explosives, in anticipation of the coming Allied invasion.[28] According to a 1943 assessment, it was "easy to penetrate into Malaya" and the Japanese were "in no way prepared for raids or coup de main acts. Their numbers—military and civilian—are few".[29] Ostensibly the guerrillas were being equipped and trained to attack Japanese positions when Allied Forces invaded Malaya, and they were instructed to limit their forays against Japanese positions in order to husband

[25] Abu Talib Ahmad, *Malay Muslims, Islam and the Rising Sun*, pp. 124–7. See Dobree, *Hujan Panas Bawa Bencana*, and Leo Tin Boon, "Force 136", pp. 55–72.

[26] H.J. Barnard, "Activities of Chinese Nationalist Military Organisation in N. Perak after the Japanese Surrender in 1945", MSS. Ind. Ocn. s. 26, Weston Library, Oxford University.

[27] Trenowder (in his *Malayan Operations Most Secret*, p. 209) claims that 371 men were infiltrated by Force 136, including 120 British officers. Clutterbuck says over 510 men were sent into Malaya (*Riot and Revolution*, p. 39). An internal report prepared in July 1945 placed the number of personnel in the field in Malaya at 187 (54 British officers, 30 British Other Ranks, 48 Gurkhas, 18 Malays and 37 Chinese). Memorandum on Force 136 for the Supreme Allied Commander, South East Asia, 17 July 1945, HS1/205. For an outline (in English) of the Force 136 operation scheme, see Shü and Chua (eds), *Malayan Chinese Resistance to Japan*, pp. 744–7 of the Chinese section.

[28] The figure of 5,000 rifles is given by Cruickshank (*S.O.E. in the Far East*, p. 210), who credits unspecified "records".

[29] L10/FE/1066 to AD/P.1, 2 Sept. 1943, HS1/114.

manpower and resources in anticipation of that event. However, the SOE treated the MPAJA with extreme caution because of the communist sympathies of its leadership, and used the organization primarily to gather intelligence for planners in India, and to disseminate information and propaganda.[30] In June 1945 the Joint Planning Staff (JPS) of the Chiefs of Staff Committee decided the MPAJA forces were unlikely to be able to coordinate extensive subversive activities with SACSEA military operations, and directed that during the planned invasion they should be used as a source of labour and intelligence, and as guides. The JPS was particularly concerned that there be no major internal security commitment after the recapture of Malaya, which would tie down forces needed elsewhere and delay the exploitation of rubber, and said for this reason the scale of the resistance, and the provision of arms, should be restricted. KMT guerrillas were to be used only as a source of intelligence, because of the political problem posed by ties with China. Malay resistance was unlikely to have a significant military impact, but was to be encouraged as much as possible because "We do not wish ... to appear to be supporting the Chinese only."[31]

The End of the War

In November of 1944 Allied bombers carried out attacks in Malaya, striking Penang and the Singapore Naval Base, a development that the *Syonan Shimbun* said was "not unexpected", and was actually an attempt to divert attention from "the disaster overtaking Douglas MacArthur's campaign in the Philippines".[32] When jittery shopkeepers in Penang closed their shops a few days later in anticipation of further attacks, the head of the *Kempeitai* warned them that shops which did not remain open would be sealed for an indefinite period.[33]

These raids caused some damage, but an attack carried out on 24 February 1945 against buildings and oil storage tanks at the Singapore Naval Base, the Empire Dock and Keppel Harbour caused widespread destruction. During a further attack on the Naval Base on 2 March, the fourth raid on the area, 50 aircraft dropped 385 500-pound bombs. A Damage Assessment Report carried out later showed that the attacks had seriously damaged buildings over an area of 650,000 sq. feet, and that most of the damage had yet to be repaired. A

---

[30] For a list of publications issued by the resistance movement, see Shü and Chua (eds), *Malayan Chinese Resistance to Japan*, pp. 71–2 of the English-language section.

[31] Report by the Joint Planning Staff of the Chiefs of Staff Committee, Resistance Movement in Malaya, J.P. (45)21, 3 June 1945, CAB 119/212.

[32] *Syonan Shimbun*, 6 Nov. 2604.

[33] *Penang Shimbun*, 15 Nov. 2604.

final assessment carried out in July 1945 concluded that outside Singapore's commercial harbour area, which had borne the brunt of the raids, damage on the island was widespread but not extensive.[34]

By this time, harassment by guerrillas and transport shortages were making it difficult for members of the Malayan administration to carry out their duties. Field officers used bicycles rather than waiting for overcrowded buses to get around, and "ran a great risk of being 'run in' by the bad elements (existing somewhere and unknown to anybody) in the performance of their duties". Many preferred not to go into rural areas.[35] Anticipating that guerrilla activity would intensify during an Allied invasion, the military authorities told the governors of the various states that they should establish Peace and Order committees, and make Japanese residents and volunteer police units responsible for preventing incidents. The *Kempeitai* intensified efforts against the guerrillas, and in April 1945 the army carried out operations against resistance groups in areas where it expected military operations to take place, in particular around Alor Star, Ipoh and Kuala Lumpur, and throughout Johore. The campaign lasted from April through July. According to a Japanese account it was successful but so preoccupied the units involved that they failed to execute their primary mission of preparing for an Allied invasion.[36] Elsewhere, as Japanese forces concentrated on strengthening defences, they found it difficult to deal with clandestine activities by the guerrillas.

In Penang, a major air raid on 11 January destroyed some government buildings, the post office and various structures near the waterfront. Another large raid took place on 1 February, and the following day the city of Georgetown was quiet and empty, with shops mostly closed. This time the government announced that those who wished to leave the city would be allowed to do so. On 19 February a massive bombing raid on Kuala Lumpur caused extensive damage to the railway workshops. The next month there was a public holiday honouring the Japanese armed forces, but many buildings did not display the Japanese flag for fear that they would become targets for Allied bombers.[37] In

[34] Detailed Interpretation Report No. DM.408. Cumulative Bomb Damage and Reconstruction Assessment Report. Commercial Harbour Area – Singapore (Malaya); Damage Assessment Report No. 47, 12 March 1945; Detailed Interpretation Report No. TM/32: Complete Damage, Clearange and Reconstruction Assessment, Singapore, from Japanese occupation to 17 July 45, in WO 208/1542.

[35] Asst DO, Batu Gajah, Monthly Report for October 2604, Batu Gajah 84/2604.

[36] JM 167, pp. 41, 49.

[37] Ahmed Meah Baba Ahmed, *Suka Duka di Georgetown*, pp. 130–1, 135, 137–9. A later raid on the Kuala Lumpur railway yards severely damaged the museum, which was situated nearby.

Illus. 10.1 Aerial photograph of the Georgetown area of Penang, showing bomb damage.

The "Fort Cornwallis Area" contained warehouses and a light railway built by the Japanese on the padang, an open field between the fort and the municipal office buildings. Photograph included in Third Phase Interpretation Report no. 44: Georgetown, Penang Island, Prai and Butterworth, Malaya (17th A.A.F. Photo Intelligence Detachment, 15 Mar. 1945).

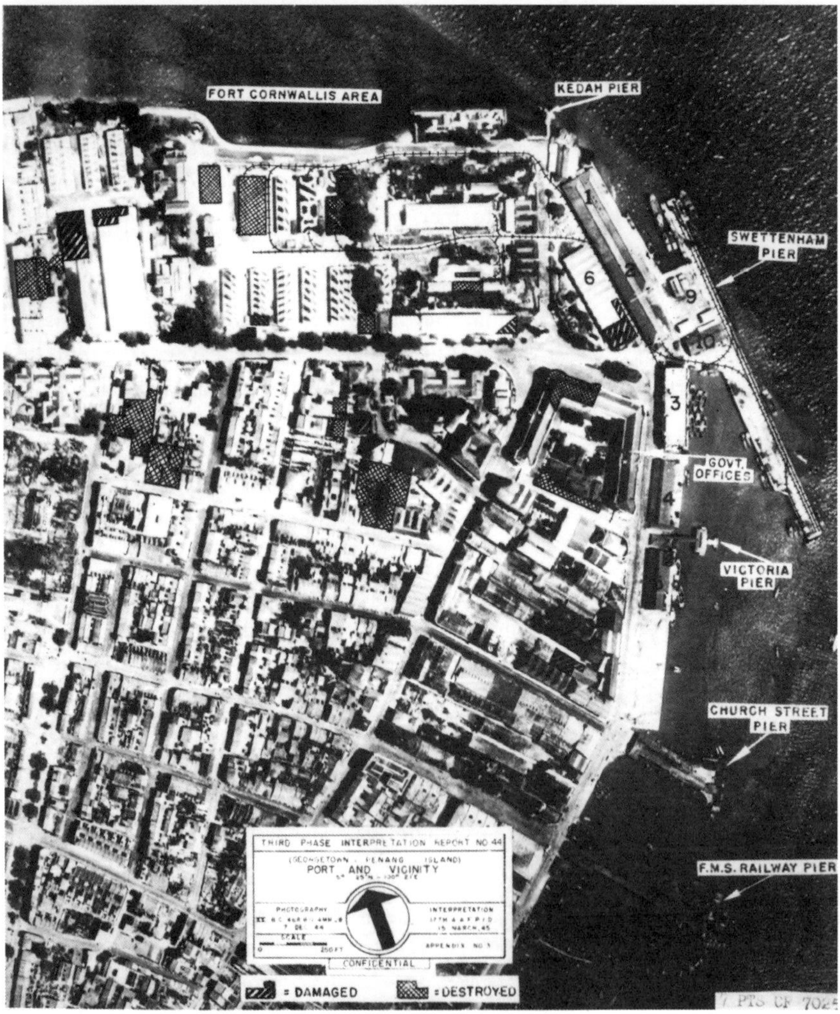

Source: NARA RG243 Records of the U.S. Strategic Bombing Survey.

Illus. 10.2 Building housing Government offices in Penang, largely destroyed by Allied bombing raids early in 1945. (See Government Offices in Illus. 10.1.)

Source: Author's personal collection.

Illus. 10.3 Aerial photograph of the Empire Dock area in Singapore, showing bomb damage. Annex I, Damage Assessment Report no. 45, Empire Dock Area, Singapore Commercial Harbour, Malaya, 7 March 1945.

Source: NARA RG226 OSS 123318.

Perak, lying in a cell in the Batu Gajah jail with her spine damaged by beatings at the hands of the *Kempeitai*, Sybil Kathigasu learned that the public had been told how to recognize the deep sound of the engines of a B29 bomber. On one occasion she saw an unfamiliar plane flying overhead in daylight hours: "It did not need the excited shouts of the other prisoners, and of the warders, to tell me that this was a B29, the herald of our freedom."[38]

Raids against the port areas of Singapore and Penang continued into March 1945, but Admiral Mountbatten then called a halt to these attacks to preserve port facilities for British use after re-occupation.[39] By April limits had also been placed on sabotage to protect resources and infrastructure that would be needed by British forces, and anti-scorch procedures had been introduced to protect the water supply, ports, bridge spans greater than 100 feet, local shipping, power stations, engineering works, rice mills, and breweries.[40]

Operation Zipper, the Allied plan for the invasion of the Malay Peninsula, involved an assault on the Port Swettenham-Port Dickson area, with troops then moving south to seize control of Singapore (Operation Mailfist), and north to recapture Kuala Lumpur. The landing was scheduled for 9 September 1945, but early in August the Allied Commander, Admiral Lord Louis Mountbatten, who had been told of the impending use of the atomic bomb against Japan, instructed his commanders to develop contingency plans in anticipation of a possible Japanese surrender. These plans called for the early re-occupation of Penang to serve as an advanced base between Rangoon and Singapore, but retained Operation Zipper as the vehicle for bringing the main body of Allied

---

[38] Sybil Kathigasu, *No Dram of Mercy*, p. 222.

[39] For information on bombing raids, see intelligence reports on bomb damage in Singapore in WO208/1541; Intelligence Section, HQ XX Bomber Command, Damage Assessment Rept no. 46 (Raid on Swettenham and Victoria Piers, Georgetown, Penang, on 1 Feb. 1945), 11 Mar. 1945, NARA RG226 123004; Third Phase Interpretation Rept no. 44 (Appendix 3: Georgetown, Penang Island Port and Vicinity), 15 Mar. 1945, NARA RG226 123669; Damage Assessment Rept no. 45 (Raid on the Empire Dock Area of Singapore on 24 Feb. 1945), 7 Mar. 1945, *NARA* RG226, 123318; Damage Assessment Rept no. 47 (Raid on the Naval Base Area of Singapore on 2 Mar. 1945), 12 Mar. 1945, NAPA RG226 123005. The Singapore Naval Base was attacked on 5 Nov. 1944, and on 11 Jan., 1 Feb. and 2 Mar. 1945. The attack on the Empire Dock area in Singapore on 24 Feb. was carried out by 105 aircraft, which dropped a total of 960 clusters of 500-pound incendiary bombs. According to photographic evaluations, the raid destroyed nearly 40 per cent of the targeted buildings and severely damaged oil storage tanks in the area. It also destroyed more than 100 business and residential buildings. Headquarters XX Bomber Command, Damage Assessment Report no. 45, 7 Mar. 1945, NARA RG226 123318.

[40] Industrial Sabotage, Malaya (1945), WO203/3285.

Illus. 10.4 Photographs showing the effects of a bombing raid on Kuala Lumpur. The circles superimposed on the Bomb Plot picture show the number of bombs that fell within 1,000 feet and 2,000 feet of the target.

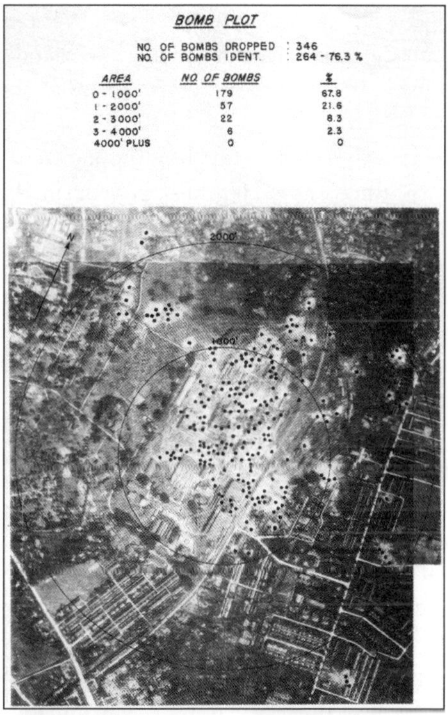

After 1st formation

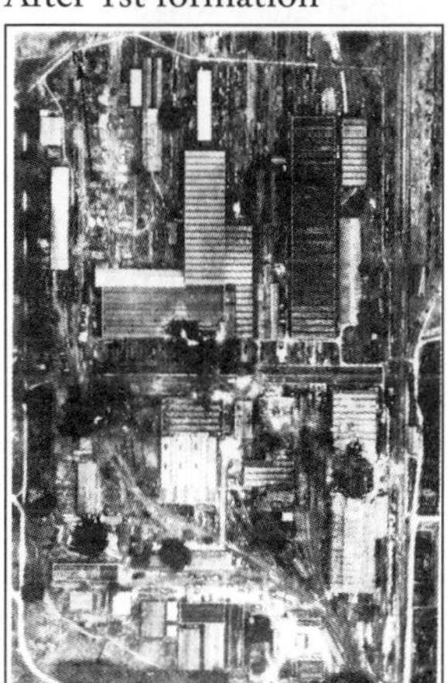

After last formation

Source: NARA RG226 123319.

troops into Malaya because shipping schedules were fixed and time was needed to assemble troops and load stores.[41]

Japan surrendered on 15 August 1945 and naval forces began to leave Trincomalee for Penang on the same day, while minesweepers sailed from Colombo on the 18th to clear the Straits of Malacca. The naval party planned to arrive at Penang on 21 August and re-occupy the island after coming to an understanding with the local garrison. However, before reaching Malayan waters the Commander received instructions to delay his arrival to allow time for dissemination of the cease-fire order issued by the Japanese commander on 16 August. On 20 August Prince Kanin Haruhito, as a cousin of Emperor Hirohito's wife a collateral member of the Imperial family, delivered the Emperor's message of surrender to Japanese forces in Singapore, and Japanese commanders were ordered to suspend all military activities as of 25 August. The next day a delegation from the Japanese High Command met with Allied representatives in Rangoon to agree on procedures for the return of Allied forces to Southeast Asia.[42] General MacArthur then delayed all landings in occupied territories until a formal surrender document could be signed in Tokyo. This event was scheduled to take place on 28 August, but had to be postponed until 2 September because a typhoon passed through Japan.

Japan's capitulation was not officially reported in Malaya until 20 August. The *Syonan Shimbun* of 15 August carried a typical range of stories concerning losses suffered by the Allied forces, an editorial telling people not to listen to foolish rumours, and a lengthy attack on the Americans for using a "super bomb" on Asian targets and against civilians. "The employment of the new super-bomb against Asiatics for the first time as a test … will remain as an imperishable memory of the insult to the Asiatic peoples."[43] War news largely disappeared on the following day, when much of the front page of the paper was devoted to further condemnations of what was now called the atomic bomb. On 20 August, newspapers in Malaya published the Imperial Rescript accepting the provisions of the Potsdam Declaration, referred to as the "joint declaration" of the United States, Britain, China and the Soviet Union. The Rescript defended Japan's war effort, which was based on "Our sincere desire to ensure Nippon's self-preservation and the stabilization of East Asia", and cited as causes for the capitulation the use of the atomic bomb and the fact that the war situation had "not developed necessarily to Nippon's advantage", while "the general trends of the world" had turned against Japanese interests. There was no admission

[41] Kirby, *The Surrender of Japan*, pp. 236–41.

[42] Ibid., JM 167, p. 52.

[43] *Syonan Shimbun*, 15 Aug. 2605.

of defeat, and a story published by the *Syonan Shimbun* alongside the Imperial Rescript noted that the Imperial Nippon Army remained "fully prepared to crush the foe if he should ever come", and said that acceptance of the declaration reflected a humanitarian desire to spare the population of Asia further suffering and the mass destruction caused by the atomic bomb. Another story explained the steps involved in terminating hostilities: a ceasefire, conclusion of a truce agreement, and the signing of a treaty of armistice. A statement by the Supreme Commander of the Imperial Nippon Army pointed out that the Japanese army for the time being remained responsible for law and order in the country, and promised severe punishment for anyone who broke the law.[44] Thus the occupation ended as it had begun, with threats. In Penang men celebrated the end of the war by appearing in public wearing neckties, forbidden under the Japanese regime.[45]

The Thai authorities announced the end of the occupation in northern Malaya with the following communication, sent to the Secretary General of Kedah (Syburi) on 27 August:

> In view of the advent of the termination of the East Asia War and the utility of illegitimate powers having gradually dwindled in noticeable degrees coupled with the fact that the gradation of the administration of the State having been well achieved, the Commander-in-Chief of the Thai Army has deemed it expedient to grant unto the State complete independence in the administration in such matters as Legislature, Court and Police without referring same for the concurrence of the Thai Authorities as was hitherto a practice.
>
> The Thai Authorities shall only retain the power of protection, guidance and consultation which the State may deem it expedient to seek in close harmony and co-operation.[46]

Under the terms of the Rangoon agreement, Japanese commanders remained responsible for safeguarding banks and public buildings, feeding the civilian population, and supplying essential services such as water and electricity until Allied forces arrived, and then were to hand over "undamaged and in good condition" their armaments and fortifications, communications equipment, food and other supplies, stocks of fuel, and all "documents, records, archives,

---

[44] Ibid., 20 Aug. 2605.

[45] Ahmed Meah Baba Ahmed, *Suka Duka di Georgetown*, p. 171. On 4 April 2602 (1942), the *Syonan Times* published a story saying that municipal and government employees were "now allowed to dress sensibly", and no longer had to wear coats, long pants and "the traditional British collar and tie".

[46] Ch. Boonyarat Pan, Ag. Military Commissioner, Syburi, 27 Singhakhom [August] 2488, SUK Kedah 52/2487.

ciphers and codes, both military and civil". Japanese troops were designated "Surrendered Personnel" rather than prisoners of war, and remained under military discipline and under the command of Japanese officers.[47]

Transition arrangements were impeded by a deterioration in Japan's will and ability to retain control in Malaya. There was looting by armed gangs, communal violence, and more focused political activity by the MPAJA. The post-war Acting District Officer for Kuala Langat, Ismail bin Dato' Haji Matsah, wrote an account of the situation in the town of Telok Datoh during this period:

> During the latter part of July 1945 there were visible signs of matters getting out of control in the district. A Japanese Officer ("Shidokan") who was supposed to be the head of the administration of the district absented himself on many occasions for days together. Certain industrial institutions run by the Japanese paid off their employees and left the district. One of the Japanese institutions which had its head quarters within a few chains of the District Office buildings began removing and vacating its premises. Worse still the Police became fearful and ceased to function on or about the 19th August, 1945 and the unruly elements swept off law and order and kept every one under fear of death.
>
> The general atmosphere was such that no one dared to get out of doors except those who claimed or posed themselves as members of the Anti-Jap army or some communist party. They generally dominated all and became supreme and threatened to meet [*sic*] out swift and drastic punishments to those who dared or attempted to question their authority or action. They carried out their threats in many ways and to quote an instance—an office clerk was forcibly taken away in the Sunday fair on the morning of 19th August, 1945 by these elements—presumably this clerk must have been murdered since, as he has never been seen again. The whole Government staff were completely demoralised and their plight was beyond description.
>
> During this period of confusion, disorder, chaos and grim out look, a good number of young Chinese entered the office in the morning of 20.8.1945 while the whole staff were in office i.e. the staff of the Courts, Treasury, Sanitary Board, District & Land Office, Customs, Agriculture, Vehicle (one was taken away in the Sunday fair) and they removed the Treasury cash and all the various and different records of all the above offices. In fact they did whatever they liked. Some later came with arms. None dared to check or restrain them in their wanton acts. They were mostly young Chinese of strange faces. While this removal or looting was taking place a car full of Japanese passed the main road firing some gun shots. The car did not stop. This brought the office staff to more panic and all ran to their houses.
>
> The people were terrorised and the whole district was under their complete sway and one could not think of anything else but solely to

[47] HQ ALFSEA, Orders for Japanese Surrender, 19 Aug. 1945, WO203/2064.

> save one's own life. In fact this went on from the latter part of July until the landing of the British Military Forces on 9.9.1945. The British Military occupied the whole District Office buildings on their arrival for some time.[48]

During the interregnum between the Japanese surrender and the arrival of British forces, the MPAJA became the dominant political force in the country, taking control of administrative offices and creating a local-level political movement, and carrying out trials and summary executions of *Kempeitai* agents and others who had supported the Japanese. When British interrogators assembled a list of 171 local agents of the *Kempeitai* in September 1945 they found that nearly all were missing, and a great many were known or rumoured to have been killed by the communists.[49] The situation was especially serious in Pahang, where the 7th Regiment of the MPAJA operated independently of Force 136:

> ... because we had no Force 136 liaison officers with them they came out of the jungle on 31st August and took over every department of Civil Administration and occupied most of the large buildings in the town from the Chinese Chamber of Commerce to the police station. They were in complete and absolute control until four Force 136 officers emerged from the jungle and came into Kuantan on 8th September; and as no troops appeared for another three weeks our takeover had to be tactful and gradual.
>
> It must be admitted that the AJUF [Anti-Japanese Union Forces] did an extremely good job. At that time the Japs in Kuantan seemed to consider the cessation of hostilities as a mutual agreement rather than surrender. They insisted on returning with their arms to Kuantan, and AJUF's position was very delicate. Though the government rice stocks disappeared in an unaccountable manner and there was the usual "bumping" off of collaborators after a mere mockery of a trial, they certainly kept order and prevented looting. Their methods did not tend to restore confidence to the Malays; the A.D.O. went so far as to say that eight days of AJUF was worse than three and a half years under the Japs....[50]

The existing civil administration had lost its moral authority. Chinese leaders had to varying degrees given clandestine support to the MPAJA, but their cooperation with the Japanese left them vulnerable to charges of collaboration,

---

[48] Investigation of problems affecting land arising out of Japanese Occupation, Telok Datoh Land Office, Kuala Langat District, reply of the Ag. District Officer Kuala Langat (Ismail bin Dato Haji Matsah) to Question No. 3, 10 Jan. 1946, BMA Sel CA436/1945.

[49] 3 MOB SEC SEATIC Translation Report no. 31, Answer to 34 Corps Questionnaire Part II, Question 12, BMA ADM/9/27.

[50] F.S. Chapman, 25 Oct. 1946, HS1/120.

and they kept a low profile until Allied forces reached Malaya. Malay leaders, who had participated in the Japanese administration to an even greater extent, were unable to prevent MPAJA cadres from entering Malay villages, where they established political organizations and interfered with people's lives. Force 136 liaison officers attempted with some success to contain these activities, but MPAJA assertiveness gave rise to racial clashes, and when British forces began arriving in the country in early September the situation in some places was potentially explosive. The MPAJA made no attempt to remain in power after the British returned, in part because it feared the strength of the forces that would oppose such a move, but also because of its own organizational and logistical weaknesses. MPAJA forces were fragmented and had to rely on Force 136 for information, supplies and finance. Leadership was also a limiting factor, because the MPAJA had never fully recovered from the loss of key figures in the Batu Caves massacre.

The Malays who made up Japan's Volunteer Army (PETA) were a potential rival to the MPAJA. Their commander, Ibrahim Yaacob, envisioned using this force as the core of an independence army, and created an organization known as KRIS (Kekuatan Rakyat Istimewa, Special Strength of the People) as his political vehicle. He anticipated that members of the pre-war Kesatuan Melayu Muda would provide the nucleus of local branches of KRIS, but it proved difficult to locate and mobilize KMM members. Ibrahim's political objective was to unite the peninsula with Indonesia, and to work for independence alongside the nationalist movement there. Japanese officials supported Ibrahim but Japan's capitulation disrupted his activities. Some Malay leaders vowed to carry on the struggle, but the Sultans opposed union with Indonesia, and nationalist figures such as Dato' Onn bin Jaafar urged caution on grounds that the Malays were economically weak. Ibrahim sought an alliance with the MCP, but the MCP had decided against revolutionary action in Malaya and rejected his overtures. On 19 August, Ibrahim together with Onan Haji Siraj travelled to Jakarta to appeal for support, but Indonesia's leaders had decided against union with the peninsula because they did not feel able to fight the British along with the Dutch. Ibrahim remained in Indonesia, and the Malay radical movement foundered following his departure. A new radical group calling itself the Malay Nationalist Party failed to secure a wide following, and the political vacuum was filled by the United Malays National Organization, which attracted support from the ruling class and from the Malay community generally by strongly defending Malay rights.[51]

[51] This summary is based on Cheah, *Red Star Over Malaya*, ch. 4. Lee Kam Heng, "Malaya: New State and Old Elites", provides a useful overview of the period.

The British party of re-occupation reached Penang on 3 September, but delayed its landing for 24 hours at the request of the local Japanese commander, who said he feared reprisals and possible rioting, and wished to evacuate his forces from Penang Island to the mainland before the British resumed control. A small number of Japanese officers and soldiers remained in Georgetown during the first day of the re-occupation, and according to an American account, "The arrogant and insolent attitude of officers and men caused much resentment among the British."[52] A formal ceremony of occupation took place at Swettenham Pier in the city of Georgetown on 5 September 1945.

Operation Zipper brought the main body of the British force to Malaya beginning on 9 September, the date of the planned invasion. The assault was to have taken place at Morib, in Selangor, where the beach proved extremely treacherous. Large numbers of vehicles bogged down in the sand, and some of the landing craft were unable to get away from the beach. Inland areas where vehicles were supposed to be de-waterproofed proved inaccessible and the job had to be done on the road leading away from the beach, creating a huge bottleneck.[53] Morib had been chosen over beaches where conditions were more favourable precisely because the Japanese were less likely to have prepared strong defences there, but the difficulties British forces experienced landing troops and equipment under non-combat conditions suggest that they were fortunate not to have made a contested landing. British and Indian forces also came ashore some 70 km further south at Port Dickson, and at two other points.[54]

There was uncertainty about how the Japanese would respond to the surrender, and concern that individual commanders might refuse to lay down arms. In the event nearly all Japanese units complied with the surrender orders. An OSS mission (Operation Young) attached to the Third Regimental Group of the MPAJA watched the withdrawal of Japanese forces and submitted the following report:

> Operation Young observed Japanese troops in Segamat, Kluang, Singapore and several times passed through the ranks of the entire Japanese Seventh Army retreating from Singapore to Kluang. These troops were in excellent physical condition, they showed high morale and superb discipline to the extent of sustaining casualties without returning fire from guerrila forces after the cease fire order had been given. They seemed infected with the initial propaganda line of the Emperor, i.e. that Japanese forces had not been defeated but were willing to declare an armistice to return the world

---

52 Maj. John T. Stark to CO OSS, Tiderace Operations Report, 16 Sept. 1945, OSS E110 Folder 2878, NARA RG226.

53 Kirby, *The Surrender of Japan*, pp. 266–71; see also Spector, *In the Ruins of Empire.*

54 *The Malaya Tribune*, 11 Sept. 1945.

> to peace. And on 13 September the Japanese Seventh Army certainly was not a defeated army and would have been a hard one to defeat.[55]

Some Japanese soldiers deserted before they could be disarmed. In Pahang, for example, two such groups remained at large as late as October 1945, though their movements were closely monitored. Guerrillas captured some deserters, but others were heavily armed and remained free until British army units could be brought in to deal with them.[56]

Between 200 and 400 Japanese evaded the British, and many of them joined the communist guerrillas. Hara Fujio suggests three reasons for soldiers taking this step: a desire to fulfill Japan's promise to liberate Malaya from colonial rule, fear of retribution at the hands of the Allies, and despair about Japan's future prospects.[57] In addition, some Japanese had married local women and wanted to stay with their families. For the Malayan Communist Party, which had decided not to fight the British when they returned, the presence of Japanese soldiers created problems. They could not blend in with the local population and had to be kept hidden, and they required food and other supplies. For the communist leader, Lai Tek, they posed a serious potential threat because he had reason to fear that some of them might know that he was a double agent, and he ordered the execution of at least 20 and possibly as many as 70 of the Japanese who joined the MCP. Over time most of the Japanese fighting with the guerrillas either died in the jungle or were killed in action. Some, disillusioned by the MCP's decision not to continue armed struggle, slipped away and surrendered or simply disappeared. When the Malayan Communist Party signed a peace agreement with the Malaysian government in 1989, two Japanese remained with the organization. One of them, Hashimoto Shigeyuki, told Hara, "Fought for 45 years in order to liberate Malayan people and to wipe off the disgrace of wicked Nippon. I have no repentance in my life."[58]

British forces completed the process of disarming the Japanese by the end of October, and on 17 October they began sending surrendered personnel to Rempang Island in the Riau Archipelago to await repatriation. Some Japanese were employed as labourers to assist with rehabilitation work, a policy that proved controversial because by international agreement the surrendered soldiers had to

---

[55] HQ OSS India Burma Theater, R&A/SEAC Memo K-153, 2 Oct. 1945, NARA RG226 XL20728.

[56] Report on the situation in Pahang written by F.S. Chapman, 25 Oct. 1945, HS1/120.

[57] Hara, "Former Japanese Soldiers Who Joined Communist Guerrillas in Malaya", p. 69.

[58] Hara Fuio, "Former Japanese Soldiers Who Joined Communist Guerrillas in Malaya: Reconstructing an Elusive History", *Journal of the Malaysian Branch of the Royal Asiatic Society* 89, 2 No. 311 (Dec. 2016): 67–99. For Hashimoto's letter, see p. 72.

be fed and housed according to a better standard than that available to many local people. Japanese figures state that there were 125,686 Japanese military personnel in Malaya when the war ended. By the end of 1945, two-thirds of the Japanese had been relocated to internment camps, while around 40,000 continued working as labourers.[59]

* * *

With the arrival of British forces in the peninsula, the Japanese occupation formally ended. Malaya would be under military administration for the next seven months, and civilian control resumed at the beginning of April 1946. The surrender ceremony put an end to open hostilities. It would take time to overcome the shortages that made life difficult, and a painful period of reconstruction lay ahead.

Describing the Malayan situation immediately before the war and occupation ended, O.W. Gilmour wrote that the population was caught between increasingly emboldened guerrilla forces and the weakening but still dangerous Japanese authorities. Summing up, he wrote that small numbers of people actively collaborated with the Japanese, others pretended to collaborate "while in fact they were feathering their own nests", while the majority tried to remain "as inconspicuous as possible". For non-collaborators, living "by honest means" was nearly impossible.[60] Japan's surrender did not automatically change this situation, and the understaffed British Military Administration (BMA) would struggle to restore normality. Individuals within it also succumbed to temptation to such a degree that the BMA, become known by the sobriquet "Black Market Administration".

---

[59] Kirby, *The War against Japan*, vol. 5, *The Surrender of Japan*, pp. 275–6; FO 371/46415 F7685/7659/61 20 Oct. 1945.

[60] Gilmour, *With Freedom to Singapore*, p. 82.

CHAPTER 11

The Aftermath

The people of Malaya were excited about the return of the British because their arrival meant the end of the Japanese regime. According to an American officer who observed the event:

> Enthusiastic and cheering crowds massed at the pier and along the streets to welcome the returning British troops. The sincerity of the welcome and joy at the end of Japanese rule appeared to be universal. Stories of terrorism and tortures were heard on every hand. The reception by the people, while unquestionably enthusiastic and friendly, should be interpreted as dominated by anti-Japanese rather than pro-British feelings.[1]

To sustain this initial euphoria the British needed to make rapid progress in overcoming the shortages that plagued the local population, but providing relief supplies and creating conditions that would promote the resumption of normal economic activities was extremely difficult, and the British Military Administration (BMA), which ran Malaya from September 1945 until April 1946, was plagued by inefficiency and corruption. Andrew Gilmour, who in April 1946 became Secretary for Economic Affairs in Singapore, observed that when the Singapore Chinese witnessed the release of British internees from prison, "the pendulum swung right over in Britain's favour; but after months of B.M.A., the pendulum had swung right back again" as a consequence of the "corruption and looting propensities of the occupying British Military Administration".[2]

A formal surrender ceremony took place in Singapore on 12 September 1945. The Japanese delegation was headed by General Itagaki, representing Field Marshall Hisaichi Terauchi, who had suffered a stroke and was too ill to attend. M.E. Dening, who witnessed the ceremony, reported that "a rather menacing noise" arose from the crowd as the Japanese officers walked toward

---

[1] Maj. John T. Stark to CO OSS, Tiderace Operations Report, 16 Sept. 1945, OSS E110 Folder 2878, NARA RG226. This remark appeared in the handwritten draft of the report, but was omitted from the final version.

[2] Gilmour, *My Role in the Rehabilitation of Singapore*, p. 6.

the building, and again as they left.[3] N.I. Low provided a fuller explanation of this "noise": "As they [the Japanese delegates] passed, the crowds shouted '*Bakaro!*' The "*bakaros*" of thousands of throats expressed the pent-up hatred of the Nip...." *Bakaro* (*bakayaro*, idiot or moron), he added, "is a word often in the mouths of the irate Nips of our acquaintance, generally going with a buffet or a kick, or both. Now, at long last, we could safely apply it to the Nip – to Nip Generals!"[4]

Illus. 11.1 Victory parade along North Bridge Road near Elgin Bridge after the Japanese surrender.

Source: 19980005701-0004 David Ng Collection, courtesy of National Archives of Singapore.

Post-war Administration

Planning for the post-war administration began early in the occupation with the creation of an informal Malayan Planning Committee involving both the War Office and the Colonial Office, and was placed on a more regular footing in July 1943 with the creation of a Malayan Planning Unit within the Civil

[3] Dening to Sterndale-Bennett, 24 Sept. 1945, British Library IOR: M/3/862.

[4] N.I. Low, *When Singapore was Syonan-to*, p. 132.

Illus. 11.2 Outside the Municipal Building in Singapore, Japanese prisoners of war fill in trenches that they had forced Allied prisoners to dig during the war.

Source: SE 4844, War Office, Central Office of Information and American Second World War Official Collection (photographs). Made by: No. 9 Army Film & Photographic Unit. Courtesy Trustees of the Imperial War Museum, London.

Affairs Directorate of the War Office.[5] Major General H.R. Hone, who had a Colonial Office background and was a former head of civil affairs in the Middle East, became Chief Planner and head of the British Military Administration (Malaya). Starting with six military officers, the staff strength of the planning unit grew by April 1945 to 162 officers, supported by 127 civilians and lower ranking military personnel.[6] The basis of a military administration lay in the declaration of Martial Law, which Hone wryly observed was "no law at all, but merely the will of the Military Commander". He noted that a military administration normally recognized existing laws, but that the commander had absolute power to suspend laws and treaties, and disregard pre-war constitutional arrangements.[7]

The Planning Unit set up departments covering trade and industry, printing and publicity, a postal service, labour and immigration, supplies, and rationing on a pan-Malayan basis. For other activities, it created separate administrations for the mainland (including Penang and Malacca) and for Singapore. The Singapore administration was described as "a shrunken form" of the pre-war government of the Straits Settlements, but the Planning Unit envisaged a future arrangement in which Singapore played a role similar to Hong Kong or Gibraltar before the war. Plans for the mainland prioritized military requirements, with a simple administration under which the military commander would legislate by proclamation, by-passing both the pre-war State Councils and the Rulers, whose "personal position of honour and dignity" was nevertheless to be protected.[8]

Phrases like "the return of the British" are often used to describe post-occupation Malaya, but a great many of the British officers who "returned" had no prior experience of the country. About 80 to 90 per cent of the officers in the pre-war Malayan Civil Service (MCS) had been interned by the Japanese, and Hone thought it unlikely that more than 30 per cent of this group would be physically able to remain in the service and return to their previous posts.

[5] Discussions of the activities of the planning unit are found in A.J. Stockwell, "Colonial Planning during World War II: the Case of Malaya", *Journal of Imperial and Commonwealth History* (1974): 333–51; A.J. Stockwell, *British Policy and Malay Politics during the Malayan Union Experiment, 1942–1948*, ch. 1–2; and C.M. Turnbull, "British Planning for Post-war Malaya", *Journal of Southeast Asian Studies* (1974): 239–54. These accounts concentrate on preparations for the creation of the Malayan Union. The definitive work on the Malayan Union is Albert Lau, *The Malayan Union Controversy*. O.W. Gilmour recounts his experiences as a member of the Malayan Planning Unit in his *With Freedom to Singapore*, pp. 23–35.

[6] H. Ralph Hone, Planning for War Establishment, Planning Directive No. 3, 3 March 1944, WO203/3877.

[7] Malayan Planning Staff, Directive No. 1 (General Plan), 10 Nov. 1943, WO203/3877.

[8] Malayan Planning Staff, Directive No. 2, 29 Nov. 1943, WO203/3877.

To provide a nucleus for the post-war civil service, he recruited most of the approximately 220 MCS officers who happened to have been outside of Malaya at the time of the Japanese invasion, as well as a small number of officers with experience in other colonies. For the remaining positions, he attempted to find men and women willing to make their careers in Malaya after the period of military administration had ended. Of 1,037 officers recruited for the BMA as of March 1945, just 244 had previously held pensionable Colonial Office appointments.[9]

Because Malaya was under British rule before the invasion and would be restored to British control, the BMA went beyond the limited range of activities normally undertaken by military commanders to administer captured enemy territory. The Key Plan called for an operational period when a rudimentary civil administration would be put in place to support the invasion force, and a post-operational period when the Civil Affairs staff would take on greater responsibilities and create a more fully developed administrative structure in anticipation of the return to civilian control.[10] With the Japanese surrender, the operational phase in the peninsula was reduced to the period needed to bring troops into the country and ended on 1 October, while in Singapore the post-operational plan was implemented immediately. Policy directives prepared by the Planning Unit covered Malayan citizenship, resident Chinese, the public services, finance and a wide range of social and economic issues (see Table 11.1). They occasioned considerable debate because some Colonial Office officials wanted to make changes immediately rather than allow business as usual to resume, while the War Office argued that policy issues should be left to the civil administration, and that the BMA should confine itself to handling the transition to civilian authority. Hone said that the Military Administration needed to consider long-term implications of any initiatives it undertook, but that responsibility for the Colonial Office should draft long-term policy directives and submit them to the War Office for implementation. The War Office wanted to end military government as early as possible and Japan's capitulation made the transition less chaotic than anticipated, but adjustments

---

[9] H.R. Hone, Statement of Progress regarding Civil Affairs Planning for Malaya ... and other Territories of the South East Asia Command, 27 Nov. 1943, and P.A.B. McKerron, Plans for the Transition Period – Malaya, 29 Dec. 1943, BMA ADM/29.

[10] Supreme Allied Commander's Policy for the British Military Administration of Malaya, WO203/13880.

to the time frame aside, the transition proceeded along the lines worked out by the planning staff.[11]

Table 11.1 BMA policy directives

Malayan Citizenship	Medical and Health
Chinese Policy	Education
Public Services	Labour and Immigration
Finance	Transport
Rubber	Posts and Telecommunications
Tin	Electricity
Primary production other than Mineral	Broadcasting
Lands, Mines and Surveys	Co-operative Department
Social Welfare	Dangerous Drugs (incl. Opium)

Source: H.R. Hone. *Report on the British Military Administration of Malaya*, p. 6.

Under the BMA, executive authority for civil administration lay with the Chief Civil Affairs Officer, a post filled by Hone. The Singapore Division and the Malay Peninsula Division were each headed by a Deputy Chief Civil Affairs Officer, with the Malay Peninsula Division sub-divided into nine regions that generally corresponded with the pre-war states. (see Table 11.2). There were no civil courts, and military courts handled criminal offences and violations of BMA Proclamations.[12] As additional staff became available, the BMA created departments to handle matters such as education, customs, civil aviation, and in January 1946 re-organized the administration in anticipation of the forthcoming transition to civil government.

The Colonial Office introduced one major change. Within the pre-war administrative structure of Straits Settlements, Federated Malay States and Unfederated States, decisions affecting the whole of Malaya required the concurrence of ten separate administrative units (the nine Malay states and the Straits Settlements). Hone opposed restoring the complex arrangements that prevailed before the war, an approach that had major constitutional implications but was consistent with a Colonial Office proposal to sign fresh treaties with

[11] Malayan Planning Staff, Directive No. 1 (General Plan), 10 Nov. 1943, and SACSEA to C-in-C ALFSEA, 28 Mar. 1945, in WO203/3877; Report on the Handover from the British Military Administration to the Civil Governments in Malaya, WO203/6077; Lau, *The Malayan Union Controversy*.

[12] The British Military Administration of Malaya, Civil Affairs Operational Plan, and Post-Operational Civil Affairs Plan for Malaya, WO203/4002.

the rulers of the Malay states in order to simplify constitutional arrangements in the peninsula.[13] The Planning Unit devised a scheme for a Malayan Union which would serve this purpose, and also allow Chinese and Indian residents to become citizens of the new entity. Singapore, as the centre of British political and military activity throughout the region, would remain outside the Malayan Union and continue to be administered as a Crown Colony. The Malayan Union scheme required changes in the terms and conditions set down in the treaties that had regulated colonial rule in Malaya, and Sir Harold MacMichael arrived in Malaya on 11 October 1945 to negotiate fresh agreements with the Malay Sultans. By the end of the year he had accomplished this task, and a White Paper on the constitutional future of Malaya appeared on 22 January 1946.

Although the Malayan Union was conceived as a mechanism to achieve improved efficiency, and to resolve questions regarding the status of non-Malays in the country, the citizenship provisions and limits on the powers of the rulers aroused considerable controversy and were the issue around which the country's first political parties took shape. The Malayan Union was inaugurated in April 1946, but intense campaigns mounted locally and among influential former members of the Malayan Civil Service in the United Kingdom let to its replacement at the end of 1947 with a new Federation of Malaya. This setback notwithstanding, Britain continued to rule Malaya until 1957, and the country's Anglophile elite inherited power.

The Question of an Enquiry into the Fall of Malaya

Many of the officers involved with the defence of Malaya submitted reports on the battle for Malaya and the fall of Singapore that blamed various parties, but the British government imposed strict limits on the circulation of these accounts.[14] In response to calls for an official enquiry to determine what had gone wrong, Winston Churchill told a secret session of the House of Commons on 23 April 1942, that a Royal Commission "would hamper the prosecution of the war". Noting that Australian accounts criticize Indian troops, other credible statements cast blame on the Australians, or on the military leadership, he said there was "an endless field for recrimination", and because many key figures were held prisoner by the Japanese they could not speak in their own defence. Accordingly, he asked the House to support the Government in rejecting calls

[13] Memorandum from C.I.C.A Headquarters, Southeast Asia Command, 24 Dec. 1943, WO203/3877.

[14] Several such reports, and a volume of telegrams dated between 16 Dec 1941 and 3 April 1942 printed for the War Cabinet, can be found in CAB 120/615.

Table 11.2 Initial administrative divisions under the BMA

Pan-Malayan Departments	*Malay Peninsula*	*Singapore*
1. Labour and Immigration	1. Civil Affairs	1. Civil Affairs
2. Postal	2. Agriculture	2. Custodian of Property
3. Printing and Publicity	3. Custodian of Property	3. Electrical
4. Rationing and Food Control	4. Electrical	4. Finance
5. Supplies	5. Finance	5. Legal and Judicial
6. Trade and Industry	6. Forests	6. Police, Prisons and Fire Service
	7. Legal and Judicial	7. Medical, Health and Veterinary
	8. Police, Prisons and Fire Service	8. Road Transport
	9. Medical and Health	9. Works
	10. Road Transport	
	11. Works	
	12. Lands, Mines and Surveys	
	13. Veterinary	

Source: The British Military Administration, Malaya: Post-Operational Civil Affairs Plan for Malaya, WO203/4002.

for an enquiry, saying the decision was "not taken in an ignoble desire to shield individuals or safeguard the administration but solely in the interests of the State and for the successful prosecution of the war".[15]

The publication of this speech in 1946 sparked renewed demands for a public enquiry, and the issue was referred to the Chiefs of Staff Committee of the Joint Planning Staff. The Committee said that any enquiry would have to be kept "within acceptable limits", which would mean avoiding discussion of general policies for the defence of the Far East, intelligence matters, reinforcements, and military equipment. These limitations automatically precluded consideration of the resources available for the defence of Malaya and Singapore, the methods used by the Japanese in attacking the peninsula,

[15] Eade, *Secret Session Speeches*, p. 55. See also *The War Speeches of the Rt. Hon. Winston S. Churchill*, Charles Eade (comp.), vol. 2, pp. 236–57.

Britain's failure to provide adequate forces for the defence of Malaya before the outbreak of fighting, and the quantity and quality of equipment supplied to British forces. What remained was the actions of men serving in Malaya, and the Committee felt it would be difficult to arrive at a reasonable assessment of this subject without considering the forbidden topics of intelligence, reinforcement and equipment. "It would moreover involve discussion of the character and ability of the higher commanders concerned, which we consider undesirable." The Committee said an enquiry confined to events surrounding the fall of Singapore was less objectionable, but feared that a limited enquiry would stimulate public demand for a wider investigation. The Prime Minister (Atlee) was already on record as opposing an enquiry, having told the Australian Prime Minister that it would do "no good but much harm." In short, the military and the political leadership agreed that a public enquiry into the Malayan Campaign was undesirable, and none took place.[16]

Treatment of War Criminals, Collaborators and the Resistance Movement

A total of 1,101 men were prosecuted for war crimes in Singapore, including a number brought from other locations. The trials, which began in January 1946 and lasted until April 1948, resulted in the execution of 135 men at Changi prison and another 79 in Malaya, and prison terms for many others. Efforts to bring to justice the Japanese responsible for the *sook ching* massacres were less successful, in part because the screenings and executions were carried out by ordinary soldiers, and it was unclear who had issued the orders. Masanobu Tsuji, the man many believe to have been behind the killings, went into hiding when Japan surrendered, and escaped retribution. Just two men received death sentences in connection with the *sook ching* in Singapore.[17]

The entire population of Malaya had of necessity collaborated with the Japanese, with the partial exception of those who joined guerrilla forces operating in the jungle. In the end, the British adopted a conciliatory attitude toward collaboration, while reserving the right to punish serious offences. In setting down his policy for the military administration of Malaya, Admiral Mountbatten specified: "The first guiding principle to be observed is that no

---

[16] Report by the Chiefs of Staff Committee of the Joint Planning Staff, signed by J.F. Stevens, J.H.N. Poett and J.H. Edwardes-Jones, 6 May 1946, CAB 119/208. Telegram No. 39 of 31 Jan. 1946, for Primet Minister from Prime Minister, in CAB 120/616.

[17] Shü and Chua (eds), *Malayan Chinese Resistance to Japan*, pp. 81–3 of the English-language section; Montgomery, *Shenton of Singapore*, p. 162.

person shall suffer on account of political opinions honestly held, whether now or in the past—even if these may have been anti-British—but only on account of previous crimes against the criminal law or actions repugnant to humanity."[18] Instructions prepared by the SACSEA Security Intelligence for Planning Section stated:

> Pro-Japanese and anti-Allied opinions expressed publicly by prominent citizens during the Japanese Occupation should not be taken invariably at face value. Many such individuals have co-operated under pressure, and have acted as intermediaries on behalf of their respective communities. Similarly, reports of "donations" made by local citizens to the Japanese war funds should be treated with reserve.[19]

The Civil Affairs directive regarding collaboration enunciated this policy in the following terms:

> It is the aim of His Majesty's Government to dissipate as speedily as possible whatever pro-Japanese sentiments may still remain, and to promote conditions under which the territories concerned may resume their position in the Empire on a basis of goodwill. To this end, and subject to what is said below, treatment of those who have collaborated with the enemy should be founded on a tolerant view of their conduct, if this will encourage the loyal support of men on whom (by reason of their administrative qualities) we must necessarily depend, but who in view of their position have in the past been employed by the Japanese.

"Prominent" renegades could be punished for carrying out propaganda work, for actively assisting enemy operations or for working against the Allied cause, but the directive warned that no one should be prosecuted "unless there is a reasonable probability of conviction".[20]

The leader of the Eurasian community, Dr C.J. Paglar, was charged with treason and put on trial in January 1946. The defence argued that community leaders such as Paglar had acted under duress, and Mamoru Shinozaki, the former head of the Welfare Department in Singapore, testified that he himself had drafted a message, said by the prosecution to be treasonable, that Paglar had read out during a ceremony to celebrate the Japanese Emperor's birthday, adding that leaders of the other communities had been given slightly different versions

---

[18] Supreme Allied Commander's Policy for the British Military Administration of Malaya, WO203/13880.

[19] SACSEA Security Intelligence for Planning Section, Proforma 'B' – Tactical: Malacca, NARA RG226 21414.

[20] Memorandum on Treatment of Renegades and Quislings, and Policy Regarding the Trial and Punishment of Disloyal Persons in Malaya Who Collaborated with the Enemy, WO203/4203A.

of the same message. The Court decided not to proceed with the trial, although the charges were not withdrawn and the case was simply adjourned, leaving a shadow hanging over Paglar but sparing him any punishment. Similar charges against other community leaders were dropped.[21]

Members of the INA posed a different problem, for they had taken up arms against Britain, and some had done so in violation of oaths taken as members of the British armed forces. Force 136 officers sent into Malaya during the occupation had been directed to attempt to persuade INA members to desert, but not to make any promises regarding future treatment.[22] After the war, surrendered INA soldiers were transferred to India where their fate became embroiled in the politics of independence. Jawaharlal Nehru, who had opposed the INA in 1942, now issued a statement of support, and public opinion in India hailed INA members as heroes. Responding to this situation, the British allowed many soldiers to rejoin their old units, and most of the rest were simply dismissed from the service. A small number of key figures were tried and sentenced to life imprisonment, but these sentences were commuted to dismissal from the army, and they were set free.[23]

Although handling wartime enemies was difficult, dealing with wartime allies was hardly less so. The MPAJA had rendered valuable service, but the agenda of the Malayan Communist Party extended beyond the defeat of the Japanese and envisioned a future re-ordering of an independent Malaya as a communist state. The politics of the MPAJA had caused concern from the outset, but immediately after the war relations were generally cordial and there was a high level of cooperation. The sacrifices of the MPAJA clearly had to be rewarded, but their presence as an armed body posed a threat to British efforts to re-establish political control. British policy was to provide honours and cash payments to guerrillas, but to demand in return that guerrilla organizations disband and turn in their weapons. Admiral Mountbatten personally presented war medals to members of the resistance, and on 1 December 1945 the British staged demobilization parades throughout Malaya at which guerrilla fighters handed in weapons and received gifts of clothing and money.[24] The MPAJA was

---

[21] Mamoru Shinozaki, *Syonan – My Story*, pp. 105–8.

[22] Brief for Head of "P" Division on Force 136 Operations in Malaya, WO203/5767.

[23] See Lebra, *Jungle Alliance*, pp. 200–10.

[24] Guerrilla forces handed in 5,497 weapons, substantially more than they had been issued, but this figure includes many captured and obsolete weapons and was by no means the entire stock of weaponary in the hands of the MPAJA. Forces of the Askar Setia Melayu and Wataniah disbanded without any complications. See Donnison, *British Military Administration*, p. 387; Leo Tin Boon, "Force 136: The Malayan Episode", pp. 79–81.

also represented at the victory parade held in London. This attempt to defuse a tense racial and political situation was only partly successful, and in the months that followed the MCP became involved in racial incidents and strikes as its political ambitions were thwarted. It finally returned to the jungle to launch an armed insurrection in 1948.

Wartime Death Rates and the Size of the Post-war Population

Death rates increased for both sexes during the occupation, and were particularly high for males. The 1931 census reported approximately 100 men for every 59 women in the Singapore population, and during the 1930s there were 100 male deaths for every 66 female deaths. For the occupation years, the ratio was 100:50, apparently because poor nutrition and harsh conditions took a heavy toll on men recruited as labourers for Japanese projects (see Table 11.3). The breakdown of these figures by race shows a significant increase in male deaths for all races, with Indians the worst affected (see Table 11.4). Infant mortality contributed significantly to the increased death rate, at least in part as a result of the poor diets available to nursing mothers (see Table 11.5).[25]

Based on data for 1941 and 1947, Malaya recorded a net population increase of 6.2 per cent during the occupation. However, the figures indicate that the Indian population declined by more than 19 per cent (from 744,202 to 599,616), while the Malay population appears to have grown by 11.5 per cent during the occupation, and the Chinese by 10 per cent (see Table 11.6). These figures are open to question.[26] Those for 1941 are estimates based on the 1931 census adjusted to take into account births and deaths, and immigration and emigration. The figures for 1947 were collected in a systematic census, but conflicted with figures the government used in issuing food rations, which showed an additional 1.1 million people. Discrepancies appeared primarily in states with large Chinese populations: Johore, for example, had 42 per cent more people drawing rations than the census figures would warrant, and Perak 32 per cent. In states with predominantly Malay populations, the difference amounted

[25] A newspaper article on beri-beri published in May 1942 suggested that breastfed children were vulnerable to infantile beri-beri if their mothers consumed insufficient amounts of vitamin B1. *Syonan Times*, Saturday Supplement, 9 May 2602.

[26] Data recorded in Malayan Union, Report on the Registration of Births and Deaths for the Year 1941 to 1946 (p. 1) are substantially different.

Table 11.3 Mortality in Singapore

	Males	*Females*	*Total deaths**
1937	8,555	5,746	14,301
1938	9,044	6,116	15,160
1939	8,508	5,689	14,197
1940	9,487	6,217	15,705
1941	9,730	6,245	15,978
1942	18,694	11,137	29,833
1943	13,718	8,212	21,936
1944	29,515	13,232	42,751
1945	24,304	11,023	35,330
1946	9,357	5,926	15,287

Note: *This column includes a small number of cases for which the sex of the deceased was not recorded.

Source: Colony of Singapore, Annual Report on the Registration of Births and Deaths for the Years 1940–47, Appendix I: Principal Causes of Deaths Registered in Singapore, and Dr Lucius Nicholls, "Colonial Office Food, Nutrition and Agricultural Survey", 12 Mar. 1946, BMA DEPT/9/4. Where there are discrepancies between these sources, I have used the former. R.B. MacGregor in his "Medical History of the War in Malaya" concluded that the mortality figures recorded for Singapore during the occupation were reasonably accurate.

Table 11.4 Mortality in Singapore according to race and sex

	Malays		*Chinese*		*Indians*		*Total*
	Male	*Female*	*Male*	*Female*	*Male*	*Female*	
1940	1,102	863	7,600	4,921	582	313	15,381
1941	n.a.	n.a.	n.a.	n.a.	n.a.	n.a.	n.a.
1942	1,914	1,717	14,164	8,514	2,314	679	29,302
1943	1,608	1,321	10,095	6,205	1,798	542	21,569
1944	7,208	2,395	18,017	9,524	3,906	1,109	41,159
1945	6,484	2,178	13,925	7,636	3,603	1,022	34,848
1946	1,171	932	6,852	4,505	1,182	399	15,041

Source: Colony of Singapore, Annual Report on the Registration of Births and Deaths for the Years 1940–47, Appendix F: Deaths by Sex and Race.

to about 10 per cent, while population figures collected in Singapore closely matched the number registered to draw rations.[27]

Table 11.5 Deaths of children under one year old in Singapore

	Malays	*Chinese*	*Indians*
1940	737	3,831	194
1941	n.a.	n.a.	n.a.
1942	n.a.	n.a.	n.a.
1943	771	4,837	353
1944	1,315	7,028	608
1945	772	3,954	496
1946	618	2,568	235

Source: Colony of Singapore, Annual Report on the Registration of Births and Deaths for the Years 1940–47, Appendix G: Deaths Grouped According to Age, Sex and Race Registered in Singapore.

Census cards were issued only on production of certificates of birth or naturalization, and it is possible that Chinese who did not have these documents avoided the census takers.[28] In Jelebu some 2,000 people spent the period when the census was taken doing work in the jungle because they were convinced the census was connected in some way with income tax, and detailed checks in other localities tended to support the contention that the census figures were too low. For Chemor, where ration cards indicated a population 12,000 but the census had reported a population of 2,750, local officials managed to locate nearly 12,000 people. Negri Sembilan, which according to the census had a population of 267,281, withdrew and reissued all ration cards, but this exercise only reduced the number of people registered to draw rations from 312,046 to 302,206.[29] The officer in charge of the census, M.V. del Tufo, strongly defended his results, and further checks of the rationing system disclosed substantial numbers of duplicate or false ration cards. By 1949 some 900,000 ration cards had been withdrawn, and the discrepancy between population figures in the census and those used by government departments responsible for issuing supplies had been

[27] MU Confidential 678/1947; C0537/2996.

[28] See, for example, "Chinese in Malaya", NARA RG59 Phil/SEA Division, Box 14, Malaya.

[29] Minute by O.H.R. Beadles, Ag. Controller of Supplies, 26 July 1948, MU Confidential 678/1947.

Table 11.6 Size of the Malayan population

State or Settlement	*Malays 1941*	*Malays 1947*	*Chinese 1941*	*Chinese 1947*	*Indians 1941*	*Indians 1947*	*Eurasians 1941*	*Eurasians 1947*	*Others 1941*	*Others 1947*	*Total 1941*	*Total 1947*
Singapore	77,231	115,735	599,659	730,133	59,838	68,978	8,321	9,110	9,582	16,866	769,216	940,824
Penang/PW	152,697	136,163	230,679	247,366	60,503	57,157	2,682	2,412	2,437	3,223	410,047	446,321
Malacca	119,913	120,327	92,125	96,144	28,587	19,718	2,481	1,978	693	1,189	236,087	239,356
Perak	335,385	360,631	450,197	444,509	196,056	140,716	1,590	1,182	5,350	6,900	992,691	953,938
Selangor	152,697	187,324	339,707	362,710	193,504	145,184	2,654	2,816	8,012	12,754	701,552	710,788
N. Sembilan	106,005	110,560	125,806	114,406	59,270	38,082	865	880	2,633	3,760	296,009	267,688
Pahang	128,539	135,772	73,925	97,329	17,226	14,744	177	79	1,305	2,254	221,800	250,178
Johore	302,104	323,680	308,901	354,770	58,498	55,044	352	478	4,178	4,279	675,297	738,251
Kedah	341,294	377,075	108,445	115,928	60,898	51,347	141	161	14,009	9,930	525,458	554,441
Kelantan	369,256	412,918	23,363	22,938	7,591	4,940	40	25	7,522	7,751	407,981	448,572
Trengganu	186,580	207,874	16,956	15,864	1,409	1,761	17	14	728	483	205,743	225,996
Perlis	46,441	55,185	8,227	11,788	1,127	1,684	10	7	2,042	1,826	57,850	70,490
Total	2,277,352	2,543,569	2,377,990	2,614,667	744,202	599,616	19,330	19,171	58,491	71,887	508,731	5,848,910

Source: Data for 1941 are drawn from *Malaya and Its Civil Administration Prior to Japanese Occupation*, Table 4. Data for 1947 are taken from the *Report on the 1947 Census of Population for Malaya*, Table 2. Columns for 1947 do not add up owing to the omission of a small number of people described as "Unlocated".

eliminated.[30] The report on the 1947 census was finally published in 1949 and differed little from the preliminary version (for example, it shows a population of 269,304 for Negri Sembilan), but the exact size of the post-war Malayan population will probably never be known.

Health

Surveys conducted by the BMA revealed that moderate malnutrition was common throughout Malaya, and that up to 30 per cent of certain groups were seriously undernourished. The incidence of diseases and of physical deterioration associated with malnutrition was high, particularly in rural areas where people had received no rice rations and often no medical supplies during the latter part of the occupation. Semi-starvation and deficiency diseases were also prevalent among Tamils on rubber estates, and people living in isolated villages. On a visit to Dusun Tua, the Civil Affairs Officer for Selangor found many residents of all ages bedridden, and described the prevailing attitude as "hopeless apathy". Industrial workers and clerical staff living in towns showed fewer signs of malnutrition.[31]

Children were especially hard hit. Although school children presented a "remarkably healthy" appearance, poor diets had retarded their growth, and researchers visiting a Malay School located on Endau Road in Johore found that children who were 10 to 14 years old differed little in terms of height and physical development from children aged 6 to 9. More extensive studies of several thousand school children in Kuala Lumpur, Pahang, Kelantan and Trengganu produced similar results: "children who appear reasonably healthy individuals of 7 or 8 years are children of 12 to 14 years". In the three east coast states, 23 per cent of the children surveyed were "grossly undersized", and for Singapore there was a marked decline in the height-to-weight ratio among children (see Table 11.7), despite the fact that most of those examined were underweight. Some 40–60 per cent of school children in Singapore were malnourished by pre-war standards, and surveys revealed a high incidence of anaemia, decayed teeth, abnormal skin conditions, ulcers and bleeding gums, all indications of malnutrition. The signs of deficiency reported by the Nutrition

---

[30] See correspondence in MU Confidential 678/1947, *inter alia* Minute by O.H.R. Beadles, 26 July 1948.

[31] I.D. Irvine to H. Ford, CAO Kuala Lumpur and Ulu Langat District, 29 Sept. 1945, Sel CA151/1945; Nutrition Unit, Monthly Report for Nov. 1945; Monthly Report for Dec. Appendix D; Proceedings and Notes of a Meeting on Nutrition, 15 Jan. BMA DEPT/1/3 Pt I; Final Report, Nutrition Unit, British Military Administration Malaya, Apr. 1946, BMA DEPT/1/3 Pt II.

Unit for children in Singapore, in order of frequency, included "underweight, anaemia (almost certainly aggravated by malaria and worm infestation), carious teeth, xerosis of the skin, crackled skin, ulcers, blue congested gums bleeding on pressure, eye abnormalities (such as excess tissue, hyperaemia, blue spots and circumcorneal injection), poor musculature, tongue abnormalities (magenta colour, depapillation and fissures), follicular hyperkeratosis, angulas stomatitis and obcilosis, Bitot's spots, beri-beri, oedema of the legs". Children also had chronic infestations of intestinal worms and other parasites, caused in part by the practice of using human waste to fertilize vegetables.[32]

Rehabilitation and Reconstruction

Malaya emerged from the occupation badly in need of physical rehabilitation. In Kuala Lumpur after the Japanese surrender:

> it was found that the streets were very dirty; there was no street or domestic lighting; the water supply was untreated and thousands of gallons were running to waste from defective and tap-less pipes; food was very scarce and no dogs were to be seen; all temporary and permanent anti-malarial work was neglected; A[nopheles] maculatus were breeding in concrete drains; any nightsoil removal was done by vegetable gardeners. The public market was full of hawkers and unauthorized stalls; the incinerator was useless and there was no scavenging or conservancy transport.[33]

The Japanese practice of denying food rations to people living in the countryside had caused large numbers of squatters to move into urban areas, and the people who had evacuated to agricultural settlements in the last year and a half of the occupation returned to the cities as soon as soon as the war ended. As people crowded into towns and cities in search of work and relief supplies, a severe housing shortage developed. A survey conducted in 1947 indicated that more than half the people in Singapore had relocated since 1940. The rooms of many buildings, some more than half a century old and in poor condition, had been subdivided into cubicles that provided accommodation for entire families.

---

[32] Nutrition Situation in Malaya, Appendix IV to Proceedings and Notes of a Meeting on Nutrition held at HQ SACSEA, 15 Jan. 1946, BMA DEPT/1/3 Pt I; Appendix E to Monthly Report of the Nutrition Unit, December 1945, BMA DEPT/1/3 Pt I; Final Report, Nutrition Unit, British Military Administration Malaya, April 1946, BMA DEPT/1/3 Pt II. The Nutrition Unit surveys covered a total of 14,696 people. In Singapore, only schoolchildren were surveyed. The sample size was 6,200 but not all were given the same examination. Dr. C.J. Oliveiro, whose investigations in 1937 provided a benchmark figure for testing the Height to Weight ratio, was part of the post-war team. See also Geoffrey H. Bourne, "Nutrition Work in Malaya under the British Military Administration", pp. 266–7.

[33] Report of the Selangor Medical Department for the Years 1941–46, RC Sel 296/1947.

Around 15 per cent of the households in Singapore did not even have a cubicle and simply occupied "space", defined as "places like bunks in passage ways, the tiered bed-lofts common in Singapore, sleeping shelves under or over staircases, sleeping arrangements in five-foot ways, kitchens and backyards and other places used for sleeping without ordinary enclosures or partitions".

Table 11.7 Height to weight ratio for Singapore schoolchildren

Age	*Height/weight (1937)*	*Ratio (1945/46)*
6	0.89	0.91
7	0.91	0.93
8	0.96	0.94
9	1.02	0.96
10	1.04	1.01
11	1.12	1.08
12	1.17	1.09
13	1.25	1.18
14	1.37	1.32
15	1.51	1.44
16	1.59	1.47

Source: Final Report, Nutrition Unit, British Military Administration Malaya, April 1946, BMA DEPT/1/3 Pt II.

Around three-quarters of the population lived in conditions defined as "overcrowded", a state of affairs that encouraged the spread of disease and created a serious fire hazard. Outside of the city proper, squatters occupied huts in settlements with no drainage or sewerage. An estimated 250,000 people needed resettlement in Singapore. Similar conditions prevailed in urban areas throughout the peninsula, and an estimated 50,000 additional houses were needed to accommodate the population there.[34] In Kedah,

> Many kampong houses were put up in all the towns to relieve the housing conjestion [*sic*]. House inspection in the towns revealed (a) A high degree of overcrowding (b) bad designing and unauthorised cubicling for 'letting" purposes (c) countless ponds and pits as an emergency measure (d) a considerable number of insanitary cowsheds.[35]

[34] AR Singapore for 1 Apr.–31 Dec. 1946, pp. 72–4; AR Malayan Union, 1946, pp. 84–6; The Singapore Department of Social Welfare, *A Social Survey of Singapore* (1947), pp. 68–84.

[35] Medical Department Annual Report of the State of Syburi for 2487, SUK Kedah 119/2487.

Conditions in urban areas were unhealthy, and waste disposal arrangements had broken down. Regulations issued in Selangor during March 1942 stipulated that rubbish had to be placed in dustbins, or deposited at designated sites, but owing to shortages of transport and fuel, a great deal of refuse had simply been tipped into rivers or dumped in open spaces. In Kedah, "controlled dumping of refuse, in the absence of incineration, is being done to fill up unwanted pools and swamps".[36] A few buildings had septic tanks and there were pit latrines in outlying areas, but "night soil"—human waste—was often dumped as well.[37] At Port Klang:

> Single bucket system sewage removal was used during the year. The night-soil in Klang South and Port Swettenham is dumped into tanks at Riverside Road, Klang, and at Camp Road, Port Swettenham, which open into the tidal part of the river. The valves are opened at ebb tide and the night-soil is carried out to sea. In Klang North, the night-soil is dumped into the river from the jetty at high tides.[38]

Supplies of water and electricity were intermittent. Pumps that normally provided about 80 per cent of Singapore's water supply had broken down, and the Pulai reservoir in Johore and the service reservoirs on Fort Canning and Pearls Hill were nearly dry. The water filtration plant no longer worked, there were numerous leaks in the delivery system, and most of the water meters in Singapore were inoperative. Klang (which served Port Swettenham and Kuala Selangor) had no treatment or purification of water at all. Chemical and bacteriological examinations in 1942 had produced results that were "not of a high standard", but were deemed "satisfactory as compared with previous years".[39] Pahang lacked fuel to run waterworks plants. The Public Works Department there managed to buy and borrow some cylinder oil in June 1942, but it was requisitioned by a Japanese military officer stationed at Mentakab to be used in connection with a proposed electricity plant. In July the Department reported that it had no chemicals to purify water, but that a Japanese officer had been "very kind to release 3 drums of cylinder oil brought from Bentong".[40] In 1944 an official report gave this summary of the water situation in Kedah:

---

[36] Ibid.

[37] Medical Questionnaire on Malaya, NARA RG226 XL11105.

[38] AR, Klang Sanitary Board, 2602, Sel Kan 108/2603.

[39] Ibid.

[40] Monthly reports of the Pahang PWD for June, July 2602, DO Temerloh 103/2602.

> There is no absolutely safe water supply anywhere in Syburi [Kedah]. The water no longer undergoes any chemical treatment, at any stage, due to absence of necessary materials. The continuous supply has become intermittent, as a war time economy.[41]

Electricity generating plants had been poorly maintained, and the distribution network had been extended to the point that it exceeded the capacity of the system. Vehicles had been used until they could no longer be repaired: "In the Works' garages great dumps of vehicles were found, but almost all were non-runners and only one, here and there, could be put on the road after extensive repairs."[42]

To overcome conditions such as these, the government needed to repair existing infrastructure and undertake major construction programmes. Under the BMA certain businesses that provided essential services to the community were designated "sponsored industries" and given military assistance.[43] These included Hume Pipe (Far East) and United Engineers (to handle repairs to vehicles and other engineering works), Far East Oxygen and Acetylene, Singapore Cold Storage, the Straits Ice Works, and Malayan Breweries (which rapidly brought production to more than 20,000 pints of beer per day, a quantity that exceeded even the capacity of the forces stationed in Malaya, and caused strains on the supplies of wooden cases). Local industries given support included the Malayan Paint Works, saw mills, and the Singapore Rubber Works.[44] These firms helped begin the process of reconstruction, but most businesses had to depend on funds obtained from the banks, and the banking system was facing difficulties.

Currency and Banking

Britain's overall economic policy called for rolling back wages and prices to pre-war levels, and the Planning Unit anticipated holding the dollar at its pre-war value of 2 shillings and fourpence. Maintaining the pre-war value of the currency seemed necessary "to restore prestige and confidence" and to prevent inflation, but it also served a compelling political need. The banks operating in Malaya had substantial liabilities in Straits dollars on their books, and these deposits were backed by sterling assets and other investments that seemed likely

---

41 Medical Department Annual Report of the State of Syburi for 2487, SUK Kedah 119/2487.

42 Gilmour, *With Freedom to Singapore*, pp. 147–64.

43 The British Military Administration, Malaya: Post-Operational Civil Affairs Plan for Malaya, BMA COM/21.

44 Trade and Industry SITREP, 2 Oct. 1945, BMA GEN/52.

to retain their value after the war. If the government reduced the sterling value of the dollar, banks would realize enormous windfall profits at the expense of the people of Malaya, an untenable situation in a context where Britain needed to recover lost prestige and restore public confidence in the government.

The policy to be adopted in connection with Japanese currency caused considerable disagreement. Officials at the Bank of England advised that "the basic monetary principle is that you *must* give some value to genuine holders of currencies legally in circulation", and they were "strongly in favour of giving value on re-occupation for any currency in the hands of the local population".[45] The Colonial Office initially agreed that if most people held only Japanese currency, it should be given some value and then progressively devalued, but strategic and economic arguments ultimately led to a decision to demonetize occupation currency. The initial concern was that Japan might attempt to impede the re-occupation of Malaya by flooding the country with currency, and when intelligence reports indicated that the Japanese currency issue had become extremely large and was causing massive inflation, a decision was taken to demonetize the wartime currency. Accordingly, the BMA issued a proclamation declaring Japanese currency valueless, and making pre-war and a new post-war currency legal tender for the country. Pending a decision on how to deal with wartime financial transactions, a moratorium was imposed on all existing debts.[46] Similar measures had been adopted for brief periods in European territories liberated from Axis control, but in Malaya the moratorium would remain in effect until 1949.

The demonetization of wartime currency pauperized much of the population. In Penang the Officer-in-Charge reported that demonetization had caused so much "indignation and alarm" that serious disturbances seemed possible, and for a brief period officials there accepted payments in Japanese currency at a large discount, but as a general policy the BMA considered it preferable to distribute supplies free of charge rather than give temporary value to wartime

[45] Fisher to Caine, 29 July 1943, emphasis in original; Cobbold (Bank of England) to Waley, 18 Dec. 1942, CO852/356/7.

[46] The Moratorium proclamation is in the BMA, Malaya, Gazette, of 1 Nov. 1945. See also Rear SACSEA to SACSEA, 6 Sept. 1945, WO203/6907.

banknotes.[47] Because large numbers of people held nothing except Japanese money, it was vital to place fresh currency in circulation as quickly as possible, and to facilitate this process the BMA paid arrears of salaries and pensions, gave advances to civil servants, made payments to help sponsored industries resume operations, purchased rice and rubber stocks held by dealers, and hired labourers for government works. It also provided small cash payments to families where the head of the household was unable to work. During the month of September some $8 million was put into circulation, and by the end of the year the figure had reached about $160 million.[48]

New banknotes worth $234 million plus about $18 million in coins had been prepared for distribution, slightly more than the pre-war issue. The Currency Commissioners held adequate sterling balances to cover the pre-war currency, and anticipated that a post-war revival of trade would support a slightly higher level of circulation.[49] The new notes were similar to but distinguishable from those used before the war, which the government gradually withdrew. In 1948 pre-war British currency ceased to be legal tender.[50] It was unclear how much pre-war currency had survived the occupation, and substantial sums proved to have been hidden away, to emerge following the Japanese surrender. The total circulation at the end of 1946 was $316 million, well above even the unusually large sums recorded in 1940 and 1941. Banks were reporting large deposits in

---

[47] Brief for Supreme Allied Commander on Penang Currency Situation, WO203/3907, brings together official correspondence concerning this issue. See also Cheah, *Red Star Over Malaya*, p. 144. In Penang there was an unofficial general strike, looting of food stocks and Hindu-Muslim clashes. Japanese 5 dollar bills were declared valid for payments to the government at a ratio of 100 to 1, but this measure did little to ease the situation, and on 7 September the offer was extended to 10 dollar bills. The British administration did not exchange Japanese money for new money, and the measure was cancelled within a week as fresh currency went into circulation, and pre-war notes appeared in increasing quantities. See materials on the re-occupation of Penang in WO203/4675.

[48] Extract from statement by W.D. Godsall (Controller of Finance and Accounts), CO852/581/1; BMA(M) to WO, 25 Sept. 1945, CO852/586/17; Financial Secretary to SCAOs, 15 Sept. 1945, SCAO Trengganu 14/1945; W.D. Godsall, *Report on the Working of the Malayan Currency Commission for the period of 1st January, 1941 to 31st December, 1946.*

[49] Turnbull, S.O. 1 Finance, 4 Dec. 1943, CO852/510/21.

[50] Turnbull, Draft Memorandum on Malayan Currency, 10 Nov. 1943, CO852/510/24.

savings accounts, prices were rising on a flourishing black market and there was concern that inflation could endanger economic recovery.[51]

The government moved quickly to promote investment and restore normal business activity. On 15 September 1945 the Financial Secretary instructed Civil Affairs Officers to encourage as many non-Japanese banks as possible to resume operations to facilitate the distribution of new currency.[52] Two days later, eight Chinese and Indian banks reopened in Singapore.[53] Because these banks had nothing but worthless Japanese currency in their vaults, the BMA authorized deposits of government funds amounting to 5 per cent of the value of pre-war deposits held by each bank (based on figures for 31 December 1941), with an assurance that the money would not be withdrawn for at least 60 days. Banks paid normal rates of interest on the deposits, and could charge no more than 7 per cent per annum in making loans from these funds. According to the Financial Secretary, the scheme involved "a certain degree of preferred treatment for local banks as against British Banks but the latter are not in a position to function and the needs of Malaya must come first".[54] One bank produced receipts for pre-war currency it had turned over to the government for destruction, and was paid $150,000 on this basis, and five others were given loans at 3 per cent interest (amounting in all to less than $1 million) against property or government securities, to be repaid within six months. The remaining banks did not seek government assistance. As an indication that substantial amounts of pre-war currency survived in private hands, the Penang branch of the OCBC on its first day of operations received deposits of $50,000 in pre-occupation Straits currency.[55]

The policy of restoring pre-war wages and prices proved unworkable because pre-war wages were out of line with post-war prices. The average cost per ton of imported rice, which had stood at $64 in 1939 and $89 in 1940, was $320 in

---

[51] See W.D. Godsall, Report on Financial and Economic Conditions in Malaya, December 1945, 30 Dec. 1945, WO203/3907; H.R. Hone, *Report on the British Military Administration of Malaya*, pp. 105–6. O.W. Gilmour notes that Japanese Surrendered Personnel were found to have some $3 million of pre-war currency, "which they apparently had faith in". *With Freedom to Singapore*, p. 134.

[52] W.D. Godsall (Controller of Finance and Accounts), Report on Finance and Economic Conditions in Malaya, December 1945, 30 Dec. 1945, WO203/3907.

[53] Chinese and Indian banks resumed operations at Kuala Lumpur on the same date, and a day later at Penang.

[54] Extract from statement by W.D. Godsall, CO852/586/1; Financial Secy to SCAOs, 15 Sept. 1945, SCAO Trengganu 14/1945.

[55] H.C. Willian, Memorandum Regarding Contracts Entered into Before and During the Japanese Occupation of Malaya, 22 Jan. 1946 (Secret), CO852/541/4.

1946. The commodities that made up a model "labourer's budget" cost $7.09 per month in 1939, and $59.05 in October 1945. By 1947 the situation had eased but the average Singapore market price for a sample list of 41 items in everyday use still stood at 4.79 times the pre-war level. Moreover, much of the population supplemented official rations with purchases on the black market, where prices were even higher. The Malayan Union and Singapore argued that high prices were a temporary phenomenon that would go away once shortages of transport and supplies had been overcome. Accordingly they held wage rates at pre-war levels, but introduced supplementary allowances for government servants in September 1946 to help deal with the high cost of living. These allowances had to be raised before the end of the year, and a commission appointed to investigate the cost of living recommended a further increase in July 1947.[56]

There was general agreement that the moratorium should be lifted as soon as possible, but the issues were complex, and affected large numbers of people. Recognizing that it was impossible to avoid all losses for all parties, the Colonial Office sought a solution which was simple and uniformly applicable, and would enable debtors and creditors to settle their affairs without going to court, thus minimizing the possibility of conflicting decisions and delays as decisions were appealed.[57] The Colonial Office initially contemplated reopening a wide range of transactions,[58] but following discussions with bankers and other interested parties, and with officials in Malaya, adopted a more conservative approach, arguing that in cases where both parties had been present during the occupation, reopening transactions seemed likely to produce as many inequities as leaving matters alone. The general lines of a policy had been worked out by April 1946, when the British Military Administration handed over power to a civil government in Malaya, but the government did not publish draft legislation to lift the moratorium until February 1948.[59] The bill made it clear that occupation-period debts already settled were not to be reopened, and that pre-occupation debts settled in occupation currency would be reopened only "when the circumstances indicated an intention on the part of the debtor to take

[56] Col. H. McFadzean, Interim Report on Prices and Wages, (30 Nov. 1945), App. A, BMA DEPT/18/13; McFadzean to Economic Adviser, 7 Mar. 1946, BMA DEPT 8/48; Malayan Union and Singapore, *Interim Report on Wages.*

[57] CO statement cited in WO to BMA(M) Secret Tel, 25 Mar. 1946, CO852/541/5.

[58] See model legislation supplied to Hong Kong, Malaya, Singapore, Sarawak, and North Borneo, enclosed in G.H. Hall to MU, Singapore, Hong Kong, North Borneo, and Sarawak, 20 Sept. 1946, CO537/1375.

[59] The bill is found in the Federation of Malaya Government Gazette (Federal), 10 Feb. 1948, pp. 175–6.

advantage of a depreciated currency to settle his obligations", or if a creditor had accepted payment as a result of "duress or coercion".[60] In such cases, payments made during the occupation were to be revalued according to a sliding scale that set values for wartime currency at different points in time, and debtors would pay the balance of the original obligation.

The legislation particularly affected banks that continued to operate during the occupation, and difficulties arose because provisions that benefitted the liquidated foreign banks worked against the interests of the local banks that had been forced to remain open. Large sums of money owed to foreign banks had been collected by the Japanese liquidator, and if these payments were validated, the foreign banks would have to write off substantial pre-war loans and incur heavy losses. If they were not validated, borrowers would have to pay twice. The bill offered a compromise by revaluing payments made to the liquidator according to the sliding scale. The Colonial Office conceded that in accepting "acts of confiscation by Japanese liquidators and custodians which were breaches of international law" the ordinance departed from "certain normal concepts of the municipal law of these colonies", but contended that the issue was a policy matter and should be decided not by legal precedents but rather by considering whether the proposed solution was "a fair and just measure" and was "warranted by the circumstances of the case".[61]

Local banks faced an entirely different set of problems arising from the fact that they held large sums deposited in connection with forced savings campaigns. Much of this money had not been invested, and at the date of liberation some banks had held more than 50 per cent of their deposit liabilities in the form of cash which the demonetization of Japanese currency rendered worthless. The draft legislation treated these deposits as debts owed by banks to their customers, and revalued them following the same principle as the revaluation of debts owed the liquidated banks. The banks argued that Japanese currency held by the public had been declared to have no value by the British military administration, and that Japanese currency which the public happened to have deposited in bank accounts should suffer the same fate, but for political reasons the government was reluctant to favour banks at the expense of their depositors.[62]

---

[60] This double formulation was needed because of the differing terminology found in the British laws used in the Straits Settlements, and the Indian legal codes used elsewhere in Malaya. S of S to MU, 1 Sept. 1947, CO852/726/1.

[61] Memorandum by J.C. McPetrie, Suggested amendments to draft Debtor-Creditor Ordinance, CO852/728/2.

[62] Gov MU to CO, 5 June 1946, CO852/728/2.

When the provisions of the proposed legislation were finally made public they generated widespread criticism, but people disagreed concerning who was likely to benefit. The Perak Chinese Chamber of Commerce claimed "the advantage lay all on the side of the creditor and the Bank" and the Malacca Chinese Chamber of Commerce complained that the bill contained clauses framed by bankers to settle accounts to their own advantage.[63] On the other side, the manager of the Penang branch of the Oversea Chinese Banking Corporation said the bill "placed bankers in a very difficult position", Singapore Chinese and Indian banks protested that it would harm their interests, and the chairman of the Hongkong Bank said it was "without justification either in law or in equity". The Indian Chambers of Commerce in Selangor, Penang, Perak, Negri Sembilan and Malacca, with support from the government of India, opposed re-opening any occupation period financial transactions, while the All-Malaya Nattukkottai Chettiars Association argued that all payments should be revalued and all sales of land and shares should be declared void.[64]

The various parties concerned generally accepted the principle of revalue transactions revaluing transactions based on a sliding scale, but the value given Japanese currency at different points during the occupation became the subject of fierce debate. The Colonial Office developed the sliding scale on the basis of estimates of the buying power of Japanese currency as developed from information supplied by real estate agents, bankers, goldsmiths and other sources. However, because wartime Japanese currency had no backing,[65] neither controlled nor black market prices provided a satisfactory basis for comparison. It was impossible to establish a realistic exchange rate between this money and pre-war currency, and the sliding scale was to a considerable extent an arbitrary mechanism created to resolve difficulties faced by the financial community. The first version proposed by the Colonial Office deliberately undervalued the

[63] Malacca Chinese Chamber of Commerce, Criticisms and/or suggested amendments ..., n.d., CO852/726/2.

[64] Report of the Select Committee ... [on] the Debtor and Creditor (Occupation Period) Bill, 1948, Federation of Malaya Legislative Council Paper No. 38 of 1948, pp. 4–7, contains these and other examples of conflicting views.

[65] The report prepared by the Select Committees that examined the Debtor-Creditor Bill stated: "The military notes issued by the Japanese were issued in great quantities for the most part without serial numbers or, apparently, proper records of the quantities issued and without backing. An occupying force may be entitled under the principles of international law to enforce its own currency in occupied territory but it is submitted that an unlimited issue of paper notes, unnumbered and without backing cover is not the issue of a currency." Report of the Select Committee [on] the Debtor and Creditor (Occupation Period) Bill, 1948, Federation of Malaya Legislative Council Paper No. 38 of 1948.

occupation currency in order to assist the foreign banks liquidated during the occupation.[66] A revised scale proposed by the Select Committees that considered the bill in the Federation of Malaya and in Singapore gave considerably more value to the occupation currency and probably more accurately reflected its purchasing power by holding the two currencies at par until July 1943. However, this version reduced to negligible levels the sums owed the liquidated banks after revaluation because liquidation proceedings began in April 1943, and the liquidator had collected a substantial proportion of the pre-war debts owed to the banks (90 per cent in the case of one bank) before July. After reviewing the proposal, the government asked the committees to reconsider the matter, and the result was a second revised sliding scale that reduced the value given to occupation currency in the first half of 1943 (see Table 11.8).

Table 11.8 Sliding scales establishing the value of Malayan $100 in occupation currency

Draft legislation		*1st revised scale*		*2nd revised scale*	
Feb. 1942	100	Feb. 1942	100	Feb. 1942	100
Apr. 1942	100	Apr. 1942	100	Apr. 1942	100
May. 1942	103	May. 1942	100	May. 1942	100
Dec. 1942	150	Dec. 1942	100	Dec. 1942	100
Jan. 1943	170	Jan. 1943	100	**Jan. 1943**	105
June 1943	375	June 1943	100	June 1943	224
July 1943	425	**July 1943**	110	July 1943	254
Jan. 1944	760	Jan. 1944	200	Jan. 1944	455
July 1944	1,700	July 1944	450	July 1944	1,010
Jan. 1945	3,600	Jan. 1945	900	Jan. 1945	2,000
1 Aug. 1945	15,500	1 Aug. 1945	5,000	1 Aug. 1945	10,300
12 Aug. 1945	105,000	12 Aug. 1945	90,000	12 Aug. 1945	95,000
13 Aug. 1945	no value	13 Aug. 1945	no value	13 Aug. 1945	no value

Note: Months shown in bold type mark the point where Occupation currency was to be given less value than British Malayan currency on each of the scales.

Sources: The original sliding scale was published with the draft legislation in the Federation of Malaya Government Gazette (Federal), 10 Feb. 1948, pp. 175–6; the scale recommended by the First Select Committee appears with the committee report in the Proceedings of the Legislative Council, Colony of Singapore, 1948, pp. C288–90, while the final version is part of the bill as passed into law. The full scale established equivalencies on a monthly basis, and on a daily basis for 1–12 August 1945.

[66] WO to BMA Tel, 25 Mar. 1946, and CO to Gov Singapore, and HC Fed. of Malaya, Secret Cypher Tel, 18 Oct. 1948, CO852/726/3.

In reporting on the deliberations of the Select Committee for the Federation of Malaya, the High Commissioner said there were "acute differences of opinion existing on practically every aspect" of the legislation. Praising the "spirit of goodwill" that had made possible a unanimous report, he warned the Colonial Office that the modified bill was the best the foreign banks could hope to achieve, and that they would have to approach the legislative councils if they wished to seek any further remedy.[67]

The legislation resolved the conflicting interests of the foreign and local banks by specifying that revaluation should be based on the rate for the day when a loan fell due or, if no due date was specified, the rate when repayment was first demanded, or, in the absence of any demand, on the rate for 12 August 1945.[68] Following this principle, money paid to the Japanese liquidator was revalued according to the date when payment was demanded in 1943, an arrangement that allowed banks to recover slightly more than half of the value of their pre-war loans. Wartime deposits in local banks were revalued according to the rate for 12 August 1945, reducing the sums that banks owed their depositors to very low levels. The two largest local banks had occupation-period liabilities of $112 million and $128 million. After revaluation, these obligations became $113,729 and $142,944 in post-occupation currency.[69]

The Debtor-Creditor bill was approved in the Federation of Malaya at the end of 1948, and in Singapore early in 1949.[70] With this legislation in place, the major obstacle to lifting the moratorium had been removed, but there remained a question concerning whether interest should be payable on revalued loans. The Debtor-Creditor legislation specified that no interest would be charged for the occupation period, and the Moratorium Proclamation had stated that no interest should be assessed during the moratorium period.[71] However, the moratorium had remained in force for more than three years and during this time borrowers had enjoyed opportunities to make good use of capital in a flourishing economy. The Select Committees noted that allowing interest to run would be unjust to debtors, while refusal to allow interest to run would be unjust to creditors, and they attempted to achieve a "balance of equities" by authorizing interest following the end of the British Military Administration.

---

[67] Gurney to S of S (Colonies), Tel, 10 Dec. 1948, CO852/726/3; Minute, 3 Feb. 1949, CO852/726/4.

[68] The reports were printed in the Federation of Malaya as Legislative Council Paper no. 38 of 1948 and in Singapore as no. 31 of 1948. See also CO852/726/3.

[69] Memorandum on the Debtor and Creditor Bill, n.d., CO852/726/2.

[70] Federation of Malaya no. 42 of 1948; Singapore no. 5 of 1949.

[71] Rear SACSEA to SACSEA, 6 Sept. 1945, WO203/6907.

Civil government had resumed on the 1 April 1946, and the Moratorium Proclamation (Repeal) Ordinances passed in the Federation of Malaya on 28 September, and in Singapore on 1 October, 1949, allowed interest after that date, subject to a ceiling of 4½ per cent.[72] Looking back on the moratorium many years later, one member of the Singapore Select Committee said their intention had been to ensure that those who had benefitted during the Japanese occupation should not benefit again.[73] The view of the Colonial Office is perhaps best summed up by an official who wrote as final preparations were underway for lifting the moratorium: "One can only trust that over the whole field rough (and doubtless very rough) justice will have been achieved."[74]

Reparations

Immediately after the war, the Allied Powers viewed reparations both as a method of assisting with the rehabilitation of territories subjected to Japanese domination, and as a punitive measure.[75] A reparations survey mission under Edwin W. Pauley suggested in 1946 that all war facilities and surplus industries existing in Japan should be removed, and that this plant might be offered to territories within the former Japanese empire to assist with their industrial development. In addition, he cited Japan's internal assets, Japanese shipping, and Japanese assets held outside of Japan as possible sources of reparations. The Far Eastern Commission, created in December 1945 by the foreign ministers of the United States, the United Kingdom, China and the Soviet Union as the policymaking body to govern Japan, undertook the implementation of Pauley's recommendations, and under a unilateral interim US directive (the "30 per cent Removals Programme"), which benefitted China, the Philippines, the

---

[72] Minutes of Joint Meeting of Select Committees of the Singapore and Federation of Malaya Legislative Councils [on] the Moratorium Proclamation (Repeal) and the Principles and Agents Rights and Liabilities (Occupation Period) Bill Fed. Sec. 13614/1949; Report of the Select Committee [on] the Moratorium Proclamation (Repeal) Ordinance, 1949, Minutes and Council Papers of the Federal Legislative Council, 2nd Session (Mar. 1949–Jan. 1950), pp. B238–44. Other legislation enacted during 1949 in conjunction with the lifting of the moratorium concerned dealings in land during the occupation, the status of land titles, and the position of agents and trustees.

[73] Interview with Tan Sri Tan Chin Tuan, 18 Jan. 1991.

[74] Minute, 26 May 1949, CO852/726/4.

[75] The Basic Post-Surrender Policy for Japan adopted by the Far Eastern Commission stated that reparations would be exacted for "acts of aggression committed by Japan and for the purpose of equitable reparations of the damage caused by her to the Allied Powers and in the interests of destruction of the Japanese war potential". Royal Institute for International Affairs, *Documents on International Affairs*, 1947–48, p. 713.

Netherlands on behalf of Indonesia, and the United Kingdom on behalf of Burma, Malaya and its other Asian colonies, there was some initial distribution of industrial plant early in 1947. Britain's colonies in fact had little interest in Japan's industrial resources, but the United Kingdom wanted as large a share as possible of Japanese gold reserves, and asked for 25 per cent of Japan's industrial assets in order to establish a claim for the gold. Malaya was allocated 5 per cent of the machinery removed from Japan, and at least half of this equipment was delivered before the programme came to an end.[76]

While negotiations on the final treaty settlement were underway, the emerging cold war altered the US perception of Japan's future role in the region. The rise of communist powers throughout the world gave rise to a feeling, enunciated by George F. Kennan, chief of the Policy Planning Staff of the US State Department, that Japanese industry could play a key role in strengthening Asia against the communist bloc, but that punitive actions which weakened Japan and impoverished the population would create opportunities for the communists. On 12 May 1949 the US government announced an end to the advance transfer programme, and adopted a policy of positive guidance leading to economic recovery under which Japan would "be permitted to develop its peaceful industries without limitation".[77] One draft version of the peace treaty suggested that because the Japanese did not have adequate resources to pay reparations and still maintain a viable economy, Japan could make available "the services of the Japanese people in production, salvaging and other work", among other things processing raw materials produced in colonial territories. This proposal aroused little enthusiasm, and with regard to reparations the treaty as signed simply recognized Japan's liability in principle to pay reparations.[78]

Apart from the war indemnity, the Chinese community considered that Japan owed a blood debt as compensation for the great loss of life during the occupation. This issue was raised as early as 1946 by the Singapore Joint Appeal Committee of Japanese-Massacred Chinese, but with the change in policy toward Japan the British government did not pursue the matter. The discovery in 1962 of a mass grave in Singapore containing the remains of several hundred

[76] D.J. Cheke (FO) to Norman Young (Treasury), 23 Dec. 1947, F16586/99/23, IOL M/4/1154; Hara Fujio, "Japan and Malaysian Economy", p. 121; Brief for Minister of State on a Bill for Carrying into Effect the Treaty of Peace with Japan, and Secy of State for Colonies to High Commissioner, Fed. of Malaya, and OAG Singapore, 30 June 1951, enclosing Secret Intel No. 135, Japanese Peace Treaty, CO1022/280.

[77] Royal Institute for International Affairs, *Documents on International Affairs 1947–1948*, pp. 728–30; Roger Buckley, *Occupation Diplomacy*, ch. 10; Takushi Ohno, *War Reparations and Peace Settlement*, pp. 18–27.

[78] See correspondence in CO1022/280.

people killed during the occupation rekindled interest in the issue, and in 1963 the Chinese Chambers of Commerce in Singapore and Malaysia asked their respective governments to approach the Japanese government. In 1967 the Japanese government agreed to settle the claim by giving Singapore loans and grants worth US$17 million (about $51 million in local currency at the prevailing rate of exchange), and Malaya ships and other capital goods valued at US$8.3 million ($24.9 million). Japan referred to these payments as "quasi-reparations". Malaysian Chinese considered this compensation inadequate, but the Prime Minister announced that no further demands would be made against Japan. Malaysia had already been provided with yen credits in 1966 covering $50 million of goods and services as project aid in connection with the country's first Five-Year Plan, and in the years following the "goodwill" agreement reached in September 1967 received massive loans from the Japanese government.[79]

War Damage Compensation[80]

Britain announced in October 1942 that it intended to provide compensation for losses of property and goods caused by fighting in the colonial empire, and in February 1946 the government issued a statement proposing that each of the British territories in the Far East occupied by Japan set up a commission to register and assess claims for lost or damaged property. Claims could be made in respect of damage caused by acts of war, including denial schemes and actions of enemy forces, or by looting. The Claims Commissioner for Malaya closed the registers in December 1947, and a compensation scheme began to take shape in 1948 with the preparation of a memorandum outlining proposals for the consideration of select committees in the Federation of Malaya and the Colony of Singapore. Claims submitted to the Commissioner amounted to $1,303 million (see Table 11.9), but the memorandum envisaged making payments on an austerity basis, and proposed a fund of $475 million (approx. £55 million). Even this figure was thought to exceed the true value of the damage eligible for

[79] Shü and Chua (eds), *Malayan Chinese Resistance to Japan*, pp. 86–8 of the English-language section; Olson, *Japan in Postwar Asia*, pp. 197, 202–3, 209; Hara, "Japan and Malaysian Economy", p. 119.

[80] Information on War Damage Compensation is drawn from *Memorandum on Proposals for a Malayan War Damage Compensation Scheme* (Kuala Lumpur: Government Press, 1948), "Joint Report of the Select Committees Appointed by the Legislative Councils of the Federation of Malaya and Colony of Singapore to Examine and Report on the Memorandum of Proposals for a Malayan War Damage Compensation Scheme", Richard Graham, "Report of the War Damage Claims Commission, 1949", and Richard Graham, War Damage Commission, Federation of Malaya and Singapore, "Report in which is included the Annual Report for 1952".

compensation, since many claims fell outside the Commission's terms of reference or were fraudulent. Additional damage valued at $196.5 million was covered by a War Risks Insurance scheme introduced in April 1941. Participation had been compulsory in cases where the value of insurable goods owned by a company within a state or settlement exceeded a certain limit (initially $10,000).

Table 11.9 Claims submitted to commission for war damage compensation

Claims in respect of	*Amount ($ million)*
Tin	190.75
Rubber	379.25
Industrial/commercial	191.00
Dwelling houses	58.75
Private chattels	163.50
Stock-in-trade	126.75
Livestock/crops	24.50
Other	173.75
Total	1,303.25

Source: Memorandum on Proposals for a Malayan War Damage Compensation Scheme, p. 7.

The war damage compensation scheme operated on the principle that business losses should be covered to the extent necessary to allow firms to resume operations, and that payments for the loss of household goods and personal effects should enable claimants to "resume their normal mode of living in a reasonable manner, though not necessarily equal to their previous standards". Compensation was allocated according to the schedule indicated in Table 11.10, with funds expected to come from a number of sources, including reparations payments from the Japanese government.[81] The original proposal gave rise to strong complaints because of the small size of the British contribution when compared with Malaya's contribution of $149 million to the British government in support of the war in Europe, and because the amount received from Japanese reparations seemed too little. The allocation of funds was revised in 1949 and despite further objections was finally accepted to allow payments to begin. A further adjustment took place when it became apparent that Japanese reparations would not be forthcoming. Money realized by the sale of Japanese assets, consisting for the most part of rubber estates and mining properties, was included in the War Damage Compensation Fund (Table 11.11).

[81] Hara, "Japan and Malaysian Economy", pp. 124–5.

Table 11.10 Allocation of payments from the War Damage Compensation Fund

	Amount (\$ million)
Rubber planting	85
Tin mining	85
Private chattels	50
Other businesses	155
War Risks (Goods) Insurance Scheme	100
Total	475

Source: Hara Fujio, "Japan and Malaysian Economy", p. 124.

Table 11.11 Malayan War Damage Compensation Fund (*\$ million*)

Source	*Amount (Sept. 1948)*	*Amount (July 1949)*	*Amount (Dec. 1952)*
Free gift from British government[a]	85.7	171.4	171.4
Japanese reparations	85.7	60.0	–
Japanese property in Malaya[b]	–	–	60.0
War Risks Insurance Fund	12.0	–	–
Assets held by Malayan CEP[C]	52.0	69.4	54.9
Malayan government contribution	239.6	–	–
Interest-free loan from British government	–	153.6	149.7
Total	475.0	454.4	435.0

Notes: [a] The British government also waived the costs it incurred during the period of Military Administration, which amounted to over \$7 million.

[b] Japanese properties sold in Malaya and Singapore realized \$72 million. Of this sum, \$49 million came from properties in Malaya, and \$46.2 million of that amount was paid into the War Damage Compensation Fund. Properties in Singapore realized \$23 million, and \$21 million was paid into the War Damage Compensation Fund.

[c] This category included looted property whose owners could not be traced.

Source: Hara Fujio, "Japan and Malaysian Economy", pp. 124–6.

Food Supplies

Food shortages caused great anxiety in Malaya immediately after the war, and apart from humanitarian considerations, the issue had strong political overtones. At the end of the occupation, the intense dislike of the Japanese gave the British a reasonable prospect of re-establishing their authority if they could improve upon the unsatisfactory features of Japanese rule. One of most important of these was chronic rice shortages, and failure to meet the country's food requirements seemed likely to damage Britain's political credibility and create opportunities for the communists.

Planning for food relief in the immediate post-war period took place between November 1943 and May 1944 when a working party under the chairmanship of Sir Hubert Young, who had earlier overseen a similar project for Europe, prepared estimates of supplies that would be needed in Malaya, Burma, British Borneo and Hong Kong during a two-year period after the Japanese were driven out. In the case of Malaya this was expected to occur following the 1946 rice harvest, which would take place between February and April. In addition to food, the Young Working Party dealt with agricultural materials, medical supplies, soap, clothing, communal needs, individual household requirements, and newsprint, while a second working party under W.B. Brett later prepared estimates for additional items.[82]

With respect to food supplies, the Young Working Party based its recommendations on the assumption that 1,700 calories per day was "the dietary necessary to meet minimum energy requirements and to prevent disease and unrest", compared with the 2,562 calories per day provided by the average pre-war diet. Enhanced scales of 2,800 and 3,600 calories applied to workers doing moderate or heavy physical labour. Using these figures, and estimates of the size of the Malayan population and the quantities of rice or other foodstuffs likely to be produced locally, the working party drafted a schedule of relief supplies. The War Office treated the figures in the Young Report as "optimum" requirements and developed a reduced schedule of "practical" requirements, taking into consideration problems of shipping, port facilities, storage and distribution. However, the BMA found less food stockpiled in the country than the Young Working Party anticipated and, based on the number of people registered to receive rations, the population appeared to be substantially larger. Moreover, rice production in Malaya had declined from an estimated 341,000 tons in 1939 to 245,000 tons in 1946, and there was little prospect of obtaining rice from this

[82] F.S.V. Donnison, *British Military Administration in the Far East, 1943–1946*, pp. 243–5. A copy of the Report of the Young Working Party (Young Report) is in BT25/75/SLA/MISC 6.

source for general distribution. Accordingly, the BMA authorities immediately appealed for increased quantities of rice to be shipped to Malaya.[83]

For a brief period after the Japanese surrender, food was readily available. Looters raided warehouses, and British soldiers distributed rice from Japanese stockpiles. Shops carried ample stocks of food, though not necessarily rice, but prices tended to be high. This time of abundance was short-lived, for as it became apparent that food shortages would continue, supplies quickly disappeared into a revitalized black market.[84]

The allocation and distribution of surplus food on a worldwide basis was regulated by the Combined Food Board, which had been created in June 1942 as an Anglo-American organization to handle the supply of food sent from the US to Britain. By the middle of 1945 the Board had begun to expand to take in other members of the United Nations organization, and it was reconstituted in June 1946 as the International Emergency Food Council (IEFC).[85] The IEFC allocated rice on the basis of projections of the quantities of grain that producing countries expected to have available for export, and requests submitted by food deficit areas. States participating in the system agreed to accept the allocations given to them, and were not supposed to import rice from sources outside the system, or to allow illicit supplies to enter their territories. Once allocations had been settled, the countries concerned had to arrange for the purchase and shipping of grain.

In Burma, Thailand and Indochina, the main rice exporting territories in the world before the war, farmers had cut back on production during the occupation when the shortage of transport to carry rice to overseas markets left them with substantial stocks of unsold grain. Post-war exports were far below pre-war levels, while recovery was impeded in Burma by war damage, and in all three countries by unsettled political conditions. Table 11.12 shows figures for rice exports from the end of the war through 1947, with 1939 figures given for comparison. A substantial part of the rice and flour allocated to Malaya in 1945 under the international system of control did not arrive on schedule, or at all, and it soon became clear that the country faced the prospect of a serious food shortage (see Table 11.13).

[83] Young Report, p. 3; SACSEA to War Office, 27 Oct. 1945, WO203/1436; Colonial Office Food and Nutrition Survey, p. 2, BMA DEPT 9/4.

[84] Proceedings and Notes of a Meeting on Nutrition, 15 Jan. 1946, BMA DEPT/1/3 Pt I.

[85] K.C. Tours, Chairman, Joint Supply Board, Memorandum on the Rice Position in Malaya, 12 Nov. 1946, RC Sel 1102/46; see also CO537/1401 and Rosen, *The Combined Boards*, pp. 244–8. For a history of the activities of the Rice Division of the IEFC, see MAF 75/72.

Table 11.12 Rice exports from Burma, Thailand and Indochina, 1945–47 (*tons*)

	1939	*July-Dec. 1945*	*1946*	*1947*
Burma	3,099,400	98,700	424,700	791,200
Siam	1,431,100	70,900	442,500	388,400
Indochina	1,832,600	7,000	96,900	42,700
Total	6,363,100	176,600	964,100	1,222,300

Source: Statistics Relating to Southeast Asia: Food and Related Economic Matters, No. 15. (Aug. 1948), CO537/2998. Figures for 1939 are from V.D. Wickizer and M.K. Bennett, *The Rice Economy of Monsoon Asia*, p. 320.

Table 11.13 Malaya: Imports of relief supplies, Sept.-Dec. 1945 (*tons*)

	Young estimates	*Quantity requested*	*Quantity received*
Rice	159,507	149,000	59,328
Flour	19,569	15,900	nil
Sugar	12,800	10,432	7,000
Salt	11,630	10,250	606
Milk	5,083	4,131	5,402
Pulses	38,954	21,098	200
Meat	5,480	3,150	200
Vegetables	1,846	1,000	741
Fish	8,246	4,466	nil

Source: CCAO, Malaya, to Lt. Gen. Sir Miles Dempsey, 5 Jan. 1946, BMA DEPT 18/13.

The rice secured through IEFC allocations was distributed under a rationing system. At the beginning of 1946 the official ration was 4.6 ounces of rice per day. In February this was supplemented with 3 ounces of wheat flour, but by April the rice ration had been cut to 3 ounces per day, which meant that the population of Malaya, which had consumed as much as 16 ounces of rice per person per day before the war, was subsisting on 3 ounces of rice and 3 ounces of wheat flour per day. The quality of rice sold on the ration varied, and while consumers occasionally found themselves issued good white rice, they also might receive glutinous rice (normally used in Malaya to make sweet desserts but not as a staple food), or rice containing a high proportion of broken grains and a great deal of dirt.

Malaya's IEFC allocations would have been jeopardized had the administration openly condoned illicit imports, and Malayan officials claimed publicly that the black market sold rice which had escaped the domestic system of requisitioning. However, those who could afford to do so supplemented their rations by purchasing smuggled rice on the black market, and the government tolerated the practice as the best way to ensure that the population received sufficient food. The Governor of Singapore told the Colonial Office in November 1946 that "it can be stated categorically that [a] large majority of the population supplement their rice ration with black market … rice",[86] and Lord Killearn, Britain's Special Commissioner for Southeast Asia, observed in 1947:

> If there is a little of the Nelson touch, a certain turning of the blind eye on the part of the authorities (which *unofficially* they are inclined to admit) to some of this smuggling it must be remembered that much of the smuggled rice is bought up by the planters and estate owners for their labourers and that the more rice for these people means less unrest throughout the country and less fertile soil for agitators to work on.[87]

At one point, British efforts went well beyond turning a blind eye. In June 1946, the Head of the British Mission in Bangkok sent an angry message to Singapore saying that Malaya Command had sent troops to protect buyers of "unofficial" exports to Malaya of "rice, cattle, hogs and opium upon which bandits were levying tribute".

> In other words British troops have apparently been employed in protecting smugglers, and this at a time when I have been engaged in urging the Siamese authorities at your request to tighten up their preventive measures against illegal exports … While I fully understand the needs of food control in Malaya, I must confess that use of british forces in a foreign country to protect smugglers against racketeers is something new in my experience.

He said he was unable to perform his work if the military authorities in Malaya "not only blatantly and deliberately ignore my advice, but treat me with entirely unmerited discourtesy and lack of consideration. Nor do I intend for one moment to put up with it." The Ministry of Defence viewed the matter as "an unfortunate local misunderstanding", and took no action.[88]

In July 1947, the rice situation had improved sufficiently for the government to lift internal controls on the movement of rice, and Malayan rice production

[86] Governor of Singapore to CO, 3 Nov. 1946, MU Secret 209/1946.

[87] Killearn to Bevin, 18 Aug. 1947, Cabinet. Official Committee of Food Supplies from South East Asia and Certain Other Countries. Report on the Activities of the Office of the Special Commissioner in South East Asia during the Second Quarter of 1947. S.E.A.F. (47)40. Burma Economic 3701/46, British Library IOR M/4/761. Emphasis in the original.

[88] Sir Geoffrey Thompson, Tel 676 to Singapore, 18 June 1946, repeated to Foreign Office, Cabinet Distribution, CAB 120/616.

reached pre-war levels in 1948 (see Table 11.14). By May 1949 black market rice cost little more than rationed rice, and large numbers of people were ignoring the rationing system and buying rice on the free market, where they could select the type and quality they preferred.[89] International arrangements for procurement and distribution of rice were also breaking down as exporting countries sold their surpluses for hard currency or entered into barter agreements, and then sought *ex post facto* approval for these irregular practices. The international allocation system ended in December 1949.

Table 11.14 Production and net imports of rice in Malaya (× *1000 tons*)

Year	*Production*	*New imports*	*Total*
1940	335	635	970
–			
1946	227	136	363
1947	257	237	494
1948	343	450	793
1949	307	495	802

Source: R.G. Heath (comp.), *Malayan Agricultural Statistics*, 1949 (Kuala Lumpur: Department of Agriculture, Federation of Malaya, 1951), Table 33.

Because imports of foodstuffs remained inadequate immediately after the Japanese surrender, the administration continued to promote local vegetable cultivation. The BMA tried to counteract "the facile but vicious supposition that because we had returned there was no need for further productive effort",[90] but people in Malaya were tired of growing food, and for many the liberation signalled the end of the need to tend vegetable plots. Something of the prevailing attitude can be seen in the Chinese press, which reported in November 1945 that black market prices were holding steady in Singapore, and described official statements urging people to conserve stocks of food and continue producing vegetables as needlessly alarmist.[91] With the food situation worsening, the *Malaya Tribune* published an editorial in February 1946 that said, "Everywhere

[89] K.G. Hamnett for Controller of Supplies, F of M, to Asst Controllers of Supplies, 21 June 1948, Perak Sec 1373/1948; DO Dindings to State Secy Perak, 30 May 1949, Perak Sec 1373/1948.

[90] Malaya's Indigenous Production of Foodstuffs, BMA DEPT 12/38.

[91] See *Hwa Chiao Jit Pau*, 23 Nov. 1945 and *Sin Chew Jit Poh*, 24 Nov. 1945 as reported in Chinese Press Summaries, Sel CA 336/45.

we see the ruins of gardens torn up with gay abandon during the delirious days immediately following the reoccupation. These gardens should be replanted at once with green vegetables and even the despised tapioca."[92] Such exhortations had little effect, and the area devoted to vegetables and root crops continued to dwindle. Table 11.15 charts the decline of foodcrop cultivation during the post-war period.

Table 11.15 Areas planted with selected foodcrops (*acres*)

	1940	*Aug. 1945*	*June 1946*
Tapioca	46,292	154,130	94,180
Sweet potato	12,366	77,661	42,661
Sago	6,976	5,938	6,268
Sugar cane	3,251	9,286	10,295
Groundnuts	2,054	4,943	4,638
Maize	8,369	17,118	5,441
Yams	1,859	2,887	2,124
Colocasia[a]	2,938	10,550	6,236
Ragi[b]	181	23,410	4,076
Soya beans	188	650	887
Pulses	–	n.a.	1,250
Misc. vegetables (market gardens)	25,406	33,757	22,806
Pineapples	60,157	25,194	19,160
Bananas	45,728	81,830	75,886

Notes: [a] Colocasia, the taro of the South Pacific, was known in Malaya as "keladi", and was unpopular as a food owing to irritating needle-like crystals found in some varieties. Before the occupation it was mainly grown by the Chinese, who used it to feed pigs. I.H. Burkill, *A Dictionary of the Economic Products of the Malay Peninsula*, pp. 647–9.

[b] Ragi (Eleusine coracana; Tamil "kepe") is a grain that grew well in Malaya, and produced reasonable crops on poor soils. It could be boiled whole and eaten like rice, or ground into flour. Before the war it was rarely cultivated in Malaya, and its consumption was generally limited to Tamil labourers.

Source: Figures for 1940 and 1946 are taken from Dir of Agr to Pvt Secy to Gov MU, 30 Oct., 1946, MU6078/1946. Those for 1945 appear as Appendix II to Proceedings and Notes of a Meeting on Nutrition, 15 Jan. 1946, BMA DEPT/1/3 Pt I.

* * *

[92] "Spectre of Famine", Malaya Tribune editorial, 23 Feb. 1946.

Japan's surrender abruptly ended the occupation of Malaya, leaving the people living there to deal with its consequences. The pre-war British administrative structure remained more or less intact. The physical restoration of the country required labour, materials, funds and time. Most buildings had survived but a great deal of the physical infrastructure had not, and businesses and other organizations had been seriously disrupted. Fear and accusations of coercion overshadowed wartime financial dealings, and rather than attempting to untangle this Gordian knot the administration sliced through it by passing legislation that simply allowed most transactions to stand.

Once the physical infrastructure was restored, the population responded to economic opportunities offered by the post-war era, and the country experienced an economic boom at the time of the Korean War. However, the consequences of malnutrition and disease, the psychological effects of constant surveillance and the ever present threat of torture, and the pain caused by the loss of friends and family members, lingered on behind the facade of renovated buildings and economic growth. Only gradually, with the passing of the generation that experienced the occupation, did these memories begin to fade away.

CHAPTER 12

Conclusion

The account of the Japanese occupation of Malaya developed in this book is based in part on memories of events found in published memoirs and in interviews such as those assembled by the Oral History Department in Singapore. These materials began to appear shortly after the war ended, but most were recorded after a considerable period of time had elapsed, and the understanding of the occupation they contain is often mediated by later events and by the concerns of the post-war era. Other materials come from wartime administrative files, intelligence papers and documents assembled by the post-war government. Information drawn from these sources deals with the administrative system, agriculture, propaganda, finance and economic affairs, and is less well known because the Japanese destroyed the administrative papers that normally would have supplied details of this sort, apparently to suppress information that might be used against the Japanese themselves or incriminate people who had assisted them.

Stories of the occupation often highlight dramatic events—mass killings, extortionate donations, torture, forced labour, severe food shortages—but for many residents of Malaya, once the shock of the invasion had passed, the war years were a dreary time when they got along with their lives as best they could. "I suppose it taught me a lesson that you can carry on or you can stop."[1] As time passed, people began to lose their sense of purpose. "Life during the war is just like an end. We were not the least worried after a time, what happen tomorrow? But we lived for the day. So we made good use of our earnings and spent our money right away if we earned it there and then."[2] Before the war life had been predictable: "… we knew where we were going. We knew … that the system would go on. But during the Occupation … there was this uncertainty. We don't know what was going to happen. There was no future."[3]

[1] OHD, interview with Mary Lim.

[2] OHD, interview with Jack Kim Boon Ng.

[3] OHD, interview with Lim Choo Sye.

The country experienced a phenomenon characterized after the war by O.W. Gilmour as "moral deterioration", a decline in respect for law and duly constituted authority, a loss of traditional values, and an overriding selfishness.[4] According to Chu Shuen Choo, "Those who got along with the Japanese had some ulterior motive and usually it was making money. That's why after the war a lot of people had plenty of money."[5] N.I. Low and H.M. Cheng wrote that a sense of betrayal had overtaken Singapore, "Gone was mutual trust and confidence. We had learnt to smile without sincerity." Neighbours and friends reported indiscreet remarks to the *Kempeitai*, or invented damaging information. One 19-year-old girl informed on her stepfather for listening to the radio. In another case, someone with a grudge against the family next door told the Japanese the man and his brother were communists. The *Kempeitai* arrested them, and then burned several women and children alive in their house. A month later the men were found innocent and set free. One wonders, Low and Cheng ruminate, if the informer "had quite bargained for all that". The pain lay not only in the brutality of the Japanese but also in "the searing discovery that our own people were lending themselves readily and willingly as instruments of that brutality. And for what? For gain, for extra rations, extra amenities, more cigarettes! Sordid boons."[6]

Some people recall positive aspects of the occupation, but in doing so often connect it with themes that emerged in Malaya after the war. For example, according to Perak resident Ibrahim bin Cheek:

> The Japanese period taught us [the Malays] to become more diligent, bad people did not dare do bad things, the spirit of love of country began because the Japanese always made the Malays aware of their rights in their own place.[7]

Other accounts credit the Japanese with teaching valuable lessons concerning the importance of unity, diligence and cooperation, and with creating a period of exemplary honesty.[8] The dedication of the Japanese soldiers also made a lasting impression. One man observed: "The British fought in order to live, the Japanese

[4] Gilmour, *With Freedom to Singapore*, p. 128.

[5] OHD, interview with Mdm Chu Shuen Choo (Mrs Gay Wan Guay).

[6] Low and Cheng, *This Singapore*, pp. 48–51, 121.

[7] Cited in Siti Zubaidah bte Kassim, "Pengalaman Penduduk Sungai Acheh yang Bekerja Sebagai Jikeidan Jepun".

[8] Instances are found in Zainuddin bin H. Ahmad, "Pendudukan Jepun di Kampung Permatang Tuan Samad, Permatang Sungai Dua, Seberang Prai"; Abdul Malek bin Samsuri, "Pendudukan Jepun di Balik Pulau, Pulau Pinang".

in order to die."[9] Moreover, the discipline of the Japanese extended beyond their capitulation. Before being regrouped, a few Japanese soldiers came to the village of Tasek Gelugur seeking work. Because they had surrendered the MPAJA left them alone, and villagers took pity on the men and hired them to cut grass. The soldiers put in ten-and-a-half-hour days, strapping bottles of water to their waists so they could drink without stopping what they were doing.

> The industry of these soldiers left such a deep impression that long after they had gone, it was customary for the people of Tasek Gelugur to say "sudah nak jadi Jepun [(you are) becoming like the Japanese] to someone found to be diligent or "cubalah jadi macam Jepun" [try to become like the Japanese] when someone was found to be lazy.[10]

People note that while the Japanese were sometimes very harsh in their treatment of the local population, they were equally hard on any Japanese who committed an offence. A Penang resident named Choong Choon Hooi, who worked with the Japanese soldiers, said the Japanese did not discriminate against him as a Chinese, and while they admittedly imposed harsh sentences such as cutting off peoples' heads, "death sentences were also imposed on Japanese who were guilty of wrong-doing".[11] According to N.I. Low and H.M. Cheng, many Japanese were either "cads" or "buffoons", but there were also "gentlemen" who "would win the suffrage of any decent company":

> A man named Mizuno stands out in my recollection. He was no egotist, nor a jingoist, nor a bully.... Never unduly familiar, he did not think it beneath his dignity to show courtesies to us, his subordinates....
>
> My heart went out to poor Mizuno when I saw the stricken look on his face when news of the surrender became known.... No congenital idiot, he had yet delivered his intelligence over to his superiors, accepting for gospel truth whatever they told him, and the shock of realization must have been terrible.[12]

Some such believers found it impossible to accept the capitulation, and felt that honour demanded they take their lives to atone for Japan's failure in war:

> We shall never how many suicides there were. Some favoured the traditional hara-kiri, scooping out entrails in the high Japanese fashion. Others preferred lone revolver-shots and yet others group-suicides, one party blowing up their house and themselves holding high revels in it.[13]

---

[9] Osman bin Senawi, quoted in Siti Zubaidah bte Kassim, "Pengalaman Penduduk Sungai Acheh".

[10] Jaafar bin Hamzah, 'The Malays in Tasek Gelugur", p. 64.

[11] Poobalan George Rajamani, untitled course essay.

[12] Low and Cheng, *This Singapore*, pp. 114–15.

[13] Ibid., pp. 164–5.

On balance, people in Malaysia and Singapore recall the Occupation with mixed feelings. They would not want to experience it again, but some see positive outcomes. In trying to convey a sense of the period, Malaysian writers juxtaposed words like "*pahit-manis*" (bitter-sweet) or "*suka-duka*" (pleasures and sorrows).[14]

Over time, a taught history took shape alongside the remembered history of the occupation. As a new generation grew to maturity with no first-hand experience of the period but vividly aware of it because of the effect on their own families, they drew on stories told by their parents and grandparents, and on textbooks and other written accounts, for information. Because the understanding of the war and occupation was influenced by post-war concerns, it changed and changed again as circumstances altered.

The first events that contributed to this process took place shortly after the Japanese surrender, when serious racial clashes took place as people sought revenge for what they had suffered under Japanese rule. The source of their grievances lay with the Japanese, but the Japanese were inaccessible, and in many cases the perceived agents of their distress were local. Violence broke out and people were killed. However, after the immediate settling of personal scores, little could be done on an individual basis, and new issues and events such as the political crisis surrounding the Malayan Union began to preoccupy the population.

Radical elements failed to secure a substantial political voice in post-war Malaya. The MPAJA emerged from the Occupation in an assertive and vengeful mood, but the Communist Party opted to work for peaceful change, but gained little political capital from its wartime activities. The MPAJA did not have an opportunity to take part in a military campaign to expel the Japanese, and so lacked this critical validation of its struggle. Moreover, while the Malayan Chinese had supported the guerrillas, either willingly or under duress, most had little sympathy with the MCP's broader social and political agenda. Even within the guerrilla organization there were many who saw the conflict in Malaya as part of a larger campaign to free China from Japanese domination, and not as a struggle to seize power in the peninsula. In 1948 the communists launched an armed rebellion that the British labelled the Emergency. The decision of the Malayan Communist Party to abandon efforts to operate within the constitutional political process negated its wartime achievements in the eyes of the leaders of Malaya and Singapore, who were now reluctant to call attention to the role played by the communists in the anti-Japanese movement. The

---

[14] Baba Ahmed, *Suka-Duka di Georgetoun*; Zainuddin bin H. Ahmad, "Pendudukan Jepun di Kampung Permatang Tuan Samad, Permatang Sungai Dua, Seberang Prai".

individual singled out to symbolize the struggle and sacrifices of the resistance was Lim Bo Seng, a genuinely heroic figure who died in Japanese custody, but a man associated with the Kuomintang rather than the Communist Party.

In Malay politics, the departure of Ibrahim Yaacob and the collapse of the organizations he had created left Malay nationalists without a political focus. Faced with British constitutional proposals that appeared to weaken the position of the Malay population, and MPAJA reprisals against Malay collaborators, Malays turned to established figures for leadership, and these men forged an alliance with Chinese businessmen against the MCP. The Indian Independence League also lost its leader when Subash Chandra Bose died in a plane crash at the end of the war. In any case, the goal of Indian independence was quickly achieved, removing the issue that had inspired Indian political activism.

The reputations of Malaya's post-war leaders rested on the struggle against the Malayan Union and their roles during the transition to independence, and not on what they did or did not do during the Occupation. The moderate figures who formed the post-war political elite included people who in various ways had cooperated with the Japanese, but apart from the radicals, the only alternative to this group was men who had spent the war years in relative comfort outside Malaya, and they were less than satisfactory precisely because they had not shared the experience of the occupation. The willingness of the colonial administration to work with and through former collaborators, whom the British found preferable to the Communists, helped rehabilitate them, while the Malayan Union issue allowed this leadership to demonstrate a capacity to force the British to make a major policy change. Britain's attempt to reform the administrative system and regularize the civil status of people with immigrant backgrounds was a racially-charged issue, and took place at a time when the Chinese were striving to gain political influence. Malay leaders saw the problem of economic marginalization they faced before the war potentially compounded by political marginalization if Chinese pretensions to power were to go unchallenged, and built a political movement around the assertion of Malay rights. The Kuantan District Officer, Dato Mahmud, caught the mood of the post-war era when he told Spencer Chapman shortly after the Japanese surrender:

> Things are not what they were before the war. In the old days everybody knew me and smiled at me. Now it is very different: the Chinese towkays are afraid to be seen talking to me; the young Chinese regard me with suspicion or even hostility. We are going to have a lot of trouble with these people in the future.[15]

[15] Lt. Col. F.S. Chapman (Force 136), "Report on A.J.U.F. 8th Sept. to 12th Oct. '45", 25 Oct. 1945, SOE Far East, Malaya no. 79, HS1/120.

The rise of communism in Asia contributed to the early rehabilitation of Japan. The Americans positioned Japan as a liberal and democratic country that had repudiated military force and was prepared to use its considerable economic might to fight against communism, and the image of Japan as a fascist power responsible for causing enormous hardships quickly faded. For its part, Japan offered loans and invested capital in Southeast Asia, becoming a major trading partner of several countries within the region.

For a time, Malaya and Singapore remained colonial territories, but the British authorities engaged in a process of localization of power that led to independence, and during the 1960s a new order settled into place. In the Federation of Malaya (after 1965, Malaysia), the Malays were politically dominant, ruling through the United Malays National Organization, or UMNO, which was the senior partner in an alliance with the Malayan Chinese Association and the Malayan Indian Congress. Singapore remained a separate entity until 1963, when it joined the Federation, but unification proved unmanageable and the arrangement ended in 1965, leaving the Republic of Singapore an independent country. There the Chinese population was in the majority and politically dominant, although the question of which Chinese party and what elements of the Chinese population would control the state was hotly contested, with the People's Action Party emerging as the winner. This sequence of events complicated interpretations of the war years. The former enemy was now a friend, people who had at the very least acquiesced in the rule of the Japanese had become key figures in the shaping of the independent Federation of Malaya and Republic of Singapore, and the organization that had spearheaded the wartime resistance had declared itself the enemy of those independent states.

An initial attempt to shape the taught history of the war and occupation came from the Japanese themselves. For nearly three weeks after the surrender, the newspapers of Malaya remained under Japanese control, and during this period they published stories that emphasized the nobility of Japan's objectives, the sorrow and regret Japan felt for the losses and suffering caused by the war, and the strong humanitarian impulse that had led the Emperor to cease hostilities even though Japan's armed forces remained capable of continuing the struggle. However, after a steady diet of propaganda over the preceding three and a half years, the Malayan population was unimpressed by Japan's final attempt to justify its failed regime, and this campaign to present the Occupation in a favourable light had little impact.

Early British accounts, beginning with a slim volume assembled during the war by Sir George Maxwell under the title *The Civil Defence of Malaya*, defended British actions at the time of the Japanese invasion, and emphasized that the end of the occupation meant a return to the *status quo ante*. The 1950s brought the first attempts to evaluate the significance of the war years. At this juncture, academic opinion credited the occupation with generating changes in the way people viewed themselves, their societies, and the world in which they lived, and with giving rise to national revolutions. Writing early in the decade, T.H. Silcock and Ungku Aziz suggested that "the sudden change of masters and the impact of violent Japanese nationalism and pan-Asianism" served as "a most intensive school for nationalist feelings and thoughts about political questions". By placing local men in senior positions, the Japanese had fostered "local professional pride" and instilled a new self-confidence in the Malayan population, while the subordination of these men to senior Japanese officials in the later stages of the Occupation, and then once again to British officials, had left them bitter and frustrated. The Malays emerged from the Occupation with a heightened sense of unity, but with patriotic sentiments and an attitude toward power that did not match "the possibilities of the situation". The Chinese, caught between the guerrillas and the Japanese, and dealing with a world in which departing from "the habits of law and order" not only paid dividends but to some extent was necessary for survival, emerged with "a vested interest in the disorder and insecurity of Japanese rule which brought them wealth at the expense of the rest of society". The Indians in Malaya were the group "most affected" by the Occupation, in that they began as "depressed and uninterested inhabitants of a political backwater", but became, "in their own estimation at least, the spearhead of a movement to liberate India", and learned the use of arms, how to organize politically and the techniques of political bargaining.[16]

A spate of histories of Malaya appeared in the late 1950s and the 1960s gave little space to the war and occupation, and after providing a bare outline of wartime events turned to post-war developments.[17] A few writers suggested that Britain's failure to protect the country against the Japanese made it difficult for the colonial administration to resume control over post-war Malaya. For example, vol. 2 of F.J. Moorhead's *A History of Malaya*, published in 1963, concluded that the experiences of the war years "made a return to the old state of affairs that obtained before 1939 impossible" because "there was now a much clearer political consciousness" among the three races.[18] Sir Richard Winstedt made a similar point, and added that the situation was made worse

[16] Silcock and Aziz, "Nationalism in Malaya", pp. 289–98.

[17] See, for example, G.P. Dartford, *A Short History of Malaya* (1956), Harry Miller, *The Story of Malaysia* (1965), J. Kennedy, *A History of Malaya* (1965), and R.O. Winstedt, *A History of Malaya* (1962, revised and expanded from a work of 1935).

[18] F.J. Moorhead, *A History of Malaya*, vol. 2, p. 203.

by insensitive behaviour on the part of post-war administrators.[19] Anticipating their discussions of the Malayan Emergency, these books mention the role played by communists in the anti-Japanese resistance, but pay little or no attention to wartime political activity among the Malays and Indians. K.G. Tregonning's *A History of Modern Malaya*, published in 1964, broke new ground by discussing both, and later textbooks routinely present the activities of the Indian Independence League, the Indian National Army, and Ibrahim Yaacob's Kesatuan Melayu Muda (KMM) and Kekuatan Rakyat Indonesia Semenanjung (KRIS) as precursors of post-war political organizations.[20]

In a radio talk delivered in the mid-1960s, Wang Gungwu, then head of the History Department at the University of Malaya, summarized the main points that formed the basis for a new interpretation of the occupation. He began with a statement of the conventional position, that for many in Malaya the occupation marked "the real beginning of the new era", but went on to suggest that the matter was "not so straightforward": "It was not the Japanese who led us to Merdeka [Independence], nor did they want us to be free and independent." Japan's role was "largely a destructive one", and the Japanese "missed a glorious opportunity to be the leader of Asia by ignoring Asian aspirations".

> What brought the new age for us were firstly, the Communist challenge against the West; secondly, the American response to the unaccustomed leadership of an anti-Communist and yet anti imperialist world; and finally, Britain's recognition that probably more could be salvaged by reason than by force.

The occupation, he continued, taught a number of lessons, among them that imperialism was not a European monopoly and Asian powers could also adopt imperialist policies, and a sense that freedom from colonial control was possible. It also left two important legacies, the fact that the Japanese had been able to take advantage of "the economic and political gulfs between communities to aggravate the differences based on cultures and religions", and the strength of the Malayan Communist Party.[21]

By the 1970s, after an outbreak of communal violence in May 1969, historians in Malaysia and Singapore were tracing nationalist initiatives to local leaders, and arguing that the Japanese period had in fact created obstacles to

---

[19] Sir Richard Winstedt, *Malaya and its History*, pp. 140–1. See also Lennox A. Mills, *Malaya: A Political and Economic Appraisal*, pp. 29–31, and Horace Stone, *From Malacca to Malaysia, 1400–1965* (1966), p. 170.

[20] See, for example, N.J. Ryan's *A History of Malaysia and Singapore* (1976) and Tan Ding Eing's school textbook, *A Portrait of Malaysia and Singapore* (1975).

[21] Wang Gungwu, "The Japanese Occupation and Post-War Malaya, 1941–1948".

national unity. In an article published in 1970, the Malaysian historian Zainal Abidin b. Abd. Wahid argued that differences in the treatment accorded to the Chinese and the Malays under Japanese rule, and particularly the use of Malay policemen against the Chinese dominated MPAJA, had a negative impact on the development of a unified Malayan nationalism and formed the starting point for inter-racial conflicts in the country.[22] A decade later another Malaysian historian, Cheah Boon Kheng, similarly argued that the enduring significance of the Occupation lay in its negative impact on race relations in Malaya, and the way this issue shaped post-war politics. "Much of the interaction of Japanese policy and local responses, especially the changing Malay and Chinese perceptions of one another during the Japanese occupation, helped to determine the direction of Malaya's post-war political development."[23]

In Singapore, as the historian Eunice Thio wrote in the 1980s, the war conclusively altered the perception of the British: "Nothing could restore the tarnished image of European invincibility and superiority", or erase the memory of "misleading British propaganda". The fact that Britain had failed to defend its subjects "called into question its right to reimpose colonial rule", and each community brought "an enhanced political consciousness" to post-war politics. She notes, too, that the Syonan years made a lasting impression on those who assumed the leadership of an independent Singapore. "Among other things, they developed a realization that in a crisis Singapore must rely upon its own resources, and a determination to ensure that the island would never again be occupied and exploited by others."[24] A 1961 statement by the then Prime Minister, Lee Kuan Yew, provides the basis for this conclusion:

> My colleagues and I are of that generation of young men who went through the Second World War and the Japanese Occupation and emerged determined that no one—neither the Japanese nor the British—had the right to push and kick us around.[25]

---

[22] Zainal Abidin b. Abd. Wahid, "The Japanese Occupation and Nationalisms", pp. 93–8.

[23] Cheah Boon Kheng, "The Social Impact of the Japanese Occupation", pp. 116–17, and personal communications. See also his *Red Star Over Malaya*.

[24] Eunice Thio, "The Syonan Years, 1942–1945", pp. 110–11.

[25] Yeo Kim Wah and Albert Lau, "From Colonialism to Independence", p. 117, citing a speech entitled "The Battle for Merger", in *Towards Socialism*, vol. 5, Ministry of Culture Series of Twelve Talks Delivered between 13 Sept. and 9 Oct. 1961 (Singapore: Government Printing Office, 1962), pp. 10–11. This passage is also quoted in a school textbook entitled *History of Modern Singapore* (p. 153), written by a Secondary History Project Team assembled by the Ministry of Education's Curriculum Development Institute.

On another occasion, during the unveiling of a memorial to civilian victims of the occupation, Lee Kuan Yew stated that the period had "served as a catalyst in building a nation out of the young and unestablished community of diverse immigrants."

> We suffered together. It told us that we share a common destiny. And it is through sharing such common experiences that the feeling of living and being one community is established.[26]

A textbook prepared by the Curriculum Development Institute of Singapore for use by students in their first year of Secondary School described the occupation as a "nightmare" when people "suffered and lived in constant fear", pointedly adding that this was "the price that a country has to pay when it is occupied by another country". People "of all races" found themselves under new masters, and were bullied by Japanese guards. The Malays "suffered under the Japanese" and some were sent to Thailand to build the Death Railway; Indians were pressured to join the INA and some who refused were killed; the Eurasians suffered because they resembled Europeans and some were imprisoned or sent to the Death Railway; but "it was the Chinese who suffered the most" because they had actively helped China to fight against Japan. The invasion and occupation provide several "valuable lessons": first, "the government and people of a country should always be well-prepared to defend the country against any enemy"; second, Britain's defeat at the hands of the Japanese, "who were Asians", demonstrated that "the Europeans were not superior to the Asians"; and third, people were shown "the need to get rid of their foreign masters".[27] Another Singapore textbook, this one used by upper level students, summarized the impact of the Japanese occupation under two headings. The first was "Economic and social disruption" (economic problems, MPAJA reprisals immediately after the war, and "the unfortunate development of anti-Chinese antagonism amongst the Malay community", which was stirred up by the Japanese). The second was "Awakening of nationalistic consciousness and change of British policy" (rejection of the "old order" by the Malays and by the communists, and the new approach to government forced upon the British by the growth of nationalist feeling and the advance of communism).[28] Another school textbook argues that the Chinese suffered most under Japanese rule, while the Indians received better treatment but "also suffered", and the "Japanese treatment of the Malays was less harsh":

---

[26] Alex Josey, *Lee Kuan Yew*, p. 541.

[27] Curriculum Development Institute of Singapore, *History of Modern Singapore*, pp. 147–53. Evelyn Sim's *A History of Malaya, Singapore and Thailand for GCE 'N' Level* offers a similar account.

[28] Nigel Kelly, *History of Malaya and South-East Asia*, pp. 91–2; emphasis in the original.

"On the whole, the Japanese treated the Malays well" because they were the indigenous people and the largest group in the country, and the Japanese wanted their support. The "strongest and most popular" resistance organization was the MPAJA, whose members "were mostly Chinese". The effects of the occupation include "crime and violence throughout the country" following the surrender, thousands of deaths, racial hostility ("deliberately created" by the Japanese, who "spread anti-Chinese propaganda"), the strengthening of the MCP, social and economic problems, the lowering of British prestige and the development of Malay nationalism.[29]

Whereas Singapore views the occupation as an experience which helped forge national unity, in Malaysia the uneven treatment of the races, the suggestion that the Japanese favoured the Malays, and other aspects of the Occupation are seen as potentially divisive issues. Moreover, post-war administrations have forged cordial relations with Japan, and the government has long since declared that matters arising from the Occupation have been definitively settled. Reflecting this perspective, an upper-level school textbook issued in 1992 by the publishing arm of the Malaysian Ministry of Education all but disregards the war and occupation. The book contends that the ethnic Malays had already achieved national awareness by 1940, and that the contribution of the Japanese Occupation was simply to elevate the struggle for national awareness, as happened in other Southeast Asian countries.[30] It moves on to a discussion of the shaping of the modern economy before 1940, before jumping to the post-war period and the struggle against the Malayan Union. In 1946, readers are told in the course of a single sentence, the Malays could not forget the unbearable hardships endured during the period of the Japanese administration, and the terror unleashed by the communist "Three Star" organization immediately after the war. The tyrannical regimes imposed by the communists in various parts of Malaya provided a lesson for the Malays, who strongly defended their rights, and as a consequence of this experience were unwilling to join together

---

[29] Marissa Champion and Joy Moreira, *History of Malaya and Southeast Asia*, pp. 203–15.

[30] "Dengan itu, jelaslah menjelang tahun 1940 telah wujud kesedaran kebangsaan di kalangan orang Melayu. Seterusnya pendudukan Jepun dari tahun 1942 hingga tahun 1945, telah secara langsung mempertingkatkan perjuangan kesedaran kebangsaan sebagaimana yang dialami oleh negeri-negeri lain di Asia Tenggara." *Sejarah Malaysia*, Tingkatan 5. Kurikulum Bersepadu Sekolah Menengah, p. 87. The authors of this volume are senior academics drawn from Malaysian universities: Siti Zuraina Abdul Majid, Muhammad Yusoff Hashim, Abdullah Zakaria Ghazali, Lee Kam Hing, Ahmad Fawzi Basri and Zainal Abidin Abdul Wahid.

with immigrant peoples in forming a common state.[31] The clear message of this textbook is that the Japanese occupation in itself was not a significant force in the shaping of modern Malaysia.

In contrast, a volume entitled *Malaysia Kita* (Our Malaysia), published in 1991 by the Malaysian Institute of Public Administration to be used by public servants in preparing for a Civil Service Examination taken as a condition for confirmation in their positions, asserted that the Japanese occupation left a deep and important impression on the people of Malaya. The defeat of the British demonstrated that an Asian nation could defeat a European power, and the spread of political awareness, and nationalist feeling after the war gave rise to an anti-colonial spirit among the Malays. Japan's Military Administration was hard and brutal. The Japanese recruited large numbers of forced labourers, particularly young Malays, who assisted the military after being subjected to indoctrination. They also chose Malay officials to fill positions as District Officers, although these men were not given real power and instead became "tools" and "ears" for the Japanese administration. Before the war, relations between the different races in Malaya—the Malays, Chinese and Indians—had been cordial and good, but the Japanese practice of giving preference to the Malays and subjecting the Chinese to harsh treatment created divisions between the two groups. When the Chinese escaped to the jungle to set up the MPAJA, the Japanese used Malay soldiers and police to attack them, thus creating a deep enmity between the two largest groups in the country. The book mentions the activities of Ibrahim Yaacob and the KMM, but says that Japan "like other imperialist powers" was simply using Malay nationalism as a tool to further its own political and economic interests, and the Malays, "as a colonized people", found the occupation a bitter experience. The "severe pressure" they experienced made the Malays politically aware, and they "rose up to oppose British imperialists" when the Malayan Union was introduced after the occupation. Force 136 is presented as a body composed of former British soldiers assisted by ethnic Malay guerrillas, and the chapter concludes with a discussion of the cruelty and brutality of the Chinese Communists during the interregnum immediately following the Japanese

[31] "Pada tahun 1946 orang Melayu masih belum dapat melupakan pendentaan semasa di bawah pemerintahan Jepun, serta peristiwa keganasan Bintang Tiga yang ditaja oleh Parti Komunis Malaya. Pemerintahan zalim selama 14 hari di sesetengah tempat oleh Bintang Tiga menjadi satu pengajaran bagi orang Melayu. Oleh itu, orang Melayu pada masa itu tetap mempertahankan haknya dan tidak mahu berkongsi negeri dengan kaum pendatang." *Sejarah Malaysia*, Tingkatan 5, pp. 122–3.

surrender. This episode came to an end when the Malays "rose up to oppose the Communists", and was a "bitter lesson for Malaysian society".[32]

* * *

With the passing of the generation that experienced the war years, the occupation ceased to provoke an immediate, emotional reaction, and with the emergence of new leaders and new concerns it lost much of its earlier potency as a symbol. The object-lessons that Malaysia and Singapore now see in the occupation have little to do with Japan or the issues that inspired the war, and the war years are used to illustrate points relating to domestic issues that have arisen since the conflict ended. Where the occupation was once viewed as a starting point for nationalist activity, the roots of nationalism are now traced to local initiatives before and after the war, and the Japanese are blamed for instigating racial antagonisms. The singularity of the occupation has all but disappeared, and 70 years after it ended, school textbooks and published memoirs treat the period as one episode among many in an eventful era, rather than as the defining moment of the twentieth century.

[32] Institut Tadbiran Awam Negara (INTAN), *Malaysia Kita*, pp. 473–7. The initial version of this book, published in 1980 under the title *Negara Kita* [Our Country] similarly emphasized the importance of the occupation, but offered a much briefer version of this story. *Negara Kita*, pp. 37–8.

Bibliography

Official Records

The following record series were consulted:

The National Archives (formerly the Public Record Office), Kew, England

BT 25 Board of Trade. Supplies to Liberated Areas Secretariat
CO 273 Straits Settlements Original Correspondence
HS 1 Special Operations Executive (SOE): Far East Files, c. 1940–46
WO 106 Directorate of Military Operations and Intelligence
WO 172 War of 1939–45: War Diaries SEAC/ALFSEA
WO 193 Directorate of Military Operations: Collation Files
WO 203 War of 1939–45; Military Headquarters Papers, Far East
WO 208 Directorate of Military Intelligence
WO 220 Directorate of Civil Affairs
WO 222 Medical Historical Papers
WO 224 Enemy POW Camps in Europe and the Far East
WO 252 Topographical and Economic Surveys
WO 325 War Crimes South-East Asia: Trials

Malaysian National Archives

Federal Records
- British Military Administration (Malaya) (BMA)
- Malayan Union (MU)

State and District Records
- Kedah: Kedah Secretariat/Setiausaha Kerajaan Kedah (SUK Kedah)
- Kelantan: Governor Kelantan, Kelantan Montri Spa, Pejabat Mentri Kelantan, Somubu (General Affairs Department), Ulu Kelantan, Pasir Puteh
- Selangor: Selangor Secretariat (Sel Sec), Selangor Kanbo (Sel Kan), Ulu Langat, Ulu Selangor, Klang
- Perak: Batang Padang, Batu Gajah, Dindings, Kinta, Kuala Kangsar, Larut, Lenggong, Telok Anson
- Pahang: Bentong, Kuantan, Temerloh

United States National Archives and Records Administration (NARA)

RG226 Records of the Office of Strategic Services (OSS)

The U.S. Army Center of Military History

Japanese Monographs (JM)

These studies were written by former officers of the Japanese armed forces for the Historical Records Section of the First (Army) and Second (Navy) Demobilization Bureaus of the Japanese Government, and translated by the Military Intelligence Service Group attached to the Headquarters of the United States Army's Far East Command. Monograph No. 107 subsequently underwent extensive editing by the Foreign Histories Division, Assistant Chief of Staff G3, Headquarters, United States Army Japan. The other monographs listed here are unedited translations. Monograph 107 bears the following cautionary note, which would apply to the others as well:

> The writers were handicapped in the preparation of the basic manuscripts by the non-availability of many operational records which are normally employed as source material in this type of study. Many official orders, plans and unit journals were lost during operations or were destroyed at the cessation of hostilities. A particular handicap has been the lack of strength reports. Most of the important orders and other information sources, however, have been reconstructed from memory and while not textually identical with the originals are believed to be accurate and reliable.

In the translated versions of these monographs, the names of ethnic groups and of places appear in upper case letters (e.g., CHINESE, SINGAPORE). For material quoted in the present volume, this convention has been abandoned.

No. 24. History of the Southern Army, 1941–45
(Written by Maj. Gen. Masami Ishii in collaboration with Col. Naritoshi Yamada, Col. Kazuo Horiba and Maj. Nizo Yamaguchi, all of whom served with the G-3 office of the Southern Army.)

No. 54. Malay Operations Record, Nov. 1941–Mar. 1942
(Compiled primarily from memoirs of Col. Sugita, Intelligence Staff Officer, Lt. Col. Kunitake, Operation Staff Officer, and Lt. Col. Hashizune, Officer of Rear-Operations. These sources were supplemented by diaries and memoirs of other officers involved.)

No. 55. Southwest Area Air Operations Record. Phase I, Nov. 1941–Feb. 1945
(A condensed instruction manual based on materials gathered by Col. Shin Ishikawa and Col. Katsui Dozonu, both instructors at the General Staff College, and enlarged and revised by Col. Minoru Miyaka, Chief Staff Officer in charge of 3rd Air Corps Operations.)

No. 102. Submarine Operations. Dec. 1941–Apr. 1942
(Compiled by Capt. Tatsuwaka Shibuya, a former staff officer of the Combined Fleet, based on his own experiences and the recollections and personal papers of Commander Yasuo Fujimori, a former staff officer (operations) with Imperial General Headquarters. This material was supplemented by battle reports of the Submarine Force, and by interrogations of Japanese Officers.)

No. 103. Outline of Administration in Occupied Areas, 1941–45
(The Malaya materials in this account are based on the personal recollections of the Malay Military Administrative Inpsector, Maj. Gen. Masuzo Fujimura.)

No. 107. Malaya Invasion Naval Operations
(Based on information provided by Commander Shiro Yamaguchi, the staff officer of the Navy General Staff in charge of planning naval operations for Malaya and Thailand.)

No. 162. Southwest Area Operations Record, Apr. 1944–Aug. 1945
(Based on information provided by Col. Yutaka Imaoka, former Chief of Staff of the Seventh Area Army.)

No. 167. Malay Operations Record. 29th Army, Jan. 1944–Aug 1945
(Based on information provided by Lt. Gen. Masuzo Fujimura and Lt. Gen. Naokazu Kawahara, former Chiefs of Staff of the 29th Army.)

Intelligence Materials

Intelligence sources included radio broadcasts, interviews with persons who escaped from Malaya or were captured, and various sorts of printed matter that fell into Allied hands. Wartime translation operations included the General Services Detailed Intelligence Centre (GSDIC), the Army Central Translation Section (ACTS) and beginning in May 1944 the South-East Asia Translation and Intelligence Centre (SEATIC). Translations of materials captured in the Pacific campaigns were prepared by the Allied Translator and Interpreter Section (ATIS), South West Pacific Area. The Foreign Research and Press Service compiled and disseminated reports based in part on translated intelligence materials, and on monitored radio broadcasts. One such collection, "Far Eastern Economic Notes" produced on 4 February 1943, includes a warning that "Since the outbreak of the Pacific War these notes have had to be compiled almost entirely from reports of enemy origin and necessarily include much mendacious propaganda: they are issued not as factual information but for whatever use can be made of them."[1] Materials based on Japanese sources used in preparing this study include the following:

[1] Foreign Research and Press Service, Balliol College, Oxford, Far Eastern Economic Notes, 4 Feb. 1943, CO273/669/50744/7.

Allied Translator and Interpreter Section (ATIS), South West Pacific Area

Hawaii-Malaya Naval Operations. Edited under the supervision of the Naval Information Department of the Imperial General Headquarters. Published by the Bungei Shunju Sha. ATIS Enemy Publications no. 6. 27 March 1943. NARA RG226 XL3138.

Intelligence Reports Issued by Yazawa Butai HQ and Oki Shudan (Group) HQ 8 Mar.–30 Sept. '42. ATIS Enemy Publications no. 28. 21 July 1943. NARA RG226 XL3161.

Yokoyama, Ryuichi. *Malaya Campaign 1941–1942*. 1942. ATIS Enemy Publications no. 278. NARA RG 165 Entry 79 Box 309.

(ATIS notes accompanying this translation indicate that the book was intended for popular consumption and was not a military instruction manual. It was acquired in September 1943, and the copy lacked its cover and a few inside pages.)

Economic Intelligence Section, Intelligence Division, HQ SACSEA. Summaries of Economic Intelligence (Far East).

Far Eastern Bureau, British Ministry of Information. Fortnightly Intelligence Reports (cited as FIR).

(Dates indicate the end of the period to which the report refers. Most of the reports issued in 1943, 1944 and 1945 are found in CO273/667/50744/7 and CO273/673/50744/7.) The Far Eastern Bureau was set up in September 1939 as a publicity bureau to disseminate information in the Far East concerning Britain and the British Empire. Its Headquarters was initially in Hong Kong, but moved to Singapore in June 1940, and to Delhi upon the fall of Singapore. Its mission changed from publicity to political warfare at the time of the Japanese declaration of war in December 1941, and it operated under the control of the Political Warfare (Japan) Committee in London. In May 1944 the Bureau began accepting operational directives from the South East Asia Command with regard to activities in that command area, and in April 1945 was placed under the Political Intelligence Department of the Foreign Office.[2]

Office of Strategic Services. Research and Analysis Branch (OSS. R&A)

The following compilations are based on Japanese radio broadcasts, printed matter that fell into Allied hands and Interrogation Reports. Some are simply assemblages of such material, but most are narratives constructed from these sources.

Assemblage No. 47.
Indians in Japan and Occupied Areas: Their Support of Indian Independence; Biographies. 20 Oct. 1944.

Current Intelligence Study no. 29. The Kempei in Japanese-Occupied Territory. 13 July 1945.

[2] The Future of the Far Eastern Bureau, WO203/5653.

R&A/SEAC 74-K. Guerilla Movements in Malaya. 10 May 1945. NARA RG226 XL9311.
R&A/SEAC 83-K. Plans for Collection of Rubber Stocks in Malaya. 18 June 1945. NARA RG226 XL11452.
R&A/SEAC 91-K. Guide to Personalities in Five Malay States: Selangor, Negri Sembilan, Malacca, Johore, Singapore. 28 July 1945. NARA RG226 XL27005. Supplement I, 10 August 1945. NARA RG226 XL11452.
R&A no. 34. Singapore. 12 Dec. 1941.
R&A no. 1433. Political and Economic Changes Effected by the Japanese in Malaya. 1 Dec. 1943.
R&A no. 1595. Indian Minorities in South and East Asia: The Background of the Indian Independence Movement Outside India. 8 Sept. 1944.
R&A no. 1791. Implementation Study of Malaya. Part I: Morale Objectives. 15 Mar. 1944.
R&A no. 2052. Thailand Biographies Assemblage 41. 2nd Edition of Assemblage 19 (31 Aug. 1943). 20 Mar. 1943. FCC intercepts of
Radio Tokyo and Affiliated Stations Dec. 27, 1941-Jan. 27, 1944 and from Far Eastern Diplomatic Lists.
R&A no. 2072. Japanese Administration in Malaya. 8 June 1944.
R&A no. 2423. Singapore under Japanese Domination. 8 Sept. 1944.
R&A no. 2589. The Rubber Industry of Southeast Asia: An Estimate of Present Conditions and Anticipated Capabilities. 16 Dec. 1944.
R&A no. 2644. Rough Summary of Information on Inflation in Southeast Asia.
R&A No. 2954. Thailand's Relations with Great Britain in the Strategic Upper Malay Peninsula. 22 Aug. 1945.

Select List of Official Reports

Appreciation of Malaya. I. Pre-Japanese Occupation. II. Post-Japanese Occupation. BMA 506/10.
Committee of Imperial Defence. Oversea Defence Committee. Singapore. "Food Supplies for the Civil Population in the Event of War". 30 Apr. 1926. CO537/937.
Far Eastern Bureau, British Ministry of Information, New Delhi. "Malaya under the Japanese". March, 1945. NARA RG226 128585. A note on a slightly different version of this document in BMA PS/412 says it was prepared by a Mrs Lindsay.
Godsall, W.D. *Report on the Working of the Malayan Currency Commission for the Period of 1st January, 1941 to 31st December, 1946*. Singapore: Government Printer, 1948.
Hone, H.R., *Report on the British Military Administration of Malaya, September 1945 to March 1946*. Kuala Lumpur: Malayan Union Government Press, 1946.
Lau Siew Foo [O.C. Chinese, M.S.S. Singapore] and Major J.C. Barry. "A Brief Review of Chinese Affairs During the Period of Japanese Occupation". N.D., BMA ADM/8/1.
Malaya – Part I and Malaya – Part II. BMA 506/10.
Malayan Union and Singapore. *Interim Report on Wages by the Joint Wages Commission, 29 July 1947*. Kuala Lumpur: Malayan Union Government Press, 1947.

Memorandum on Proposals for a Malayan War Damage Compensation Scheme. Kuala Lumpur: Government Press, 1948.

Military Intelligence Service, War Department, Washington, DC. "Notes on Japanese Warfare on the Malayan Front". Information Bulletin no. 6. 9 Jan. 1942. NARA RG226 19072.

________. "Notes on Japanese Warfare". Information Bulletin no. 10. 21 Mar. 1942. NARA RG226 19072.

Psychology Division, Divisional Report no. 47. (Originally prepared for the Foreign Information Service.) Social Conditions, Attitudes and Propaganda in British Malaya with Suggestions for American Orientation Toward the Malayans. BMA 522/00.

Report of the Young Working Party. BT25/75/SLA/MISC 6.

Research and Analysis Branch, Interim Research and Intelligence Service, Department of State. Japanese Penetration of the Rubber Industry. 12 Oct. 1945. NARA RS226 XL23029.

Security Intelligence for Planning Section, SACSEA. Proforma 'A' – Strategical.
Kedah and Perlis. NARA RG226 XL21421
Penang and Province Wellesley. NARA RG226 XL21417
Singapore. NARA RG226 XL21416

Security Intelligence for Planning Section, SACSEA. Proforma 'B' – Tactical.
Johore. NARA RG226 XL21412
Kedah and Perlis. NARA RG226 XL21419
Malacca. NARA RG226 XL21414
Negri Sembilan. NARA RG226 XL21415
Pahang, Kelantan and Trengganu. NARA RG226 XL21409
Pahang, Kelantan and Trengganu. Addenda No. 1, NARA RG226 XL21420
Penang and Province Wellesley. NARA RG226 XL21413
Perak. NARA RG226 XL21411
Selangor. NARA RG226 XL21410
Singapore. NARA RG226 XL21407

Singapore Department of Social Welfare. *A Social Survey of Singapore* (1947).

Supplementary Guide to JIFC (Indian) Activities (Malaya). HQ Allied Land Forces, South East Asia Command, 16 Aug. 1945. WO203/2298.

War Damage Commission, Federation of Malaya and Singapore. *Report*. Kuala Lumpur: Government Press, 1953.

Newspapers

Syonan Times/Syonan Sinbun/Syonan Shimbun
Penang Shimbun
Perak Times

Miscellaneous

"The Good Citizen's Guide". *Syonan Shimbun*, 2603.

A compendium of "declarations, orders, notifications, rules and regulations, etc." issued by the administration in Syonan-to and Johore, and published "with a view to helping the people to make themselves good, law-abiding citizens".

Del Tufo, M.V. *Malaya, comprising the Federation of Malaya and the Colony of Singapore: A Report on the 1947 Census of Population.* The Governments of the Federation of Malaya and the Colony of Signapore. London: Crown Agents for the Colonies, 1932.

Vice Admiral the Earl Mountbatten of Burma. *Report to the Combined Chiefs of Staff by the Supreme Allied Commander South-East Asia, 1943–1945.* London: HMSO, 1951; repr. New Delhi: English Book Store, 1960.

Nathan, J.E. *The Census of British Malaya*, 1921. London: Government of British Malaya, 1922.

C.A. Vlieland. *British Malaya: A Report on the 1931 Census and on Certain Problems of Vital Statistics.* London: Crown Agents for the Colonies, 1932.

Bibliographies

Corfield, Justin J. (comp. and ed.) *A Bibliography of Literature Relating to the Malayan Campaign and the Japanese Period in Malaya, Singapore and Northern Borneo.* Centre for Southeast Asian Studies, University of Hull, 1988.

From Singapore to Syonan-to, 1941–1945: A Select Bibliography. Singapore: Reference Services Division, National Library, 1992.

Sbrega, John. *The War Against Japan, 1941–1945: An Annotated Bibliography.* New York: Garland, 1989.

Published Collections of Documents

Benda, Harry J., James K. Irikura and Koichi Kishi. *Japanese Military Administration in Indonesia: Selected Documents.* Translation Series No. 6. New Haven: Southeast Asian Studies, Yale University, 1965.

Boeicho Boei Kenshujo Senshishitsu (Defence Agency, Defence Studies Institute, War History Library). *Mare shinko sakusen* [Malaya Offensive Operation]. Tokyo, 1966.

________. Shiryoshu Nanpo no gunsei. Tokyo, 1985.

Garcia, Mauro (ed.). *Documents on the Japanese Occupation of the Philippines.* Manila: Philippine Historical Association, 1965.

Great Britain. Cabinet Office. Cabinet History Series. *Principal War Telegrams and Memoranda, 1940–1943.* vol. 4. *Far East.* Nendeln: KTO Press, 1978 (includes Sir Robert Brooke-Popham. Despatch on Far East. 27 May 1942); vol. 7. Miscellaneous. Nendeln: KTO Press, 1978.

Kurasawa, Aiko. *Marei Koho.* Tokyo: Ryukei Shosha, 1990. (Bulletins of the Japanese Military Administration in Malaya issued between May 1943 and January 1944.)

________. *Tomi Koho.* Tokyo: Ryukeisha, 1990. (Bulletins of the Japanese Military Government in Singapore [the Tomi Shudan Gunseikanbu] issued between 1 October 1942 and 15 April 1943.)

Lebra, Joyce (ed.), *Japan's Greater East Asia Co-Prosperity Sphere in World War II: Selected Readings and Documents.* Kuala Lumpur: Oxford University Press, 1975.

Royal Institute for International Affairs. *Documents on International Affairs, 1947–1949*. London: Oxford University Press, 1952.

________. *Survey of International Affairs: The Far East, 1942–1946*. London: Oxford University Press, 1955.

Trager, Frank N. (ed.). *Burma: Japanese Military Administration, Selected Documents, 1941–1945*. Philadelphia: University of Pennsylvania Press, 1971.

Books and Articles

A[bdul] Samad Ismail. *Ketokohan dan Kewartawanan* [About Leaders and Journalists], compiled by A. Karim Haji Abdullah. Kuala Lumpur: Dewan Bahasa dan Pustaka, 1991.

Abdul Aziz bin Satar Khan. "Terengganu 1940–1945: Satu Kajian Mengenai Kemunculan Golongan Kiri Melayu" [Trengganu 1940–1945: A Study of the Emergence of the Malay Left]. In *Terengganu: Dahulu dan Sekarang* [Trengganu: Past and Present], ed. Abdullah Zakaria Ghazali. Kuala Lumpur: Persatuan Muzium Malaysia, 1984.

Abdul Aziz bin Zakaria. *Leftenan Nor: Pahlawan Gerila* [Lieutenant Nor: Guerrilla Hero]. Kuala Lumpur: Dewan Bahasa dan Pustaka, 1963.

Abdul Latiff Abu Bakar. *Ishak Haji Muhammad: Penulis dan Ahli Politik sehingga 1948* [Ishak Haji Muhammad: Writer and Politician, until 1948]. Kuala Lumpur: Penerbit Universiti Malaya, 1977.

Abdul Samad bin Idris (comp.). *Askar Melayu 50 Tahun* [Malay Soldiers, 50 Years]. Kuala Lumpur: Pustaka Budiman, 1983.

Abdul Wahab. *Medical Students during the Japanese Invasion of Singapore, 1941–1942*, ed. Cheah Jin Seng. Singapore: Academy of Medicine, 1987.

Abdullah Hussain. *Terjebak* [Trapped]. Kuala Lumpur: Pustaka Antara, 1965.

Abdullah Zakaria Ghazali. *Pentadbiran Tentera Jepun dan Thai di Terengganu, 1942–1945* [The Japanese and Thai Military Administrations in Terengganu, 1942–1945]. Kuala Lumpur: Penerbit Universiti Malaya, 1996.

Abu Talib Ahmad. "The Impact of the Japanese Occupation on the Malay-Muslim Population". In *Malaya and Singapore during the Japanese Occupation*, ed. Paul H. Kratoska. Singapore: Journal of Southeast Asian Studies, 1995.

________. *The Malay Muslims, Islam and the Rising Sun: 1941–45*. Kuala Lumpur: Malaysian Branch of the Royal Asiatic Society, 2003.

Adnan bin Ibrahim. "Pendudukan Jepun dan Keadaan Sosio-Ekonomi di Negeri Kelantan" [The Japanese Occupation and Socio-Economic Conditions in Kelantan]. In *Pendudukan Jepun di Tanah Melayu, 1942–1945*, ed. Paul H. Kratoska and Abu Talib Ahmad. Pulau Pinang: Pusat Pengajian Ilmu Kemanusian, Universiti Sains Malaysia, 1989.

Ahmad Kamar. "The Formation of Saberkas". In *Darulaman*, ed. Asmah Haji Omar. Kuala Lumpur: Perpustakaan Negara Malaysia, 1979.

Ahmed Meah Baba Ahmed. *Penaklukan Jepun: Suka Duka di Georgetown* [The Japanese Conquest: Pleasures and Sorrows in Georgetown]. Kuala Lumpur: Media Indah, 1992.

Aisha Akbar. *Aisha Bee at War: A Very Frank Memoir*. Singapore: Landmark Books, 1990.

Akashi, Yoji. "Japanese Military Administration in Malaya: Its Formation and Evolution in Reference to Sultans, the Islamic Religion and the Moslem Malays, 1941–1945". *Asian Studies* 7 (Apr. 1969).

________. *The Nanyang Chinese National Salvation Movement, 1937–41*. Lawrence, KA: Centre for East Asian Studies, University of Kansas, 1970.

________. "Japanese Policy towards the Malayan Chinese, 1941–1945". *Journal of Southeast Asian Studies* 1 (Sept. 1970): 61–89.

________. "Education and Indoctrination Policy in Malaya and Singapore under the Japanese Rule, 1942–45". *Malaysian Journal of Education* 13 (Dec. 1976): 1–46.

________. "The Japanese Occupation of Malaya: Interruption or Transformation?". In *Southeast Asia under Japanese Occupation*, ed. Alfred W. McCoy. New Haven: Monograph Series no. 22, Yale University Southeast Asia Studies, 1980.

________. "Bureaucracy and the Japanese Military Administration, with Specific Reference to Malaya". In *Japan in Asia, 1942–1945*, ed. William H. Newell. Singapore: Singapore University Press, 1981.

________. "Japan and 'Asia for Asians'". In *Japan Examined: Perspectives on Modern Japanese History*, ed. Harry Wray and Hilary Controy. Honolulu: University of Hawaii Press, 1983.

________. "The Japanese Occupation of Melaka, January 1942–August 1945". In *Melaka: The Transformation of a Malay Capital, c. 1400–1980*, ed. Kernial Singh Sandhu and Paul Wheatley. Kuala Lumpur: Oxford University Press, 1983.

________. "Japanese Cultural Policy in Malaya and Singapore, 1942–45". In *Japanese Cultural Policies in Southeast Asia during World War 2*, ed. Grant K. Goodman. Houndmills: Macmillan, 1991.

________. "Notes on Japanese Sources on the Occupation of Malaya, 1941–45". *JCC Bulletin* (Bulletin of the Japan Cultural Centre, Kuala Lumpur) 23 (May–June 1994): 1–4 and 24 (July–Aug. 1994): 1–7.

________. "The Anti-Japanese Movement in Perak during the Japanese Occupation, 1941–45". In *Malaya and Singapore during the Japanese Occupation*, ed. Paul H. Kratoska. Singapore: Journal of Southeast Asian Studies, 1995.

Aldrich, Richard J. "A Question of Expediency: Britain, the United States and Thailand, 1941–42". *Journal of Southeast Asian Studies* 19 (Sept. 1988): 209–44.

________. *The Key to the South: Britain, the United States and Thailand during the Approach of the Pacific War, 1929–1942*. Kuala Lumpur: Oxford University Press, 1993.

Allen, Louis. *The End of the War in Asia*. London: Hart-Davis, MacGibbon, 1976.

________. *Singapore: 1941–42*. Singapore: MPH, 1977. (First published London: Davis-Poynter, 1977.)

Andaya, Barbara Watson, and Leonard Y. Andaya. *A History of Malaysia*. London: Macmillan, 1982.

Arena Wati. *Cherpen Zaman Jepun: Suatu Kajian* [Stories of the Japanese Period: A Study]. Kuala Lumpur: Pustaka Antara, 1968.

Azahar Raswan Dean b. Wan Din. "Pengeluaran dan Perdagangan Padi dan Beras di Negeri Kedah dari Pendudukan Jepun Hingga Pentadbiran Tentera Thai, 1942–1945" [The Production and Trade in Padi and Milled Rice in Kedah from the Japanese

Occupation through the Thai Military Administration, 1942–1945]. *Kajian Malaysia* 5 (June 1987): 40–62.

Barber, Noel. *Sinister Twilight: The Fall of Singapore*. London: Collins, 1968 (Reprinted London: Arrow, 1988).

Barker, Ralph. *One Man's Jungle: A Biography of F. Spencer Chapman, DSO*. London: Chatto and Windus, 1975.

Barnhart, Michael A. "Japan's Drive to Autarky". In *Japan Examined: Perspectives on Modern Japanese History*, ed. Harry Wray and Hilary Conroy. Honolulu: University of Hawaii Press, 1983, pp. 293–300.

Batson, Benjamin A. "The Fall of the Phibun Government, 1944". *Journal of the Siam Society* 62 (July 1974): 89–120.

________. "Siam and Japan: The Perils of Independence". In *Southeast Asia under Japanese Occupation*, ed. Alfred W. McCoy. New Haven: Yale University Southeast Asia Studies, 1980, pp. 267–302.

Bayly, Christopher and Tim Harper. *Forgotten Armies: The Fall of British Asia, 1941–1945*. Cambridge, MA: The Belknap Press of Harvard University Press, 2005.

Beasley, W.G. *Japanese Imperialism, 1894–1945*. Oxford: Clarendon Press, 1987.

Benjamin, D. *Japan's Imperial Conspiracy*. London: Heinemann, 1971.

Bennet, Henry G. *Why Singapore Fell*. London: Angus and Robertson, 1944.

________. "Review Article: The Conquest of Malaya". *Journal of Southeast Asian History* 2 (1961): 91–100.

Bhargava, K.D. and K.N.V. Sastri. *Official History of the Indian Armed Forces in the Second World War, 1939–45: Campaigns in South-East Asia, 1941–42*, ed. Bisheshwar Prasad. Calcutta: Combined Inter-Services Historical Section, India and Pakistan, 1960.

Bose, Romen. *A Will for Freedom: Netaji and the Indian Independence Movement in Singapore and Southeast Asia, 1942–1945*. Singapore: VJ Times, 1993.

Bourne, Geoffrey H. "Nutrition Work in Malaya under the British Military Administration". *International Review of Vitamin Research* 21 (1949): 265–307.

Brailey, Nigel J. *Thailand and the Fall of Singapore: A Frustrated Asian Revolution*. Boulder: Westview Press, 1986.

Buckley, Roger. *Occupation Diplomacy: Britain, the United States and Japan, 1945–1952*. Cambridge: Cambridge University Press, 1982.

Burkill, I.H. *A Dictionary of the Economic Products of the Malay Peninsula*. 2 vols. Kuala Lumpur: Ministry of Agriculture and Co-operatives for the Governments of Malaysia and Singapore, 1966.

Caffrey, Kate. *Out in the Midday Sun: Singapore, 1941–1945*. London: Andre Deutsch, 1973.

Chalou, George C. (ed.) *The Secrets War: The Office of Strategic Services in World War II*. Washington: National Archives and Records Administration, 1992.

Chapman, F. Spencer. *The Jungle is Neutral*. New York: W.W. Norton, 1949.

Cheah Boon Kheng. "Some Aspects of the Interregnum in Malaya (14 August–3 September 1945)". *Journal of Southeast Asian Studies* 8 (Mar. 1977): 48–74.

________. "The Japanese Occupation of Malaya 1941–45: Ibrahim Yaakob and the Struggle for Indonesia Raya". *Indonesia* 28 (Oct. 1979): 85–120.

________. "The Social Impact of the Japanese Occupation of Malaya, 1942–45". In *Southeast Asia under Japanese Occupation*, ed. Alfred W. McCoy. New Haven: Yale University Southeast Asia Program, 1980.

________. *Red Star Over Malaya: Resistance and Social Conflict during and after the Japanese Occupation, 1941–1946*. Singapore: Singapore University Press, 1983.

________. "The Erosion of Ideological Hegemony and Royal Power and the Rise of Postwar Malay Nationalism, 1945–46". *Journal of Southeast Asian Studies* 19 (1988): 1–26.

Chelvasingam-MacIntyre, S. *Through Memory Lane*. Singapore: University Education Press, 1973.

Chen Su Lan. *Remember Pompong and Oxley Rise*. Singapore: The Chen Su Lan Trust, 1969.

Cheng Kok Peng. "A Brief Study of the Situation in Batu Pahat during the Japanese Occupation". In *Pendudukan Jepun di Tanah Melayu, 1942–1945*, ed. Paul H. Kratoska and Abu Talib Ahmad. Pulau Pinang: Pusat Pengajian Ilmu Kemanusian, Universiti Sains Malaysia, 1989.

Chin Kee Onn. *Malaya Upside Down*. Kuala Lumpur: Federal Publications, 1976. (Originally published in Singapore by Jitts & Co, in 1946.)

Chin Kee Onn. *Ma-rai-ee*. Sydney: Australian Publications, 1946.

"Chop Suey". *A Selection from a Host of Gruesome Events that Happened in Malaya during the Japanese Occupation*. 3 vols. Singapore: Ngai Seong Press, 1946.

Chua Chong Bin. "Japanese Occupation in Kelantan – A Focus on Pasir Puteh". In *Pendudukan Jepun di Tanah Melayu*, 1942–1945, ed. Paul H. Kratoska and Abu Talib Ahmad. Pulau Pinang: Pusat Pengajian Ilmu Kemanusian, Universiti Sains Malaysia, 1989, pp. 58–72.

(Churchill, Winston S.) *The War Speeches of the Rt. Hon. Winston S. Churchill*. Compiled by Charles Eade. 3 vols. London: Cassell, 1952.

Clutterback, Richard. *Riot and Revolution in Singapore and Malaya, 1945–1963*. London: Faber and Faber, 1973. Reprinted with some additional material as *Conflict and Violence in Singapore and Malaysia, 1945–83*. Singapore: Graham Brash, 1984.

Collier, Basil. *The War in the Far East, 1941–45*. London: Heinemann, 1969.

Corner, E.J.H. *The Marquis: A Tale of Syonan-to*. Singapore: Heinemann Asia, 1981.

Corr, Gerard H. *The War of the Springing Tigers*. London: Osprey Publishing, 1975.

Cross, John. *Red Jungle*. London: Robert Hale, 1957.

Cruickshank, Charles. *SOE in the Far East*. Oxford University Press, 1983.

Curriculum Development Institute of Singapore (Secondary History Project Team). *History of Modern Singapore*. Rev. ed. Singapore: Longman Singapore, 1994.

van Cuylenburg, John Bertram. *Singapore through Sunshine and Shadow*. Singapore: Heinemann Asia, 1982.

Danaraj, T.J. *Japanese Invasion of Malaya and Singapore: Memoirs of a Doctor*. Kuala Lumpur: T.J. Danaraj, 1990.

Dartford, G.P. *A Short History of Malaya*. London: Longmans, Green, 1958.

Das, S.K. *Japanese Occupation* and *Ex Post Facto Legislation in Malaya*. Singapore: The Malayan Law Journal, 1960.

Dobree, Peter George James. *Hujan Panas Bawa Bencana* [Hot Rain Brings Danger]. Kuala Lumpur: Dewan Bahasa dan Pustaka, 1994.

Dol Ramli. "History of the Malay Regiment, 1933–1942". *Journal of the Malayan Branch of the Royal Asiatic Society* 38 (July 1965): 199–243.

Donnison, F.S.V. *British Military Administration in the Far East, 1943–1946*. London: HMSO, 1956.

Drabble, John H. *Malayan Rubber: The Interwar Years*. Basingstoke: Macmillan, 1991.

Eade, Charles (comp.) *Secret Session Speeches by the Right Hon. Winston S. Churchill.* London:" Cassell, 1946.

Elphick. *Singapore: The Pregnable Fortress.* London: Coronet, 1995.

Elsbree, W.H. *Japan's Role in Southeast Asian Nationalist Movements.* New York: Russell and. Russell, 1970.

Emerson, Rupert. *Malaysia.* New York: The Macmillan Co., 1937. (Reprinted Kuala Lumpur: University of Malaya Press, 1964.)

Falk, Stanley F. *Seventy Days to Singapore: The Malayan Campaign, 1941–42.* London: Robert Hale, 1975.

Farrell, Brian. *The Defence and Fall of Singapore.* Port Stroud, Glouc: Tempus, 2005.

Fawzi Basri. "Kosaku dan Operasi Matador: Satu Kajian Mengenai Per-tempuran Jepun-British di Kedah, 1941–42" [Kosaku and Operation Matador: A Study of the Japanese-British Conflict in Kedah, 1941–42]. In *Beberapa Aspek Sejarah Kedah*, ed. Khoo Kay Kim. Kuala Lumpur: Persatuan Sejarah Malaysia, 1983.

Fay, Peter Ward. *The Forgotten Army: India's Armed Struggle for Independence, 1942–1945.* Ann Arbor: University of Michigan Press, 1993.

Flood, Thadeus. "The 1940 Franco-Thai Border Dispute and Phibun Songram's Commitment to Japan". *Journal of Southeast Asian History* 10 (Sept. 1969): 304–25.

Frei, Henry P. "Japan Remembers the Malaya Campaign". In *Malaya and Singapore during the Japanese Occupation*, ed. Paul H. Kratoska. Singapore: Journal of Southeast Asian Studies, 1995.

________. *Japan's Southward Advance and Australia: From the Sixteenth Century to WWII.* Carlton, Vic: Melbourne University Press and Honolulu: University of Hawaii Press, 1991.

Fujii, Tatsuki. *Singapore Assignment.* Tokyo: Nippon Times, n.d. (ca. 1943).

Fukuda Shozo. *With Sweat and Abacus: Economic Roles of Southeast Asian Chinese on the Eve of World War II*, trans. Les Oates, ed.George Hicks. Singapore: Select Books, 1995. (Originally published in Japanese as *Kakyo Keizai-Ron.* Tokyo: Ganshodo Shoten, 1939.)

Ghazali bin Mayudin. *Johor Semasa Pendudukan Jepun, 1942–1945* [Johore during the Japanese Occupation, 1942–1945]. Bangi: Jabatan Sejarah, Universiti Kebangsaan Malaysia, 1978.

Ghosh, K.K. *The Indian National Army.* Meertu: Meemakshi Prakashan, 1969.

Gilchrist, Andrew. *Malaya 1941: The Fall of a Fighting Empire.* London: Robert Hale, 1992.

Gilmour, Andrew. *My Role in the Rehabilitation of Singapore, 1946–1953.* Singapore: Oral History Pilot Study No. 2, Institute of Southeast Asian Studies, 1973.

Gilmour, O.W. *With Freedom to Singapore.* London: Ernest Benn, 1950.

Godley, Michael R. *The Mandarin-Capitalists from Nanyang; Overseas Chinese Enterprise in the Modernization of China, 1893–1911*. Cambridge: Cambridge University Press, 1981.

Goodman, Grant K. (ed.). *Japanese Cultural Policies in Southeast Asia during World War 2*. New York: Macmillan, 1991.

Gough, Richard. *SOE Singapore, 1941–42*. London: William Kimber, 1985. Reissued as *Special Operations Singapore, 1941–42*. Singapore: Heinemann Asia, 1987.

________. *The Escape from Singapore*. Singapore: Mandarin, 1994.

Hack, Karl and Kevin Blackburn, *Did Singapore Have to Fall?* London: Routledge Curzon, 2004.

Hamond, Robert. *A Fearful Freedom: The Story of One Man's Survival Behind the Lines in Japanese Occupied Malaya, 1942–45*. London: Leo Cooper/Secker and Warburg, 1984.

Hara Fujio. "Former Japanese Soldiers Who Joined Communist Guerrillas in Malaya: Reconstructing an Elusive History". *Journal of the Malaysian Branch of the Royal Asiatic Society* 89, 2 No. 311 (Dec. 2016): 67–99.

________. "Japan and Malaysian Economy: An Analysis of the Relations Started with Reparations after the End of World War II". In *Formation and Restructuring of Business Groups in Malaysia*, ed. Hara Fujio. Tokyo: Institute of Developing Economies, 1993.

________. "The Japanese Occupation of Malaya and the Chinese Community". In *Malaya and Singapore during the Japanese Occupation*, ed. Paul H. Kratoska. Singapore: Journal of Southeast Asian Studies, 1995.

Haseman, John B. *The Thai Resistance Movement during the Second World War*. DeKalb: Northern Illinois University Center for Southeast Asian Studies, 1978.

He Wen-Lit. *Syonan Interlude*. Singapore: Mandarin Paperbacks, 1992.

Hicks, George L. (ed.) *Overseas Chinese Remittances from Southeast Asia, 1910–1940*. Singapore: Select Books, 1993.

________. *Chinese Organisations in Southeast Asia in the 1930s*. Singapore: Select Books, 1996.

Hills, Carol and Daniel C. Silverman. "Nationalism and Feminism in Late Colonial India: The Rani of Jhansi Regiment, 1943–1945". *Modern Asian Studies* 27 (1993): 741–60.

Ho, Ruth. *Rainbow Round My Shoulder*. Singapore: Eastern Universities Press, 1975.

Holman, Dennis. *The Green Torture: The Ordeal of Robert Chrystal*. London: Robert Hale, 1962.

Hon, Joan. *Relatively Speaking*. Singapore: Times Books International, 1984.

Hsü Yün-Tsiao. "Record of Malayan Chinese Victims during the Japanese Occupation". *Journal of the South Seas Society* 11 (June 1955): 1–112.

Huff, Gregg and Shinobu Majima (translators and editors). *World War II Singapore: The Ch-ōsabu Reports on Syonan*. Singapore: NUS Press, 2018.

Ibrahim Ismail, General Tan Sri. *Have You Met Mariam?* Johore Bahru: Westlight, 1984.

Ibrahim Ismail. *Sejarah Kedah Sepintas Lalu* [A Passing Glance at the History of Kedah]. Jitra: Jawatankuasa Penerbitan, University Utara Malaysia, 1987.

Ienaga, Saburo. *The Pacific War: World War II and the Japanese, 1931–45*. New York: Pantheon Books, 1978.

Ike, Nobutaka. *Japan's Decision for War: Records of the 1941 Policy Conference*. Stanford University Press, 1967.

Ismail Babu. *Kisah Seorang Perajurit* [Story of a Warrior]. Kuala Lumpur: Dewan Bahasa dan Pustaka, 1988.

Itagaki, Yoichi. "The Japanese Policy for Malaya under the Occupation". In *Papers on Malayan History*, ed. K.G. Tregonning. Singapore: University of Malaya, 1962.

Itagaki, Yoichi and Koichi Kishi. "Japanese Islamic Policy: Sumatra and Malaya". *Intisari* 2, (n.d.).

Jaafar bin Hamzah. "The Malays in Tasek Gelugur during the Japanese Occupation". *Malaysia in History* 21 (Dec. 1978): 56–64.

Jones, F.C. *Japan's New Order in East Asia: Its Rise and Fall, 1937–45*. London: Oxford University Press, 1954.

Josey, Alex. *Lee Kuan Yew*. Singapore: Donald Moore Press, 1968.

A. Karim Haji Abdullah. *A. Samad Ismail, Ketokohan dan Kewartawanan*. Kuala Lumpur: Dewan Bahasa dan Pustaka, 1991.

Kathigasu, Sybil. *No Dram of Mercy*. London: Neville Spearman, 1954.

Kawashima, Midori. "The Records of the Former Japanese Army Concerning the Japanese Occupation of the Philippines". *Journal of Southeast Asian Studies* 27 (Mar. 1996): 124–31

Kee Yeh Siew. "The Japanese in Malaya before 1942". *Journal of the South Seas Society* 20 (1965): 48–88.

Kelly, Nigel. *History of Malaya and South-East Asia*. Singapore: Heinemann Asia, 1993.

Kennedy, J. A *History of Malaya*. Kuala Lumpur: Macmillan, 1965.

Khan, G. Mohammed. *History of Kedah*. Penang: Penang Premier Press.

Khoo Kay Kim. "The Malay Left, 1945–48: A Preliminary Discourse". *Sarjana* 1 (Dec. 1981): 167–92.

Kirby, S. Woodburn. *History of the Second World War: The War Against Japan*, 5 vols. London: HMSO, 1957–69.

Kirby, S. Woodburn. *Singapore: The Chain of Disaster*. London: Cassell, 1971.

Kobkua Suwannathat-Pian. "Thai Irredentism and the Return or the Four Malay States to Thailand in 1943". In *Sumbangsih, Kumpulan Esei Sejarah*, ed. Nik Hassan Shuhaimi Nik Abdul Rahman, Nik Anuar Nik Mahmud and Yahaya Abu Bakar. Bangi: Universiti Kebangsaan Malaysia, 1988.

________. "Thai Japanese Bargaining over the Return of the Four Malay States to Thailand". *Jebat* 17 (1989): 29–38.

Kratoska, Paul H. "The Post-1945 Food Shortage in British Malaya". *Journal of Southeast Asian Studies* 19 (Mar. 1988): 27–47.

________. "Banana Money: Consequences of the Demonetization of Wartime Japanese Currency in British Malaya". *Journal of Southeast Asian Studies* 23 (Sept. 1992): 322–45.

________. "Labor in the Malay Peninsula and Singapore under Japanese Occupation". In *Asian Labor in the Wartime Japanese Empire: Unknown Histories*, ed. Paul H. Kratoska. Armonk, NY: M.E. Sharpe, 2005, pp. 237–48.

________. "Malayan Food Shortages and the Kedah Rice Industry during the Japanese Occupation". In *Food Supplies and the Japanese Occupation in South-East Asia*, ed. Paul

H. Kratoska. Houndmills, Basingstoke: Macmillan Press, and New York: St. Martin's Press, 1998, pp. 101-34.

________. (ed.). *Penghijrah dan Penghijrahan: Kumpulan Esei Sejarah Malaysia oleh Pelajar-Pelajar Universiti Sains Malaysia* (Migrants and Migration: A Collection of Essays on Malaysian History by Students at Universiti Sains Malaysia). Pulau Pinang: Kertas-kertas Berkala dari Pusat Pengijian Ilmu Kemanusian No. 1, Universiti Sains Malaysia, 1982.

________. (ed.) *Malaya and Singapore during the Japanese Occupation*. Singapore: Journal of Southeast Asian Studies, 1995.

Kratoska, Paul H. and Abu Talib Ahmad (eds). *Pendudukan Jepun di Tanah Melayu, 1942–1945: Kumpulan Esei Sejarah Malaysia oleh Pelajar-Pelajar Universiti Sains Malaysia* [The Japanese Occupation in Malaya, 1942–1945: A Collection of Essays on Malaysian History by Students at Universiti Sains Malaysia]. Pulau Pinang: Kertas-kertas Berkala dari Pusat Pengajian Ilmu Kemanusian No. 4, Universiti Sains Malaysia, 1989.

Lau, Albert. *The Malayan Union Controversy, 1942–1948*. Singapore: Oxford University Press, 1991.

Lebra, Joyce. *Japanese-Trained Armies in Southeast Asia: Independence and Volunteer Forces in World War II*. New York: Columbia University Press, 1977.

________. *Jungle Alliance: Japan and the Indian National Army*. Singapore: Donald Moore for Asia Pacific Press, 1971.

Lee Geok Boi. *Syonan: Singapore under the Japanese, 1942–1945*. Singapore: Singapore Heritage Society, 1992.

Lee Kip Lee. *Amber Sands: A Boyhood Memoir*. Singapore: Federal Publications, 1995.

Lee Kam Heng. "Malaya: New State and Old Elites". In *Asia: The Winning of Independence*, ed. Robin Jeffrey. London and Basingstoke: Macmillan Press, 1981.

Lee Say Lee. "A Study of the Rice Trade in Kedah Before and During the Japanese Occupation". *Malaysia in History* 24 (1981): 109–16.

Lee Siow Mong. *Words Cannot Equal Experience*. Petaling Jaya: Pelanduk Books, 1985.

Lee Ting Hui. "Singapore under the Japanese, 1942–1945". *Journal of the South Seas Society* 17 (Apr. 1961): 31–69.

Leong, Stephen. "The Malayan Overseas Chinese and the Sino-Japanese War, 1937–41". *Journal of Southeast Asian Studies* 10 (Sept. 1979): 293–320.

Lim Pui Huen, P. "Memoirs of War in Malaya". In *Malaya and Singapore during the Japanese Occupation*, ed. Paul H. Kratoska. Singapore: Journal of Southeast Asian Studies, 1995.

Loh Kok Wah, Francis. *Beyond the Tin Mines: Coolies, Squatters and New Villagers in the Kinta Valley, Malaysia, c. 1880–1980*. Singapore: Oxford University Press, 1988.

Low, N.I. and H.M. Cheng. *This Singapore (Our City of Dreadful Nights)*. Singapore: Ngai Seong Press, 1946.

Low, N.I. *When Singapore Was Syonan-To*. Singapore: Eastern Universities Press, 1973.

McCoy, A.W. (ed.). *Southeast Asia under Japanese Occupation*. New Haven: Yale University Southeast Asia Studies, 1980.

McDonald, Lawrence H. "The OSS and Its Records". In *The Secrets War: The Office of Strategic Services in World War II*, ed. George C. Chalou. Washington, DC: National Archives and Records Administration, 1992.

Macgregor, R.B. "Medical History of the War in Malaya". *The Medical Journal of Malaya* 3 (Mar. 1949): 145–72.

McIntyre, W. David. *The Rise and Fall of the Singapore Naval Base, 1919–1942*. London and Basingstoke: The Macmillan Press, 1979.

Mackenzie, Compton. *Eastern Epic*. London: Chatto and Windus, 1951.

Malaya and Its Civil Administration Prior to Japanese Occupation. London: The War Office, 1944.

Malaysia Kita (Our Malaysia). Kuala Lumpur: Institut Tadbiran Awam Negara Malaysia, 1991.

Marshall, Jonathan. *To Have and Have Not: Southeast Asian Raw Materials and the Origins of the Pacific War*. Berkeley, Los Angeles and London: University of California Press, 1995.

Maxwell, Sir George, et al., comp. *The Civil Defence of Malaya: A Narrative of the Part Taken in It by the Civilian Population of the Country in the Japanese Invasion*. London: Hutchinson, n.d., but ca. 1944.

Miller, Harry. *Menace in Malaya*. London: George G. Harrap, 1954.

________. *The Story of Malaysia*. London: Faber and Faber, 1965.

________. *Prince and Premier: A Biography of Tunku Abdul Rahman Putra Al-Haj, First Prime Minister of the Federation of Malaya*. London: George G. Harrap in association with Donald Moore, Singapore, 1959.

Mills, Lennox A. *Malaya: A Political and Economic Appraisal*. Minneapolis: University of Minnesota Press, 1958.

Mohamad Isa Othman. *Pendudukan Jepun di Tanah Melayu, 1942–1945 (Tumpuan di Negeri Kedah)* [The Japanese Occupation in Malaya, 1942–1945 (With Special Reference to Kedah)]. Kuala Lumpur: Dewan Bahasa dan Pustaka, 1992.

Mohd. Rafdi Mohd. Taha. "Serangan dan Pendudukan Tentera Jepun terhadap Kampung Pak Amat dan Pengkalan Chepa" [The Japanese Military Attack and Occupation at Kampong Pak Amat and Pengkalan Chepa]. In *Pendudukan Jepun di Tanah Melayu, 1942–1945*, ed. Paul H. Kratoska and Abu Talib Ahmad. Pulau Pinang: Pusat Pengajian Ilmu Kemanusian, Universiti Sains Malaysia, 1989, pp. 91–7.

Montgomery, Brian. *Shenton of Singapore: Governor and Prisoner of War*. London: Leo Cooper, Secker and Warburg, 1984.

Moore, Donald, and Joanna Moore. *The First 150 Years of Singapore*. Singapore: Donald Moore Press, 1969.

Moorhead, E.J. *A History of Malaya*. 2 vols. London: Longmans, Green, 1957, 1963.

Morley, James William (ed.). *The Fateful Choice: Japan's Advance into Southeast Asia, 1939–1941*. New York: Columbia University Press, 1980.

Murfett, Malcolm *et al. Between Two Oceans: A Military History of Singapore*. Singapore: Times Academic Press, 1999.

________. *Fool-Proof Relations: The Search for Anglo-American Naval Cooperation during the Chamberlain Years, 1937–1940*. Singapore: Singapore University Press, 1984.

Nadarajan Rajoo. "The Estate Food Supply and Distribution Network before and during the Japanese Occupation". In *Penghijrah dan Penghijrahan*, ed. Paul H. Kratoska. Pulau Pinang: Pusat Pengajian Ilmu Kemanusiaan, Universiti Sains Malaysia, 1982.

Nakahara, Michiko. "Asian Laborers along the Burma-Thailand Railroad". *Waseda Journal of Asian Studies* 15 (1993): 88–107.

Nantawan Haemindra. "The Problem of the Thai-Muslims in the Four Southern Provinces of Thailand". *Journal of Southeast Asian Studies* 7 (Sept. 1976): 197–225 and 8 (Mar. 1977): 85–105.

Negara Kita: Sejarah, Pentadbiran dan Dasar-Dasar Pembangunan (Our Country: History, Administration and Development Policies). Kuala Lumpur: Institut Tadbiran Awam Negara Malaysia, 1980.

Neidpath, James. *The Singapore Naval Base and the Defence of Britain's Eastern Empire, 1919–1941*. Oxford: Clarendon Press, 1981.

Ng Teong Kiat. *Anti-Nip Memoir of Mr. Ng Teong Kiat*. Chinese by Wong Yiet Mun, English by Lim Cheng Tek. Privately published, 1946.

Nik Anuar Nik Mahmud. "Kelantan di bawah Pentadbiran Tentera Jepun dan Pentadbiran Tentera Thai, 1941–45: Suatu Kajian Sepintas Lalu" [Kelantan under Japanese Military Administration and Thai Military Administration, 1941–45]. In *Malaysia: Sejarah dan Proses Pembangunan*. Kuala Lumpur: Persatuan Sejarah Malaysia, 1982.

Ohno, Takushi. *War, Reparations and Peace Settlement: Philippines-Japan Relations, 1945–1956*. Manila: Solidaridad Publishing House, 1986.

Olson, Lawrence. *Japan in Postwar Asia*. New York: Praeger Publishers, 1970.

Ong Chit Chung. *Operation Matador: Britain's War Plans against the Japanese, 1918–1941*. Singapore: Times Academic Press, 1997.

Ooi Keat Gin. *The Japanese Occupation of Borneo, 1941–1945*. London: Routledge, 2011.

________ (ed.) *Japanese Empire in the Tropics: Selected Documents and Reports of the Japanese Period in Sarawak, Northwest Borneo, 1941–1945*. 2 vols. Athens, OH: Ohio University Center for International Studies, Monographs in International Studies, Southeast Asia Series No. 101, 1998.

Oong Hak Ching. "Kerjasama British dengan Parti Komunis Malaya dan Kuomintang: Kesan-kesannya terhadap Dasar-Dasar British di Tanah Melayu (1941–45)" [British Cooperation with the Malayan Communist party and Kuomintang: Effects on British Policies in Malaya (1941–45)]. *Jebat* 18 (1990): 129–44.

Palit, D.K. *The Campaign in Malaya*. Dehra Dun: Palit and Dutt, 1971.

Percival, A.E. *The War in Malaya*. London: Eyre and Spottiswoode, 1949 (Reprinted New Delhi: Sagar Publications, 1971).

Purcell, Victor. *The Chinese in Southeast Asia*. 2nd ed. Kuala Lumpur: Oxford University Press, 1980.

Ramlah Adam. *Ahmad Boestamam: Satu Biografi Politik*. Kuala Lumpur: Dewan Bahasa dan Pustaka, 1994.

Reynolds, E. Bruce. *Thailand and Japan's Southern Advance, 1940–1945*. New York: St Martin's Press, 1994.

Robertson, Eric. *The Japanese File: Pre-War Japanese Penetration in Southeast Asia*. Singapore: Heinemann Asia, 1979.

Roff, William R. *The Origins of Malay Nationalism*. Kuala Lumpur: University of Malaya Press, 1967.

Rohaini bte Kamsan. 'Keadaan Kehidupan Masyarakat Luar Bandar Melayu Pulau Pinang dimasa Pendudukan Jepun Secara Am" [Living Conditions for the Rural

Population of Penang during the Japanese Occupation in General]. In *Pendudukan Jepun di Tanah Melayu, 1942–1945*, ed. Paul H. Kratoska and Abu Talib Ahmad. Pulau Pinang: Pusat Pengajian Ilmu Kemanusian, Universiti Sains Malaysia, 1989.

Rosen, S. McKee. *The Combined Boards of the Second World War: An Experiment in International Administration*. New York: Columbia University Press, 1951.

Rosnani Ibrahim. "Pendudukan Jepun di Hulu Langat" [The Japanese Occupation in Ulu Langat]. In *Selangor: Dahulu dan Sekarang*, ed. Khoo Kay Kim et al. Kuala Lumpur: Persatuan Musium Malaysia, 1985.

Ryan, N.J. *A History of Malaysia and Singapore*. Kuala Lumpur: Oxford University Press, 1976.

Saravanamuttu, Manicasothy. *The Sara Saga*. Penang: Privately published, 1969; reprinted Penang: Areca Books, 2010.

Sato, Shigeru. *War, Nationalism and Peasants: Java under the Japanese Occupation, 1942–1945*. St Leonards, NSW: Asian Studies Association of Australia in Association with Allen & Unwin, 1994.

Sejarah Malaysia. Joint authors: Siti Zuraina Abdul Majid, Muhammad Yusoff Hashim, Abdullah Zakaria Ghazali, Lee Kam Hing, Ahmad Fawzi Basri and Zainal Abidin Abdul Wahid. Tingkatan 5, Kurikulum Bersepadu Sekolah Menengah. Kuala Lumpur: Dewan Bahasa dan Pustaka, 1994.

Sheppard, Mubin. *Askar Melayu: Taat dan Setia, 1933–47* [Malay Troops: Obedient and Loyal]. Kuala Lumpur: Department of Public Relations, Malay Peninsula, 1947.

Sheppard, M.C. *The Malay Regiment, 1933–1947*. Port Dickson: Askar Melayu Diraja, 1978.

Shinozaki, Mamoru. *Syonan – My Story: The Japanese Occupation of Singapore*. Singapore: Asia Pacific Press, 1979.

Shü Yün-Ts'iao and Chua Ser-Koon (eds). *Malayan Chinese Resistance to Japan, 1937–1945: Selected Source Materials*. Based on documents collected by Col. Chuang Hui-Tsuan. Singapore: Cultural and Historical Publishing House, 1984.

Sidhu H. *The Bamboo Fortress: True Singapore War Stories*. Singapore: Native Publications, 1991.

Silcock, H.T. and Ungku Aziz. "Nationalism in Malaya". In *Asian Nationalism and the West*, ed. L.W. Holland. New York: Macmillan, 1953.

Silverstein, Josef (ed.) *Southeast Asia in World War II: Four Essays*. New Haven: Yale University Press, 1966.

Sim, Evelyn. *A History of Malaya, Singapore and Thailand for GCE 'N' Level*. Singapore: Federal Publications, 1993.

Simson, Ivan. *Singapore: Too Little, Too Late. Some Aspects of the Malayan Disaster in 1942*. London: Leo Cooper, 1970.

Singh, Gurchan. *Singa: The Lion of Malaya*. Kuala Lumpur: Printcraft, n.d.

Smith, Bradley F. *The Shadow Warriors: O.S.S. and the Origins of the C.I.A.* London: André Deutsch, 1983.

Spector, Ronald H. *In the Ruins of Empire: The Japanese Surrender and the Battle for Postwar Asia*. New York: Random House, 2007.

________. *The Eagle against the Sun: The American War with Japan*. New York: Vintage Books, 1985.

Stockwell, A.J. *British Policy and Malay Politics during the Malayan Union Experiment, 1942–48*. Kuala Lumpur: Monograph no. 8, The Malaysian Branch of the Royal Asiatic Society, 1979.

________. "Colonial Planning during World War II: the Case of Malaya". *Journal of Imperial and Commonwealth History* 2 (May 1974): 333–51.

Stone, Horace. *From Malacca to Malayasia, 1400–1965*. London: Harrap, 1966.

Suchasingh, Christina Anne. "Food Rationing in Penang during the Japanese Occupation 1941–1945: How Effective Was It?" In *Pendudukan Jepun di Tanah Melayu, 1942–1945*, ed. Paul H. Kratoska and Abu Talib Ahmad. Pulau Pinang: Pusat Pengajian Ilmu Kemanusian, Universiti Sains Malaysia, 1989.

Swan, William L. "Thai-Japanese Relations at the Start of the Pacific War: Insight into a Controversial Period". *Journal of Southeast Asian Studies* 18 (Sept. 1987): 270–93.

Swinson, Arthur. *Defeat in Malaya: The Fall of Singapore*. London: MacDonald, 1969.

Syonan, Singapore under the Japanese. A Catalogue of Oral History Interviews. Singapore: Oral History Department, 1986.

Tan Chong Tee. *Force 136: Story of a WWII Resistance Fighter*. First published in Chinese in 1994. Trans. Lee Watt Sim and Clara Show. Singapore: Asiapac Books, 1995.

Tan Ding Eing. *A Portrait of Malaysia and Singapore*. Singapore: Oxford University Press, 1975.

Tan, Y.S. "History of the Formation of the Oversea Chinese Association and the Extortion by J.M.A. of $50,000,000 Military Contribution from the Chinese in Malaya". *Journal of the South Seas Society* 3, 1 (1947): 1–12 (English-language section).

Thamsook Numnonda. "Pibulsongkram's Thai Nation-Building Programme during the Japanese Military Presence, 1941–45". *Journal of Southeast Asian Studies* 9 (Sept. 1978): 234–47.

________. *Thailand and the Japanese Presence, 1941–45*. Singapore: Research Notes and Discussion Series No. 6, Institute of Southeast Asian Studies, 1977.

Thio Chan Bee. *Extraordinary Adventures of an Ordinary Man*. London: Grosvenor Books, 1977.

Thio, Eunice. "The Syonan Years, 1942–1945". In *A History of Singapore*, ed. Ernest C.T. Chew and Edwin Lee. Singapore: Oxford University Press, 1991.

Thomas, Mary. *In the Shadow of the Rising Sun*. Singapore: Maruzen Asia, 1983.

Toye, Hugh. *The Springing Tiger: Subhash Chandra Bose*. Bombay: Jaico Publishing House, 1978.

Tregonning, K.G. *A History of Modern Malaya*. Singapore: Eastern Universities Press for University of London Press, 1964.

Trenowden, Ian. *Malayan Operations Most Secret – Force 136*. Singapore: Heinemann Asia, 1983. (A reprint of *Operations Most Secret SOE: The Malayan Theatre*. London: William Kimber, 1978.)

Tsuji, Masanobu. *Singapore: The Japanese Version*. New York: St Martin's Press, 1960.

Turnbull, CM. "British Planning for Post-War Malaya". *Journal of Southeast Asian Studies* 5 (Sept. 1974): 239–54.

________. *A History of Singapore, 1819–1975*. Kuala Lumpur: Oxford University Press, 1977.

________. *A History of Malaysia, Singapore and Brunei*. Sydney: Allen & Unwin, 1989.

Van Thean Kee. "Cultivation of Taiwan Padi in Perak during the Japanese Occupation". *Malayan Agricultural Journal* 31 (Apr. 1948): 119–22.

Wan Hashini b. Hj. Wan Teh. *Pejuang Gerila Force 136* [The Guerrilla Struggle of Force 136]. Kuala Lumpur: Biro Politik dan Pelajaran, Pergerakan Pemuda UMNO Bahagian Grik, 1984.

________. *Perang Dunia Kedua: Peranan Askar Melayu* [World War II: The Role of Malay Troops]. Kuala Lumpur: Dewan Bahasa dan Pustaka, 1993.

Wang Gungwu. "The Japanese Occupation and Post-War Malaya, 1941–1948". In *History of the Malaysian States*, ed. Wang Gungwu. Singapore: Lembaga Gerakan Pelajaran Dewasa [Adult Education Board], 1965.

Ward, Ian. *The Killer They Called a God*. Singapore: Media Masters, 1992.

Warren, Alan. *Singapore 1942: Britain's Greatest Defeat*. London: Talisman, 2002.

Wee, Peter H.L. *From Farm and Kampong....* Singapore: Graham Brash, 1989.

Wickizer, V.D. and M.K. Bennett. *The Rice Economy of Monsoon Asia*. Stanford, CA: Food Research Institute, 1941.

Wigmore, Lionel. *The Japanese Thrust*. Canberra: Australian War Memorial, 1957.

Winstedt, R[ichard] O. *A History of Malaya*. Rev. ed. Singapore: Marican, 1962.

Winstedt, Sir Richard. *Malaya and Its History*. 5th ed. London: Hutchinson University Library, 1958.

Wong Moh Keed (ed.). *To My Heart, with Smiles ... The Love Letters of Siew Fung Fong & Wan Kwai Pik (1920–1941)*. Singapore: Landmark Books, 1988.

Wyett, John. *Staff Wallah at the Fall of Singapore*. Sydney: Allen & Unwin, 1996.

Yahya Abu Bakar. "Kebangkitan Tok Janggut Menentang Jepun" [The Uprising of Tok Janggut against Japan]. *Malaysia in History* 19 (Jan. 1976): 22–37.

Yap Pheng Geck. *Scholar, Banker, Gentleman Soldier: The Reminiscences of Dr. Yap Pheng Geck*. Singapore: Times Books International, 1982.

Yap Siang Yong, Romen Bose and Angeline Pang. *Fortress Singapore: The Battlefield Guide*. 2nd ed. Singapore: Times Books International, 1995.

Yen Ching Hwang. *The Overseas Chinese and the 1911 Revolution*. Kuala Lumpur: Oxford University Press, 1976.

Yeo Kim Wah and Albert Lau. "From Colonialism to Independence, 1945–1965". In *A History of Singapore*, ed. Ernest C.T. Chew and Edwin Lee. Singapore: Oxford University Press, 1991.

Yeo Tiam Siew. *Destined to Survive: The Story of My Life*. Singapore: Published by the author, 1993.

Yip Yat Hoong. *The Development of the Tin Mining Industry of Malaya*. Kuala Lumpur: University of Malaya Press, 1969.

Yong, C.F. *Chinese Leadership and Power in Colonial Singapore*. Singapore: Times Academic Press, 1992.

Yuen Choy Leng. "Japanese Rubber and Iron Investment in Malaya, 1900–41". *Journal of Southeast Asian Studies* 5 (Mar. 1974): 18–36.

________. "The Japanese Community in Malaya before the Pacific War: Its Genesis and Growth". *Journal of Southeast Asian Studies* 9 (Sept. 1978): 163–79.

Zainal Abidin b. Abd. Wahid. "The Japanese Occupation and Nationalisms". In *Glimpses of Malaysian History*, ed. Zainal Abidin b. Abd. Wahid. Kuala Lumpur: Dewan Bahasa dan Pustaka, 1970, pp. 93–8.

Zhou Mei. *Elizabeth Choy: More than a War Heroine*. Singapore: Landmark Books, 1995.

Dissertations and Academic Exercises

Brett, Cecil Carter. "Japanese Rule in Malaya, 1942–1945". MA, University of Washington, 1950.

Halinah Bamadhaj. "The Impact of the Japanese Occupation of Malaya on Malay Society and Politics (1941–1945)". MA, University of Auckland, 1975.

Horner, Layton. "Japanese Military Administration in Malaya and the Philippines". PhD, University of Arizona, 1973.

Kang Jew Koon. "The Chinese in Singapore during the Japanese Occupation, 1942–1945". BA, Department of History, National University of Singapore, 1981.

Koh Soo Jin, Denis. "Japanese Competition in the Trade of Malaya in the 1930s". BA, Department of History, National University of Singapore, 1991.

Kwok Siu Fun, Stephanie. "Extraordinary Lives: Catholic Missionaries during the Japanese Occupation of Singapore". BA, Department of History, National University of Singapore, 1994/95.

Lai, N.G. "The Japanese Occupation in Singapore's Collective Memory". BA, Department of Sociology, National University of Singapore, 1992/93.

Lee, Karen. "The Japanese Occupation in Selangor". BA, University of Malaya, 1973.

Lee Beng Kooi. "The Japanese Occupation in Penang, 1941–1945". BA, University of Singapore, 1974.

Leo Tin Boon. "Force 136: The Malayan Episode". BA, Department of History, National University of Singapore, 1986/7.

Ng Sze Syn, Alvin. "Nippon-go: Japanese Language Instruction during the Occupation of Singapore, 1942–1945". BA, Department of Japanese Studies, National University of Singapore, 1992/93.

Ooi, Ophelia. "Inquiry into the Political Activities of the Japanese in Singapore, 1930–1942". BA, Department of History, National University of Singapore, 1979.

Ramdas, Kamalini. "Spectacle, Surveillance and Resistance: The Politics of Space in Syonan-to, 1942–45". BA, Department of Geography, National University of Singapore, 1994/95.

Rodziah Haji Shari'ia. "Japanese Settlement Schemes: Endau and Bahau, 1942–1945". BA, Department of History, National University of Singapore, 1986/87.

Siow Hung Woo, Ron H. "Singapore through the *Syonan Shimbun*: Daily Life in Syonan-To under the Japanese Occupation (1942–45)". BA, Department of Japanese Studies, National University of Singapore, 1994/5.

Toong Lei Ling. "Japanese Occupation in Malaya and its Effects on Malaya Nationalism". BA, Department of Japanese Studies, National University of Singapore, 1990.

Twang Peck Yang. "Indonesian Chinese Business Communities in Transformation". PhD, Australian National University, 1987.

Yap Hong Kuan. "Perak under the Japanese, 1942–1945". BA, University of Malaya at Singapore, 1957.

Published Oral History Materials

Force 136 (1). Interviewee: Tsang Jan Nam. Interviewer: Tan Kim Hong. Pulau Pinang: Siri Sejarah Lisan Pendudukan Jepun, no. 2. Jawatankuasa Sejarah Lisan dan Perpustakaan Universiti Sains Malaysia, 1991.

Force 136 (2). Interviewee: Lim Hong Pei. Interviewer: Tan Kim Hong. Pulau Pinang: Siri Sejarah Lisan Pendudukan Jepun, no. 3. Jawatankuasa Sejarah Lisan dan Perpustakaan Universiti Sains Malaysia, 1991.

Reminiscences of Tunku Abdul Rahman on the Japanese Occupation. Interviewers: Y. Bhg. Datuk Profesor Sharom Ahmat and Profesor Madya Dr Cheah Boon Kheng. Pulau Pinang: Siri Sejarah Lisan Pendudukan Jepun, no. 1. Jawatankuasa Sejarah Lisan dan Perpustakaan UniversitiSains Malaysia, 1989.

Syonan: Singapore under the Japanese. A Catalogue of Oral History Interviews. Singapore: Oral History Department, 1986.

Unpublished Materials

Since the 1980s students in history courses at Universiti Sains Malaysia have been writing essays on the Japanese occupation, drawing on oral sources as well as archival materials and published works. In addition to the published collections listed above (see the entries for Paul H. Kratoska), Abu Talib Ahmad gave me access to further student essays that he has collected, and they were an extremely valuable supplement to the archival record in understanding the experiences of the local population. The essays are written in Bahasa Malaysia, the national language of Malaysia.

I consulted following items:

Abd. Hamid bin Md Isa. "Pendudukan Jepun dan Kesannya di Kawasan Bukit Selambau Daerah Kuala Muda Kedah" [The Japanese Occupation and Its Impact in Bukit Selambau, Kuala Muda, Kedah].

Abdul Malek bin Samsuri. "Pendudukan Jepun di Balik Pulau, Pulau Pinang" [The Japanese Occupation in Balik Pulau, Penang].

Ahmad Zuber Lebai Abdul. "Kesan Pendudukan Jepun di Mukim Lambor Kiri, Daerah Perak Tengah, Perak 1941–1945" [The Impact of the Japanese Occupation in Mukim Lambor Kiri, Central Perak, 1941–1945].

Ahmat Puat bin Moh. Basir. "Mukim Gersik Semasa Pemerintahan Jepun di Tanah Melayu, 1942–1945" [Gersik Mukim during the Japanese Administration of Malaya].

Anbalakan Kailasam. "Pendudukan Jepun di Tanah Melayu: Tumpuan kepada Kesan-Kesannya di Kalangan Buruh-Buruh Estet (Bagan Serai)" [The Japanese Occupation in Malaya, with Emphasis on its Impact among Estate Workers (in Bagan Serai]).

Aripin b. Othman. "Suatu Tinjauan Teoritis: Kehidupan Buruh (Paksa) Pembinaan Lapangan Terbang Zaman Jepun di Kuala Pilah, N. Sembilan" [A Theoretical

Enquiry: The Lives of Forced Labourers Building the Airfield at Kuala Pilah, N. Sembilan during the Japanese Period].

Azwana bt Abu. "Pendudukan Jepun di Telok Kumbar, Pulau Pinang dan Kesannya terhadap Aspek Sosial dan Politik" [The Japanese Occupation at Telok Kumbar, Penang, and Its Impact on Society and Politics].

Chan Moi. "Kesan Pendudukan Jepun terhadap Kaum Cina di Kawasan Kulai, Johor" [The Impact of the Japanese Occupation on the Chinese Population in Kulai, Johore].

Cheong Peng Yeap. "Sejauh Manakah Pendudukan Jepun di Taiping Mempengaruhi Kehidupan Seharian Komuniti Cina di Sana?" [To What Extent Did the Japanese Occupation Affect the Daily Life of the Chinese Population of Taiping?].

Lynley Ruth Gomez. "Satu Tinjauan Umum Mengenai Keadaan Sosioekonomi di Tanah Melayu dan Sarawak pada Masa Pendudukan Jepun dengan Memberi Tumpuan kepada Daerah Jasin (Melaka), Muar (Johor), Layang-layang (Johor) dan beberapa Bandar Besar Sarawak" [A General Examination of Socio-Economic Conditions in Malaya and Sarawak During the Japanese Occupation, with Emphasis on Jasin District (Malacca), Muar (Johore), Layang-layang (Johore) and some Large Cities in Sarawak].

Hairani Mohd Khalid. "Satu Tinjauan Am tentang Kehidupan Penduduk Mukim Relau, Kedah semasa Pendudukan Jepun" [A General Enquiry Concerning the Lives of Residents of Relau Mukim in Kedah during the Japanese Occupation].

Hasnilawati bt Awang Embon. (Untitled essay concerning food supplies during the Occupation, covering the consumption of root crops and bananas in place of rice, and the problem of starvation.)

Kalavathy a/p Ponnampalam. "Murid-Murid India di Pulau Pinang semasa Pendudukan Jepun" [Indian Schoolchildren in Penang the Japanese Occupation].

Lee Kit Yeng. "Sook Ching dan Perkembangannya di Pulau Pinang" [The Sook Ching in Penang].

Leong Lai Wan. "Masyarakat Cina di Sungkai semasa Pendudukan Jepun dari Segi Ekonomi dan Sosial" [Chinese Society in Sungkai during the Japanese Occupation from the Economic and Social Perspective].

Mary Florence Meera Diridollou. "Semasa Pendudukan Jepun di Tanah Melayu Kaum India Tidak Terlepas Daripada Kekejaman Jepun" [During the Japanese Occupation of Malaya Indians Were Not Exempt from Japanese Cruelty].

Mohd Noor Zam Yusoff. "Sejauhmanakah Pendudukan Jepun Bertanggungjawab Mencetuskan Pertikaian Kaum Melayu-Cina di sekitar tahun 1945?" [To What Extent was the Japanese Occupation Responsible for Malay-Chinese Ethnic Conflicts that Took Place in 1945?].

Noraziah Hashim. Untitled Paper on the following subject: "Mohamad Isa Othman berpendapat: 'Ditinjau dari Segi Kehidupan Rakyat, Ternyata Jepun Tidak Dapat Memenuhi Impian Kemakmuran Asia'" [According to Mohamad Isa Othman: "Considered from the Perspective of the Life of the People, the Japanese Occupation Clearly Did Not Fulfill the Dream of Asian Prosperity"].

Norrizan bt Seman. "Perjuangan Gerila Melayu Melalui Dua Tokoh" [The Malay Guerrilla Struggle under Two Leaders].

Poobalan George Rajamani. (Untitled paper concerning the political, economic, social and educational impact of the Japanese Occupation in Pulau Pinang.)

Ramesh a/l Nagayah. (Untitled paper concerning hardships experienced by the Indian population of southern Perai.)

Romsina bt Abdul Karim. "Corak Pendidikan yang telah diterima oleh Penduduk di Tanah Melayu semasa Zaman Pendudukan Jepun" [The Pattern of Education Received by Residents of Malaya during the Japanese Occupation].

Rozita bt Nordin. "Pentadbiran Tradisional Peringkat Daerah di Zaman Pendudukan Jepun di Tanah Melayu, 1942–45" [Traditional District-Level Administration during the Japanese Occupation, 1942–45).

Selva Rani Raman. "Pendudukan Jepun di Panchor, Muar, Johor" [The Japanese Occupation in Panchor, Muar, Johor].

Shasitharan, R. "Keadaan Sosio-Politik Orang-Orang India Semasa Pendudukan Jepun 1941–1945 (Harvard Estet)" [Socio-political Conditions of the Indian Population during the Japanese Occupation 1941–1945 (Harvard Estate)].

Siti Zubaidah bte Kassim. "Pengalaman Penduduk Sungai Acheh yang Bekerja Sebagai Jikeidan Jepun pada Waktu Pendudukan Jepun di Tanah Melayu" [The Experiences of the Residents of Sungai Acheh who Joined the Japanese Jikeidan during the Japanese Occupation of Malaya].

Zainuddin bin H. Ahmad. "Pendudukan Jepun di Kampung Permatang Tuan Samad, Permatang Sungai Dua, Seberang Prai" [The Japanese Occupation in Kampung Permatang Tuan Samad, Permatang Sungai Dua, Seberang Prai].

Index